"[AN] AMAZING, ENTERTAINING AND ENLIGHTENING ENCYCLOPEDIC ACHIEVEMENT."

—Mortimer J. Adler

"As comfortable with science as with art, with mathematics as with poetry, Charles Van Doren—in tracing the history of knowledge—makes us comfortable too. A born teacher, he has a rare gift of catching us up in his own enthusiasms and perhaps more important, of making even the most complex ideas clear, accessible, and compelling."

—Joy Gould Boyum
Professor of English and Communication Arts
New York University

"At once authoritative and delightful, this engaging explanation of the development of knowledge in the West brings fresh insight even to those matters that are most familiar to well-educated men and women. As for the young, Van Doren's contagious enthusiasm for the Great Ideas will be a welcome alternative to dry and uninspired text books."

—James O'Toole
The University Associates' Chair
University of Southern California

"A clear, concise, unpretentious survey of all human knowledge—and what remarkable talent Charles Van Doren has exercised in pulling it off so deftly! . . . chiefly by insightfully pinpointing those spellbinding and towering breakthroughs, which collectively define that unique human achievement we call knowledge. Each page reveals another enthralling landmark in the history of ideas."

—Julian Krainin
Producer of the television series
Heritage: Civilization and the Jews and
The World of James Michener

A
HISTORY
OF
KNOWLEDGE

Past, Present, and Future

Charles Van Doren

Ballantine Books • New York

To

Gerry, Liz, Sally and John

Contents

Acknowledgments

THIS BOOK is the result of a lifetime of reading, thinking, and talking. Its seeds were planted nearly fifty years ago, when I was a student at St. John's College and was introduced to the world of ideas by Scott Buchanan, Jacob Klein, and Richard Scofield.

I made my first acquaintance with the literature of universal history thirty years ago, when I was writing *The Idea of Progress* (Praeger, 1967). My mentor at the time—as he continues to be today—was Mortimer J. Adler. We have discussed many of the themes treated here repeatedly over the years, and he has given me many useful bibliographical suggestions. We have agreed on many points, and differed on others. His intellectual judgments are represented in many places in this book, usually without credit. I offer it here.

Students of the history of knowledge owe much to the work of F. J. Teggart and G. H. Hildebrand, whose carefully chosen collection of classic readings, *The Idea of Progress* (University of California Press, 1949), is a consistently useful guide to works from three millennia.

For broad interpretations of this literature I am indebted to many philosophical historians, from Ibn Khaldun to Oswald Spengler, from Arnold J. Toynbee to Fernand Braudel. The last, in particular, taught me to pay close attention to the small details of everyday life, which tell us so much about the way people live, whatever they say or write.

For the history of science, I am indebted to various works by James Burke (especially *Connections*, Little Brown, 1978), Herbert Butterfield (especially *The Origins of Modern Science*, Macmillan, 1951), and Erwin Schrödinger (especially *Nature and the Greeks*, Cambridge, 1954).

Among anthropologists, I have learned most from Bronislaw Malinowski, Claude Lévi-Strauss, and Lord Raglan, author of *The Hero* (Vintage, 1956). Robert L. Heilbroner's *The Worldly Historians* (Simon and Schuster, 1953, 1986) has helped me to understand and utilize a number of works in economics.

Every time I reread Marshall McLuhan's *Understanding Media* (McGraw Hill, 1965) I am again impressed by the power of his insights and the accuracy of his predictions.

No recent book about the worldwide experience of modernity seems to me so thoughtful and provocative as Marshall Berman's *All That Is Solid Melts Into Air* (Simon & Schuster, 1982). I have not met its author, but I have engaged Professor Berman in many silent conversations in the watches of the night.

It was my brother, John Van Doren, who brought Berman's book to my attention; he also made me read for the first time, many years ago, John Masefield's perfect lyric of world history, "Cargoes." I am grateful for these recommendations, among many others; for his thoughtful comments on parts of the manuscript; and for conversations over five decades, during which I doubtless got more than I gave.

I am grateful, indeed, to all my friends and seminar students over the past six years who, in the course of discussions more or less formal and more or less heated, have given me ideas and helped me to understand points that had baffled or irritated me. They could not have known this at the time, nor could I now more precisely enumerate my debts.

My twenty years as an editor of Encyclopaedia Britannica taught me much about many things. In particular I grew to have a profound respect not only for my colleagues but also for the work that they produce. Hardly a day has passed when I have not consulted the Britannica on some matter, major or minor. I am well aware that the editors of Britannica have been engaged for more than two centuries in the same task that I have here undertaken for myself—that is, the preparation of a history of the knowledge of the human race. They have, of course, gone about it in a very different way.

It is my pleasure to record here three other debts. The first is to Patrick Gunkel, the inventor of ideonomy and my friend of two decades. In a hundred lengthy conversations over the years Pat has brought me to understand that there is a history of the future as well as the past. I have shamelessly employed some of his insights, including the idea of companion computers (CCs). The most valuable thing he has taught me is that the future has a hard substantiality and may be even more intelligible than the past. It is, of course, the present that is hardest to understand.

I owe a large debt to my editors, Hillel Black and Donald J. Davidson, who insisted ruthlessly on clarity and demanded that I write, rewrite, and rewrite until they were satisfied I had said what I intended. If the book has merit, they deserve much of the credit. Its faults are mine alone.

My wife, Geraldine, read every page of the manuscript twice and made a thousand suggestions, most of which I adopted. More important, she allowed me to experiment with ideas, as I proposed theses that either outraged, delighted, or amused her. The book could not have existed without her help.

Cornwall, Connecticut
August 1991

Author to Reader

THE VOLUMINOUS LITERATURE dealing with the idea of human progress is decidedly a mixed bag. While some of these writings are impressive and even inspiring, many of them are superficial, perhaps even ridiculous, in their reiteration (especially during the nineteenth century) of the comforting prospect that every day in every way we are growing better and better.

This kind of foolishness is manifested especially in discussions of such matters as economic, political, and moral progress, and of progress in art. In fact, it is hard to argue effectively for the proposition that progress in mankind's overall wealth, in general governance, in the average or typical behavior of human beings, or in the production of great works of art has occurred over the entire history of the human race on earth.

From time to time, there seems to be real and measurable improvement in these areas. At other times the opposite seems equally to be the case. Thus the fervent belief of writers like the French sociophilosopher Auguste Comte in the inevitability of progress in all fields of human endeavor must be viewed as insupportable. We cannot accept it any longer, even if we once thought it was true.

Progress in Knowledge

Progress in human knowledge is another matter. Here it is possible to argue cogently that progress is in the nature of things. "Not only does each individual progress from day to day," wrote the French philosopher, mathematician, and mystic Blaise Pascal, "but mankind as a whole constantly progresses . . . in proportion as the universe grows older." The essence of man as a rational being, as a later historian would put it, is that he develops his potential capacities by accumulating the experience of past generations.

Just as in our individual lives we learn more and more from day to day and from year to year because we remember some at least of what we have learned and add our new knowledge to it, so in the history of the race the collective memory retains at least some knowledge from the past to which is added every new discovery.

The memories of individuals fail and the persons die, but the memory of the race is eternal, or at least it can be expected to endure as long as human beings continue to write books and read them, or—which becomes more and more common—store up their knowledge in other mediums for the use of future generations.

The rate at which the totality of human knowledge increases varies from age to age; sometimes the rate is very fast (as, for example, it is today or it was during the fifth century BC), while at other times it is very slow (as, for example, it was during the Dark Ages). Nevertheless, this progress essentially never ceases and, most probably, never can cease as long as man is man.

Kinds of Progress in Knowledge

The knowledge that thus expands and accumulates is of several kinds. We know more today about how nature works than we knew a hundred years ago, or a thousand, and we can expect to know even more a hundred years hence. It is easy to understand and accept the idea of progress in know-how, or technology, and to be optimistic about its continuing in the foreseeable future.

Progress in other kinds of knowledge *may* have occurred. For example, as long as historians are free to write about the past, and readers are free to read their books (neither has always been true, as the Roman historian Tacitus reminds us), we will never forget the new ideas about just government that were advanced and fought for during the revolutions of the eighteenth century in England, America, and France. This does not mean that better governance is inevitable; the time may come when we look back with a sigh to those happy days when democracy flourished throughout much of the globe. But even then we will *know* more about governance than we once did.

Similarly, the glowing examples of Socrates, Jesus, St. Francis of Assisi, and Dr. Martin Luther King, Jr., to name only a few, will not be lost while we can read or otherwise recall the stories of their lives and realize how they challenge us to live like them. This does not mean we will necessarily be better human beings, but we will know more about what human excellence is and can be.

Universal History

Progress in knowledge was painfully slow as long as the racial memory was transmitted only by oral traditions. For example, some primitive man or woman discovered long ago that the great enemy, fire, could be forced to obey and to make life better. Without any organized means of communication, it may have taken many generations for this new knowledge to become universal. With the invention of writing, the process of building up a body of knowledge available, essentially, to all human beings accelerated. Today, devices for storing and recalling the accumulated knowledge of the human race, such as computers, are *themselves* subject to progressive efforts to improve them.

These things being so, the history of mankind is the history of the progress and development of human knowledge. Universal history, at least, which deals not so much with the deeds of individuals or even of nations as with the accomplishments and the failures of the race as a whole, is no other than an account of how mankind's knowledge has grown and changed over the ages.

Universal history, thus conceived as the history of knowledge, is not a chronology of every discovery and invention ever made. Many of them—perhaps most—are ultimately of little value. Instead, it is and must be the story, told in the broadest and most general terms, of the significant new knowledge that humanity has acquired at various epochs and added to the growing store. It is also the story of how, at certain times, knowledge has changed more than it has grown, and how at other times major elements of knowledge have been given up or lost completely, because these seemed irrelevant to a succeeding age.

For example, the fall of the Roman empire was a nearly universal cataclysm, resulting in misery and suffering everywhere in the European world. Despite that, or perhaps even because of it, new kinds of knowledge emerged in the following centuries. Most of that new knowledge has not endured, but it remains as an example of a remarkable way of life that we have discarded, but to which it is possible that we may some day return. And when the classical Greek and Roman knowledge, which had been forgotten, was rediscovered during the Renaissance it had an energizing effect and helped to create the world in which we live today.

For another example, the seventeenth century saw more than its share of war and conquest, in both East and West, as well as a great number of relatively minor inventions and discoveries that led to increases in human comfort. Yet all those pale to insignificance when compared to that age's discovery of scientific method, which has proved to be the key to enormous progress in many kinds of knowledge in the past three centuries.

Finally, the "knowledge explosion" of our own time is a phenomenon that it is futile to try to define if the attempt is made to describe every bit and piece of new knowledge. But our century has seen a number of very significant advances in knowledge that will probably continue to affect the way human beings live (not necessarily for the better) for generations to come. Most of these advances build on progressive developments of knowledge in the past; they are significant primarily because that is so. They are therefore part of universal history.

These great advances, changes and, perhaps, temporary losses of knowledge are the subject matter of this book. It is a general history of man's accumulation of knowledge about the world he lives in and about himself—and, sometimes, his failure to understand either or both. Since that accumulation reveals perceptible patterns over the centuries, the book can also attempt a forecast of future progress in knowledge. The more clearly we see how knowledge has changed and grown in the past, particularly the recent past, the more accurately we can predict the changes that are likely to occur in the future—at least the near future.

The far future, a century or more away, is another matter. Here, one can only guess what will happen. I shall offer some guesses that I believe are plausible in the last chapter.

Primitive Man

Other animals have physical advantages over human beings: they see, hear, and smell better, they run faster, they bite harder. Neither animals nor plants need houses to live in or schools to go to, where they must be taught what they have to know to survive in an unfriendly world. Man, unadorned, is a naked ape, shivering in the cold blast, suffering pangs of hunger and thirst, and the pain of fear and loneliness.

But he has knowledge. With it he has conquered the earth. The rest of the universe awaits his coming with, I suspect, some trepidation.

It is very difficult to reach into and understand someone else's mind, even someone you know well, someone you live or work with, someone you see every day. It is even more difficult to reach into and understand the minds of a pair of naked apes, the first man and woman, who may have lived as much as a quarter of a million years ago. But it is worth trying, if only in imagination.

Our ancestors would have looked like us. The male would have been small, the female even smaller, both of them less than five feet tall. Imagine them standing before you. Imagine looking into their eyes. What would you see there? What would they see in you?

Leave aside the fear you would probably feel, and they surely would.

Suppose you can overcome this mutual fear; imagine that you are free to try to know one another. Do not assume you could talk to them; they might not have language as you understand it. Even so, they can communicate with one another, as you can see. Watch them do things, and let them watch you. That way, you might arrive at some notion of what they know.

As you imagine them standing before you, as you imagine them moving, gesturing, communicating; catching, killing, or gathering their food, preparing it, eating it; cleaning themselves; covering themselves against the cold; caressing one another and making love—as you imagine all this, you would have to conclude that they know a great deal.

Some of what you know, these creatures must know, too. But they must know other things that you do not know, unless you are an experienced survivalist. As you come to this conclusion, you realize that a large part of the things you know, you know the *way* they would. The great majority of what you know, furthermore, is *like* what they know.

Knowledge of Particulars

They know where they are, well enough to get around and to survive; and if they do not have names for the places they know, like West Fourth or Downtown, they must recognize markers both in things and in their memories that allow them to know where they are at any time. They also know there are other beings beside themselves, and they must have invented signs or markers of them as well.

In fact, as you think about it, they must possess innumerable bits of knowledge of this kind: A squirrel has a nest in that tree; tigers come to drink in this spring in the evening, but it is safe to draw water in the morning; the stones in that stream make good arrowheads. We all know innumerable things of this kind. They are what mostly fill our minds and memories.

That kind of thing is what mostly, and perhaps exclusively, fills the minds and memories of animals, too. Animals know where they are; they resist being lost, the tales being legion of how they came home through unfamiliar territory. My black dog knows many things about her environment—which men and vehicles are safe and which are not, where the deer and the woodchucks are likely to be found, that breakfast is always followed by one or two pieces of toast for her, with butter and jelly. My cat also has many bits of particular knowledge in her mind, and I am sure the birds in our yard, the foxes that cross our field in the night, and the mice that inhabit the barns know a vast number of things about the world around them. For the mice certainly, and probably for the cat and perhaps for the dog, all the things they know are particular things.

General Knowledge

There is another kind of thing that we know and they do not. We know that the sun rises in the morning, crosses the sky, and sets in the evening; we know that the sun does this every day, even when clouds obscure its passage, and always will as long as the world exists. We know that winter follows summer, and summer winter. We know that all living things were born and will also die, sooner or later. In short, we know the causes of things—at least some things.

Those and others like them are bits of general knowledge, which we state in language that is different from the language we use when divulging our knowledge of particulars.

> A squirrel has a nest in that tree.
>
> All living things are born and also die.

How different, in their weight and beauty, are those statements! The first, ordinarily of no account, might be important if you were hungry. But it requires such particular circumstances. The second is majestic and true at all times and places.

I have said that animals do not possess general knowledge—concepts, as they are called—and we do. Personally, I am not certain of that, in the case of some animals—for example, my dog; but I cannot prove she does possess that kind of knowledge, for she cannot speak and tell me so. She is a dumb animal—all animals are dumb—and therefore we can never rightly know what is in their minds apart from what we can deduce must be there because of the way they behave.

We can easily deduce that they have many bits of particular knowledge, but we cannot say that they possess general knowledge. We have supposed that we could not talk to our imaginary pair of naked apes. We could only stare at them and watch them act. Watching them, can we deduce that they know the sun always rises in the morning and sets in the evening? Do they know that all living things are born and also die? Do they, too, know the causes of some things?

If they do not, there is a simple explanation: We have gone back too far in time. Move the clock forward, quickly. Sooner or later we will come upon primitive men and women who know in both the ways we do, who are fully human because they know as we know.

They may still be naked, they may still be fearful, they may still try to flee from us or, alternatively, try to kill us. But they will be like us in the only way that is really essential. And probably, very soon, they will be able to speak and tell us so.

When this first happened to mankind is truly beyond our knowledge. Perhaps it happened a million years ago, perhaps only ten thousand. How it happened is equally mysterious. What is important is that it did happen, and that human beings began to know in this new way, not shared with the animals, and became conscious that they did. Thus began the great story that is this book.

Certain Knowledge

For the most part our knowledge of particulars is certain. When it comes to knowing where we are, for instance, we may be right or we may be wrong, but if we are right, we are certainly right. If we are Downtown, and say we are, there is no doubt about its being so.

Our general knowledge about the way nature works and the way human beings behave is always to some extent doubtful. Even when it comes to the rising of the sun, we realize that it is at best highly probable, and not certain. Something could happen to the earth or the sun so that it would not rise tomorrow. (Of course, if it did not, we would not be here to see it.)

Two types of our general knowledge are characterized by certainty. One is our knowledge of self-evident propositions. The other is faith.

There are not many self-evident propositions; some philosophers claim there are none. We do not have to become involved in philosophical disputes to understand what is meant here. Take, for example, the general proposition:

A finite whole is greater than any of its parts.

When we understand what is meant by "finite whole," "part," and "greater," we see that this proposition is true beyond doubt.

Another self-evident proposition is this:

A thing cannot both be and not be at the same time
and in the same respect.

Again, if we understand the meaning of the terms, the proposition is indubitably true.

Thomas Jefferson said that the general proposition with which he began the Declaration of Independence, namely, that all men are created equal, was self-evident. Most do not agree that this is self-evident, even if they accept it as true. In fact, there are not many propositions beside the two I have mentioned that are widely accepted as self-evident.

Many mathematical statements are certainly true if we accept the assumptions on which they are based. If we define "two," "plus," and "equals" in a certain way (although it is not easy to do that), then "two plus two equals four" is certainly true. The same goes for the proposition that "the sum of the angles of a triangle is equal to two right angles," as well as for other, more complicated mathematical statements. But the world of mathematics is not the real world; the certainty we find in it is the certainty we put there, so it is not surprising that we find it. The certainty of self-evident propositions is inherent in the nature of things. But there are only a few such propositions.

Faith is also certain knowledge; it is knowledge that is revealed to us by God. If the revelation is direct, as it was, Moses said, in his case, then there is no question about it. It is more difficult for some than for others to accept with utter finality and certitude any second-hand revelation. It is said, in fact, that no one can fully accept such a revelation without God's help, his grace. No matter how hard you try, according to this line of argument, you cannot have faith—which is absolute certainty that God exists, for instance—without God's grace. If you ask, How do I know I have received God's grace? the answer is: If you know with certainty that God exists, then you have received it; if not, not.

Despite the apparent circularity of this reasoning, it is sufficient to multitudes. At any rate, there are many who possess faith not only that God exists, but that other consequential propositions are also certainly true: God made the world, God rules the world, God loves mankind, and all that happens is for the best. All of these are unquestionably propositions about the real world, just as much as the statement that the sun rises every morning and sets every evening.

Faith is not a recent acquisition of human beings. It seems very likely that our imaginary couple would have known or believed some things with the same tenacious certainty that characterizes believers of our own day.

Assuming they knew the sun rises and sets every day, they may also have known, or believed with even greater certainty, that the sun would cease to rise if they ceased to please it. They may have believed with equal certitude that births, at least human ones, did not occur unless some other god was pleased or placated, and that death finally came only to those who were displeasing to the gods.

In other words, they might have felt that they certainly understood the world because they understood the gods, and that the world, because of their relation to it and to the gods, must be what they believed it to be.

The notion that the world must be what we believe it to be *because* we believe it to be that way has been the source of great comfort to billions of persons, including perhaps our naked ancestors, but it has also been a source of discomfort to others. The reason is that a long time ago (nobody knows how long), human beings began to think that their systems of knowledge and faith were so crucial to the meaning of their lives that they had to kill other human beings who had different systems. That is only one reason why knowledge does not always make us happy.

Knowledge and Happiness

Animals do not seem to be unhappy, at least in the way human beings are. As Walt Whitman wrote in "Song of Myself":

> I think I could turn and live with animals,
>   they are so placid and self-contain'd . . .
> Not one is respectable or unhappy over the whole earth.

Many human beings are unhappy either because of what they know or because of what they do not know. Ignorance remains bliss only so long as it is ignorance; as soon as one learns one is ignorant, one begins to want not to be so. In the case of cats this is called curiosity. In the case of mankind it is something deeper and even more essential.

The desire to know, when you realize you do not know, is universal and probably irresistible. It was the original temptation of mankind, and no man or woman, and especially no child, can overcome it for long. But it is a desire, as Shakespeare said, that grows by what it feeds on. It is impossible to slake the thirst for knowledge. And the more intelligent you are, the more this is so.

Knowledge of particulars lacks the quality of essential insatiability. So it is, also, with the faith that passes understanding. Immemorially, therefore, the only effective cure for the disease of insatiable desire for knowledge has been faith, the grace of God.

Our ancient ancestors may have had a primitive equivalent of faith. Millions of more recent ancestors possessed it, or said they did. But do many human beings living today rest comfortable in the knowledge that they possess, without desiring more? Or has the disease of insatiable knowledge become epidemic among all the peoples of the earth?

Outline of the Book

This book is divided into fifteen chapters. The first, "Wisdom of the Ancients," beginning with written history, around 3000 BC, describes the most significant elements of general knowledge shared by the peoples of the ancient empires, from the Egyptian to the Aztec and the Inca. Essentially, this is what mankind knew before the explosion of Greek thought that occurred in the sixth century BC. Chapter 2, "The Greek Explosion," describes that epochal event and shows how what the Greeks knew has affected all subsequent progress in knowledge.

Greek civilization was absorbed into and adapted by the Roman empire, which looked upon much that the Greeks knew with suspicion. Nevertheless, the Romans insured that the most important elements of Greek knowledge would survive, even if they did not like them. As Chapter 3, "What the Romans Knew," reveals, the Romans also possessed important knowledge of their own, some of which forms the foundations of our knowledge today.

The Roman empire fell to the barbarian hordes in the fifth century AD. Chapters 4 and 5, "Light in the Dark Ages" and "The Middle Ages: The Great Experiment," describe the world that succeeded the empire. Life was very different, and so was knowledge. In particular, a great experiment in governance was undertaken during the thousand years after the fall of Rome, an experiment that failed, but one that holds lessons for our future.

Chapter 6, "What Was Reborn in the Renaissance?" describes the changes in knowledge produced by the rediscovery of classical civilization after ages of neglect. It also shows how the effort to understand the ancient world and to incorporate its newfound knowledge into the culture of the Middle Ages broke that culture apart and launched mankind on its tumultuous journey to the present day.

Around 1500 AD, universal history, the story of progress in knowledge, enters a new stage. It had taken perhaps a hundred thousand years for the human population to reach 400,000,000, the level it enjoyed in 1500; the earth's population will *increase* by a similar amount in the five years between 1995 and 2000. Chapter 7, "Europe Reaches Out," attempts to explain this extraordinary change. Major emphasis is placed upon the achievement of Columbus, who inherited a world divided and bequeathed to us a world well on the way to the unity that it experiences today, and that will be even more complete tomorrow.

Human progress is more than merely the progress of knowledge of Western man. Nevertheless, during the period between about 1550 and about 1700 Western man invented a method of acquiring knowledge that would soon be employed everywhere on earth. There are other kinds of knowledge beside scientific knowledge, as Chapter 8, "The Invention of Scientific Method," affirms, but none of them, at the present time and in the foreseeable future, has the power, prestige, and value that scientific knowledge has. Science has become the most distinctive of human activities, and the indispensable tool for the survival of the billions who now inhabit the planet.

Newton's *Principia* was published in 1687 and imbued the succeeding age with the idea that mechanical principles ruled the world. This idea accomplished a great deal, including inaugurating the Industrial Revolution, but it was another kind of revolution that more truly characterized the eighteenth century. Chapter 9, "An Age of Revolutions," deals in succession with the Glorious Revolution of 1688 (in England), the American Revolution of 1776, and the French Revolution of 1789, showing how radically new ideas about governance were discovered, leading to knowledge about how men may best live together that has come to ultimate—or almost ultimate—fruition in our own time.

Chapter 10, "The Nineteenth Century: Prelude to Modernity," covers the eventful hundred years from 1815 and the Battle of Waterloo to 1914 and the onset of the Great Twentieth-Century War. The chapter shows how a complete change in social and economic institutions, brought on primarily by the Industrial Revolution but also at least in part by the political revolutions of the previous century, was preparing the way for the new and fundamentally different world that we inhabit today. The elements of this change are all to be found in nineteenth-century thought, even if the concrete realization of the change often had to wait for the twentieth century.

Chapter 11, "The World in 1914," sets the stage for the birth of this new world, which is the one we now know. By that date, hardly anything could happen in one place on the globe that did not affect events in another, and so it is not surprising that the war that began in that year was termed a world war. But why did the war have to destroy the old civilization in order for the new to come into being? The reasons are found in the very nature not only of knowledge but of man.

Chapter 12, "The Triumph of Democracy," Chapter 13, "Science and Technology," and Chapter 14, "Art and the Media," treat the twentieth century. Together these three chapters deal with the great achievements in the progress of knowledge, and only secondarily with the events that have occurred during the approximately seventy-five years since the onset of World War I. Many living persons have seen these things happen and these great changes in what we know occur. Perhaps no living individual, including myself, can have a totally unbiased perspective on this splendid, cruel, and creative century. But most readers will recognize the emergence of the new knowledge described, and concede its significance.

Chapter 15, the last, is "The Next Hundred Years." It describes several changes in human knowledge and, especially, in the uses of knowledge that I think are quite likely to occur before the year 2100. The chapter also treats some things that may occur by that date, although I am by no means sure. If they do occur, they will be among the most important events in the history of human knowledge, that is, in human history.

A History of Knowledge

1

Wisdom of the Ancients

By THE TIME written history began, some fifty centuries ago, mankind had learned much more than our primitive ancestors knew.

Human beings in many different parts of the world had discovered not only how to use the skins of animals and birds for clothing, but also how to weave wool, cotton, and flax to make cloth. They had discovered not only how to hunt animals and fish for food, but also how to grow grains and make bread, both leavened and unleavened, as well as cakes made out of rice. They had learned how to sow seeds in the wild, and how to clear the land and till the soil, and to irrigate and fertilize it. They had learned not only how to make homes in caves and other natural shelters, but also how to build houses and monumental structures out of wood, stone, bricks, and other materials, some existing naturally, others man-made. They had also learned how to make and replicate statues and other works of art, and how to mine ores from the earth, smelt them, and make new metals by combining those found in nature.

A large part of mankind's ingenuity had gone into inventing new ways of killing and torturing other human beings, and the threat of pain or death had been found to be the best, and often the only, means of ruling large numbers of people. In several parts of the world, in Egypt, in Mesopotamia, in Persia, in India, in China, empires had been formed or were in the process of being formed to rule over vast areas and millions of subjects. These empires gave their people law, which is to say, a measure of peace and security against the violence of other people like themselves. But they provided no security against the rulers themselves, who ruled by violence and guile, and whose will was absolute.

Almost everywhere priests, whose business it was to interpret the equally absolute and despotic will of the gods, joined with the temporal rulers to keep the people in submission. The ruled submitted because they had no choice. Probably they did not even imagine an alternative. No-

3

where in the world did people think that they could rule themselves instead of either dominating others or being ruled by them.

Everywhere, in short, a state of war existed, between one people and another and between a ruler and his people. Everywhere, as Thucydides wrote, the strong did what they wished and the weak suffered what they had to. There was no arbiter except force, and justice and the right was everywhere and always no other than the interest of the stronger.

Even so, the human race prospered, and its numbers grew. Competing for dominance with the larger animals, it had begun its work of ridding the planet of "enemies," as it called them: the saber-toothed tiger, the mammoth, and dozens of other species. By the second millennium before the Christian era, almost all of the larger animals had either been hunted to extinction, domesticated, or denominated as "game." In other words, they were used for pleasure, for work, or for food.

In one small corner of the world, a race of men grew up calling themselves Jews and affirming a novel story of the creation. In the beginning, these people said, the one God had made a paradise from which man, through his own fault (or rather the fault of woman), was exiled. Henceforth, God told man, he would have to work for a living. But since God loved man, he gave him the earth and all it contained for his sustenance and survival. The exploitation of the animal and vegetable kingdoms was therefore justified by divine decree.

This, too, was the law of force, justice being the interest of the stronger. Since it was divine, it was also right.

Egypt

The first empires grew up in major river valleys of Africa and Asia. Egypt, which believed itself to be born of the Nile, was probably the first of all. It was organized and unified sometime between 3100 and 2900 BC, and it endured as a semi-independent state for about three thousand years, until the Roman conquest in 30 BC.

Egypt's remarkable and indeed unique persistence over three millennia may be accounted for in part by the country's relative freedom from competition, owing to its geographical isolation. It was surrounded on three sides by practically impassable deserts, so the invasions, when they occurred, usually came across the Isthmus of Suez. This narrow piece of land could be defended fairly easily.

Other empires also enjoyed isolation, but they did not last. The Egyptians had a great secret, which they did not forget for thirty centuries. They feared and hated change, and they avoided it wherever possible.

The Egyptian state lacked much that we feel is necessary for efficient government today. But it worked well enough. No people has ever so completely accepted the rule: If it works, do not try to fix it. Once they had established a kingdom and an economy based on the agriculture made possible by the annual inundations of the Nile, the rulers of Egypt, together with those they ruled, became fiercely determined to avoid progressing in any way. And they managed to progress remarkably little in three thousand years.

Like all ancient empires, Egypt was organized on hierarchical principles. The gods stood at the top of the hierarchy; beneath them were ranged the vast assembly of the dead. At the bottom of the hierarchy lay humanity as a whole, by which was principally understood the Egyptians.

The pharaoh occupied a unique and powerful position, standing as he did between humanity and the dead above him (and the gods above the dead). In this hierarchy of beings he was the only individual being, the sole link between the living human world and the world of spirits.

The pharaoh was human, but he was also more than human, not so much in his person as by virtue of his role in the cosmic hierarchy. He was feared, adored, and obeyed, because not to do so was to call everything in question, including the regularity of the inundations of the river—on which the life of the community depended—as well as *ma'at*, "social order." In that supremely conservative and tradition-bound society, order was of the essence.

Egyptian agriculture was efficient and fruitful partly because of the fertile soil the great river brought down each year. Consequently, there was usually a surplus of labor. According to the Egyptian interpretation of social order, no one should be idle, and so the surplus was used for immense construction projects. The building of the Great Pyramids during a four-hundred-year span from about 2700 to about 2300 BC would tax modern abilities, yet the Egyptians did not even have metal tools with which to work the stone (their knives and chisels were made of obsidian, a black volcanic glass). Daunting as were the physical challenges, the economic ones surpassed them. And the army of workers, who for the most part were not slaves, appears to have labored willingly.

Why were the Egyptians so tradition-bound and conservative? Why was social order so important that change and progress of every kind had to be sacrificed to it? Was it because the river that had given the society its birth remained unchanging in its course? Was it a habit into which the Egyptians fell early in their history, a habit they could never break? Or was there something about the Egyptian temperament that led this remarkable people to choose the road of immutability toward the immortality that all men seek?

It is difficult if not impossible to answer these questions. One fact is to be noted: Ancient Egypt, in keeping with its extreme conservatism, seemed to be in love with death. Men lived but to die, and they spent their lives and their fortunes preparing for death. However, death was not as we conceive of it, but a kind of hovering, phantasmagoric immortality. The dead were all around them, in the air, in the ground, in the waters of the Nile. Their presence gave this ancient people of the river a certain comfort.

Perhaps that does not answer the question of why the Egyptians were the way they were. Probably it suffices to say that even today many individuals adopt the Egyptian attitude toward life, preferring the status quo to almost any change, even if change is shown to be improvement. In other words, the Egyptians were acting in a fundamentally human way. The only surprising thing is that they were all acting in the same way.

It is also important to recognize the wisdom of their stance. Change for the sake of change alone is a principle of dubious merit. If life is acceptable as it stands, why change it? From the point of view of tyrants, that rule is all the more important to follow. Any change, for a tyrant, is for the worse. Thus the Egyptians had discovered a secret of great value for tyrants down the centuries. The tyrants of our own time have not forgotten it.

India

The ten centuries beginning about 2500 BC saw the rise and fall of an ancient river valley culture based on the Indus River, which today flows through western Pakistan. Two major cities, Mohenjo-daro and Harappa, each having a population of more than fifty thousand persons, and numerous other smaller settlements grew up in an area considerably larger than modern Pakistan. At its greatest extent, around 2000 BC, the Indus Valley civilization covered an area larger than either Egypt or Mesopotamia, making it the largest empire up to that time.

Mohenjo-daro came to a sudden end around the middle of the second millennium, apparently in an attack by Aryan invaders, who left hundreds of dead lying in the abandoned streets. Farther south, the civilization survived and probably merged slowly into subsequent cultures of central and western India.

Little is known about the social organization of the Indus Valley civilization, but its descendants all reveal a principle of hierarchical ordering known as the caste system. For many centuries it has been a powerful tool for controlling a large population in which there are severe differences in wealth, power, and privileges.

In modern India there are thousands of castes, but only four main groups of castes, a division that goes back to well before the time of Christ. At the top of the hierarchy stand the Brahmans (priests), then the barons or warriors, then the commoners or merchants, and lastly the Sudras (artisans and laborers). As such, the system does not markedly differ from that of other ancient hierarchical societies. The genius of the caste system is its powerful feedback mechanism. One is not only born a Sudra; one also becomes a Sudra by the occupation one follows, which Sudras alone must follow and which only Sudras may follow. Everyone is "polluted" by his occupation, his dietary habits, his customs; since "pollution" is unavoidable, it is accepted by all.

It is everywhere true that those at the bottom of the social hierarchy are the majority, in the past often the great majority. Their lives are nastier, more brutish, and considerably shorter than the lives of their more fortunate contemporaries. Why then does the majority remain deprived? The minority at the top may have a near monopoly of force, but force alone is not the answer. A system of social differentiation must be found in which all believe, not just some. The universal acceptance of the caste system ensures its perpetuation.

It is easy to blame the Indians for living under a caste system when we do not. However, social classes have many affinities to the castes of India. Members of the lowest class often feel they rightfully belong to it; the same goes for the members of the higher classes. Members of any class are intensely uncomfortable when they find themselves in the company of persons of another class. There are certain occupations that upper-class people simply do not follow, and the same goes for lower-class people. Different classes also eat different foods differently and have different customs in family life, courtship, and so forth.

The ancient cultures of the Indian subcontinent may have been the first to discover this powerful means of maintaining social order. But they were by no means the only cultures to use the principle once it was discovered. It thrives today. Class differentiation is the great foe of the equally great idea of social equality. It is also much older.

China

Human settlement in what is now China dates to about 350,000 years ago. The first dynasty for which historical materials survive, the Shang, ruled over a large part of modern China from about 1750 to 1111 BC. In the latter year the Chou, a subject people of the Shang, defeated them and instituted a dynasty that endured until 255 BC. A time of troubles ensued, which was ended by the first true unification of China, in the year 221 BC.

This was accomplished by the Ch'in, one of four or five different but closely related peoples inhabiting the area. Their king took the name Shih Huang-ti: "First sovereign emperor." His dominions defined China from that time. In later epochs China sometimes held other territories, but the lands of Shih Huang-ti remained the indivisible area of China proper.

The new emperor immediately set about consolidating his gains. His first major project was to build a network of roads. The second involved connecting and strengthening the walls guarding his northern borders. Hundreds of thousands of men labored on what is probably the greatest construction project ever undertaken. They completed the wall, stretching some fifteen hundred miles from the Gulf of Chihli to Tibet, in a little over ten years. For two millennia the Great Wall defined the frontier between civilization and barbarism, in the minds of Chinese.

The most important change made by Shih Huang-ti had to do with social organization. At one stroke he abolished the feudalism that had shaped Chinese society for a thousand years and replaced it with a complex state bureaucracy based on Confucian principles.

Confucius was born in 551 BC and died in 479. A member of the impoverished nobility, he was orphaned and grew up poor. Although largely self-educated, he was famous as the most learned man of his time. Despite this achievement and his other merits, he was unable to obtain a position allowing scope for his talents. He therefore gathered about him a group of disciples and began to teach them. He ended up being the most famous teacher in Chinese history and one of the most influential men of all time.

Confucian doctrine is complex and has changed much over the centuries. One essential principle has not changed, which is that all eminence should be based entirely on merit. Ability and moral excellence, according to Confucius, rather than birth, fitted a man for leadership. Merit was based on learning—in later centuries, when Confucianism became the state orthodoxy, on knowledge of Confucian texts.

Shih Huang-ti was imbued with Confucian teachings, and he based his new bureaucracy on its principle of moral excellence. Entry into the bureaucracy was supposed to be based on merit alone, except for the highest posts, which were reserved for the emperor's family. This was a far cry from the feudalism which the new bureaucracy replaced, where power was achieved by birth and military might.

The feudal lords did not give in without a struggle. In particular, a number of intellectuals objected to the abolition of the old system. Shih Huang-ti did not tolerate any dissent. Four hundred and sixty protesting intellectuals were tortured, then buried alive. That was shocking, for intellectuals had usually been safe from the anger of Chinese tyrants. Even more shocking was the emperor's order that all books other than those dealing with law, horticulture, and herbal medicine be burned. That odd trio of subjects alone was safe. All other kinds of knowledge were dangerous, and speculation about any other field of knowledge was banned.

Shih Huang-ti wished above all to be immortal. Every divinity that might in any way be helpful to this aim was propitiated, at state expense, and messengers fanned out over the empire to seek an elixir of life. None was found, and the emperor died only twelve years after founding his state.

The empire collapsed after the death of Shih Huang-ti, but the seeds of unity had been planted. As it turned out, Shih Huang-ti's innovations were crucial to the task of ruling a nation as large as China, at the time, from about 200 BC to about 200 AD, the largest and most populous in the world. These included the establishment and maintenance of a bureaucracy based more or less on merit, with merit determined by learning; the careful control of the economy, effected by mass construction projects that employed all surplus labor; and the idea that most knowledge is dangerous.

The Chinese have never forgotten those three precepts. The present Communist regime adheres to all of them, two thousand years after Shih Huang-ti. But those principles have been adopted by other historical tyrants, and even some democratic regimes. Until very recently, entry into the British foreign service depended on knowledge of Greek and Latin and the ability to translate classical texts into elegant English prose. It was taken for granted that if a man could learn Greek and Latin well, he could learn anything else equally well, including diplomacy.

The major totalitarian regimes of our time have engaged their peoples in massive construction projects, partly for the glory of the regime, partly so that no one should suffer—or enjoy—the restlessness of the unemployed. And every tyrant in history has attempted to insulate his people from all kinds of knowledge except the most practical. A knowledgeable populace will always seek both freedom and justice, precisely those things tyrants do not wish to give them.

Mesopotamia

The earliest examples of Chinese writing date from the Shang Dynasty (eighteenth to twelfth century BC). By 1400 BC Chinese script contained more than twenty-five hundred characters, most of which can still be read. The script was fixed in its present form during the Ch'in period (the reign of Shih Huang-ti, from 221 to 206 BC).

Chinese script is the precursor of written Japanese and Korean as well, although the spoken languages are entirely different. Chinese writing is thus both very old and very influential.

It is not the oldest in the world, however. The honor of being the first to invent writing belongs to the Sumerians, who inhabited lower Mesopotamia (now southern Iraq) during the fourth and third millennia BC.

The Tigris and the Euphrates, the two great rivers of West Asia, rise in the mountains of eastern Turkey and flow southeasterly through northern Syria and Iraq. Both rivers have traversed more than two-thirds of their courses before reaching the fringes of the Mesopotamian Plain, the fruitful, silt-filled depression that is the joint delta of the rivers. At the lower end of this plain the rivers join and flow together, as the Shatt al-Arab, one hundred slow and meandering miles to the Persian Gulf.

Mesopotamia, "the land between the rivers," is the site of the earliest human civilization. A kind of primitive writing was developed in this extremely fertile region as early as about 8000 BC. By 3500 BC this system of writing had become coherent. By 3100 BC it is unambiguously related to the Sumerian language.

The cuneiform markings of ancient Sumerian comprised some twelve hundred different characters representing numerals, names, and such objects as cloth and cow. The earliest use of the written language was therefore to record the number of cows or bolts of cloth possessed by such and such a person. For centuries writing was used primarily for accounting purposes. But as life grew more complex and more things had to be recorded, the written language became more complex, too. This was particularly so when the Sumerian script was adopted by the Akkadians during the third millennium BC. The Akkadians, conquerors of the Sumerians, inherited much from their victims, but they possessed a social structure and a system of ownership that was different from that of the Sumerians. The Babylonians and Assyrians, successors to the Akkadians as rulers of Mesopotamia, added complexities of their own.

Mesopotamia went through numerous political changes from the fourth millennium, when part of it was first unified under the Sumerians, until it was finally conquered by the Persians under Cyrus the Great in 529 BC. But the knowledge of writing never was lost. Perhaps no other civilization besides our own has been so dependent on literacy, even though probably only one percent or fewer of Mesopotamians were ever literate, even in the best of times. Scribes, who wrote letters and kept records and accounts for kings and commoners alike, always possessed great power. As ancient advertisements for pupils and apprentices proclaimed, scribes wrote while the rest of the people worked.

Knowing how to read and write was the way to wealth and power among the Sumerians, the Akkadians, the Babylonians, and the Assyrians. It remains the case that literacy, even today, is often the key to advancement. Skill at interpreting small black marks on a piece of paper opens the way for the majority of Americans, for example, while the lack of it consigns a minority to a life of many deprivations. The percentages have changed since Assyrian times, but the principle has not.

Aztec and Inca

When the Spanish conquistadores reached the Valley of Mexico in 1519, and the high Valley of the Andes thirteen years later, in 1532, they were astonished to discover flourishing cities with large populations ruling over empires that rivaled in extent the largest countries of Europe. The Aztec, in Mexico, and the Inca, in Peru, were both remarkable civilizations. Both crumbled before the challenge of European arms. The Aztec empire was gone within a year after the arrival of Hernan Cortés. The Inca lasted a little longer, but their empire fell within three years to Francisco Pizzaro and his 168 Spanish soldiers, who defeated a large and superbly organized army standing at the head of a nation of 12 million persons.

The Aztecs were not the first people to organize a rich and powerful state in Mesoamerica. They were preceded by the Toltecs, and they by other peoples going back into the mists of prehistory. The population of what is now Mexico rose and fell as empires came and went. Under the Aztecs, at the time of the Spanish conquest, there were at least five million souls under the direct control of Montezuma II, the last of the Aztec rulers. Smaller states and tribes in the vicinity paid tribute to their Aztec overlords.

The Aztecs had discovered writing, they possessed a highly accurate calendar, and they were able to construct large and beautiful buildings out of stone, although they lacked metal tools. Perhaps their most notable achievements were in agriculture. They practiced an intensive system of crop diversification aided by complex irrigation works. They grew many grains, vegetables, and fruits that were unknown to their Spanish conquerors. Today, some 60 percent of all the foodstuffs in the world are descendants of crops grown in Mexico and Peru five hundred years ago.

The Inca empire stretched from modern Quito, Ecuador, to modern Santiago, Chile, a distance of more than three thousand miles. Like the Aztecs, the Inca were rich, although they seemed to love gold and silver more for their beauty than for the monetary value that the Spaniards saw in them. When they realized how mad the Spaniards were for gold, the Inca were happy to give them as much as they wanted, if they would only go away. The Spaniards did not leave, and the Inca fell.

The Inca were great builders, and their beautiful city of Machu Picchu, on its lofty peak in the Peruvian Andes, is one of the most thrilling archaeological sites in the world. Pizzaro never entered it, for the Inca themselves had forgotten the city by the time he came to Cuzco, their capital, in 1532; it was not discovered until the American explorer Hiram Bingham stumbled upon it in 1911. It had lain empty for five hundred years, for a reason that we will probably never know.

The Inca were also great road builders, constructing a system of royal roads that linked all the cities of the empire, up hill and down over distances of thousands of miles. But the Inca never discovered the wheel, so their roads were built for foot travel only and sometimes proceeded up and down the sides of mountains in a series of steps cut out of the rock.

The Inca also never discovered writing. They had lived for many centuries within a few hundred miles of the civilizations of Mesoamerica, but they did not know anything of them or their achievements. Their knowledge and skill in some things, and their ignorance in many others, are both extraordinary.

Why were the Spaniards able to destroy two flourishing civilizations so quickly and easily, so that today little is known of them and hardly anything survives except the ruins of monumental buildings, a few gold ornaments out of the millions that were made, and the foods that they grew? (The last is far from insignificant.) The answer may lie in the principles by which both empires were organized.

Fear and force ruled both empires. Both the Aztec and the Inca were relative *arrivistes*. In each case a ruthless, semibarbarian minority had taken over a previous, probably decadent civilization. These new rulers, having conquered by the merciless use of military power, saw no reason not to rule by it, too. They did not bother to try to acquire the love and loyalty of those they ruled. They had nothing they wished to give their subjects, except a measure of security against want and external enemies. But the enemy within—the rulers themselves—were more fearsome than any foreign foe. And the price exacted for freedom from want turned out to be very high.

It was paid in the blood of children and young people. Human sacrifice was practiced by both these unregretted civilizations of the recent past. Among the Aztec, the toll of sacrifice stuns the mind. In the last years before the Spanish conquest, a thousand of the finest children and young people were offered up each week. Dressed in splendid robes, they were drugged and then helped up the steps of the high pyramids and held down upon the altars. A priest, bloody knife in hand, parted the robes, made a quick incision, reached in his other hand and drew forth the heart, still beating, which he held high before the people assembled in the plaza below. A thousand a week, many of them captured in raids among the neighboring tribes in the Valley of Mexico. A thousand a week of the finest among the children and youth, who huddled in prisons before their turn came. It is no wonder that all the enemies of the Aztec rushed to become allies of the conquering Spaniards and helped to overthrow that brutal regime. Not that doing so helped these fervent allies. They were also enslaved by the victorious conquistadores.

The Inca did not regularly sacrifice large numbers of human beings, but whenever an Inca emperor died, the toll was terrible. Hundreds of maidens would be drugged, beheaded, and buried with the dead ruler. Hundreds of others would die whenever the state faced a difficult problem or decision. Stolid priests proclaimed that only thus would the gods be pleased to help, and so the beautiful boys and girls died on the reeking altars.

Pizzaro did not receive the aid of allies, for the Inca had conquered everyone within reach. But internal dynastic quarrels had rent the Inca, and one ruler, fighting with his rebellious family, welcomed the Spaniards because he supposed that they had come to help him. He was imprisoned and then executed, and the other claimants to the throne were soon in terminal disarray. Within fifty years, the population of twelve million had fallen to half a million, as thousands of Indians a week died in the mines high in the Andes, sacrifices to the unremitting desire of the Spanish monarchy for gold and silver.

Human Sacrifice

Sacrifice, one of the most fundamental and ubiquitous of religious rituals, was or is practiced in almost all of the religions that have ever existed. Great latitude is found in the types of living beings or other things that are or have been sacrificed, as well as in the ritual itself.

In the sacrifice that was central to all the ancient religions, the sacrificial object was usually an animal, frequently a valuable one: an ox or a ram, whose strength and virility were given to a god in return for a divine gift of strength or virility. Often, inanimate entities like wine or water, bread or corn, were substituted for the living victim. But in a sense, these entities were not "inanimate." They possessed a kind of life, given to them by the god, which was returned to him in the hope that he would once again instill life in the wine or corn.

Human sacrifice seems to have originated among the first agricultural peoples. Apparently rarely practiced by the hunter-gatherers who preceded them, it existed in all of the most ancient religions. The early Greeks and Romans, the earliest Jews, the Chinese and Japanese, the Indians, and many other ancient peoples sacrificed human beings to their gods. The victim was often dressed in magnificent garments and adorned with jewels so that he or she might go in glory to the god. The victims, often chosen for their youth and beauty (the god wanted the best), were drowned or buried alive, or their throats were cut so that their blood might bedew the ground, fructifying it, or be spattered upon the altar. The throats of bulls, rams, and goats were also ritually cut, their blood spilled upon the ground in the effort to please the god or produce a communion between the god and those who sought his help.

Two basically different types of ritual sacrifice seem to have been practiced in most parts of the earth. In one, the victim was killed, a part of the body was burned (and thus given to the god), and the remainder was eaten in a joyous meal of communion among the people, and presumably with the god as well. In the other, the victim was destroyed completely. If the sacrifice was to the gods of heaven, the sacrificial object was burned so that the smoke might rise to the divine abode; if to the gods of the underworld, the victim was buried.

Homer reveals that the first type of sacrifice was common among the Achaean besiegers of Troy. On many occasions in the *Iliad* bulls or oxen are sacrificed, their blood spilled upon the ground, and the fat thrown upon the flames so that the ritual smoke may rise to heaven. The soldiers then feast on the remainder of the beast. But in the *Odyssey*, Odysseus, desiring to visit the Underworld, sacrifices animals to its gods but does not eat them; what is not consumed by the flames is buried, as a propitiary offering. Such sacrifices the Greeks called Mysteries. They usually were practiced at night, in caves or other dark places, and the initiated alone were permitted to participate.

The story of the sacrifice of Isaac by his father Abraham is now believed to date from the beginning of the second millennium before Christ. It is told in the twenty-second chapter of Genesis.

And it came to pass after these things that God did tempt Abraham, and said unto him, Abraham: and he said, Behold, here I am.

And he said, Take now thy son, thine only son Isaac, whom thou lovest, and get thee into the land of Moriah; and offer him there for a burnt offering upon one of the mountains which I will tell thee of.

And Abraham rose up early in the morning, and saddled his ass, and took two of his young men with him, and Isaac his son, and clave the wood for the burnt offering, and rose, and went into the place of which God had told him. . . .

And they came to the place which God had told him of; and Abraham built an altar there, and laid the wood in order, and bound Isaac his son, and laid him upon the altar upon the wood.

And Abraham stretched forth his hand, and took the knife to slay his son.

And the angel of the Lord called unto him out of heaven, and said, Abraham, Abraham: and he said, Here am I.

And he said, Lay not thine hand upon the lad, neither do thou any thing unto him: for now I know that thou fearest God, seeing that thou hast not withheld thy son, thine only son from me.

And Abraham lifted up his eyes, and looked, and behold behind him a ram caught in a thicket by his horns: and Abraham went and took the ram, and offered him up for a burnt offering in the stead of his son.

Were the Jews the first people to decide that human sacrifice was wrong, that is, that God did not desire it? Possibly. Apparently the Jews never again sacrificed human beings to their Lord. The Christians, following the traditions of the Jews, never practiced human sacrifice, although their religion is based on one supreme sacrifice: Jesus Christ, the Lamb of God and the Only Begotten Son of the Father, died that all men might live. And for Roman Catholics at least, this supreme sacrifice is repeated in every mass, for Jesus is present in the wine (blood) and bread (flesh) that is consumed in joyous communion with God and the other participants in the ritual.

Buddhism and Islam, among the other great religions of the world, were also free of human sacrifice from the beginning to this day. Would that the primal lesson given by God to Abraham had been known by the Aztec and the Inca and the many other relics of a more primitive time!

Judaism

Abraham was the founder of Judaism. The account of his life in Genesis, though considered today to be not entirely historical, is nevertheless in accord with historical facts dating from the beginning of the second millennium BC. According to the story, Abraham, his father Terah, his nephew Lot, and his wife Sarah left Ur of the Chaldees, in southern Mesopotamia, and journeyed slowly, always under the command and watchful eye of their God, toward the land of the Canaan (modern Israel and Lebanon). After the death of Terah, Abraham became the patriarch, and a covenant between God and him was established. This covenant, or promise, involved the certainty that Abraham's seed would inherit the land of Canaan.

Was there such a journey between Ur, a real place, and Canaan, another real place? There is historical and archaeological reason to think so, apart from the biblical narrative. Why did Abraham leave Ur? Was he fleeing religious persecution, seeking new economic opportunities, or was he driven by some divine command, real or imagined? At any rate, within a few hundred years there were many Jews in Canaan, worshiping one god, Yahweh. In a world full of polytheistic religions, they had become monotheists—the first, probably, in the history of the world.

Yahweh at first was the God of Abraham, Isaac, and Jacob. Did that mean he was not the God of mankind, the only God? It is impossible to determine when Yahweh, or Jehovah, took on the universal character that he possessed by the time of Jesus, and that he possesses to this day. Suffice it to say that the God of Abraham, perhaps once a tribal deity and as such one (perhaps the greatest) among many, is now the One God worshiped by Jews, Christians, and Moslems the world around.

According to Jewish belief, the Jews were the chosen people of God. What did that mean to them? They believed that they had been chosen by God to have a special and permanent relationship to him. This relationship involved three things. First, they were given the law, both the commandments which Moses received on Mount Sinai and the rules of diet, behavior, and social intercourse incorporated in the Torah or holy books (the word of God). Second, they were given a promise, or covenant, that God would never desert them throughout history and would insure that their career on earth would be successful. Third, they were required by God to be a witness to his being, goodness, and justice. This witness was to be carried by them to all the other peoples of the world.

The history of Judaism and of the Jews is a long and complicated story, full of blood and tears. The Jews have endured as a witness to the truth of the One God, but they have also denied that God and his prophets when they came, at least according to the Christians and the Moslems. They have tried to live at peace with the rest of mankind, but this has been difficult for them, for a number of reasons. In our time they have suffered from the Holocaust and the unremitting enmity of the Arab neighbors of Israel.

With all that, the Jews are still, essentially, the same stubborn, dedicated people, now, and forever maybe, affirming the same three things. First, they are a people of the law as given in the holy books of Moses. Second, they are the chosen people of God, having an eternal covenant with him. Third, they are a witness that God is and will be forevermore.

The ancient wisdom of the Jews, which has been passed down from father to son for nearly four thousand years and which at the same time is given to the rest of mankind, is complex. But it may be summed up in those three great concepts.

Christianity

Jesus Christ was a Jew, and he accepted without demur all three of those things that he received from his forefathers. But he changed them all.

Born in Bethlehem, in a manger, because there was no room at the inn, on December 25 of the year by which much of the world measures the passage of all subsequent time, Jesus of Nazareth had been proclaimed by some as the King of the Jews. He died at the hill of Golgotha, the Place of the Skull, in Jerusalem, on Good Friday of the year 30 AD. He perished on a cross, his death partly the fault of the Roman governor of the province.

According to the Christian creed, he then descended into hell, "harrowed" it—that is, bore up to paradise the souls of Adam and Eve and the patriarchs—and then himself rose again on the morning of the third day after his death, which is celebrated by all the Christians of the world as Easter Sunday.

Jesus said that he would not change any "jot or tittle" of the Jewish law, but he added to it a kind of supernumerary law, based on love, as he said, and not only on justice. Christians interpret this to mean that by his own death he bought for mankind the forgiveness of the original sin of Adam and Eve and the promise of eternal life in paradise, at least for all those who would believe in his new witness, or testament, to the being and goodness of God. The most trenchant statement of the new doctrine is contained in Christ's Sermon on the Mount, in which he spelled out the modifications of the law of Moses for which he stood.

The Gospel according to Matthew tells of this famous occasion, when Jesus "went up into a mountain" and taught his disciples, saying:

Blessed are the poor in spirit, for theirs is the kingdom of heaven.
Blessed are they that mourn: for they shall be comforted.
Blessed are the meek: for they shall inherit the earth.
Blessed are they which do hunger and thirst after righteousness:
    for they shall be filled.
Blessed are the merciful: for they shall obtain mercy.
Blessed are the pure in heart: for they shall see God.

Jesus almost always spoke in parables, which required interpretation in those days and still do today. The wisdom of some of these parables, while profound, is perhaps not so different from the wisdom of other ancient religious teachers. But there was also a core of uniqueness in the teachings of Jesus the man. He combined the earthiness of the Jews with the mystical vision of the Christians.

He is supposed to have established the Christian Church, founding it, as he said, upon a rock, that is, by a play upon words, upon his disciple Peter (the name means "rock" in Greek). Thus Christians everywhere believe that the Church was the actual creation of Christ and cleaves to his teachings.

Others wonder about this, remembering one of his most trenchant sayings, recorded by the simple St. Mark. "Whosoever will save his life shall lose it," said Jesus; "but whosoever shall lose his life for my sake and the gospel's, the same shall save it. For what shall it profit a man, if he shall gain the whole world, and lose his own soul?"

As if that were not challenge enough to the splendid, rich, and powerful

Christian Church, Jesus also said: "Whosoever will come after me, let him deny himself, and take up his cross, and follow me."

Is there any more perfectly succinct summing up of the teachings of Jesus than those wonderful, and terrible, words?

Wonderful, because those words can inspire anyone to rise above the dross of the everyday and live a life that is charged with meaning and purpose.

Terrible, because they ask of so many men and women more than they can give.

Judaism and Christianity Compared

The Old Testament is the Jewish holy book. It is holy, too, for the Christians, but in a different way. Besides being read as the history of the Jews, out of whose history would be born Jesus Christ and the religion which he founded, it is read by Christians as a prophecy of the coming of Christ. Every event in the Old Testament is viewed as having a double meaning. For example, while the sacrifice of Isaac is seen as symbolic of the ending of human sacrifice by the Jews, it is also seen as prefiguring the Passion of Christ. Abraham offers his only begotten son as a sign of his obedience; once he has passed the test, his son is saved. God the Father offers up his only begotten son so that all men may be free of original sin; his son also rises to heaven to sit at the right hand of the Father.

The Jewish God is an angry God, justice is his mark. The Christian God, although he, too, will judge the quick and the dead, is a God of mercy. Mankind is redeemed by the sacrifice of Christ and will attain ultimate salvation.

Christians accepted the idea that the Jews were chosen by God as a witness to his rule over mankind. But the refusal of the Jews to accept Christ as not merely one of the prophets but as the son of God and as one of the three persons of God—Father, Son, and Holy Ghost—created a deep and unbridgeable gulf between the two religions. Furthermore, the part that the Jews played, historically, in the death of Jesus of Nazareth was conceived by many Christians as the ultimate betrayal, not just of Christ, but of the Jews' own faith. The unfounded charge that "the Jews killed Christ" is one of the heaviest burdens Jews have had to bear in the Christian world throughout the centuries.

The New Testament is uniquely Christian. Mostly written in Greek, by Greek-speaking Jews, it consists of several accounts of the life and sayings of Jesus, an eschatological work (Apocalypse of St. John the Divine), and a number of letters by St. Paul and others to new Christian communities, indicating the course they should follow in establishing the new religion.

The epistles of Paul are distinctly different from anything in the Old

Testament. The older work was primarily historical; the letters of Paul are primarily theological. Paul was a Jew, but he was also very much a Greek in his thought. The infusion into Christianity of Greek theological subtlety and speculation characterized Christianity for the next two thousand years and differentiated Christianity from Judaism.

The historical Jesus was probably a member of a sect of Jews called Essenes, who were themselves more mystical and theological than many previous Jewish groups. Most of the sayings of Jesus are parables, giving rise to heady and speculative interpretation by sixty generations of subsequent thinkers. The mysterious figure of the man Jesus is hard to discover. That he was a great man and teacher, whether or not he was the son of God, is undeniable.

Islam

Born in Mecca around 570 AD, Muhammad had lost his father before he was born and his grandfather when he was eight. This double orphaning left him without a male protector and guide in the masculine-oriented society of medieval Arabia. A lesser man would probably have faded away into a historical nonentity. But Muhammad had managed, by the time he died in Medina in 632, not only to found a new religion and to unite all the Arabs of Arabia into one nation, but also to inspire a fervor that would, within twenty years of his death, lead his followers to conquer most of the Byzantine and Persian empires and, within a hundred years, to create a land empire rivaling in size and organization the Roman empire at its greatest.

Around 610, when Muhammad was about forty years old, he received his first direct message from God. It came in the form of a vision of a majestic being (later identified with the angel Gabriel) who announced to him: "You are the Messenger of God." This marked the beginning of his great career as a messenger, or prophet. At frequent intervals, from then until his death, Muhammad received revelations—verbal messages that he believed came directly from God. Eventually they were collected and written down and became the Koran, the sacred scriptures of Islam.

Muhammad began to preach to his immediate family and close acquaintances, but he soon found himself beset by opposition at Mecca, the most prosperous center of Arabia in his time. Within ten years, it was apparent that his position had become very difficult, and he began to plan an escape from his native city. He left Mecca for Medina, accompanied by about seventy-five followers, on September 24, 622, the date of the Hegira, or "emigration"; in that year, the traditional starting point of Islamic history, the Islamic calendar begins.

Muhammad was admired by his contemporaries for his courage and impartiality, becoming for later Moslems the exemplar of virtuous character. He founded not only a state, but also a religion that would eventually be adopted by nearly a billion persons. His moral sternness and seriousness are almost unique in his time. He is one of the most remarkable and charismatic men in history.

Judeo-Christianity and Islam Compared

Mecca possessed a large Jewish community during Muhammad's lifetime; he was certainly influenced by it and learned much from Jewish historians and thinkers. He was also conversant with Christian lore. He accepted Abraham as the first patriarch (so that Abraham is a holy man in all three religions) and believed that Christ had been the greatest of the prophets before himself. But he did not accept Jesus' claim to be (or the claim of Jesus' followers that he was) the son of God.

Muhammad's view of both Judaism and Christianity was, at least at the beginning, primarily sympathetic. Jews and Christians were "people of the book" and so were allowed religious autonomy; however, they had to pay a per capita tax, and that, in fact, led many of them to convert to Islam in the century after the Prophet's death. Their status was very different from that of pagans, who were forced to choose between conversion and death. From the beginning, Islam was a fierce, warrior faith; its outward manifestation was *jihad*, or holy war. This faith established a clear, clean line between the rest of the world and themselves, and the sense of close, fraternal community thus engendered led to rapid and astounding victories over societies and cultures not so bound together.

Christ, in his saying to St. Peter concerning the tribute money, had marked out a clear distinction between "that which is Caesar's and that which is God's." In other words, there are two distinct realms, the religious and the secular, which need not be in conflict but which also must not be confused. Judaism recognized a similar distinction, but Islam did not. At the beginning Islam acquired its characteristic ethos as a religion that united both the spiritual and the temporal in one community and sought to control not only the individual's relationship to God but also his social and political relationships with his fellow men.

Thus there grew up not only an Islamic religious institution but also an Islamic law and Islamic state. Only in the twentieth century, and then only in a few Islamic countries (for example, Turkey), has any distinction been made between the religious and the secular. The enormous power Ayatollah Khomeini exercised in Iran can be explained by the fact that he combined in himself, as *imam*, both the religious and the political leadership of a nation; as such, he acted no differently from many Islamic leaders before him.

Do these three great connected but conflicting religions still have a viable and vital message for mankind? Billions of people in the world think and say so. Although six million Jews died in the Holocaust of World War II, and European Jewry was almost wiped out, Judaism survives as a vital commitment of millions of men and women in Israel, Russia, the United States, and other lands. Christianity, in its many manifestations, perhaps attracts more adherents than any other religion. And Islam has enjoyed a recent renaissance, as conservative movements in many countries have reinstated traditional practices, including the enforcement of traditional sharia law, the subjection of women, and the total control of education by religious leaders. The *jihad* has acquired new strength, and a new sense of brotherhood among Moslems worldwide seems to be abroad.

Buddhism

The first Indian empire came into existence about 325 BC. The Mauryan dynasty, so-called after Chandragupta Maurya, the founder, ruled the subcontinent for several hundred years. At its greatest extent, under Asoka (who ruled from about 265 to 235 BC), this first organized Indian state probably included an area of nearly a million square miles and a population of over fifty million persons.

Soon after Asoka ascended to the throne, as behooved a new monarch, he undertook a military campaign. He was victorious, but his victories did not make him happy. Instead, he was struck by the suffering his campaigns had produced, for both the victors and the vanquished. At the time of his enlightenment, Asoka was probably about thirty years old.

Siddhartha Gautama, the Buddha ("Enlightened One"), had been born about 563 BC to a princely family of northern India. He married and lived in luxury. But when he was twenty-nine he awoke to the recognition of man's fate, which is to grow old and sick, then die. Overwhelmed with sadness, he began to seek some means of allaying the pain of life.

He left his wife and infant son and wandered south to the Magadha kingdom, hoping to find teachers who could give him the answers to his questions about the meaning of suffering. With them he attained to a state of mystical contemplation, as was traditional in Indian religion of the time. But he was not satisfied merely to contemplate existence. Other teachers promised him deep understanding if he would undertake a life of extreme asceticism. For months he ate and drank little and exposed his body to the elements. In this way he came to understand what it was to suffer, but he still failed to comprehend the reasons for suffering.

He thereupon renounced asceticism, began to eat, and regained his health. But he would not give up his quest. And on a certain morning in May 528 BC he sat down cross-legged under a great bo tree (banyan), at a

place called Buddh Gaya, and determined not to move until he had
achieved the enlightenment that he sought.

He thought for hours, turning and turning in his mind. Mara, the evil
one, appeared and tempted him to give up the search. "Do meritorious
deeds," said Mara. "What is the use of your continuous striving?"
Gautama ignored him; he was proof against any temptation. Mara departed, defeated. Gautama spent the rest of the night in contemplation.
By the next morning, the morning of May 25, when he was thirty-five, he
had attained the Awakening, and became a supreme Buddha.

What had he learned? "I have realized this Truth," he thought to
himself, "which is deep, difficult to see, difficult to understand. . . . Men
who are overcome by passion and surrounded by a mass of darkness
cannot see this Truth which is against the current, which is lofty, deep,
subtle, and hard to comprehend."

The truth the Buddha found cannot be adequately described in a few
sentences. Perhaps it requires a lifetime to understand it. The Buddha
described it in a parable. A man should seek the middle path between self-
indulgence and self-mortification. This middle way, known as the Noble
Eightfold Path, consisted of right view, right thought, right speech, right
action, right mode of living, right endeavor, right mindfulness, and right
concentration.

The great truth of the Buddha, as he explained it, consisted of Four
Noble Truths. The first, which he understood before he left on his pilgrimage, is that man's existence is full of conflict, sorrow, and suffering.
The second noble truth holds that all this difficulty and pain is caused by
man's selfish desire. The third holds that there can be found emancipation
and freedom—Nirvana. The fourth noble truth, the Noble Eightfold Path,
is the way to this liberation.

In a sense Buddhism is not a religion, for it worships no god. But this
primarily ethical doctrine soon spread far and wide, partly because of the
fervent speculation which it everywhere engendered, partly because of its
revolutionary overtones. The Buddha, a man of profound understanding
and deep sympathy and compassion, had held that all men are equal in
their common destiny. He had therefore opposed the idea of caste. His
followers carried the principle of social equality throughout southern Asia,
causing both political troubles and enlightened political progress in many
ancient states.

After his own enlightenment, which came to him three hundred years
after the death of the Buddha, Emperor Asoka renounced war and violence, sought peace with his people and with his neighbors, and inaugurated for India what later came to be viewed as a Golden Age.

Buddhism continues to play a vital role in the politics of many Asian
countries. Its emphasis on social equality, and its doctrine that many

human ills are caused by poverty, have inspired liberal reform movements in numerous places. Buddhists also usually support the aspirations of nationalist movements against colonial regimes or the domination of unfriendly or inimical ethnic groups. Hence Buddhism remains one of the most vigorous systems of ethical thought in the world. This is true even though Buddhists are hardly anywhere a majority (except in Burma). But the mystical power of the Buddha's thought retains its age-old influence over the minds of human beings.

Lessons from the Past

Most of the ancient kingdoms and empires arose out of the turmoil of warring families, villages, or tribes. For almost all of them, the establishment of political and social order became the most important task. Often, order was imposed by force alone. When threatened by immediate and painful death, most people, then as now, would remain quiet and obedient—as long as the force remained. The problem became, then, how to keep order when force was not present, as it could not be at all places and times.

We have seen that the Egyptian solution entailed an aversion to change. Things as they stand may not be perfect, but any change is likely to be for the worse. The Egyptians carried the principle farther than any other people ever has. All civilizations have adopted it to some extent.

The Indian solution involved the establishment of a caste system. Basically, this meant widespread agreement that a person's birth both explained and justified his social position. This, too, is a useful principle, for about a person's birth there can be no argument. My parents were who they were; therefore I am who and what I am. If it does not seem just that the haves should always be the haves, from father to son for endless generations, and the have-nots always the have-nots, the answer is that social order, which the Egyptians called *ma'at*, is worth almost any cost in injustice. For what is the alternative? Nothing but constant turmoil and conflict, invariably leading to destruction.

The Chinese justified social inequalities in a novel manner. Birth alone fits a man for nothing; only he may advance in life and occupy a superior position who is inherently superior. This principle did not need to be observed at all times and places. It made sense for the emperor to reserve the highest posts for his family. That was practical. Who would act otherwise? But the idea that superiors were superior because they deserved to be, obtained widespread acceptance. It was perhaps somewhat harder to accept the idea that superiority should be exhibited by superior knowledge of Confucian texts. But there had to be some objective test of superiority, and Confucian texts were better than many tests that might be used.

In our day superiority is exhibited by high scores on a different kind of objective test, the so-called SATs (Scholastic Aptitude Tests). The tests have nothing whatever to do with Confucius, but the principle is the same.

As literacy was developed in various Mesopotamian civilizations, it turned into a different kind of test of superiority. Literacy did not establish a man's social or political position. Instead, it was the entrée into a powerful minority that controlled most of the business of the state, both public and private. Literacy conferred control over a society's information systems, and those have always been crucial to a society's life. They are all the more crucial today. It has been estimated that the information industry represents more than half the gross national product of modern industrial states. Information was a burgeoning business in ancient Mesopotamia. It is the biggest business of all in our time.

It is a curious but undeniable fact that all of the great teachers and founders of religions whose doctrines come down to us were opposed to the principles of social organization that have been enumerated here. They were all rebels, revolutionaries, who fought against the interests and powers of their times. Do we not have to conclude, therefore, that their rebelliousness explains their success—at least in part?

Abraham and the other Jewish patriarchs and prophets began by proclaiming that their tribal god was the greatest god of all and ended by insisting that there was only one God, Jehovah, for all men. Pagan polytheists inevitably worshiped at least two kinds of gods, good ones and evil ones. The good gods were responsible for the good things that happened, the evil ones were responsible for the bad things; to worship the latter was to concede their existence, which in turn was to try to avoid their influence. The Jews were the first to insist that man himself is responsible for his acts; he cannot blame them on the gods.

Jesus and his Christian followers and interpreters carried that revolutionary doctrine farther. Eve had been tempted by Satan, and Adam by Eve. Both had fallen prey to sin and death. But the Devil could not be blamed for man's disobedience. Man had brought his exile from Eden upon himself, and he and woman would have to bear the consequences forever. God, because he loved Adam and Eve and all their seed, could and did ransom and redeem mankind with the blood of his only begotten son. But responsibility remains where the Jews had said it was: within the individual human soul.

Confucius, perhaps for reasons arising out of the special circumstances of his own life, rebelled against the feudal system of his time, which based social organization upon birth. Merit alone fitted a man for a high position in the society or the state, and merit should be determined by learning. Superficially, this principle was adopted by the Chinese state. But if Confucius were to return, would he say that true merit is adequately exhibited by the knowledge of any set of texts, whether written by him or not? Did he not mean something deeper and more revolutionary than that?

Buddha fought against the caste system that already held sway in the India he knew. All men are equal, he said, in their suffering; all men face the same challenges and must seek to follow the same path. The deep-seated equality which he foresaw in the brutally unequal society of his time was also foreseen by David, Jesus, and Muhammad. No accident of birth or even of learning can earn favor with God. All men and women are equally beset, and all can gain the kingdom of heaven if they will seek it with loving hearts.

The idea of social equality is inherently revolutionary. More than two thousand years would elapse before it would begin to be taken seriously as the principle of justice in social organization. But the influence of the ancient Jews, of the early Christians, of Muhammad and his immediate followers, as well as of the Buddha, Confucius, and other eastern sages—to say nothing of the pagan Socrates—was always present through the centuries.

Alphabets

The first alphabets probably came into existence in Mesopotamia around the middle of the second millennium before the Christian era, but the Phoenicians deserve the credit for developing the first standard alphabet. Many letters used today descend from those used by Phoenician scribes as early as 1100 BC. But the Phoenician alphabet contained only consonants and could not be used efficiently to transcribe any Indo-European language. The Greeks, around the middle of the eighth century BC, invented symbols for vowels. The resulting alphabet—which we use to-day, with minor changes—was one of the most valuable contributions the Greeks, that ingenious, creative people, made to posterity.

Not all writing is alphabetical. Chinese writing is not alphabetical. This was also true of ancient Egyptian, ancient Sumerian, even ancient Hebrew. Languages like Chinese and Japanese are highly expressive but hard to write down unambiguously. Alphabetical languages like Greek, Latin, German, and English, to name only a few, possess a clarity when written that no other kinds of languages have. The reason is the alphabet itself.

Ancient Hebrew, Aramaic, and other northern Semitic languages of the first millennium before Christ were highly inflected, but differences in meaning were usually indicated by context rather than by the spelling of individual words. To this day, Hebrew uses no vowels; a system of dots over certain letters can be used for extra clarity, but the dots are not needed for correct writing. English, a language employing few inflections, could not be written meaningfully without vowels. Consider the letters *bt*. Then consider the five words *bat, bet, bit, both*, and *but*. They mean completely different things. There is no semantic connection between any two of them. In writing, the difference is expressed by the five vowels, *a, e, i, o*, and *u*. In writing, the difference is unambiguous. (When spoken, by speakers with different accents, the difference may not be so clear.)

Written Chinese employs thousands of different signs to transcribe its thousands of different sounds, each having a different meaning. English has as many different sounds as Chinese, and probably more words and meanings, but only twenty-six signs are needed to write all the words in the language. Such efficiency takes the breath away.

Scholars disagree about whether the Phoenician alphabet was in fact a real alphabet, since it contained no signs for vowel sounds. In that case the Greek alphabet was the first in history. There is credit enough to go around. The Greek invention is no less astounding because it built on a prior invention.

The Inca failed to discover the art of writing. They also failed to understand the underlying principles of the tools they used. They made particular tools to accomplish particular tasks, but the abstract idea of a lever, for example, escaped them. Similarly, the Egyptians and Mesopotamians of various eras seem to have failed to understand general ideas, although they were adept at solving the specific problems they faced.

The spoken language of the Inca was sophisticated and expressive. Without any language at all they would have been no more than animals. But the lack of a written language may explain their lack of general knowledge—and their rapid defeat by a people who did not lack it. Perhaps the human race is unable to think and know generally if individuals cannot write down their thoughts so that others can clearly understand them.

It is true that oral tradition carried mankind a long way. The earliest empires were built without writing; great art, even great poetry, was produced by men who did not know the art of writing. Homer himself, the first and in some ways still the greatest poet, was nonliterate. Most of the world was nonliterate in his time (around 1000 BC).

en where men had learned to write, as in Mesopotamia, in Egypt, in ey used the wonderful new skill only to keep records. They did g as an incomparable way to think better.

soon as they had a complete alphabet to work with, were

the first to understand that fact. And so the world we know and live in began to come into existence.

Zero

The Greeks were typically quick to recognize the benefits to be obtained from writing based on the alphabet. They were not nearly so ready to adopt another important invention of the Babylonians: positional notation in computation.

When we write any number, say, 568, we are usually not aware of the extraordinarily efficient shorthand device we are employing. If we desired to be absolutely accurate, we would have to write 568 in one of two different ways. One is this:

$$(5 \times 100) + (6 \times 10) + 8 = 568$$

The other is even more general.

$$(5 \times 10^2) + (6 \times 10^1) + (8 \times 10^0) = 568$$

If we had to use such cumbersome notation, it is obvious that we would never get much calculation done in a reasonable time. Computers might not be troubled. But schoolchildren would be abashed, even more than they ordinarily are when they learn arithmetic.

Positional notation is second nature for all of us. We never even think of it when we are writing numbers. But not all civilizations in human history have enjoyed this useful shortcut to calculation.

Nevertheless, more than one of the ancient empires we have discussed in this chapter discovered positional notation, apparently quite independently. When the Spanish reached the Valley of Mexico in the sixteenth century, they were astonished to learn that the Mayans had used positional notation in calculating dates in their complex calendars. The Egyptians may have independently discovered position notation some four thousand years previously. But the Babylonians deserve the credit for having discovered it first.

The Sumerians and Babylonians were redoubtable calculators when most of the rest of humankind were still counting on their fingers, if at all. Their use of positional notation in their sexigesimal number system (a system built on a base of sixty instead of ten) may have occurred as early as 3500 BC, according to historian Eric Temple Bell.

For a long time, the Babylonians had no way of avoiding the ambiguities involved in another sort of number, for example, 508. This number does not seem much different to us from 568. But for centuries it was a puzzle for the Babylonians as well as the Egyptians.

The number 508 can be written this way:

$$(5 \times 100) + (0 \times 10) + 8 = 508$$

To us, there is no problem. To the Babylonians, there was. They did not really understand what "no tens" was doing in the middle of this number. And so they often did not bother to record that there was nothing in the tens position.

Positional notation fails if the positions are not retained in all circumstances, even when there is nothing in the position. In the number 508 the symbol 0 is extremely important. Leave it out, and 508 become 58. The Babylonians often left it out, with the result that their computations were often hopelessly confusing unless close attention was paid to the context.

The Babylonians did not discover the need for a zero symbol until late in their history, perhaps around 350 BC, which may have been more than three thousand years after they discovered positional notation. The Egyptians may have employed a zero symbol a little earlier. But they were not consistent in its use, which shows they did not fully understand it.

After 350 BC, Babylonian tables of astronomical numbers (all in the sexigesimal system) regularly employed a zero symbol. The late Greek astronomers, leading up to Ptolemy in the second century AD, followed the Babylonian practice, even employing the symbol $\bar{o}$ to denote zero. But they also retained the sexigesimal number system for astronomy, which, despite the benefits of the notation, was needlessly cumbersome.

Around 1200 AD, or perhaps a few hundred years earlier, the Hindus began to use zero (0) in their decimal system. They are often mentioned as the discoverers of zero. It is probable that they learned of it from the Greeks. Their combination of positional notation in the decimal system, together with a consistent use of 0, proved to be the final solution of an important computational difficulty, and the world by and large has used it ever since.

Our debt to the Babylonian and Egyptian mathematicians is therefore great. But we should recall one rather puzzling fact. The early Greek mathematicians, so famous for their profound intuitions and their brilliant success in geometry, simply did not catch on to the importance of positional notation. There is no doubt that they built on a mathematical base constructed by the Babylonians, and in geometry they went far beyond their teachers. But they were not good calculators. There was something about simple arithmetic that seems to have escaped, even baffled them.

2

The Greek Explosion

THERE HAVE BEEN two knowledge explosions in human history, not just one. The second began in Europe four or five centuries ago and is still going on. The first began in Greece during the sixth century BC.

The Greek explosion also had a long life. Like ours, it spread quickly and finally affected the entire known world. Like ours, it commenced with the discovery of a new communications device and a new method for acquiring knowledge, continued with the help of striking advances in mathematics, and culminated in revolutionary theories about matter and force.

The Greek knowledge explosion did not advance as far as ours has in the investigation, understanding, and control of external nature. But despite the vaunted contributions of our "human" sciences of economics, sociology, and psychology, it could be claimed that the ancient Greek investigators understood at least as well as we do what can and cannot be reasonably said about human nature and a good life. If we have seen physics advance farther than the Greeks ever dreamed it could, the Greeks probably carried philosophy, especially ethical philosophy, farther than we have been able to do.

When we recognize that the progress in the physical sciences that we have made, and of which we are justly proud, has been partly based on Greek ideas that went underground for more than a thousand years and were revived and reapplied in our own time, the Greek knowledge explosion may even seem to be the more widely influential of the two.

Of course, the Greeks made serious errors, not only about nature but also about human nature. Some of these errors had disastrous consequences, up until our day. But our knowledge explosion has also made mistakes, some of which may ultimately lead to disaster for the human race as a whole.

In both cases the errors were and are due to arrogance: a kind of

29

overweening presumption implying an impious disregard for the limits
that an orderly universe imposes on the actions of men and women. The
Greeks gave human arrogance a special name: *hubris*. Hubris was a sin,
they thought, and they worshiped a goddess, Nemesis, who punished
those who committed it.

We have no special name for human arrogance in our time, nor do we
worship Nemesis. But the signs of her work are all around us.

The Problem of Thales

The mainland of Greece is a peninsula, deeply indented by the sea, that
juts down into the Mediterranean from the Eurasian landmass. Its eastern
coast faces Anatolia, the westernmost province of modern Turkey, lying
south of the Dardanelles. Between Greece and Anatolia there is a sea full
of islands and resplendent with light—the Aegean. Perhaps it is the most
famous body of water of its size in the world.

Some ten or a dozen centuries before the birth of Christ, men and
women who spoke Greek voyaged across the Aegean and established
colonies on the western coast of Anatolia. They did not penetrate deeply
into the hinterland, but they founded cities and controlled the coastal
area, which has many natural harbors where their ships could safely ride
at anchor. They called this new colonial empire Ionia.

Of the Greek cities of Ionia the largest and most prosperous was
Miletus. It was the most southerly of the Ionian cities, situated close to the
point where the coast of Anatolia turns eastward to form the narrow end
of the Mediterranean that Crete dominated then as it does now. Nothing
remains today of Miletus except ruins, because its two fine harbors silted
up and became unusable nearly twenty centuries ago.

From the site of Miletus to the capital of ancient Egypt is scarcely an
hour's flight in a commercial jetliner, but in those far-off times it was a
long journey, by land or by sea. By the middle of the eighth century BC,
the ambitious Milesians were making it regularly, trading with the Egyptians, carrying to them Greek ideas and goods and bringing home Egyptian ideas and gold. One was a discovery the Egyptians had made perhaps
two millennia earlier, namely, that from the papyrus plant, which grows
along the Nile, it was possible to make a smooth, thin, tough material that
would last a long time and on which you could write.

There is no evidence that Greek was a written language prior to the
middle of the eighth century BC. Suddenly, with the importation of
papyrus, Greek written materials began to be produced, and commercial
records and treatises on technical subjects began to be distributed
throughout the Greek world. The center of this activity was Miletus,

which gained a reputation not only as a commercial power but also as a source of inventions and ideas.

Around 625 BC, a man was born in Miletus who was uniquely capable of taking advantage of the special opportunities afforded by his native city. His name was Thales. He has been called the first philosopher and the first scientist.

Very little is known about his life or career. He may have been a successful politician. He was known as one of the Seven Wise Men, and all the others were Greek political leaders. He was revered, first by the Greeks and then by the Romans, for other achievements. He was supposed to have discovered some of the theorems of the first book of Euclid's *Elements*. He was said to have predicted an eclipse of the sun in the year 585; if so, he may have been the first person ever to foresee this phenomenon.

According to the ancient commentators, Thales was best known for being the first thinker to propose a single universal principle of the material universe, a unique substratum that, itself unchanging, underlay all change. The commentators agree that Thales' substratum, or first principle, was water.

To comprehend what Thales meant by this it is necessary to understand the problem he was trying to solve, and that he may have been the first to see the importance of solving it. If so, he was truly the first philosopher.

As we look around us, we perceive a vast assortment of different things, all of which, as far as we can tell, are in a state of constant change. Living beings are born, grow to maturity, and pass away. Plants spring from the earth, flourish, and die. The sea is in constant motion, and even the great mountains weather away. Even Earth, our Mother, changes. Does everything change, then, or is there something that does not?

As we think about the question, we begin to realize that there must be something about every given thing that does not change, else how could we recognize it as the same thing over time, even while it changes? Take a lump of clay. I rub it with my fingers, and it becomes smaller before my eyes. But it is still a lump of clay. "It" is something that does not change, while many aspects of "it," the qualities of "it," as we may say, as well as the quantity of "it," change. In fact, all of the qualities change, but the thing itself in some sense remains the same; otherwise we could not even say that "it" changes.

We give the name *clay* to the substratum of change in the case of my lump. But I have not solved Thales' problem by thus naming a piece of clay. I can fritter away the entire lump, dust my hands together, and depart. The clay of my lump has now been dispersed, but it has not ceased to be, even if I now turn my back on it.

I may drop some of it into a pool of water. I may throw other bits up into the air, where they are taken by the wind. I may even feed some of the lump to my chickens. When it reappears a day later, it is not clay any longer. But the new stuff was not generated out of nothing. It came from the clay. Something endured, underlying even so radical a change.

Over years, over centuries, even deeper and more far-reaching changes occur. Peoples and families change, nations change, the continents are washed away, and new, young mountains rise where seas once existed. Even the universe changes. Galaxies are born and die over billions of years, and black holes swallow up millions of suns, converting their matter into something we do not comprehend.

Is there one primordial thing that underlies all this change? Is there one thing that remains the same when everything else is different from one moment, or one eon, to the next?

In the case of any individual thing, we can always find an unchanging substratum. The United States of America has grown in two centuries from a nation of three million to a country of two hundred and fifty million, and the number of states has grown from thirteen to fifty. But it still is accurate to refer to one underlying thing that has not changed, namely, the United States of America. Similarly for a man or a woman we know, or a place where we live, or a book that we read, or a word that we speak. But our success in such endeavors does not seem to guarantee success in what Thales was trying to do. Is there one thing that underlies *all* change, over *all* time, in *all* places of the universe?

If not, how can we even conceive of such a thing as the universe? How can we give it a name? Is that name merely the sound of an illusion? Or is there really such a thing? Is there such a persistent, enduring, perhaps eternal thing?

Thales said yes, there is such a thing as the enduring universe, or cosmos (the Greek word), and its underlying principle—that which *undergoes* change—is water. We cannot be certain what he meant. He surely did not mean that everything is literally "made of" water. He knew that stones, for example, are not.

But stones, ground up like dried clay, when thrown into water are dissolved. Perhaps he meant that water is the universal solvent. Or perhaps he was referring to the liquidness of water, to its perpetual mutability, when he said the underlying principle was water, or wetness. Also, water, when heated, becomes steam (gas), and when cooled becomes ice (solid). It is not such a bad candidate.

Whether it a good candidate or not, and whatever Thales meant by saying that "all is water," he was performing a significant mental feat by proposing that a single physical entity, or element, underlay all the different things in the world. His doing so showed that he had come to understand the world in a new way.

Thales had done two remarkable things. First, he had not resorted to animistic explanations for what happens in the world. That is, he had not explained the otherwise unexplainable by saying: "I do not know why this happens, and therefore I will assume that the gods made it happen."

Second, he had made the extraordinary assumption that the world—the cosmos—was a thing whose workings the human mind *can* understand.

Thales possessed tools and simple machines; he knew how they worked. He lived in a house and knew how it worked. He may have understood how the solar system works. But his hypothesis that "all is water" went far beyond those bits of general knowledge. The hypothesis was almost as far as the mind *can* go. For it implied that Thales believed that the totality of things in the world, which is the world itself, is intelligible as a whole. The world is ordered, framed, and constructed in a manner that can be understood by human minds. It is not, at bottom, a mystery, or a plaything of the gods.

In the preface to his book *Early Greek Philosophy*, John Burnet has this to say:

> It is an adequate description of science to say that it is "thinking about the world in the Greek way." That is why science has never existed except among peoples who came under the influence of Greece.

I remarked that Thales' hypothesis went almost as far as the mind can reach in assuming that the world is an intelligible entity, whose workings can be understood and explained in terms of one or more underlying elements. It is important that he did not go all the way. He did not include everything in the intelligible world. Thus, Thales was not only the first scientist; he was the first to become enmeshed in a serious problem of knowledge that has not been adequately solved to this day.

The world that Thales attempted to understand and explain consisted of the material cosmos, the sensible universe. That is, it was the totality of things that can be perceived by our senses. As such, it included the bodies of other human beings, as well as the body of Thales himself: the hand and arm he could see, the hair on the back of his head that he could feel, the scents his body gave off that he could smell, the sounds he made that he could hear.

But it did not include the minds of other persons, or Thales' own mind, which are not sensible things. We can remember, which is a kind of sensing, things that are not present to our senses at the moment, we can dream of them, we can even imagine things that never were, like unicorns or gryphons, things that are, nevertheless, made up of sensible parts. But we cannot sense minds, other persons' or our own. Minds are immaterial things.

It is one thing to say that all the material things in the world are made of water, or are somehow built up out of a single element that does not change while everything else does. It is quite another to claim that everything, including minds, consists of a material element or elements. Probably Thales did not say that, although other philosophers did later.

None of the writings of Thales survive, but he must have written works that were widely distributed. As a result of his writings, his new idea, that the world is basically intelligible and that there is a deep commensurability between the external world and the human mind, even if the mind is not a part of the external world, spread throughout Greece and beyond. Soon many Greeks, not just Thales, were "thinking about the world in the Greek way." All over Ionia, and in the lands Greece influenced, men began to speculate about and propose other primary elements that might be what is unchanging, and therefore intelligible, in a changing world.

The Invention of Mathematics: The Pythagoreans

The island of Samos lies a few miles off the Ionian coast, not far from Miletus. In ancient times it was the site of a prosperous city-state that vied with other Ionian city-states for the leadership of Greek Asia Minor. Samos reached the height of its power under Polycrates, who became tyrant of the city in 532 BC. Polycrates was apparently an enlightened despot who attracted sculptors, painters, and poets to his island kingdom. But he did not get along with the most famous man in Samos.

This was Pythagoras, who had been born in Samos around 580 BC. Because he did not like or approve of Polycrates, he left Samos in the year that the tyrant assumed power and journeyed with a group of followers to southern Italy, where he established a kind of philosophocracy, a philosophical brotherhood ruled by Pythagoras himself. Many myths grew up about him, for example, that he had a golden thigh. His followers never used his name but referred to him as "that man" and claimed authority for their statements by proclaiming: "That man says so!" (*Ipse dixit*).

Both the arrogance and the mystical fervor of Pythagoras and his disciples seem to have offended his new Italian neighbors, as they had offended the Samians, and after a few years the philosophocrats were driven out of Croton, now Crotona. Pythagoras moved to a nearby town on the Bay of Taranto, where, it is said, he starved himself to death around the year 500 BC.

Many mystical beliefs were ascribed to Pythagoras by his contemporaries. For example, he claimed to remember inhabiting the bodies of four men who had lived before his time; one was the soldier who, in the *Iliad*, wounded Patroclus, the friend of Achilles, so badly that Hector was able to kill him. Pythagoras believed in the transmigration of souls, a doctrine that he may have learned from the Egyptians and seems to have transmitted to Plato. Copernicus, the medieval astronomer, claimed that he received the idea of the so-called Copernican system from Pythagoras, although what Pythagoras actually believed about the arrangement of the solar system is unknown.

Pythagoras is also the apparent inventor of the idea of the music of the spheres, which was in line with his general thinking about mathematics. One day, the legend goes, while sitting with a musical instrument in his lap, Pythagoras suddenly realized that the divisions of a taut string that produced its harmonies could be described in terms of simple ratios between pairs of numbers, to wit, 1 to 2, 2 to 3, and 3 to 4. We now write these ratios as 1/2, 2/3, and 3/4. This extraordinary fact astonished Pythagoras, who loved music, for it seemed to him exceeding strange that there should be a connection between numbers, on the one hand, and the notes of a string, on the other, which could move a listener to tears or exalt his spirit.

As he reflected on this strange relationship, Pythagoras began to feel that numbers might have an even greater influence on material things. He and his disciples soon arrived at the conclusion that things *are* numbers and numbers *are* things. Thus was discovered the intimate connection between mathematics and the material world that has both inspired and puzzled thinkers since this day.

Probably Pythagoras himself did not understand very well what he was talking about when he tried to describe the external world in mathematical terms. Much of what he said had mystical meaning, if any. For example, he is supposed to have thought that 10 is the number of justice, because the numbers 4, 3, 2, and 1, when arranged in a triangle, add up to 10.

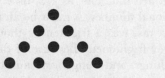

But his original insight, that there is something about the real world that is intelligible in mathematical terms, and perhaps only in mathematical terms, is one of the great advances in the history of human thought. Few ideas have ever been more fruitful.

After the death of Pythagoras, his disciples, despite being hounded from one city to another for their political views, continued their mathematical researches, giving posthumous credit to the Master for all their important discoveries. One such discovery was the proof of the so-called Pythagorean theorem, which states that in a right triangle, the square on the side opposite the right angle, the hypotenuse, is equal to the sum of the squares on the other two sides. For example, if the sides of a right triangle are three, four, and five, then three squared (nine) plus four squared (sixteen) is equal to five squared (twenty-five).

Since any triangle inscribed on the diameter of a circle is a right triangle (another theorem the Pythagoreans were the first to prove), and since such triangles in semicircles are the basis of trigonometry, the Pythagorean theorem is one of the most useful mathematical truths.

Pythagorean researches in mathematics ceased around the middle of the fourth century BC. The brotherhood never lost its offensive characteristics and was eventually wiped out. More important from our point of view, the researches stopped because the Pythagoreans, in the course of their work, came upon a problem so difficult, and, they thought, so dangerous, they could see no way to deal with it.

The problem is this. All right triangles are not like the example given above, where the three sides are all whole numbers, or integers. In fact, right triangles with three integral sides are rare. The great majority of right triangles, even those in which the two sides joining at the right angle are integral, do not have an integral hypotenuse.

The simplest of triangles, as the Pythagoreans found, poses the problem. Imagine a right triangle whose shorter sides are both one. One squared is one ($1 \times 1 = 1$), and one squared plus one squared is therefore two ($1 + 1 = 2$). But two is not a square number; that is, there is no integer which, when multiplied by itself, equals two.

As the Pythagoreans found, the square root of two (that number which, when multiplied by itself, equals two) is a very strange number indeed. They realized that the square root of two is not a rational number; that is, it cannot be expressed as a ratio between two integers. (Rational numbers are sometimes called fractions, as 2/3, or 4/17). But if the square root of two is not a rational number, it must be an irrational number. And that, to the Pythagoreans, was a frightening thought.

Why were they frightened? Because of their original assumption that numbers were things, and things were numbers. And also because of the insight of Thales, which lay behind all the researches of the Pythagoreans, namely, that the world is intelligible to the human mind. But the power of the human mind is reason, it is man's rationality; if the world is irrational, or has irrational things in it, then either Thales must be wrong, or Pythagoras—and if both were right, then there must be an equivalent irrationality in man to correspond to the irrationality in nature. But how could unreason know anything, to say nothing of knowing the world?

It is to the credit of the Pythagorean researchers that they did not deny what they had learned. They faced it and admitted that there must be some deep imbalance somewhere. That took courage. But they did not have enough courage to forge on and work through the problem. The trouble was their mystical belief that things, including the world itself, are numbers simply. A thing is not a number, simply. Just because some real thing, for example, the ratio between the side and the diagonal of a square, can only be described by an irrational number does not mean that the thing is irrational in itself, in the sense of being so unreasonable that it cannot be reasoned about, or understood.

We are no longer frightened by the problem the Pythagoreans failed to solve. We have come to understand that numbers have a different kind of existence from things, even though numbers and things continue to manifest the intimate relationship that the Pythagoreans were the first to recognize. Today, we use even more arcane numbers than the irrational numbers of which the Pythagoreans were the discoverers. Irrational numbers are not frightening at all; each one (this will be a little technical) is the root of an algebraic equation with integral coefficients. But there are an infinite number of numbers that are not even that, some of them very famous, for example, π, which is the ratio between so simple a pair of things as the circumference and the diameter of a circle. And then there are the so-called imaginary numbers, which are made up of two parts, $a +$ bi, where a and b are real numbers and i is the square root of minus one (that is, it is the number that, when multiplied by itself, equals minus one). And there are numerous ranks and grades of numbers that far exceed even those in complexity and, mathematicians might say, in beauty.

The Pythagoreans may have suspected that irrational numbers did not exist in the real world. But if not there, then where? Were these strange and dangerous numbers a door into the chaos that all Greeks always feared? Were they the signs or symbols of unknown, malevolent gods? Some such belief may explain why the Pythagoreans, and other Greek mathematicians as well, stopped mathematizing in a creative way around the middle of the fourth century BC.

Euclid compiled his *Elements of Geometry* around 300 BC, and this great textbook, which is almost as famous as the Bible, remained in use in most schools of the West until very recently. But Euclid was not an original thinker in mathematics, although he was an incomparable teacher. Original work continued to be done in mechanics, astronomy, and some other mathematical fields. But the great creative impulse had been spent.

Similar stoppages of scientific work have occurred, or at least been threatened, in recent history. After World War II, many persons, scientists and nonscientists alike, urged that no further research be done into atomic energy, because of the danger such research might pose to all life on earth. In our own time, voices are heard calling upon biotechnologists to cease their experiments in genetic engineering. In neither of these cases have the stoppages actually occurred, despite the dangers involved. Are we more courageous than the Pythagoreans? Perhaps. Or are we more foolhardy?

The Discovery of Atomic Theory: Democritus

Democritus was born around 460 BC in Abdera, a small city in the southwestern corner of Thrace, a few miles from the border with Macedonia. His father was wealthy and is supposed to have entertained Xerxes, the Persian emperor, when the Persian army passed through Thrace twenty years before Democritus was born. When Democritus's father died, leaving three sons, his fortune was divided into three parts: land, buildings, and money. The money was the smallest part, but Democritus chose it as his portion because he wanted to be free to travel.

With the one hundred talents of his inheritance he set out to see the world. He traveled first to Egypt, where he learned geometry from the priests. He went to Persia to study under the Chaldean masters, and then across what is now Pakistan to India, where he visited the Gymnosophists, ascetic Hindu philosophers who went naked and gave themselves up to mystical contemplation. He returned to Greece via Ethiopia and Egypt, ending up, some say, in Athens. He scorned the great city, perhaps because it scorned him.

He lived to be very old, and although he became blind, he remained cheerful; he posited cheerfulness as an important good. He returned to Abdera in his last years. He had exhausted his fortune, but to an assembly of the chief citizens he read one of his books, whereupon the council voted him another hundred talents. Because he laughed at everything, including himself, he is known as the Laughing Philosopher.

Democritus is supposed to have written some seventy books dealing with a wide range of subjects, from ethics to mathematics, from physics to music, from literature to medicine, history, and prognostication. It is a pity that none survives. According to Aristoxenus, who lived a century later, Plato wanted to burn all of Democritus's books but was dissuaded by his disciples, who pointed out that the books were already so widely distributed that burning them would do no good. Hundreds of pages of Plato's dialogues came down to us; not a single complete page of Democritus.

Democritus, like every Greek thinker of his time, was fascinated by the problem of Thales, and he developed a solution that revealed the brilliance of his thought. Every material thing, Democritus believed, is made up of a finite number of discrete particles, or atoms, as he called them, whose joining together and subsequent separation account for the coming to be of things and their passing away. The atoms themselves, he said, are infinite in number and eternal. They move, according to a necessary motion, in the void, which we would call space; the void is the principle of nonbeing, the atoms that of being.

There is a finite number of different *kinds* of atoms, round and smooth ones, for example, of which water is made, which slips and slides over itself because of the shape of its atoms. Others have hooks and indentations that allow them to cleave together to make dense, heavy things like iron or gold.

If the universe were finite in extent, an infinite number of atoms, no matter how small each might be, would fill it completely. Democritus, being aware of this and also knowing that we do not perceive a universe that is full of matter, posited an infinite universe containing many other worlds like our own.

In fact, according to Democritus, there are an infinite number of worlds, at least one of which, and perhaps more than one, is an exact copy of our own, with persons in it just like you and me. The concept of an infinite universe containing many different worlds was also accepted by other thinkers, including the philosopher Friedrich Nietzsche.

A few fragments of Democritus survive. One of them is famous because it was often quoted by later critics of his atomic theory. In a passage from his writings the Intellect is introduced in a kind of dialectical contest with the Senses.

Intellect. Ostensibly there is color, ostensibly sweetness, ostensibly bitterness, actually only atoms and the void.

The Senses. Poor Intellect, do you hope to defeat us while from us you borrow your evidence? Your victory is your defeat. (Fragment D125)

The world of atoms and the void is colorless, cold, without qualities. It must be. Yet all the evidence of its existence belies this. What kind of madness is that? It is science. It is thinking about the world in the Greek way.

Democritus's intuition that at the basis of all material things there is nothing but atoms and the void has been triumphantly confirmed. At the same time it is equally indubitable that the basis of our thinking is the report our senses give us. The mental tension produced by this antinomy, as the German philosopher Immanuel Kant (1724–1804) called it, is perhaps the source of much of our intellectual energy.

What were the main tenets of the atomism of Democritus?

Most were astonishingly modern. First, the atoms were invisibly small. They were all of the same stuff, or nature, but there was a multitude of different shapes and sizes. Though impermeable (Democritus did not know that atoms could be split), they acted upon one another, aggregating and clinging to one another so as to produce the great variety of bodies that we see. The space outside the atoms was empty, a concept that most of Democritus's contemporaries could not accept.

Second, the atoms were in perpetual motion, in every direction, throughout empty space. There is no above or below, before or behind, in empty space, said Democritus. In modern terms, empty space was therefore isotropic, a sophisticated notion.

Third, the continual motion of the atoms was inherent. They possessed what we would call inertial mass. The notion that the atoms kept on moving without being pushed, besides being another remarkable intellectual concept, was not acceptable to Aristotle and others. Only the celestial bodies, Aristotle thought, kept on moving of and by themselves, because they were divine. The general refusal by Aristotle and his influential followers to accept the law of inertia stood as an obstacle to the development of physics for two thousand years.

Fourth, weight or gravity was not a property of atoms or indeed of aggregates thereof. Here Democritus was as wrong as wrong could be.

Whether Democritus was right or wrong about a fifth point is not definitely decided to this day. He held that the soul is breath, and because breath is material, and therefore made up of atoms, so must the soul be.

All the old words for soul originally meant breath: psyche, spiritus, anima. So far so good. But is it acceptable to maintain that the soul, or the mind, is material? If it is a physical thing like stones or water, it must be determined by physical laws; it cannot be free. But how can we say that the soul or the mind or the will is not free? We are more certain of our freedom than of anything else—our freedom to lift or not to lift a finger, to walk forward rather than backward, to get up in the morning or to lie abed. If we accept the notion of a determined, material mind and soul, we are faced with the absurdity of morality, for if we are not free to act as we wish, then how can we be held responsible for our actions?

Again we have an antimony. We can accept Democritus's assumption that our bodies at least, including our breath, are part of the material universe, which we can understand by assuming it to be made up of atoms and the void. But we cannot accept that our minds and souls and wills are material and belong to that world. Even the hardy thinkers who claim to accept this theory do not act as if they do. They may deny the innate freedom of others, but they act as if they believe in their own.

The tension built up by this antinomy, too, has proved to be fruitful over the centuries. However, the notion that the soul was material proved so unacceptable to both the Aristotelians and the Christians that for nearly two millennia the atomic hypothesis languished.

The Problem of Thales: The Ultimate Solution

If the seventy books of Democritus had survived, would their author be as famous as Aristotle? Would Democritus's dialogues now be preferred to those of Plato, who got his wish? It is interesting to speculate about this. Why did the books of Democritus perish? Was it because they were wrong or uninteresting? Why did those of Plato and Aristotle survive? Was it because they were better and more true? Or was there something about what Democritus believed that was so offensive and perhaps even dangerous that his reputation had to be destroyed, with a consequent destruction of his books?

Regarding Plato, it is not so hard to see why he might have wanted to burn them. Plato's master, Socrates, had been uninterested in scientific research; he was concerned only with ethics and politics. He did not even enjoy being in the country, for there he was too close to nature and there were too few people to talk to and about.

Plato inherited this basic prejudice against the systematic study of the material world, and added to it a kind of contempt for matter itself. Like all Greeks, he was more interested in what underlay matter, but this he believed was immaterial, not material: the Forms, as he called them, of things like tables and cats and men, as well as of things that we call "good," "true," and "beautiful."

What is shared by all the things we call cats? It is catness, said Plato, a Form; catness is not material, even though all cats are material beings. What is shared by all things that are good, by virtue of which we call them "good"? It is goodness, another, and higher, Form; it, too, is immaterial, although many good things may be material.

Here was still another updated and highly sophisticated solution of the problem posed by Thales. From a philosophical point of view the solution proved to be splendid and required little modification. From the scientific point of view it was useless.

Aristotle, Plato's pupil, recognized a lack of balance in Plato's solution of Thales' problem. He corrected it in a series of dazzling metaphysical strokes. Matter, said Aristotle, is pure potentiality; it is nothing yet, but it has the capacity to be anything.

Form is what Matter becomes when it becomes something. Both Matter and Form are necessary for the existence of any thing; Matter is the wax that is imprinted by the Form. Considered merely as Matter, which is different from the kind of material stuff that we know in the world, a human being does not exist, yet. He is only potentially himself. Considered as Form, he is intelligible, which Matter is not, because it *is* not, but only abstractly. He is merely a set of descriptors, of measurements, of coordinates, or of predicates, as Aristotle would have said: he does not yet breathe, fear, and love. Matter and Form must come together to make him, or any real thing, exist. (Aristotle thought that in the case of a living thing, like a cat or a man, the mother contributed the Matter, the father the Form. This was another reason, if another was needed by the ancients, to prove the inferiority of females.)

In Aristotle's view, Matter did not exist by itself, nor did Form. He disagreed with Plato about the latter point, for Plato had posited the independent existence of Forms. Thus the world that Aristotle taught us to understand and philosophize about is the very world we see. It is full of real objects which he called substances, having a potential aspect, which allows them to change, and a formal or essential aspect, which makes them intelligible and allows us to understand them. For it is the Forms of things that we understand, not the things themselves, since Forms can be in our minds as well as in things, whereas the things themselves are not in our minds. In this respect, said Aristotle, in a famous phrase, the knower is one with the thing known.

Here was an even more sophisticated solution of Thales' problem. From the philosophical point of view, it is the ultimate solution; no one has improved upon it. From the point of view of science, however, there was some question whether the theory would work. Aristotle was not, like Plato, anti-matter. He did not assume a world of immaterial essences, or Forms, floating about our heads. For Aristotle, real things were real things, and there was nothing else. But the concept of Matter as pure potentiality and as such having no real existence might cause trouble. And what about the atoms of Democritus? Were they matter or Matter? Aristotle did not say, and left it to us to struggle with the problem.

Moral Truth and Political Expediency: Socrates, Plato, and Aristotle

Plato and Aristotle were more than just ontologists, experts about being; they had something to say about everything, not just Form and Matter. It is time to introduce them, together with their great predecessor and teacher, Socrates.

Socrates was born in Athens about 470 BC. He served with distinction as an infantryman during the Peloponnesian War between Athens and Sparta. According to Plato he saved the life of the Athenian general Alcibiades. He was a sophist, or teacher of philosophy, but unlike the other sophists he refused to take money for his teaching. Instead, he claimed that he knew nothing himself, and he spent his time interrogating his fellow citizens, and especially the professional sophists, who claimed that they did know.

If he did not know anything else with certainty, he surely knew how to argue and to ask hard questions. In fact, as a philosopher he may almost be said to have discovered all the hard questions there are to ask. His lifetime of questioning did not endear him to many of the Athenians, and in 399 he was indicted and charged with impiety and corrupting the young, who liked to listen to him quizzing their elders and who enjoyed the discomfort that Socrates produced. He was found guilty, by a majority vote of the jurors, and forced to drink a fatal poison made from hemlock.

Socrates wrote nothing, but many actions of his life and especially many conversations he had with eminent men and sophists of his day are recounted in Plato's dialogues. Plato was born in Athens in 427 or 428 BC of a distinguished family. After the execution of Socrates, Plato and other "Socratics" took refuge in Megara and then spent years traveling about Greece. During that time he became a friend of Dion, the tyrant of Syracuse, whom he tried to instruct in philosophy in hopes of making him a "philosopher-king." He founded the Academy in Athens in 387 for the systematic conduct of research in philosophy and mathematics, presiding over it for the rest of his life. He wrote dialogues that included Socrates as the chief speaker and others in which an "Athenian stranger" takes the leading role. It is tempting to assume that the latter represents Plato himself, but in fact it is difficult if not impossible to distinguish between the thought of Plato and Socrates.

Aristotle was born in Stagira, Macedonia, in 384 BC. Hence he was often called the Stagirite. He was sent to Athens to the Academy in 367 and spent twenty years there as Plato's most famous pupil and, doubtless, as his burr, for the two men disagreed about many things. On Plato's death in 348 or 347, Aristotle left Athens and traveled for twelve years, founding new academies in several cities and marrying the daughter of a king. Returning to Macedonia, he spent three years tutoring Alexander, the son of King Philip. He opened the Lyceum in Athens in 335. This school, as opposed to the Academy, was devoted to scientific work. In 323 Alexander died, and an anti-Alexandrian movement arose in Athens. Aristotle, as the former teacher of the dead hero, was suspect. Saying that it was not fitting for two philosophers to be killed by the Athenians, Aristotle retired to Chalcis, where he died in 322.

Aristotle taught us to reason about the world we see and know: he invented the science of logic, which is the rules of thinking, as grammar is the rules of speaking and writing. His contribution did not stop there. He also invented the idea of the division of the sciences into fields distinguished both by their subject matters and by their methods, and he made many useful observations about natural things, like fish, men, and stars.

Despite his deep interest in natural science, which he would have called natural philosophy, Aristotle shared with Plato, as Plato shared with Socrates, an overweening concern and fascination with politics and morality. None of them ever questioned the idea that the most important being in the world is man. Mankind in the abstract, for only men, they agreed, have rational souls. Real men, also, because with them we must live, our happiness or misery depending on how well or badly we do so.

In the case of Socrates and Plato, and to their great credit, "man" included all human beings, even women, even foreigners, even, perhaps, slaves. In the case of Aristotle the term was hardly all-inclusive. Slaves were inferior—else they would not permit themselves to be enslaved. Women were inferior—else they would not be the ones to run the household, while men ran the city-state. Non-Greeks, too, were inferior, because they did not speak Greek or know how to philosophize.

For Aristotle, the inferiority of slaves and women was innate. It could not be cured. Non-Greeks might be teachable, but this was risky. Aristotle therefore cautioned his pupil Alexander to prohibit his captains from intermarrying with barbarians, lest the virus of inferiority infect the superior race.

Indeed, it is sad to have to report that for Aristotle almost everyone was inferior except the Greek male aristocrats whose economic and other interests he shared and among whom he believed he was fit to be numbered. In his famous and great book, the *Nicomachean Ethics*, he arrived, after a series of brilliant *coups de raison*, at a conclusion that is deeply flawed.

The Fallacy of the Consequent

The *Nicomachean Ethics* is about virtue, and about its reward, which is happiness. Who is virtuous? He—rarely she—who makes right choices habitually, not just once in a while, accidentally. But what are right choices? They are choices of action, Aristotle said, that are characterized by being means between extremes. Courage, for example, is a mean. It lies between the extremes of timidity and rashness.

So far so good. But, Aristotle recognized, the analysis of actions in terms of means and extremes is theoretical and of little practical value. A better way to identify habitual choices that must be virtuous is to observe the actions of a virtuous man. The right choices are those that are made by a good man; a good man is one who makes the right choices. The circularity of the reasoning is amusing until you reflect on the consequences.

Such circularity in reasoning survives to our day. When one holds that women, or blacks, or homosexuals, or Hispanics, or the poor, or natives—you name it—are treated as inferiors *because* they are inferior, one is really thinking along the same lines. There is a name for this kind of logical error, given to it by Aristotle himself: the "fallacy of the consequent." It also works in reverse. One is treated as superior because one *is* superior. Justice reigns: what we have, we deserve; what others do not have, they do not deserve.

The fallacy of the consequent is often used to determine the membership of clubs. This person *belongs*; that person *does not*. Good old boys are good because they do and think and feel the right things; the right things are the things that good old boys do, think, and feel.

In Plato's great dialogue about justice, the *Republic*, he had defended the thesis that rulers only deserve to rule if they have undergone an intensive and far-reaching education, so that they have become philosophers.

> Until philosophers are kings, or the kings and princes of this world have the spirit and power of philosophy, and political greatness and wisdom meet in one, and those commoner natures who pursue either to the exclusion of the other are compelled to stand aside, cities will never have rest from their evils—no, nor the human race, as I believe.

Socrates is speaking here. He goes on to say that until such time, mankind must be content with a kind of shadow of justice, characterized by a "Royal Lie" to the effect that those who rule deserve to do so, and those who are ruled deserve that, too.

There is profound irony in the thesis, which we came upon in another form in the last chapter. Confucius, whose lifetime overlapped that of Socrates (although they surely knew nothing about one another), had also proclaimed that only those who merit leadership should enjoy it. Superficially, such a meritocracy is the same as the aristocracy of Socrates. But there is an underlying difference of great importance.

The implication of the Confucian doctrine is that men are inherently unequal, and their inequality is manifested by their greater or lesser understanding of certain written texts. In the case of Socrates, there is serious question whether men are inherently unequal. At least we can be certain that Socrates believed there was no way to tell whether one man—or woman, he was also certain about that—was superior or inferior to another prior to a series of examinations based on absolutely equal opportunity for schooling. Any superiority manifested on such examinations—which we must assume would have been fair—would then be based on merit, but this merit need not be assumed to be innate. A superior performance might be based on greater effort as well as on greater native skill or intelligence. What would it matter? The end in view was to obtain rulers who knew well how to rule. Nothing else was so important. How they managed to arrive at such knowledge—by working harder or by being more intelligent—was relatively unimportant.

For Socrates, in short, an underlying equality existed in the human species. All men and women were equal, at least until they proved themselves to be otherwise. That was a splendid thing for someone living in the fifth century BC to believe. The irony of the doctrine of the Royal Lie consisted in Socrates' belief that the underlying equality should not be used to justify direct democracy. That is, it did not follow, according to Socrates, that because all men and women are equal they are all equally qualified to rule. That being so, the state must propagate the doctrine that all are *not* equal in order to obtain able rulers. Most people, he thought, would not accept those who ruled over them unless they felt that the rulers were inherently superior.

The passage just quoted about the philosopher-king is famous. In another passage in the *Republic*—not nearly so famous—Socrates treats the kind of society in which human equality, which he believed was the true condition of man, could be publicly recognized.

Socrates is seeking the meaning of justice. That is a hard thing to find, he admits. He therefore proposes trying to locate it in a state, where the meaning of justice should be larger and more visible than in an individual human being. And so he begins his quest, which is a very long one as it turns out, by describing a very simple kind of state. Here is how the men and women will live in it.

Will they not produce corn, and wine, and clothes, and shoes, and build houses for themselves? And when they are housed, they will work, in summer, commonly, stripped and barefoot, but in winter substantially clothed and shod. They will feed on barleymeal and flour of wheat, baking and kneading them, making noble cakes and loaves; these they will serve up on a mat of reeds or on clean leaves, themselves reclining the while upon beds strewn with myrtle or yew. And they and their children will feast, drinking of the wine which they have made, wearing garlands on their heads, and hymning the praises of the gods, in happy converse with one another. And they will take care that their families do not exceed their means; having an eye to poverty or war.

Glaucon, Socrates' young interlocutor at this point in the dialogue, objects. "Yes, Socrates," he says, "and if you were providing for a city of pigs, how else would you feed the beasts?" He goes on to insist on more comfort than Socrates has provided the citizens of his ideal little city, wherein he hopes to find justice. Socrates replies:

> The question you would have me consider is, not only how a State, but how a luxurious State is created; and possibly there is no harm in this, for in such a State we shall be more likely to see how justice and injustice originate.

Commentators throughout the ages have seldom taken Socrates seriously in his apparent preference for a "city of pigs" over a city "at fever heat," as he later remarks. Perhaps they are right, in the sense that Socrates may not have believed that men, constituted as they are, would be content with the simple life of the city of pigs. But that he really preferred it I have no doubt. And not least because in such a city no Royal Lie would be needed; all are equal there, and all are qualified to rule, because there, rule requires no special expertise.

Another kind of irony emerges when Aristotle's fallacy of the consequent is applied to the doctrine of the Royal Lie. When that happens, the doctrine becomes a theory of injustice. Suppose that all men and women are equal. Also suppose that some are rulers and others are ruled, and that this principle is accepted because the ruled accept the Royal Lie. By the fallacy of the consequent, this is to assume that the Royal Lie is not a lie; in other words, some persons—namely, the rulers—really are superior, else they would not be rulers. And, in fact, Aristotle allowed this fallacy to blind him to the Socratean truth of the equality of all persons; that is, he argued that the Lie was true. In a just state, he said, the rulers would deserve to be rulers because of their innate superiority, not just because of their superior qualification as rulers. And if persons ruled a state who did not deserve to do so, then the state itself was unjust and bad and should be amended.

"If all men were friends, there would be no need of justice," Aristotle proclaimed. This famous statement is one of the bulwarks of the argument for the necessity of government, for clearly all men are not friends, and government, imposing justice upon them, is therefore needed. Again, the statement can be turned upon itself and used for ill purposes. It can mean, for example, that the members of a club do not need rules to govern themselves; they only need rules to keep other people out, the ones that do not belong. Justice is only needed when dealing with "others," usually inferiors. Justice helps to keep them in their place.

I am being hard on Aristotle, but not without reason. His greatness as a philosopher and protoscientist is undeniable. Yet his errors have had enduring harmful effects. His doctrines of natural inferiority and female inferiority, respectively, justified, or helped to justify, slavery and the inequality of the sexes until our own time. His great authority also helped to defend tyranny, in the name of "benevolent" despotism, and his doctrine of ethnic inferiority helped to justify racism. All of these errors— for that is what they are—might have endured without Aristotle. But it would have been harder to justify them.

Ironic Socratean confusions about the Royal Lie are still with us. Consider this question. When you enter the voting booth to record your fateful choice for the next ruler of your country, do you choose the man or woman whom you believe to be the better person, or the one you think is likely to be the better ruler? Or is there no difference in your mind between these two considerations?

Perhaps there should be. Could you imagine circumstances in which a worse man or woman—not really a bad one, but simply a man or woman who is not as good as the other candidate—would be a better ruler? Is virtue, as such, a qualification for leadership or rule? Of course, virtue is important, but is it all-important? What about knowledge and experience? Are they not important, too?

Do you believe, with Socrates, that all men and women are equal as human beings? But does that mean that all are equally qualified to be leaders?

Some of the Greek city-states acted on that last assumption. They chose their rulers by lot, on the grounds that there is no such thing as special qualifications for the rule of equals over equals. At the same time they reduced the time when anyone could rule to a few months, perhaps on the assumption that no one can do much harm in so short a time.

That kind of extreme democracy, as he thought of it, enraged Socrates. We choose everyone else for his experience and expert knowledge, he pointed out: our generals, our doctors and advocates, our horse trainers, house builders, and shoemakers. Yet we choose our leaders by lot. What folly!

Greece versus Persia: The Fruitful Conflict

Greece was a small, relatively unpopulated, out-of-the-way country on the outskirts of civilization, consisting of a number of city-states having in common language, religion, and extreme litigiousness. The last characteristic led to frequent quarrels and made political unity hard to create and harder still to maintain.

The Persian empire that the Greeks feared and also admired for so long and finally conquered under Alexander the Great rose in the open spaces of central Asia in the seventh century before the Christian era. First organized by Medes, it was soon ruled by Persians under Cyrus the Great (from c.550 BC) and Darius the Great (from c.520 BC). At its greatest extent, under Darius's successor Xerxes (ruled 486–465 BC), the empire rivaled in size the later Roman domain, extending from India westward over the lands below the Caspian and Black seas to the east coast of the Mediterranean and including Egypt and Thrace. Its great cities, joined by the famous Royal Road, were Sardis, Nineveh, Babylon, and Susa. East of Susa lay Persepolis, a vast religious monument that, while not the political capital of the empire, was its spiritual center. For its austere beauty and its grandeur Persepolis was one of the wonders of the world.

To the north were the lands of the Scythians, whom the Persians never conquered (nor did the Romans). The uninhabitable desert of Arabia lay to the south. To the west was the small, rough, poor peninsula inhabited by Macedonians and Greeks. To Darius it appeared both inevitable and easy to extend the Persian power over these troublesome foreigners who refused to worship the Great King and who liked to organize their cities into what they called democracies, that is, tiny city-states governed by the *demos*, or "people."

The first concerted Persian attack on Greece occurred in 490 BC, when an army of Persians was defeated at the famous battle of Marathon by Greeks led by Miltiades. The Persians, astonished, retired for ten years, returning in 480 BC, under the personal leadership of their new king, Xerxes, with a much greater army and a powerful fleet.

The Spartans delayed the land forces heroically at Thermopylae, but they could not stop them. The army kept on coming, invested Athens, took and burned its citadel on September 21, 480, and prepared to conquer the rest of Greece. But the Persian navy was trapped and destroyed at Salamis by an Athenian fleet commanded by Themistocles (September 29), and a combined Greek army stymied the Persian land forces in a great battle at Plataea (August 27, 479). Before that, Xerxes, distressed or perhaps just bored by these frustrating proceedings, had returned to his luxurious palace at Susa, and for a century the Greeks were left to boast and enjoy their victory. They had a right to glow, for by their wits and their courage their small and relatively poor nation of independent city-states had defeated the greatest army in the world and sent the ships of the greatest navy to the bottom of the sea.

How had they managed to do it? The Greeks were fighting for their homes against an invading foreign foe, which is always an advantage (*vide* the Russians against the French in 1812 and the Germans in 1941). The Greeks themselves perceived another difference between them. The Persian soldiers and sailors often had to be whipped into battle. We are free, said the Greeks. Our discipline is that of free men, able to choose. We fight because we wish to, not because we are forced to do so. And, they said, we will never give in, for that would be to betray our freedom, which is the most precious thing to us.

The Persians did not give up, either, although they ceased sending armies into Greece. Instead, they sent "Persian archers," which were gold coins with an archer on one side. Persian gold succeeded where Persian soldiers had failed, bribing both sides—at different times—during the Peloponnesian War, the destructive civil conflict between Athens and Sparta and their allies that lasted, with intermittent truces, from 431 BC to 404 BC. In the end, Sparta defeated Athens, but her victory was short-lived, for her involvement during the next century in the Persian civil wars in Ionia led to her defeat by other Greek forces and a long decline. Thus both Athens and Sparta were destroyed, with Persian help.

Even the destruction of these city-states was not the final word in the long and bitter conflict between the pesky Greeks and the ponderous, powerful Persians. Alexander the Great, the Macedonian pupil of Aristotle, inherited the throne of Macedonia in 336 BC. After he consolidated his power in Greece, he set out in the spring of 334 on his celebrated Persian expedition. The winter of 334–333 saw his conquest of western Asia Minor, including Miletus and Samos. In July 332 he stormed the island city of Tyre, where he won his most famous victory. During the following months he conquered Egypt, leaving Greeks to rule that country until the Roman conquest three hundred years later (Cleopatra was a Greek, not an Egyptian). In 330 Alexander reached Persepolis, after having conquered all the Persian royal cities, and burned it to symbolize the end of his Panhellenic war of revenge.

Still, there is a sense in which the Persians had the last word. When the kings and rulers of all the far-flung nations of the Persian empire had journeyed to Susa or Persepolis to pay their homage to the Great King, the King of Kings as he was called, they had prostrated themselves before him, crawling on their bellies, eyes averted, until they reached his feet. The Greeks called this ritual *proskynesis*, "worship"; their contempt for a people who would worship a man as though he were a god had originally been great.

By the time Alexander died, he had been corrupted by the Persian idea of greatness, which involved being worshiped as a god. And so he adopted the ritual of *proskynesis*, demanding that his followers, even Macedonians and Greeks, prostrate themselves before him. The tough old Macedonian warriors laughed at the new requirement, and Alexander, embarrassed, quickly abandoned the ritual. (He later killed the man who had led the laughter.) But nothing more pathetically revealed that he had forgotten the idea of personal freedom that had helped to place him on his throne.

The Persian wars of the early fifth century BC were an inspiration to the

Greeks, particularly to the Athenians, who, prior to the battles at Marathon and Salamis, had been a minor power in Greece compared to the Spartans. The Athenians rebuilt the burned Acropolis, and the Parthenon has remained for twenty-three centuries as a symbol, as they themselves viewed it, of the victory of freedom over imperial despotism.

Poets sang the victories in dramatic verse so innovative and powerful that it, too, has lasted for millennia. And the two historians Herodotus and Thucydides invented a new science and a literary form to memorialize, and try to understand, what had happened.

The Tragedy of Athens

Aeschylus (c.525–c.465 BC) has to be credited with being the inventor of drama, for he is said to have introduced the second actor into the plays that were presented every year in Athens in honor of the god Dionysus. Prior to Aeschylus, plays had consisted of primarily religious verse exchanges between a single figure representing a god or a hero and a chorus representing the people. Once there were two actors, interacting with one another, true drama began. At first the chorus continued to play an important role, but as time passed, the chorus disappeared, and the whole burden of development of the action and thought was taken by the actors. So it is today.

Aeschylus fought with the Greeks against the Persians at the battle of Marathon. This fact was recorded on an ancient grave marker; his plays were not mentioned. Those plays are among the great treasures of Greek antiquity. Stately and magnificent, they deal in sublime verse with the age old problems of the conflict between man and god. In his greatest surviving work, the trilogy about the hero Agamemnon, his murderous wife, and his avenging son Orestes, Aeschylus showed how the hubris of Agamemnon led to his death and to the never-ending woes that afflicted his house, pursued by Furies and condemned to Hades. Justice, said Aeschylus, "is the smoke of common men's houses"; the great are arrogant, as Xerxes had been, and are brought low by the anger of the gods.

Sophocles (c.496–406) added valuable elements to the developing tragic drama. Not just the great, but all men, he saw, were caught in the same inexorable trap. Forced by the condition of their life to act as if they had knowledge of the future, they were bound, like King Oedipus, to suffer because they actually lacked such knowledge and therefore could not avoid the errors that would inevitably bring them to ruin. The choral verses of Sophocles are unsurpassed for their limpid grace and sweetness, but the stories Sophocles told, as Aristotle the critic knew, compressed within their brief span a horror that no viewer could evade.

These lines from *Oedipus at Colonus* tell the tale:

> Not to be born surpasses thought and speech.
> The second best is to have seen the light
> And then to go back quickly whence we came.

Euripedes (c.484–406 BC) was the third and last of the great Athenian tragedians of the fifth century BC. He could not surpass Aeschylus or Sophocles, but he saw the path of drama in the future and opened the way to it. Bringing the gods and heroes down to earth and making them mere mortals having the vanity, greed, anger, envy, and pride of common men and women, he presented pictures of human life that were sometimes tragic, sometimes almost comic, but always and undeniably real. Peopling his plays with women and slaves and making the heroic figures of the past mere cardboard masks of men, he showed the Athenians, who were fascinated by his art but did not like him, what was really in their hearts and minds.

Aeschylus died before the Peloponnesian War began, but Sophocles and Euripides lived through it, from the beginning almost to the end (both died in 406 BC, two years before the final Athenian defeat). The suffering caused by the war, both physical and moral, particularly imbues their later plays, which are cries to unheeding heaven against the injustice, cruelty, and folly of war, which wasted all the pride and treasure built up by the Greeks in their victory over the Persians a half century before. The tragedy of Athens, as the playwrights saw, was the very same hubris that had brought Agamemnon and Oedipus down to Hades, all their riches scattered and with no one to beweep their fate.

> The god of war, money changer of dead bodies,
> held the balance of his spear in the fighting,
> and from the corpse-fires at Ilium
> sent to their dearest the dust
> heavy and bitter with tears shed
> packing smooth the urns with
> ashes that once were men.
> They praise them through their tears, how this man
> knew well the craft of battle, how another
> went down splendid in slaughter . . .
> There by the walls of Ilium
> the young men in their beauty keep
> graves deep in the alien soil
> they hated and they conquered.
>
> Aeschylus, *Agamemnon*

When the people vote on war, nobody reckons
On his own death; it is too soon; he thinks
Some other man will meet that wretched fate.
But if death faced him when he cast his vote,
Hellas would never perish from battle-madness.
And yet we men all know which of two words
Is better, and can weigh the good and bad
They bring: how much better is peace than war!
First and foremost, the Muses love her best;
And the goddess of vengeance hates her. She delights
In healthy children, and she glories in wealth.
But wickedly we throw all this away
To start our wars and make the losers slaves—
Man binding man and city chaining city.

Euripides, *Suppliant Women*

Herodotus, Thucydides, and the Invention of History

For centuries men had recorded the events of the past, in Egypt, in Mesopotamia, in China. But before Herodotus, no one had ever tried to put down a coherent story, with a beginning, a middle, and an end, and with an explanation of why things happened the way they did.

Again it was the Greek victory over the Persians in 490–480 BC that inspired the Athenian historians, as it had inspired the dramatists. Nothing had ever happened before that was so astonishing and so wonderful, they thought; this momentous victory required them to try harder to understand it than men had ever before tried to understand such events.

They were also inspired by the Ionian philosophers of the previous century, from Thales on down, who had taught the Greeks to look at the world in a new way, as we have seen. Just as external nature must have underlying principles that would make it comprehensible, so must the actions of men have an intelligible substratum that would make it possible to understand why men did what they did, and so perhaps what they would do in the future.

Herodotus was born around 484 BC and thus grew up with tales of the Greek triumph ringing in his ears. He was a great traveler. His wide journeys, over many years, took him to most parts of the Persian empire, to Egypt, and to most of the cities of Greece. He apparently made careful notes wherever he went, recording his observations and his interviews with eminent persons. His curiosity was boundless, and he spent his life indulging it. And writing his history, or, as he called it, his Researches into the causes and events of the Persian wars.

The causes lay far in the past, he realized, so he began by writing the story of the rise of the Medes and then the Persians from a scattered desert folk into the rulers of the greatest empire on earth, as he believed it. In the process, and because he had spent many fascinated months in Egypt, he told the story of that ancient kingdom. But he never forgot the central question of his labors, which was how a relative handful of Greek soldiers and sailors had been able to defeat a force ten times their number, not just once, but many times over a period of years.

His answers to the question have shaped our thinking ever since. On the one hand was the undaunted Persian arrogance and pride. When Xerxes arrived at the Hellespont, the waves were very high, forcing his army to delay its crossing of the narrow strait. Xerxes, in a rage, commanded that the waters should be whipped, as though they were disobedient slaves. How different were the Greeks, who, having driven the Persians back, forbore to harass them further, content to have saved their homes. These were lessons, Herodotus thought, which all Greeks should learn.

According to Herodotus, Xerxes had a philosophical streak. This passage is famous.

And now, as he looked and saw the whole Hellespont covered with the vessels of his fleet, and all the shore and every plain about Abydos as full as possible of men, Xerxes congratulated himself on his good fortune; but after a little he wept.

Then Artabanus, the king's uncle . . . when he heard that Xerxes was in tears, went to him, and said:—

"How different, sire, is what thou art now doing, from what thou didst a little while ago! Then thou didst congratulate thyself; and now, behold! thou weepest."

"There came upon me," replied he, "a sudden pity, when I thought of the shortness of man's life, and considered that of all this host, so numerous as it is, not one will be alive when a hundred years are gone by."

Herodotus died before 420 BC, too soon for him to be able to comprehend the tragic self-destruction of the Peloponnesian War. Thus the task of trying to make sense of that suicidal conflict was left to his successor, Thucydides.

Born some time before 460 BC, Thucydides as a young man determined to write an ongoing account of the war that filled his lifetime and that of his contemporaries. He was himself a prominent soldier. Although he was removed from his command and exiled because of his failure in an important battle, he concentrated on the military history of the drawn-out conflict. He enlivened this with a device of his own invention, the insertion into the narrative of speeches by important war figures which, for their eloquence and apparent verisimilitude, are almost unique in history.

Thucydides has often been criticized for his innovation: he could not have been present at the actual speeches of important men on these occasions. He admitted that this was so, and justified his practice by stating that he had investigated the facts as deeply as possible. He believed his efforts to be valuable even if he was not able to ascertain exactly what was said; in other words, the judgment of an informed and unbiased researcher concerning what must or ought to have occurred during an historical event was a genuine part of history.

To this practice of Thucydides we owe the moving funeral oration by Pericles (c.495–429 BC), the Athenian leader during the early years of the war, in which he praised his countrymen for their daring and their willingness to take risks of all sorts, intellectual as well as military.

We throw open our city to the world, and never by alien acts exclude foreigners from any opportunity of learning or observing, although the eyes of an enemy may occasionally profit by our liberality; trusting less in system and policy than to the native spirit of our citizens; while in education, where our rivals from their very cradles by a painful discipline seek after manliness, at Athens we live exactly as we please, and yet are just as ready to encounter every legitimate danger. . . .

We cultivate refinement without extravagance and knowledge without effeminacy; wealth we employ more for use than for show, and place the real disgrace of poverty not in owning to the fact but in declining the struggle against it. Our public men have, besides politics, their private affairs to attend to, and our ordinary citizens, though occupied with the pursuits of industry, are still fair judges of public matters; for, unlike any other nation, regarding him who takes no part in these duties not as unambitious but as useless, we Athenians are able to judge at all events if we cannot originate, and, instead of looking on discussion as a stumbling-block in the way of action, we think it an indispensable preliminary to any action at all. . . .

In generosity we are equally singular, acquiring our friends by conferring, not by requiring, favors. Yet, of course, the doer of the favor is the firmer friend of the two, in order by continued kindness to keep the recipient in his debt. . . . It is only the Athenians, who, fearless of consequences, confer their benefits not from calculations of expediency, but in the confidence of liberality.

In short, I say that as a city we are the school of Hellas. . . .

No people has ever been more lovingly praised by a leader, and for a time, Thucydides thought, no people ever deserved more praise.

But Athenian love of freedom and justice could not survive the horrors of continual warfare and the yearly invasions of the homeland by Spartan troops who mercilessly killed the country people and burned the crops and the orchards and the olive groves. As in so many subsequent wars, what may have been the more virtuous side became less virtuous under the exigencies of force, and in time the Athenians became as cruel and tyrannical as their enemy. This, Thucydides implied, was the real tragedy of Athens, that in winning the battles she was losing her soul.

Thucydides' history ends prior to the conclusion of the war. It is probable that he died before the war ended in 404 BC, although there is no other evidence for this inference. Some commentators have wondered whether he failed to finish his book because of a broken heart.

The Spirit of Greek Thought

Before Thales, most knowledge had been practical, comprising pragmatic rules for success in enterprises from hunting to growing crops, from organizing households to governing cities, from creating art to waging war. The slow accumulation of such practical know-how, which persisted for thousands of years, did not cease because the Greeks began to philosophize about the nature of things. To the contrary, it accelerated, as the curious Greeks ranged far from their sea-locked peninsula, following the example of the culture hero, Odysseus:

> Many were the cities he saw
> Many were the men whose minds he learned,
> And many were the woes he suffered on the sea.

The Greeks suffered many reversals, but mostly they learned, about cities and men's minds. And so knowledge grew apace, knowledge of husbandry, viticulture, pottery making, commerce and salesmanship, finance, metals, weapons, and warfare.

> Many the wonders but nothing walks stranger than man.
> This thing crosses the sea in the winter's storm,
> making his path through the roaring waves.
> And she, the greatest of gods, the Earth—
> ageless she is, and unwearied—he wears her away
> as the ploughs go up and down from year to year
> and his mules turn up the soil.
>
> Gay nations of birds he snares and leads,
> wild beast tribes and the salty brood of the sea,
> with the twisted mesh of his nets, this clever man.

He controls with craft the beasts of the open air,
walkers on hills. The horse with his shaggy mane
he holds and harnesses, yoked about the neck,
and the strong bull of the mountain.

Language, and thought like the wind
and the feelings that make the town,
he has taught himself, and shelter against the cold,
refuge from rain. He can always help himself.
He faces no future helpless. There's only death
that he cannot find an escape from. He has contrived
refuges from illnesses once beyond cure.

Clever beyond all dreams
the inventive craft that he has
which may drive him one time or another to well or ill.

Sophocles, *Antigone*

The Greeks learned not just because they were curious and traveled to alien places. More important was their revolutionary discovery of how to learn systematically, which is to say, their invention of organized knowledge itself. Before Thales, knowledge, the possession of which had insured success and conferred happiness rather than misery, had been a monopoly of the ruling class, that is, of kings and priests. Thales and his followers changed knowledge from a "mystery" into a public thing. Anyone who could read might share in its benefits. Anyone who could understand its principles might add to it, for others' benefit as well as his own.

Here as in so many other realms of knowledge Aristotle was the knower *par excellence.* He established different methods and different criteria of knowledge for a variety of subject matters. When approaching any subject, he always reviewed the contributions of his predecessors and contemporaries, criticizing what he believed to be wrong and adopting what he thought was valuable. Moreover, he created research teams to study particularly difficult subjects, like botany and current political theory.

Most important, Aristotle wrote and published many books, and they were carried everywhere Greeks went. It was a stroke of fortune, too, that Alexander the Great had been his pupil. The conqueror enlisted himself as one of Aristotle's researchers, sending back reports to his old teacher, together with zoological and botanical samples for the master to analyze and categorize.

In short, there was suddenly a new thing in the world, which the Greeks called *episteme,* and we call science. Organized knowledge. Public knowledge, based on principles that could be periodically reviewed and tested—and questioned—by all.

There were enormous consequences. First, the idea grew that there was only one truth, not many truths, about anything: men might disagree, but if they did, then some must be right and others wrong. Furthermore, what was true now had always been true and always would be true: truth was not subject to modification by the mere passage of time or the change of opinions. This did not mean that all the truth about anything was already known. The understanding of truth could change and improve. But truth itself stood outside of man's thinking, like a beacon guiding him home.

Second, there came into existence the idea of a fundamental relationship between the knower and the thing known, the fit, as it might be called, between the exterior world and the interior mind. The world is essentially rational, and therefore, since we possess reason, we can understand it. Perhaps we do not yet understand the rational world, or all of it; perhaps we will never understand it completely. But that is not because the world is essentially unintelligible, as men before the Greeks had believed. It is just because it is too hard for us to know everything about so complicated a thing as the world.

Third, a new concept of education took hold. Fathers had always taught their sons the rules of their "art"; mothers had taught their daughters the rules of theirs; and the state had insisted that all young subjects learn the rules of living in it. The penalty for not learning the rules was banishment or death. But there was no body of organized knowledge that all could be taught, or that all young people should be expected to learn. Suddenly, there was another new thing, which the Greeks called *paideia*: a curriculum for everyone (with the usual exceptions: women, slaves, foreigners, and so forth) to study, that they might become good men as well as good citizens.

Finally, there was the idea of science itself, and its young queen, mathematics. The eagerness with which the Greeks everywhere threw themselves into the scientific study of everything, and especially mathematics, the science of pure reasoning, is both beautiful and terrifying. Perhaps the beauty goes without saying. The terror needs some comment.

In their eternal restlessness, the Greeks were exhilarated by learning new things, and they took their ideas wherever they went and explained them to more settled peoples. They were essentially and eternally iconoclastic; more than anything else, they enjoyed questioning old beliefs and tipping over other peoples' sacred applecarts. This was especially true of the Greek rulers settled upon the Egyptians by Alexander. They wanted to "modernize" Egypt, even though Egypt had worked so very well for so many centuries.

Iconoclasm can be exciting. It can also be frightening. It challenges the old, safe belief that you should leave well enough alone. The human race, on the whole, had survived, even flourished, for thousands of years on that philosophy. And so the Greeks, bringing this gift of a new, questioning spirit, which required re-examination of everything, were not loved by all to whom they brought it.

The Greeks were mariners and explorers. The sea was home to them. Like Odysseus they set out in their frail craft to see the world, to establish colonies in far-flung lands, to trade with friend and foe alike.

It was therefore natural enough for them to set off on intellectual craft to explore unknown seas of thought. With their unprecedented and inexplicable genius they undertook this adventure, over and over, for nearly a thousand years, from the first stirrings of philosophy in Miletus at the beginning of the sixth century BC to the triumphs of Alexandrian scholarship in the fourth century AD. In so doing they set before the human race an image of what it might become.

In our time, we have indeed all become like those ancient Greeks. Iconoclasts and adventurers, we question every tradition and seek to change every established rule.

3

What the Romans Knew

Homer's Odysseus, that questing, mythical figure out of the remote Greek past, had by classical times become the culture hero of the Greeks. As late as the fifth century BC the Homeric poems were still the curriculum of a Greek education. Only under the influence of Aristotle, a century later, did the ideal of *paideia* begin to incorporate regular and systematic study of history, philosophy, and nature. But the fame of Odysseus never dimmed, as it has not to our own day.

Odysseus was a wanderer, an adventurer, who gloried in his questing. Certain that his beloved Penelope would always await him, he explored strange cities, made new conquests, and loved other women.

When, at the end of the first century BC, Virgil (70–19 BC) wrote his own great Latin epic, the *Aeneid*, to teach the Romans about their glorious past and reveal to them their character as a people, he chose Odysseus as his model. He made his hero, Aeneas, a quester, too. But with what a difference!

Aeneas, by contrast with Odysseus, is a homebody. He is driven from Troy, his old home, and forced to wander across the sea in search of a new one. He finds it in Italy and settles down, marries a local girl (his first wife did not survive the fiery conquest of his native city), and establishes a new community of Trojan exiles. He never ceases to complain of his sad fate. He is a quester, but a reluctant one. Home is where his heart is, as it was for most Romans—not Greeks.

Aeneas fled the burning towers of Ilium in mythical times—let us say about 1150 BC. Upon his shoulders in his flight he carried his old father, led his young son by one hand, and in the other held the gods of his household and his city. (He literally carried small clay figures that were the gods.) For seven years, according to Virgil, he wandered throughout the world of the eastern Mediterranean, seeking a place where he and his men might find a a new home for their gods. On the northern shore of

Africa, Dido, the mythical founder and queen of Carthage, offered herself and her kingdom to the wandering Trojan exile. But he spurned her, driven by his fate and the will of Jupiter. Once more he fled across the inland sea, landing in Latium, on the western shore of Italy, near the mouth of the river Tiber. There he found a friendly king, Latinus, ruler of a native tribe called Latins. Latinus had a daughter, Lavinia. He offered her to Aeneas as his bride. Turnus, who had loved her, was jealous, and war ensued between Aeneas and Turnus. Finally victorious, Aeneas had a new home for himself, his men, and his gods.

Aeneas was not the founder of Rome. The traditional date of its founding is centuries later. According to the story, Numitor, last of the Alban kings of Latium, had a daughter, Rhea Silvia. A Vestal, she was supposed to remain a virgin, but she was seduced by the god Mars and bore twin sons, Romulus and Remus. A new king, who had usurped Numitor's throne, ordered that they be drowned in the Tiber, but they were miraculously saved and later suckled by a she-wolf. The king's shepherd, Faustulus, discovered the little boys in a thicket and brought them up. Eventually recognized for who they were, they determined to found a city where they might live safe from the wrath of the usurper's descendants.

But strife grew up between them, and they fought one another. Remus was killed, and Romulus went on to establish the city on the Tiber that would bear his name. The traditional date was 753 BC. Archaeologists now assert that the date was probably earlier.

At first, starved for citizens, Romulus made the new settlement a refuge for runaway slaves and murderers. Thus there were plenty of men in the rough new town, but few women. By a ruse, the Roman bachelors captured their neighbors' women and carried them away to be their wives. The rape of the Sabine women led to another war, but peace soon followed, and the Romans and Sabines together formed a new state under the rule of Romulus.

After the death of Romulus and his apotheosis, the rulers of Rome became Etruscans, from Etruria, north and east of the city (modern Tuscany). The Etruscan kings, being more interested in their splendid old cities of Tarquinia, Volterra, and Cortona, paid little attention to the frontier outpost at the Tiber's mouth. Around 500 BC the Romans rose up and after a hard fight claimed their independence. They thereupon formed a republic, famous in antiquity for its virtue and justice and its longevity.

The motto of the state was *Senatus Populusque Romanus*, the Senate and the People of Rome. (The famous abbreviation, SPQR, still appears everywhere in Rome.) The origins of the Senate are lost in antiquity. An advisory group of patrician families, the senate predated the overthrow of the monarchy in 509 BC. Under the republic the senate continued its advisory role, giving advice to the consuls, who were elected officials, in their task of ruling the state.

At first the "people" consisted of only a few of the wealthiest and most powerful citizens. Nevertheless, it was more than merely a figment that the republic was a partnership between the senate and the people. As the centuries passed, the franchise, and thus the effective rule, was extended to more and more persons. Furthermore, the Roman bureaucracy included representatives of the common people, called tribunes. From time to time the tribunes came into conflict with the consuls. Such conflicts were usually resolved peacefully, for the leading men of Rome knew well how much the power and prosperity of the commonwealth depended on the common people, even the poor, even slaves.

This working partnership may have been modeled on the Greek city-state. Sparta had originally had a similar constitution, as did Corinth in historical times. But the Greek cities constantly struggled with the question whether they should be ruled by the many (democracy) or the few (oligarchy). In effect the Roman republic proclaimed that it was ruled by both. Like so many Roman adaptations of Greek ideas, it was a pragmatic and very successful compromise.

Now in the fourth century BC the restless Greeks controlled most of the eastern Mediterranean world through which Aeneas and his men had wandered. The Greeks explored and carried their commerce everywhere, and under Aristotle's extraordinary pupil, Alexander the Great, they conquered Egypt and the East, the ancient empires falling before them like nodding grain before the sickle.

Alexander died in 323 BC, at Babylon, which he had hoped to make the capital of his empire. He was only thirty-two. He had marched with his army from Macedonia, where he had been born, through Thrace to the Bosporus, thence to Susa and Persepolis, which he burned, then to Samarkand, deep in Asia, then down the valley of the Indus to the Arabian Sea, then back to Persepolis again and finally to Babylon. He had covered ten thousand miles in about ten years, and conquered three empires, Egyptian, Persian, and Indian.

His death marked the apex of Greek temporal power, which, deprived of his genius, quickly began to wither. But it declined more slowly than it might have, because at first there was nothing to take its place. At the time, the Romans were having problems of their own.

Not Greece but Carthage, the populous city on a bay northeast of modern Tunis, was the great early competitor of Rome. Founded by Phoenician colonists from Tyre a little later than Rome itself, Carthage (the name in Phoenician means New Town) was inhabited by a people whom the Romans called Poeni, from which is derived the adjective Punic. Romans and Carthaginians fought for dominion in three Punic wars, which slowed the growth of both civilizations during the century between about 250˙BC and about 150 BC. Carthage was overcome for the first time in 201, its famous general, Hannibal, having been defeated by Scipio Africanus on the plains of Zama, in northern Tunisia. But Carthage rose again only to be finally destroyed in 146, the city walls torn down, the land sown with salt.

Its western flank secure, Rome turned its attention to the east. The end of Greek hegemony in the eastern Mediterranean came during the last decades of that same second century BC. Thereafter Greek and Roman history are one.

The ensuing three centuries, from about 150 BC to about 150 AD, were the high tide of classical civilization and the highest point that Western man attained until after the discovery of the New World. For the first hundred years Roman expansion continued, with little to hinder it, at an increasing pace. Civil wars disrupted Roman life, but the territorial entity that would be called the Roman empire grew inexorably until, by the time of Christ, it included most of what the Romans knew as "the world." (Of course, it did not include India, China, or Japan, or the two as yet undiscovered continents of North and South America.)

The Roman republic came to an end during this period, as we shall see, but it had been eroding for a long time and probably would have died of its own accord even if Julius Caesar and the future emperor, Augustus, had not brought about its death. In fact, Augustus (63 BC–14 AD) tried to restore the republic during his long reign as the first Roman emperor, from 30 BC to 14 AD. He kept the final power in his own hands, but he shared the administrative power with the senate, the consuls, and the tribunes, who continued to be elected. In effect, he was the chief executive officer, while others shared with him the operating authority. His successors converted this partly free government into a totalitarian state.

When Augustus died (14 AD), the area of the empire extended eastward from what is now Belgium, with hardly a break to what is now Syria, southward to Egypt, westward along the coast of North Africa to what is now Algeria, across the sea to Spain and north to Belgium again. During the following century further pieces were added; Britain, Mauretania (modern Morocco), most of present-day Germany west of the Rhine, Dacia and Thrace (modern Romania and Bulgaria), the wealthy lands lying east of the Black Sea (Armenia, Assyria, Mesopotamia, and Cappadocia), and that part of the Arabian peninsula adjoining Judaea and Egypt.

The reign of the emperor Trajan (98–117 AD) coincided with the apex of Roman territorial power. Until the time of Trajan the *limites*, or boundaries, of Rome had been in the minds and wills of the soldiers, who camped here and there, in desert or forest, along the banks of rivers and seas, and accepted no frontiers as such, because the very idea of a frontier implied that there was something stable and permanent on the other side of it. Trajan and his successor Hadrian converted the *limites* to a line of stone walls and forts, protecting the Romans from external dangers, but also walling them in. Hadrian, furthermore, decided to abandon certain holdings in the East, and from then on the emperors gave up more land, on balance, than they acquired.

Edward Gibbon (1737–1794), author of *The Decline and Fall of the Roman Empire* (1776–1788), believed that the apex not just of Roman but of world history had been reached during the Age of the Antonines, the period of eighty-two years from the accession of Trajan in 98 to the death of Marcus Aurelius in 180. Of the four men who successively ruled Rome in those years, Antoninus Pius, who succeeded Hadrian in 138 and nominated Marcus Aurelius as his heir at his death in 161, may have been the most fortunate, although all were fortunate rulers in their different ways.

The twenty-three years when Antoninus Pius ruled the empire are almost a blank in history, so few and short-lived were the wars and other foreign troubles, so rare the civil strife, so prosperous and happy the people of all ranks. Above all, Antoninus, a modest and intelligent man, obeyed the laws as if he were not an all-powerful tyrant but a private citizen. Marcus Aurelius (121–180), whose private *Meditations* come down to us as one of the treasurers of antiquity, believed that it was an incomparable privilege to have lived during those years and to have received the reins of power from "that man," his adoptive father. But Marcus Aurelius, with all his brilliance, was not able to hold things together as his predecessor had. Gibbon may have been right in seeing his death in 180 as the beginning of the end of Roman greatness.

The city on the Tiber that Romulus had founded would survive for three more centuries as the putative ruler of the known world, and for fifteen centuries beyond that as a center of Western civilization. (There was a hiatus during the Middle Ages, when goats cropped the grass on the Capitoline and Hadrian's great tomb at the riverside was converted into a fortress by the popes to keep the starving populace at bay.) But those final years of rule were mostly a relentless decline, or *Untergang*, as the German historian Oswald Spengler (1880–1936) called it. The *limites* were drawn ever inward, barbarians sacked the imperial cities, not excluding Rome itself, and the centers of culture, power, and ambition were scattered afar.

During the fifth century AD the empire was divided, with the western part being ruled not from Rome but from Ravenna, the eastern from Constantinople (modern Istanbul), situated at the juncture of the Mediterranean and Black seas. For three centuries after its founding, the Eastern empire continued to speak and write Latin and to retain Roman institutions. But about 750 Constantinople began to speak and write

Greek. Thus, after nearly a thousand years, the Greeks had finally won the war, although they had lost all the battles.

Greek Theory, Roman Practice

A visit to any museum of classical antiquities will reveal the immense influence exerted by Greek culture on the peoples of the Italian peninsula. Even Italic culture, which preceded Etrurian, seems Greek in spirit. Etruscan art and religion were notably Greek; and when the Romans conquered Etruria in the fourth and third centuries BC, they, too, soon found themselves infected by Greek ideas, images, and world views.

The Romans renamed the Greek gods and adopted them as their own. Zeus became Jupiter, Athena became Minerva, Artemis became Diana. Apollo bore the same name. They also adopted the Greek alphabet, that brilliant invention, which served as well for their own language as it had for Greek. It still serves us today, although the form of some of the letters has changed over time. The Romans copied the Macedonian order of battle and Spartan steel weapons and armor, and they conquered everywhere with them. They learned about poetry and drama from Greek authors, they studied Greek philosophy (without understanding its subtleties because, it is said, Latin could not express them), and they imitated all forms of Greek plastic art. Roman fascination with things Greek extended even to domestic matters, and Greek life-styles came to be preferred by many Romans to traditional Roman ones.

Other Romans drew the line at living like Greeks. It was all right to read Plato, or at least to read a Roman like Cicero expounding Platonic doctrine. You could hire a Greek sculptor to reproduce a statue of the classical age and install it in a corner of the garden, or on a grave. You could laugh at the Greek-style comedies of Plautus and Terence or be afrighted by the Greek-style tragedies of Seneca. It was also all right to imitate Greek pottery shapes and decorations, and Greek coins.

But when it came to living like Greeks, men such as Cato the Censor (234–149 BC) were adamantly opposed. In 184 BC, Cato was elected one of the two censors, or assessors both of property and of moral conduct. He aimed at preserving ancient Roman customs and tried to extirpate all Greek influences, which he thought were undermining the old Roman moral standards. He believed that most if not all Greeks were weak, dissolute, and immoral, especially in sexual matters. Cato thought their luxurious life-styles and their cynical lack of belief in religious and moral codes had led to their defeat by the Roman armies, and, if adopted, would lead to the defeat of Roman armies by the barbarians.

One of the most pervasive characteristics of ancient Rome consisted of the ambivalence Romans felt about Greece. Romans on the one hand were attracted to Greek ideas and on the other hand were repulsed by warnings like those of Cato. Greek elegance, subtlety, taste, and charm were widely admired—and feared. Similar ambivalences have marked other epochs. The English were fascinated by the French throughout the eighteenth century, but that did not keep the two countries from fighting each other almost continuously. Nor did it prevent English moralists from expressing their severe disapproval of French behavior. The English gentleman, in turn, was the *beau idéal* of the German upper classes in the decade before World War I. Today, Americans feel a similar ambivalence about many things Japanese.

One reason for the Roman fascination with Greece was the almost total lack of an indigenous Roman culture. In a thousand years of Roman history there is scarcely a single work of art that is truly Roman, that is not derivative and imitative. This does not mean that Roman life in the imperial age was lacking in polish or style. The Romans did, after all, have the Greeks to teach them how to live. More important, the Romans brought to this curious amalgam of different but complementary cultures some crucially important ideas that they had *not* learned from the Greeks, ideas, in fact, that were opposed to what most Greeks believed.

In a way it is easy to answer the question, What did the Romans know? Most of what they knew they learned from the Greeks; the Romans knew what the Greeks knew. But there were a few other things that they knew that the Greeks had never known. Perhaps it was these things primarily that helped the Romans defeat the Greeks whenever they fought them. With all their brilliance, perhaps because of it, the Greeks had seldom been a practical people. Essentially iconoclastic, in love with risk taking, they had feverishly sought novelty in all things, discarding the old simply because it was old and not necessarily because it was bad. The Romans, on the contrary, were consistently and habitually practical. Their practicality was manifested in many ways. They watered down the great Greek philosophies, in the process making them much more palatable to the multitudes. They reduced *paideia*, the noble and complex Greek system of education developed by Aristotle and others, to a course in rhetoric or oratory, because knowing how to make persuasive speeches was the way to success in business and politics. In modern terms, this view resulted in the reduction of liberal to vocational education. The Romans also converted the Greek concept of immortal fame to mere mortal honor, and it became customary to worship emperors as living gods, thus further muddying the distinction between honor and fame. Finally, the triumph of Augustus converted the glorious but ultimately unworkable republic to a dreary and dangerous, but efficient, totalitarian empire.

Underlying all these changes was one very important belief that the Romans embraced but the Greeks did not: A grand idea that does not work is less valuable than a smaller one that does. On this principle the Romans constructed a city-empire that endured for a thousand years.

Law, Citizenship, and Roads

The great aim of the Greek philosophers concerned abstract standards of justice. Socrates, Plato, Aristotle, and others contributed to this search, which has had an enduring effect upon Western thought. Otherwise, very little survives of Greek law, either statutes or procedures. This is partly because each city-state possessed its own code of laws; there was never such a thing as a common law of the entire Greek nation, even in Hellenic times.

By contrast, Roman law was first codified in the Twelve Tables of about 450 BC and remained in daily use in the West until the barbarian invasions of the fifth century AD and in the Eastern empire until its fall in 1453. Roman law continues to this day to be an influence upon almost all legal systems in the Western world.

The Romans always possessed a fierce respect for and love of law. They considered their ancient laws and customs to be the lifeblood of the state. They were also avid students of law, and they constantly sought to improve their legal system. This was especially true during the two centuries of rapid Roman expansion after the defeat of Carthage in 146 BC. Everywhere that Rome conquered they took their law with them and gave it to the peoples they ruled. As a consequence, during the greatest days of the empire one law ruled all men from Britain to Egypt, from Spain to the Black Sea.

The Twelve Tables, tablets of wood and, later, bronze, were inscribed with the laws of the state and erected in the Roman forum so that they became public property and could be appealed to by every citizen. In the famous phrase of John Locke, writing two thousand years later, they thus became "a standing rule to live by," which applied to every man, great or small, rich or poor. Copies of the tablets were carried by the Roman legions and erected in conquered cities so that the defeated might know what kind of people had been victorious over them.

Roman law was complex and ingenious, but Romans never forgot that its purpose was to regulate the lives of ordinary mortals. Thus there were laws of succession and inheritance, laws of obligations (including contracts), laws of property and possessions, and laws of persons (which included family, slaves, and citizenship). Originally, these laws were easy to understand, and this was true as well of Roman legal procedure, which was not arcane and complicated, like the Greek, but accessible to all citizens.

The body of Roman law had grown enormously by the end of the fifth century AD. Many attempts had been made to simplify it, but none had succeeded, partly because the law itself was so successful as a regulatory system for the millions of Roman citizens throughout the world. Finally, in 529 AD the emperor Justinian (ruled 517–565), resident in Constantinople, promulgated the famous Codex Constitutionum, which thus became the chief source and authority of Roman law. Henceforth no law not included in this great code was considered to be valid. The Code of Justinian remained in effect for more than a thousand years and still forms the basis of the legal systems of most European countries as well as of the state of Louisiana. It is the prime legacy of Rome to legal history.

The Greeks, led by their incomparable military genius Alexander, were brilliantly successful at conquering faded empires. But those conquests did not last.

Alexander had been taught by his schoolmaster, Aristotle, that barbarians were inferior to Greeks and should not be taken for wives or offered a role to play in governing the conquered state. Intuitively, Alexander, who as a Macedonian and not a true Greek was a bit of a barbarian himself, recognized the error in this, and he married a barbarian princess, Roxana, the daughter of the Bactrian chief Oxyartes. He also urged his generals to marry barbarian women, and made some effort to share the rule with members of the vanquished aristocracies.

After Alexander's death, which Roxana did not long survive, the traditional Greek exclusiveness became the rule. But the inbred Greek rulers of Alexander's empire were subtle, vain, ambitious, and frightened of the peoples they governed. Their theories of government were logical, but for the most part they did not work in real life.

It took the Romans the better part of three centuries to learn the trick of governing conquered peoples. As they spread out over the Italian peninsula during the years between the founding of the republic and the final defeat of Carthage, they conquered all their neighbors and incorporated the lands into the Roman state. At first they tended to enslave many of the men and women they had beaten.

But these slaves did not work well or willingly. They objected bitterly to being slaves. Even if they had been defeated, they wanted to remain free. Although we must have slaves, the practical Romans decided, we will find them somewhere else, and make citizens of the Italians. At a stroke the subject Italian peoples became Romans, with all, or most, of the privileges that went with the title.

Even the poorest Roman citizen, if he fought for the senate for a stated period (usually twenty years), was given land to work and build on. If he was a city man, he was provided with a daily ration of grain. If he had nothing else to do on a sunny afternoon, there was the Circus, where he might view a chariot race—admission free—or the Arena, where the gladiators fought and the Christians suffered, also free. No man was better than another, although some, naturally, were richer, sometimes a great deal richer, and that made a difference. But in his heart one Roman citizen felt himself the equal of any other Roman citizen. It was a title to which one might well aspire.

Aspire to it men did, all over the world. In Spain, in North Africa, in those parts of the old Persian empire that the Greeks turned over with hardly a fight, in Egypt, armies threw down their arms and pleaded to be Roman citizens. Seldom did the victors refuse. Citizenship cost little to confer. Why withhold it, then, since its promise made winning easier? It was an excellent example of Roman practicality.

Then there were the Roman roads. Greeks had always been redoubtable seafaring travelers and enterprising merchants. But their empire had never reached far inland, except in the domain of the old Persian empire, whose royal roads they inherited. Essentially, the Greeks never seemed to understand the importance of roads. Lacking internal communications, their empire soon fell apart.

The Romans knew about roads: how to build them and where, how to make them to last. The durability of Roman roads is legendary. Hundreds of miles of Roman road still exist, after twenty centuries of continuous use. The Via Appia, for instance, which runs south from Rome to Naples and Brindisi, is driven on by modern automobiles.

There had always been roads, of course. The Greek colonists in southern Italy built a network of narrow roads, and the Etruscans built roads in Tuscany. In fact, the Etruscans may have taught the Romans a lot about building them. But as usual the Romans, with their genius for applying the good ideas of other peoples, improved on the existing models. The Greek roads, hastily built, had required much maintenance. Roman roads required very little. Etruscan roads had wandered here and there. Roman roads went straight where they could, climbed mountains where they had to, spanned gorges, crossed rivers, burrowed through natural barriers.

With the dogged persistence that marked everything they did, the Romans dug deep, filled the trench with sand, gravel, and crushed stone for drainage, and then faced the crown of the road with cut stone blocks so well fitted that they did not move under the feet of men or horses or the wheels of wagons. Where those blocks of stone have been left to lie, and not been taken up to build something else, which happened to most of them over the centuries, they are often still usable as a roadbed.

The first of the major Roman roads was the Via Appia, begun by Appius Claudius the Blind, consul in 312 BC, and consequently named after him. For many years this was the only road of its kind, but as a result of the military demands of the Second Punic War, at the end of the second century BC, more roads were built, up the coast from Rome to Genoa,

across the mountains to Ravenna, on the Adriatic, and even beyond the
limites, since teaching a conquered people to build roads was as useful
when it came to rule as giving them law or citizenship. By the time of
Trajan, in the first century AD, there were thousands of miles of Roman
roads, over which the traffic and communications of the empire moved.

The arch was another idea that the Romans used to practical effect.
The arch had been known both in Egypt and Greece, where it had been
used for small-scale, mostly decorative, purposes, but it had not been
considered suitable for monumental architecture. Both the Egyptians and
the Greeks preferred four-square buildings in which to worship their gods
and make their laws. The Romans used the arch not only for temples and
basilicas, but also for bridges and aqueducts.

The latter usage was crucial. The plain of Latium is arid, and as Rome
grew, it quickly outstripped its supplies of fresh water. Aqueducts brought
water from the faraway mountains, and then there was no limit to how
populous Rome could become. Under Trajan, Rome contained more than
a million persons and was one of the largest cities in the world.

Later, aqueducts were constructed to supply water to all imperial cities
that were not blessed with sufficient groundwater. Many bits and pieces of
the Roman aqueducts survive to this day, to remind us of their practical
genius.

Lucretius

Perhaps the best way to understand what the Romans knew is to compare
the Roman versions of some important Greek ideas with the originals.
Four Roman authors can show us the way.

T. Lucretius Carus was born in 95 BC and died in 52 or 51 BC. Because
of an enigmatic remark in an ancient text, he is thought to have committed suicide. His epic poem, *On the Nature of Things*, was dedicated to a
friend in the year 58 BC. A version of the work must therefore have been in
existence then. It was never completed. This does not matter much, as the
poem is not a narrative, and if it had been finished, it could not have been
more admired than it is.

On the Nature of Things is an exceedingly strange poem. It is a philosophical tract that is also supremely beautiful. It is about the science of
physics, yet it contains profound wisdom about human life. It is dedicated
to "pleasure," yet it leaves readers with the impression that happiness is
produced by the virtue of moderation.

Lucretius was a devoted follower of the Greek philosopher Epicurus
(341–270 BC), who was born in Samos and lived the last half of his life in
Athens. There Epicurus set up an informal school in a garden which came

to be known simply as the Garden. The school accepted women and at least one slave, a young man with the curious name of Mouse.

Epicurus held that happiness is the supreme good. By happiness he seems to have meant, primarily, the avoidance of pain; a life without pain, worry, and anxiety would inevitably be happy, man being constituted as he is. The avoidance of pain meant for the Garden avoidance of political life. Epicurus said it was so difficult to be happy in public life that anyone was well advised to retire from it altogether. Life in the Garden was simple. Water was the preferred drink, and barley bread was the staple of the diet.

Epicurus had studied under Democritus as a young man, and he was consequently a confirmed atomist. He wrote thirty-seven books on nature, or physics, in which he advanced the atomist doctrine. Hardly any of his works survive. He also wrote tender letters to his friends, some of which do exist, in which he urged upon them a life of simplicity, ease, and moral rectitude.

In later centuries, Epicurus's "happiness" came to be interpreted as "pleasure," and Epicureanism consequently gathered about it the bad connotations that it possesses to this day. Lucretius, when he came to write his adoring paean to the memory of Epicurus, expressed his fervent desire to have it understood that this pleasure, or happiness, was based on virtue, and was the reward of a virtuous life.

Lucretius was also influenced by the doctrines of another Greek philosopher, Zeno the Stoic (c.335–c.263 BC), who, as his dates reveal, was almost an exact contemporary of Epicurus. Zeno set up a school in Athens during the first half of the third century BC. He taught his pupils in the Stoa Poikile, or Painted Colonnade, hence the name of his philosophy. Stoicism taught that happiness consists in conforming the will to the divine reason, which governs the universe. A man is happy if he fully accepts what is and does not desire what cannot be.

Both Epicurus and Zeno were influential throughout the ancient world in their own right. But Epicurus was often misunderstood, even by his followers, and Zeno's Stoicism was too narrow, harsh, and unworldly for most Romans, even if they could read Greek. The doctrine advanced by Lucretius in his beautiful poem combined Stoicism and Epicureanism in a way that made sense two thousand years ago and still does to many readers.

Lucretius said he wanted to bring philosophy down to the human level. He was aware that Greek philosophy often seemed rarified and inaccessible to Romans. He wanted ordinary people, like himself as he claimed, to understand and appreciate philosophical thought.

Even this concept was not original. Socrates had also been acclaimed as the thinker who brought philosophy "down into the marketplace," where common people could talk about ideas. Nevertheless, Socrates remained a rather austere figure who demanded more of his followers than they could give. However much we may love Socrates the man, we never get over the feeling that we cannot live as he said we should.

Lucretius, while inheriting the "divine simplicity" of Socrates in his interpretation of Epicureanism and Stoicism, did not make the mistake of humiliating his readers and followers. Instead, he tried to present a delectable picture of the universe as Epicurus had conceived it, whose attractions would convince more persons than argument could.

Much of Lucretius's poem consists of verse expositions of the scientific doctrine of his Greek masters. But Lucretius is not remembered today because he happened, more or less by accident, to support a particularly scientific theory. Instead, he is loved for his humanity. He was a progenitor of that special kind of person that we call the Mediterranean type, the modern examples of which include the sardonic Spaniard and the life-loving Italian. Both seem to be able to do what is, strangely, so difficult for many persons: they are able to forgive themselves, as a wise man once said, for being human. That is, knowing that life is hard and virtue rare, they keep the ancient faith that it is better to love than to hate, to live fully even if imperfectly.

Epic poets always begin by invoking the assistance of a muse. Lucretius's muse is none other than Venus herself, the goddess of love. She was said to have been the mother of Aeneas by a mortal man, Anchises his father, and so he addresses her thus at the beginning of his poem, in lovely words:

> Mother of the Aeneadae, darling of men and gods, increase-giving Venus, who beneath the gliding signs of heaven fillest with thy presence the ship-carrying sea, the corn-bearing lands, since through thee every kind of living thing is conceived, rises up and beholds the light of the sun. Thou . . . are sole mistress of the nature of things and without thee nothing rises up into the divine borders of light, nothing grows to be glad or lovely.

Cicero

We know very little about the life of Lucretius, author of *On the Nature of Things*. We probably know more about the life of Marcus Tullius Cicero than about any other person of classical times.

A voluminous author and the leading lawyer of his day, Cicero became famous for his orations in defense of his clients and against his enemies.

His works were widely read and copied. But the main reason we know so much about Cicero, and also about the times in which he lived, is that he was an inveterate letter writer who kept copies of his own correspondence and seemingly never threw away a letter from anyone else.

Perhaps as many as three-quarters of Cicero's letters are now lost, although many more were known in antiquity. But over eight hundred letters remain. They constitute the most important source of our knowledge, not only of his own life, but also of the events of that wonderful and dreadful period during the middle of the first century BC when Caesar and Pompey vied for the rule of the Roman world, Pompey was defeated and victorious Caesar murdered in the senate, and Mark Antony and Octavian (later to become the emperor Augustus) inherited the power all had sought for so long.

Cicero was born in 106 BC, the son of a wealthy family that lacked a noble lineage. He was well educated, both in Greece and by Greek teachers at Rome. He began his legal career and, while still in his twenties, gained important electoral posts. In 63 BC, still only forty-three, he was elected one of the two consuls, a signal honor for a man who did not come from the old senatorial aristocracy.

Cicero soon found himself caught up in the struggle between Caesar and Pompey for world dominion that ultimately led to the fall of the republic. He was sought as a supporter by both men, and he made the wrong choice. He believed Pompey (106–48 BC) was a less dangerous threat to ancient institutions, so he agreed to support him. This was a mistake, not only because Pompey lost, but also because Caesar, for all his capriciousness and ambition, was a man more capable of appreciating the complex Cicero. And Cicero understood the complexity of Caesar, although he did not like him. Pompey, by comparison, was a relatively simple person who failed to appreciate the great advantage of Cicero's friendship.

Caesar (100–44 BC) was willing to forget the past, because he did know how to value Cicero. But Cicero never trusted Caesar, and he was therefore not sorry when Caesar was murdered, stabbed to death at the base of a statue of Pompey by Brutus and Cassius and other conspirators. Cicero himself had no part in that famous affair on the Ides of March (March 15). Afterward, he acted heroically, if imprudently, in attacking Mark Antony and Octavian for their illegal encroachments on ancient Roman freedoms. Antony (81/82–30 BC), provoked (he was a brutal man), had Cicero murdered in 43 BC; he cut off the hands of the corpse and nailed them to the senate rostrum as a warning to other men who might wish to write the truth.

During most of the last decade of Cicero's life he was unable, for political reasons, to participate in public life. He therefore devoted his abundant energy to literary activity. If he could not be active in law and politics, he could write books.

Cicero boasted of his political successes. Concerning his intellectual work he was always modest. He claimed that he was merely a popularizer who had taken up the task of translating Greek thought so it could easily be understood by his countrymen. He made no truly original discoveries. Yet he helped many persons to discover the brilliant and original insights of his great predecessors.

He also set himself a hard challenge, to apply the principles of Greek ethical thought to the rough life of a Roman businessman or politician. A man could always retire from the fray, as Lucretius, the Epicurean, had recommended. But what if he did not wish to retire? Could he still live a virtuous life?

Cicero's last book, *On Duties*, dealt with a wide range of homely problems. How honest did a businessman have to be? Did shortcuts exist that could honestly be taken? How should a good man respond to the unjust demands of a tyrant? Was it all right to be silent, or should a person always speak up, even if to do so would prove dangerous? How should a man treat his inferiors, even his slaves? Did inferiors have rights that ought to be respected?

Cicero's solution of all such problems seems simple: Always do the right thing, he insisted, because a wrong action, although perhaps apparently advantageous, can never be *really* advantageous because it is wrong.

What *is* the right thing? How do you know? Cicero does not dodge the question. First, the right thing is what is legal, what is required by law. But beyond that, for the law itself is not always just, the right thing is what is honest, open, and fair. Keeping your word, no matter the consequences. Telling the truth, even if you have not taken an oath. And treating everyone—foreigners, slaves, and women—alike, because they are all human beings. All are equal in their humanness, although in no other way. Their humanness gives them the right to be treated with respect.

It is easy to mock Cicero's simple rule that one should always do what is right because the wrong can never be truly advantageous. Bad men have always found such mockery a convenient excuse.

In fact, Cicero's very simplicity is his strength. Admit it! he exclaimed. We do know when we are doing right and when we are doing wrong. We do feel that we should do right. In the course of a whole life the number of cases where we cannot be sure is invariably small. We also believe we would be happier if we always did what we knew was right, even if that meant we might be poorer or less successful.

Cicero's simple rule of life defined the practical Roman version of the grand scheme of institutionalized state education as set forth by Socrates and Plato in the *Republic*, and of Aristotle's searching and subtle analysis of virtue as presented in his *Ethics*. Both of those books are incomparably greater than Cicero's *On Duties*. But, as a practical matter, neither of them gives us a rule of life that is as easy to understand and to follow as Cicero's modest yet profound directive.

Cicero lived in one of the most glorious, and dangerous, periods in history. Throughout the Roman world men struggled with the greatest of all political problems, namely, how to live together in peace *and* freedom. It seemed to most Romans during the climactic half century before the fall of the republic and the triumph of Augustus that a choice had to be made between those two ultimate political goods.

You could have freedom, but then you would have to forsake peace. Conflicts would necessarily arise, it seemed, among men who were free to seek their different goals. Or you could have peace, but at the cost of freedom, for how could peace endure if it were not imposed from above by a supreme power which alone would remain free, while all others bore the yoke of tyranny?

The Greek example was no help. Anyone could see that the Greeks, for the most part, had chosen freedom, but at the high cost of nearly constant conflict. Romans in the early days had also chosen freedom. Their wars of conquest had permitted them to avoid internal conflict. Because they were always fighting others, they did not have to fight among themselves.

Now, when Roman power had extended itself throughout the Mediterranean world, civil conflict had become epidemic. A series of ruthless men offered themselves as tyrants in order to secure peace. All of them were beaten down. The last of them, Catiline (108–62 BC), had been personally defeated by Cicero when he was consul. The double threat of Caesar and Pompey proved harder to deal with.

Caesar removed Pompey from the scene by first defeating him in battle and then having him murdered in 48 BC. But that left Caesar himself, the most dangerous threat of all. A handful of aristocrats, fearful of what a brilliant *arrivé* like Caesar might do to the traditional Roman aristocracy, removed him, too, by assassinating him, in an act that Cicero considered to be noble and that, for a time, most Romans believed to have been both necessary and just. But the freedom for which Brutus (85–42 BC) and Cassius (d. 42 BC) had murdered Caesar was not freedom for all, and so the aristocrats soon lost their support among the people. In any event, the faith in freedom was not strong enough to resist these repeated crises. Mark Antony and Octavian (later Augustus) offered still another chance at tyranny, combined with a guarantee of security, and it was accepted. The republic fell, and Augustus, who survived his own falling out with Mark Antony, inaugurated the system of institutionalized tyranny that was the Roman empire.

The change was not immediate. Octavian rid himself of Mark Antony in 31 BC, when he defeated him and his paramour, Cleopatra of Egypt, in the harbor of Alexandria. From 31 to 23 he ruled as consul, although there was no question of his being elected to the post; he had elected himself. In 23 Augustus received imperial power to be exercised only in emergencies, which soon occurred, as well as the power of the tribune of the people. After his death in 14 AD he was deified. The *proskynesis* the Macedonian veterans of Alexander laughed at had won the day.

For two millennia the demise of the Roman republic has been regretted by those who have loved liberty. But freedom did not really have a chance there. Too few men believed it could survive, or perhaps even wanted it to survive, since a republican form of government makes demands upon the citizens that a tyranny does not (a tyranny makes other kinds of demands). Perhaps no one believed in a republic so deeply as Cicero.

He saw a third solution to the great political problem. If everyone was master over himself, then there would be no need to have a single master over all the others. If everyone did what he knew was right, peace would be secure, and freedom, too, could be preserved. In other words, he believed in a government of laws and not of men.

Cicero was probably mistaken in thinking that there existed a "constitution" subtle enough to ensure the survival of the republic, over any extended period of time, as a government of laws. Lacking such a constitution, a government of men (as it happened, of *a* man) was probably the only practical alternative.

But Cicero was not mistaken in his intuitive sense of how to solve the problem. There is only a difference in detail between his solution of the Roman problem and that of the Founding Fathers of the American republic. They were the first to show how, as a practical matter, a government of men could be replaced by a government of laws. But Cicero, as they well knew, had pointed the way.

The U.S. Constitution establishes an executive branch and gives it the means of defending itself against attack: by law it holds a monopoly of authorized force. Besides the armed forces, these protections include the Federal Bureau of Investigation, the Central Intelligence Agency, the T-Men, the Secret Service, and various other police forces. But it is not these military and paramilitary organizations that ensure that the United States will remain a government of laws, not of men.

The Constitution is a piece of paper. It cannot fight for itself. If Americans do not believe in it, it will become mere paper.

Most Americans wholeheartedly accept the Constitution as the law of the land. They may disagree about everything else. But they know they must not intentionally and knowingly act unconstitutionally. In that realm, they agree they should always do right. Not to do so is to challenge the basis of American government: the Constitution has no protection except the people's belief in it. Soldiers and police could not protect the Constitution if the people ceased to believe in it, although they might destroy it by turning the American democracy into a police state.

Belief cannot be legislated. It is an act of the free will of the citizens. Cicero failed to persuade enough of his fellow citizens to save the Roman republic. Nevertheless, he was perhaps the first man ever to realize that nothing less than near-universal belief of this sort could ensure both peace and freedom in a state.

Seneca

The Romans, in setting themselves adrift from the legal and quasi-constitutional protections of their republican institutions, were gambling that they would be so fortunate as to find men to rule them who would be both strong and just. The rich hoped to become richer in safety; the poor expected to be free from the uncontrolled rapacity of the rich. And for a little while the gamble seemed to have been won. Life under Augustus, even when he became emperor in name as well as in fact, was noticeably better than it had been under the senate and the consuls in the last days of the republic.

A major defect of the imperial system lay in its lack of legal and customary machinery for arranging the succession of power from one emperor to another. Augustus, who was inventing institutions as he went along, decided to choose his successor ten years before he died. He chose Tiberius (42 BC–37 AD), the son of one of his wives—not his own son. Tiberius would have been an excellent choice some years before. When Augustus chose him in 4 AD, however, he had become as proud as he was powerful, as violent as he was cunning.

Augustus died in 14 AD, and Tiberius accepted the "election" as emperor. His rule at first seemed prudent and wise, although the force often showed through. In 23 his son Drusus died. From that time he seems to have lost interest in the empire and occupied himself with his pleasures, which grew more and more perverse. In 27 he visited the island of Capri in the Bay of Naples. He had intended to stay for only a short time, but he never returned to Rome. From then on, his reign was marked by an unending series of cruel and violent acts: torture, murder, and the theft of the property of distinguished citizens, who were accused of crimes, convicted, executed, and their property confiscated at a word from Tiberius, who usually did not care whether they were guilty or not.

Shortly before he died, Tiberius, like his predecessor Augustus, decided upon an heir. He had no son, so the choice fell upon the least undesirable of an undesirable lot. His name was Gaius Caesar, nicknamed by the soldiers Caligula (12–41 AD), "Little Boots." Caligula succeeded in 37 AD. Within a year he had either gone mad or wished to pretend he had. At any rate, the pretense was persuasive. If he was only pretending to be mad, he was certainly cruel. His cruelty was so ruthless and unpredictable that in 41, after only four years as emperor, he was murdered by the tribune of the palace guard.

Afterward, the guard found Claudius, the nephew of Tiberius and a grandson of the wife of Augustus, cowering in a corner of the palace, expecting to die. Instead, the guard made him emperor. Claudius (10 BC– 54 AD) had been no one's first choice; he was an unattractive man, over fifty at the time, shy, unused to public speaking, a scholar. He had written several books of history under the tutelage of the historian Livy. But he managed to be a good emperor, as emperors went. He made innovations in administration and restored some ancient religious traditions that pleased both the patricians and the populace. Nevertheless, he was so awkward and ugly that he could never achieve popularity.

His greatest mistake came in 48, after he had been emperor for seven years, when he married his niece Agrippina. This marriage went against Roman law, so he changed the law. Agrippina was beautiful and sensual, but she did not love her husband. She was able to persuade him to renounce the claims of his own son, whom he liked, for her son by an earlier marriage, who consequently was chosen as Claudius's heir. His elevation accomplished, Agrippina poisoned Claudius with a mess of mushrooms in 54.

Her son, when he succeeded to the throne, took the name Nero (37–68 AD). He was for nineteen centuries the most despised and hated tyrant in Western history. It is possible that some of the famous stories are untrue. For example, it is unlikely that he fiddled while Rome burned, or that he started the conflagration himself in order to clear a large space for a new palace, for he was far away from Rome when the fire broke out in 64 AD. He did take advantage of the fact that the center of the city was gutted and began building his Golden House, which would have been the largest palace ever built by one man for himself and would have covered a third of Rome if it had been completed.

By 59 Agrippina had obviously become insane, and she screamed in fury that her son Nero was slipping out of her control. With possible regret, Nero had her murdered, and his own wife Octavia three years later, because he had fallen in love with another woman. From that time forth he descended deeper and deeper into a kind of religious delirium. It had been customary to worship the emperors posthumously as gods. Nero wished to be not just a god but to create God while he was alive, perhaps in his own person. His acts became more and more wild and unintelligible. In 68 the soldiers, who had become impatient with their mad master, chose Galba as a successor while Nero was still alive. He committed suicide shortly after.

There had been conspiracies against Nero for several years, the most widespread coming to a head in the year 65. Led by a patrician named Caius Piso, the plot soon involved a large number of nobles and even some members of Nero's praetorian guard. The conspiracy was betrayed by slaves of one of the conspirators, and Nero managed to escape. Fourteen of the conspirators were either executed or forced to commit suicide.

One of the latter was Lucius Annaeus Seneca, Rome's leading intellectual figure during the middle of the first century AD. Born in Spain in 4 BC, the son of a wealthy family, his early promise was hindered by a sickly frame. That later saved him from the mad hatred of Caligula, who did not kill him because he was told Seneca could not live long in any event. When he was forty-five Claudius banished him, but Agrippina brought him back to Rome and made him the tutor of her son, the future emperor Nero.

The murder of Claudius in 54 placed Seneca at the pinnacle of power. The new emperor, Seneca's pupil Nero, was seventeen and sought his teacher's advice in every decision. For eight years Seneca was *de facto* ruler of the Roman world. But as the historian Tacitus said, "Nothing in human affairs is more unstable and precarious than power unsupported by its own strength." Seneca was a favorite of a tyrant, and the tyrant was turning mad. Furthermore, he was falling out of love with his old teacher; he had begun by adoring him, but now he grew to hate him, for Seneca was frank in his criticisms of Nero's cruelty and extravagance.

In 59 Seneca and his colleague, Burrus, were ordered to contrive the murder of Agrippina. Three years later Burrus died, and Seneca realized he was alone at the edge of a precipice. He asked the emperor for permission to retire. It was given to him. Three years later, in 65 AD, the conspiracy of Piso gave Nero his opportunity. Seneca and Piso knew each other, but Seneca did not like Piso and had refused to speak to him when called upon by the patrician, probably to have the conspiracy broached to him. This mere hint of complicity proved enough. Soldiers surrounded Seneca's house and informed him of the emperor's sentence of death.

Seneca asked permission to write his will, but the soldiers refused. He turned to friends who were present and, regretting that he was unable to requite them, offered them "the noblest possession yet remaining to him," as Tacitus wrote, "the pattern of his life, which, if they remembered, they would win a name for moral worth and steadfast friendship." He then pleaded with his wife, Paulina, whom he loved, not to die with him, but she insisted that she would accompany him into death, and they put their arms together and severed their veins with one stroke of a dagger.

Nero, hearing of this attempted suicide, ordered his soldiers to save

Paulina's life. Unconscious, she was bound and taken away, to live for a few more years in mourning for her husband. There was no mercy for Seneca. Scrawny and tough, although nearly seventy, his blood did not flow easily, and he found it hard to die. He begged a relative for poison, but it, too, failed to kill him. Seeking to increase the flow of blood, he ordered his slaves to prepare a hot bath, and when he entered it, the steam apparently suffocated him.

Seneca cannot be acquitted of at least a few of Nero's crimes, and his personal vanity colored his judgment in some matters. But there seems little question that he was a man of integrity who adhered to the Stoic doctrines that he tried to instill in Nero. He was also learned and did not fail at the end of his life to recognize that, whereas Aristotle, his predecessor in philosophy as he liked to suppose, had survived being the tutor of one emperor, Alexander, he, Seneca, was not likely to survive such a relationship with another.

Seneca wrote many letters on philosophical and moral subjects in which he advanced and argued for the dour doctrines of Zeno the Stoic. He was also a renowned tragedian, although his plays were seldom produced on the stage but instead were read to a company of friends. He believed himself to be the heir of Aeschylus, Sophocles, and Euripides, the Greek masters of tragedy, but he so changed the form that it was hardly recognizable.

Classical Greek tragedies had dealt with cruel murders and unnatural acts, such as incest and parricide. The stories were usually religious myths, which could be understood on many levels, and the poet-authors had filled their plays with profound psychological examination and analysis of the ancient myths. Seneca retained the lurid Greek stories, such as the series of dynastic murders in the House of Atreus (source of Aeschylus's trilogy of the *Oresteia*), but he by and large left out the psychology.

Seneca's plays became influential in later centuries, especially during the Renaissance. Their Grand Guignol devices, their ghosts and murders most cruel were popular in England, for example, during Shakespeare's youth. But Shakespeare outgrew such juvenile dramatic habits, as did drama generally.

However, audiences remained fascinated by the kind of cruel, violent, and dramatically crude plays that Seneca had written, supposing he was imitating the great Greeks. Audiences are fascinated today. It is Senecan rather than Sophoclean or Shakespearian drama that we watch, with avid interest, on television in the late twentieth century. Except that we have added a fillip. Our television dramas, no matter how bloody and violent, always have happy endings. Even Seneca did not stoop so low.

In short, Seneca was a man of many accomplishments. He was not a great writer, but within the narrow bounds of his talent and understanding he tried to keep alive the great tradition of his Greek predecessors in philosophy and drama, and he also made a real, though finally unsuccessful, effort to guide the mad young man who had graduated from his tutorship to become the ruler of the world.

Tacitus

The conspiracy of Piso, and Seneca's death, occurred in 65 AD. Nero himself was dead three years later. He was succeeded by three different emperors within a year. The palace was in chaos. Yet the empire continued to thrive, despite the lack of a ruler at its head. This strange contradiction fascinated Tacitus, the historian.

Born in Gaul around 56 AD, Publius Cornelius Tacitus studied rhetoric in preparation for administrative office and married the daughter of a consul, Gnaeus Julius Agricola, the future governor of Britain. Tacitus was probably helped in his career by his father-in-law, but since he was also in his own right the possessor of talent and administrative skill, he continued to advance even after Agricola's death in 94. Tacitus attained the consulship in 97, under the emperor Nerva, and continued until his death around 120 to fill high posts in the imperial bureaucracy, as well as to practice law.

The literary career of Tacitus began in 98 AD, when he wrote two works, one a biography of his father-in-law, renowned for its cool objectivity, the other a descriptive essay on the Roman frontier country on the Rhine. He emphasized the simple virtues of the Germanic tribes, which he compared to the sophisticated vices of the Romans, and predicted that the barbarians in the north could be a real threat to Rome if they acted together. But these short books were just the prelude to the real work of his lifetime, the *Histories* (which began with the death of Nero and was written first), and the *Annals*, which covered the period from the beginning of Tiberius's reign to the end of Nero's (it was written second).

To the regret of all students of Roman history, much is lost of both these long and fascinating accounts of the first hundred years of the empire. (Will the missing pages be discovered one day, hidden away in some ancient attic or in the basement of a ruined monastery? It is every classical scholar's dream that he will be the one to find them.) Only a portion of the *Histories* survives, covering the years 69–70, when a trio of adventurers, successively occupying the throne, attempted to control the careering Roman state. Of the *Annals*, only those books dealing with the early career of Tiberius, and some of those treating the reigns of Claudius and Nero, survive.

What a treasure the surviving pages are! We see the progressive madness of Tiberius creeping over him; the isolation of Claudius, which finally became unbearable; most memorable of all the uncontrollable juvenile wildness of Nero, who, if he had been a teenager in a twentieth-century American suburb might have grown out of it, but who happened to be the world's most powerful man, with no one to tell him where or why to stop. The subject matter that Tacitus chose to treat was, and is, irresistible, and therefore we must forgive him for not always treating it as coolly or judiciously as Thucydides portrayed his chosen subject matter. Although Thucydides is certainly the greater historian, Tacitus has been for many centuries the more popular. His vivid writing does not let the reader go.

Here are two examples, chosen from a multitude. After the great fire that destroyed the major part of Rome in 64 AD, a rumor spread that Nero had ordered the conflagration in order to clear a large space for his new palace.

Consequently, to get rid of the report, Nero fastened the guilt and inflicted the most exquisite tortures on a class hated for their abominations, called Christians by the populace. Christus, from whom the name had its origin, suffered the extreme penalty during the reign of Tiberius at the hands of one of our procurators, Pontius Pilatus, and a most mischievous superstition, thus checked for the moment, again broke out not only in Judaea, the first source of the evil, but even in Rome, where all things hideous and shameful from every part of the world find their centre and become popular. Accordingly, an arrest was first made of all who pleaded guilty; then, upon their information, an immense multitude was convicted, not so much of the crime of firing the city, as of hatred against mankind. Mockery of every sort was added to their deaths. Covered with the skins of beasts, they were torn by dogs and perished, or were nailed to crosses, or were doomed to the flames and burnt, to serve as a nightly illumination, when daylight had expired.

Nero offered his gardens for the spectacle, as if he was exhibiting a show in the circus, while he mingled with the people in the dress of a charioteer or stood aloft on a car. Hence, even for criminals who deserved extreme and exemplary punishment, there arose a feeling of compassion; for it was not, as it seemed, for the public good, but to glut one man's cruelty, that they were being destroyed.

A year later the conspiracy of Piso was discovered, and Nero embarked on a frenzied attempt to identify all who had wished to kill him. A certain Epicharis, a beautiful freedwoman of a liberal cast of mind, had made attempts to stir the leading officers of Nero's guard to revolt against him. She was arrested.

Nero . . . remembering that Epicharis was in custody . . . and assuming that a woman's frame must be unequal to the agony, ordered her to be torn on the rack. But neither the scourge nor fire, nor the fury of the men as they increased the torture that they might not be a woman's scorn, overcame her positive denial of the charge. Thus the first day's inquiry was futile. On the morrow, as she was being dragged back on a chair to the same torments (for with her limbs all dislocated she could not stand), she tied a band, which she had stript off her bosom, in a sort of noose to the arched back of the chair, put her neck in it, and then straining with the whole weight of her body, wrung out of her frame its little remaining breath. All the nobler was the example set by a freedwoman at such a crisis in screening strangers and those whom she hardly knew, when freeborn men, Roman knights, and senators, yet unscathed by torture, betrayed, every one, his dearest kinfolk.

Tacitus was still a boy when Nero died, and he lived far away in Gaul. But the magnet of Rome drew him, and he spent the last five years of Domitian's reign in the city. They were terrible years, a period of terror unprecedented even in that ghastly century, which had seen the perverse cruelties of Tiberius, Caligula, and Nero. Domitian died, or rather was murdered, in 96; he was succeeded by Nerva, and he by Trajan, in 98. A new era had begun, and it would endure for the eighty-two years of the Antonines.

During those years, a golden age, the emperors were neither mad nor evil, and they obeyed their own laws. In the introduction to his *Histories*, Tacitus described the exceptional conditions under which he was now able to write following the death of Domitian in 96. He wrote:

I have reserved as an employment for my old age, should my life be long enough, a subject [the history of the empire from the death of Nero to that of Domitian] at once more fruitful and less anxious in the reign of the Divine Nerva and the empire of Trajan, enjoying the rare happiness of times, when we may think what we please, and express what we think.

Think what we please, and say what we think—how better to sum up the happiness of political freedom? And the reverse is pure tyranny.

A few other trenchant remarks can be found in the works of Tacitus. In the *Agricola* he describes a Roman commander who has brutally put down a rising of a barbarian tribe, afterward reporting that he has brought "peace" to the region. Tacitus sees it differently. *Faciunt solitudinem*, he writes, *et pacem appellant*: "They make a wilderness and call it peace." How better to depict the famous Pax Romana as it was created by the later empire?

Such moments of flashing insight are rare. Most of the time Tacitus is content—even eager—to regale us with stories of the cruel and lascivious actions of the emperors. A master of the type of history that can be termed "life-styles of the rich and powerful," he is the ancestor of such cultural institutions as *People* magazine, although he never falls to the depths reached by the *National Enquirer*.

There is no denying the fascination of such tales, true or not. To give Tacitus his due, he tried to tell the truth, insofar as he could ascertain it. But a really good story, he must have felt, was worth a thousand truths.

What the Romans Did Not Know

The Romans continued to try to build a state that worked even when they suffered under the worst of their emperors. They constructed more roads. They spread the educational ideas of their Greek teachers wherever they conquered, and then sent Greek teachers to educate the new subservient populace. By the second century AD every Roman, provided he was not a woman or a slave, from Britain to Persia, could obtain an education practically as good as any other provided for Romans. The work of applying everywhere the body of Roman law never ceased. And Greek know-how in a number of fields—ceramics, metallurgy, alchemy—was summed up in Latin treatises that were distributed all over the empire.

Nevertheless, Roman science lagged. There was a remarkable lack of interest in science and technology. Rumors persisted until our own day that certain Greek inventions were actually rejected by the later emperors. It is known, for instance, that a Greek named Hero of Alexandria invented a kind of steam engine in the first century AD. Called an aeolipile, it consisted of a hollow sphere mounted so that it could turn on a pair of hollow tubes that provided steam from a cauldron below. It could have achieved useful work, but it was apparently treated as an amusing toy.

Steam power would have solved some of the more vexing problems of the empire. Despite its fine system of roads, communications remained slow. A message could be carried no faster than a horse could run, and a running horse could not carry much more than its rider and a packet of letters. After a thousand years of progress, the freight of the empire still moved on ships and barges, the latter often pulled along by mules or men harnessed together.

This meant that severe problems of distribution continued to beset the empire five hundred years after the republic had fallen, partly because of the same problems. For example, a famine in one region could not be relieved by surpluses in other regions, with the result that famines were always politically perilous. Soldiers, rather than food, would be sent to control the starving population, because it was quicker to send armed men. Fifteen centuries later steam power began to solve these problems when it was finally applied to the movement of goods.

If the Roman leaders did reject technological innovations, it was not out of mere ignorance or stubbornness. Even some of the worst emperors—for example, Tiberius and Nero—adopted innovative changes in administration. Attempts were made during both the third and fourth centuries AD to reorganize the entire political structure of the state. Such changes were always conceived of as involving law and custom, not technological improvement. It is easy for us to see how and why the Romans were wrong. It was not at all easy for them.

The Roman system of government, though fundamentally tyrannical, worked well enough everywhere except in the city of Rome itself. Roman citizens—that is, citizens of the central city—did not have to work in order to live, as everyone else did; the state supported them with free daily rations of grain. As many as half a million persons in Rome during the third century had little to do except to amuse themselves.

They could also be used by politicians to cause trouble, which was why the politicians retained the ancient custom of free rations. A political orator could sway the mob, control it, and get it to do what he wanted. The Roman mob, once galvanized by an effective orator, became a fearsome political force. It could guarantee the election of one person rather than another, get laws passed or revoked, and destroy political parties by killing or frightening away their leaders.

The army could also control the mob, but only by force. The mob, essentially, could not be reasoned with. Thus, while good government could prevail in the provinces, at home government was a dangerous game played for the highest stakes. The mob or the army could raise a man to the throne; it could also kill him. When life and death are the stakes in politics, the best do not enter the profession.

Rome in the latter days of the empire, at the end of the fourth century and the beginning of the fifth, was like Beirut in our time. An emperor would be chosen by a gang and would rule only so long as he pleased the assassins. When he ceased to do so, he was replaced. Emperors who knew they might not have long to live were seldom benevolent toward their subjects, whom they did not trust—and for good reason.

The ancient empire, which self-consciously celebrated the one thousandth anniversary of its founding in the middle of the fifth century AD, was thus crippled at its heart by a political disease which no one knew how to cure. The barbarians who ringed the empire had a solution, which was to wipe it out. And that is what they did.

4

Light in the Dark Ages

A GES MAY BE CALLED dark for one or both of two reasons. First, they may be largely unknown to us, in which case we think of them as obscured from us, unknowable. Or they may be infused with troubles, misery, and woe, when all the prospects of life are bleak.

The period from the fall of the Roman empire of the West, in the middle of the fifth century AD, to roughly the year 1000 has traditionally been referred to as the Dark Ages, for both reasons. But the first reason no longer applies, as modern historical scholarship has discovered a great deal about a period that used to be considered practically unknowable.

What about the second reason? Those five centuries were a stagnant time with little apparent life. Economic and political troubles continued throughout the period, and the lives that most people led—from our modern point of view—were bleak, deprived, and miserable. Did the people of the Dark Ages feel the same way about their lives as we do? Or did they see a light that we no longer see?

The Fall of Rome

The empire of the West fell to a series of invasions by barbarians from the East that started in 410 AD and continued for more than fifty years. Who were these barbarians? Where did they come from?

The Great Wall of China was completed around 220 BC to keep maurauding tribes of nomadic warriors out of Shih Huang-ti's new Chinese empire. It succeeded for a time, but it also had another result that walls often have; it provided a haven outside the wall in which the northern nomads could gather their forces. The Roman *limites*, once they had become a line of stone walls and forts instead of just an idea in the minds of the soldiers, had a similar result.

The barbarians who eventually overran Europe originated as the Hsiung-nu, nomads. They gathered outside the Great Wall of China, becoming unified and growing in power, cunning, and military skill. In the first century AD they exploded southward into what was now the Han empire, devastating and depopulating large areas. The Han recovered and drove the barbarians back, but at the cost of much destruction and of the brutalization of Han institutions, which changed in order to meet the challenge of the barbarian attack.

Little is known about the Hsiung-nu even today. They were probably almost universally illiterate, so no written records survive. They surely possessed almost no knowledge of agriculture. They owned herds of goats, cattle, and horses, which they pastured wherever they found good grass.

They knew everything about horses—how to break them, ride them, breed them, and how to fight from horseback. They would swoop down on their prey, shooting deadly arrows from short, powerful bows made of layers of animal bone combined with wood for flexibility. They would appear without warning, thunder into a settlement, kill everyone they found, and disappear again, taking with them whatever they could carry on a horse. If they could not carry away much from any given settlement, there were always other settlements, with their accumulations of food, weapons, and sometimes gold, guarded by men who, compared to the barbarians, were both morally and physically soft, that is, men who were not utterly ruthless. The ruthlessness of the barbarians, and the panic it engendered, proved their most effective weapon.

The Chinese adopted the military tactics of the Hsiung-nu, hired some of them as mercenaries, and managed to drive the rest westward, away from China proper, during the second and third centuries AD. In the vast empty plain of central Asia there was little to impede the fleeing nomads until they reached the lands around the Black Sea.

Here the Hsiung-nu, now called Huns, encountered other nomadic peoples. The Huns quickly displaced the native tribes, the Goths and the Vandals, and settled down for a while. The Goths and the Vandals were forced to flee westward in turn.

And then the Huns moved again, only to stop once more, at the borders of Europe, around 400 AD. The Goths, displaced again, split into two groups. One branch continued westward into Gaul, forcing the native Germanic peoples to flee southward. The other branch of the Goths, called Visigoths, headed straight south into Italy. There they found the Roman empire, weakened by luxury, corruption, and civil strife, trembling before them. In the year 410 the Visigoths sacked Rome and devastated the countryside around it. The Roman emperors during the next thirty years tried to deal with the Visigoths, offering them land to hold and live on, and giving them military tasks to perform. Most of these efforts were in vain, for the barbarians knew well that they were the stronger force.

The Vandals continued to move westward, pillaging as they went (their name to this day is a synonym for willful desecration or destruction), and then turned southward through Gaul and into Spain. Spain had been one of the richest provinces of the empire. The Vandals ravaged and cut it off from its headquarters in Italy. They then crossed into Africa, conquering all of Roman Africa, including the flourishing city of New Carthage, built on the site of the Phoenician city destroyed by the Romans six hundred years before. The Vandals then recrossed the Mediterranean into Italy and sacked Rome in 455.

The capital of the empire had moved from Rome to Ravenna, on the Adriatic, in 402. From this walled citadel, helpless emperors tried to stem the tide of conquest, but in vain. In 493 another group of barbarians, the Ostrogoths, took Ravenna and most of the rest of Italy, and their king, Theodoric, ruled this ancient land which had once held sway over all the world.

The feverish energy of the barbarian hordes, which had brought the Huns all the way from Mongolia and the Goths and the Vandals from western Asia, could not endure. Under Attila, their last leader, the Huns invaded Gaul but were defeated in 451 by a combined Roman and Visigothic army. It was Attila's first defeat, and he died a year later. The Huns then descended into Italy, but they were defeated again and soon disappeared from history, their ferocity played out. They left nothing but a name that could still inspire fear centuries later.

The Ostrogoths and the Vandals also ceased to be a significant power within a few years of the turn of the fifth century AD. They, too, had played out their role in history. The Visigoths lasted a little longer. They held a strip of southern France and much of the Iberian peninsula for two centuries. But eventually they, too, were absorbed into the new society that was being born in what is now western Europe.

Post-Roman Europe

Energetic emperors in Constantinople continued to rule their eastern portion of the old empire, and during the middle of the sixth century AD armies funded by the emperor Justinian and commanded by the famous general Belisarius (himself a barbarian, as most generals were by this time) reestablished Byzantine control over Italy, most of Gaul, and a part of North Africa. But this was not the same kind of control that the Romans had once exerted. By comparison, it was almost no control at all.

Western Europe, once so tightly held together, had simply fallen apart.

Where one great social and economic organization had existed, there were now hundreds of small communities. The Roman empire had been an open world, with a single language, Latin, that was understood everywhere; with a single code of law that everyone obeyed; with good roads that joined its far-flung regions; and, most important, with Greek teachers and cultural ambassadors available to travel anywhere they were needed to instruct newly civilized peoples in how to live well.

Now most of the Greeks were sequestered in Constantinople, the capital of the Eastern empire. The roads were mostly empty of travelers and freight, people spoke different languages and few could read, and there was little law except that of force. In the century between about 450 and about 550 AD, a hundred years of fire and death, most of the openness disappeared, and the world that anyone could know became small and closed in.

You were well enough aware of a narrow region around your home, and you had notions, often wrong, about your neighbors over the horizon, but beyond that you knew next to nothing. You had no time to read, even if you knew how, for life had become hard, with most people dependent on what they could scratch with their hands from the earth around their homes, and much of that was likely to be stolen as a matter of course by stronger and more ruthless men.

Since there was little or no law, you had to protect yourself and your family, and that, too, took time from the leisure activities that Roman citizens had enjoyed a century before. Art, philosophy, and discussion simply ceased to occur. Government (except on a primitive level) no longer operated. Even hope seemed to stop.

Those hundred years from 450 to 550 were among the most terrible periods in Western history. It is hard to imagine them. Historically, they are almost a blank; we only know that at the end of this period of rapine and death the region now called Europe was utterly changed.

It has never been the same. Europe has never again been one nation, ruled from a single central city, speaking one language, obeying one set of laws, enjoying the creation and the fruits of a single culture.

Life went on, but owing to the constant warfare and the breakdown of most social and health services, there were fewer people than before in most places. For example, the population of Rome itself consisted, during the second century, of more than a million souls. By 550, the city's residents had dwindled to fewer than fifty thousand. Due to the wholesale destruction of the barbarian invasions, there were fewer houses, public buildings (temples, churches, markets, law courts), monuments, forts and walls, and structures like aqueducts. There were also many fewer domestic animals and fewer acres under cultivation. It was hard to find a place to educate your children, or teachers to instruct them. There were almost no books, because books are almost always among the first things to be destroyed in a cataclysm.

There was little news, for news is only meaningful to persons who have the leisure to care about what happens to others, often far away. When life is a constant struggle, the hardships of others cease to be of interest. There was also little ready money, for the old imperial coins were soon used up, hidden, or lost, so that most commerce had to be conducted by barter. This was an adequate system for the times, as there was little commerce anyway in an economy essentially lacking a surplus of goods.

Nor were all of these changes merely temporary. A century of devastation had plunged western Europe into a Dark Age that lasted for five hundred years. Only with the start of a new millennium, around the year 1000, did Europeans begin to try to live again in something like the old way. That long period of darkness raises many questions in our minds.

Is it necessarily true that a catastrophe—war or invasion or plague— should induce hundreds of years of decline before there is a recovery? In later times Europe experienced all these, and did not experience another Dark Age. The terrible plague that is known as the Black Death may have killed half of all Europeans in the middle of the fourteenth century. The statistics are not precise, but a study of death tolls indicates that at least twenty-five million died during a period of little more than five or ten years. Europe did not surpass the level of population it had before 1348 until the beginning of the sixteenth century. But in other ways that devastating loss was quickly overcome. Within a generation post-plague Europe was experiencing an economic boom.

Similarly, Germany was ravaged by the Thirty Years' War (1618– 1648). Most of the armies that crossed and recrossed the country consisted of ill-paid mercenaries, who robbed, pillaged, and murdered as a matter of course. But that experience, in some respects quite similar to the barbarian invasions of the fifth and sixth centuries, was also overcome within a generation.

Western Europe after World War II seemed totally and perhaps permanently destroyed. Germany, Italy, and Austria were in ruins, and the victors, notably France and Britain, were hardly better off. Once more, Europe came back to a prosperous, flourishing life in less than thirty years.

And the barbarians who destroyed the Western empire also devastated the East, but with much less of a lingering effect. Earlier, they had decimated northern China. But China, too, had rebounded fairly quickly.

Why, then, did the barbarian invasions of the fifth century change Europe so profoundly, and for such a long time? We will return to this question in a moment.

The Triumph of Christianity: Constantine the Great

Constantine was born in what is now Yugoslavia in about 280 AD, the son of an army officer who was raised to the rank of Caesar. The title meant that Constantine's father would eventually be a Roman emperor, which he was, but only after many vicissitudes. Constantine himself was named Caesar, and after even more difficulties brought on by a complex series of civil wars, he, too, became the sole emperor of both the West and the East.

His ascension to the throne was ensured by his victory over an army led by his brother-in-law, Maxentius, at the Milvian Bridge near Rome. It is one of the most famous battles in history, because during the night before the battle Constantine, lying asleep in his tent, dreamt that an angel had descended from heaven. The angel held a cross and spoke to him, saying, "In this sign thou shalt conquer!" (*In hoc signo vinces*). On waking, Constantine ordered that Christian symbols be painted on the standards and the shields of his army, and from that time forward he was a deeply committed Christian.

Constantine inherited an empire whose official religion was paganism. Christianity, now three centuries old, could count several million adherents, but they were far from a majority of the population. Furthermore, their numbers had been sharply reduced during the reign (285 to 305) of Constantine's predecessor, the dour, efficient administrator Diocletian. Diocletian's efficiency had gone far to restore the economic and political health of the empire after a century of near-chaos, with emperors chosen and deposed at the whim of the army and few enforceable controls over commerce and trade. But for reasons which are not well understood, Diocletian had also undertaken the last and probably the most terrible persecution of Christians, during 304–305 AD. As a youth in the Eastern provinces of the empire, Constantine had seen many Christians tortured, burned at the stake, and crucified, and their martyrdom may have affected him deeply.

In any event, Constantine's religious beliefs were strong and lasting. He made Christianity the official religion of the empire, supported the Church with rich gifts and, more important, wide privileges and immunities from taxation, and promoted Christians to high posts in the army and bureaucracy. In a letter written in 313 to the proconsul of Africa he explained why the Christian clergy should not be distracted by secular offices or financial obligations: "When they are free to render supreme service to the Divinity, it is evident that they confer great benefits upon the affairs of state."

Constantine died in 337, after a reign of twenty-five years, during which Christianity penetrated so deeply into the fabric of the Roman state that even the return to paganism of one of Constantine's successors had no effect upon it. Julian the Apostate tried to make paganism the official religion during his short reign of twenty months in 361–363, but his early death left Christianity still the faith of the majority of Romans, which it remained from then on.

Constantine not only adopted Christianity as the Roman religion, he also founded Constantinople, endowed it with wealth taken from pillaged pagan temples, and made it the headquarters of his empire. The West continued to be ruled from Ravenna, but it had less and less power, as the East grew wealthier and more populous. The city of Rome never lost its symbolic importance as the ancient center of the empire, and it also remained rich both culturally and economically. But the main impetus toward the future shifted under Constantine from West to East, and his successors never modified this new national direction.

Nor did they modify the Christian character of the state. As time went on, Christianity became more and more a guiding principle of Rome, and the Church a leading institution. Thus when the barbarian invasions began in 410 AD with the first sack of the city of Rome, it was a Christian country that was devastated and conquered. And that fact had profound consequences.

The Promise of Christianity: Augustine

Edward Gibbon, in *The Decline and Fall of the Roman Empire*, identified two reasons for the fall of the ancient civilization that he admired so much. He called them barbarism and religion. By barbarism he meant not only the barbarian invasions, but also the deep changes in Roman life brought on by the presence of barbarians, first outside the state but impinging on it, later within the very citadels of Roman power. By religion he of course meant Christianity.

The suggestion shocked Gibbon's eighteenth-century readers, but it was not new. As the city of Rome lay in ruins in the wake of the Visigoth conquest in 410, voices were raised everywhere in the empire, accusing the Christians of having brought about this terrible defeat, and blaming the debacle on the disregard of the old pagan deities that the adoption of Christianity as the official religion had entailed.

Christians were quick to defend their faith. Sermons were preached and apologias were produced. Out of the dust of this moral and intellectual battle one great writer emerged. He wrote a book that was not only the most eloquent of all the defenses of Christianity produced at this time, but also a new version of history based on Christian principles.

Aurelius Augustinus was born in the North African town of Tagaste (modern Souk-Ahras, Algeria) in 354 AD. His exceptional potential was realized, and his family invested their entire financial resources to send him to New Carthage, then one of the major cities of the empire, to acquire the education that would fit him for a high government post. In Carthage the young man read Cicero's lost treatise *Hortensius*. It filled him with enthusiasm for philosophy, which he viewed as a rational system for understanding the world.

Augustine's mother, Monica, was a devout Christian, but his father was not. Despite his mother's early attempts to lead him to her faith, the young scholar found himself repelled by what he considered the antirational mysticism and intellectual confusions of Christianity. Instead, he was drawn to Manichaeanism, a philosophico-religion which held that there were two universal principles, one of Good and one of Evil, that warred for dominance in the cosmos. Although Manichaeanism was also mystical, it struck Augustine at the time as being a more realistic explanation.

However, Augustine had serious questions, and he found to his disappointment that the Manichaeans with whom he conversed could not answer them to his satisfaction. He began to shift his philosophical allegiance to the doctrines of Plotinus (205–270), the founder of Neoplatonism. Plotinus had died at Rome less than a hundred years before Augustine was born, and the young man found himself attracted by Plotinus's calm but intense quest, as manifested in his teachings and in his life, for mystical union with the Good through the exercise of pure intelligence.

The patient efforts of his mother, who is revered as Santa Monica because she helped to convert that extraordinary man St. Augustine, and his constant reading of Plotinus led Augustine to recognize the superhuman characteristics of Christ. But as Augustine tells us in his *Confessions*, it was a child's voice, overheard in a garden in Milan, that led him to take up the Bible and read a verse (Rom. 13:13) that made him perhaps the most famous convert in the Church's long history.

The year was 386. Augustine was thirty-one. He resigned the lucrative teaching posts that his family had worked to procure for him and went back to Tagaste. Soon he became a priest, and not much later bishop of Hippo, a Roman city in what is now Algeria that is famous only because of him. He spent the rest of his long life engaging in religious controversy, performing the numerous judicial duties that fell to bishops in those days, and writing books. The most important and influential of these was *The City of God*.

This was Augustine's response to the charge that Christianity had been the cause of the sack of Rome in 410. But he went farther than merely disproving that charge. He also laid out a plan of world history, showing how two cities had vied with each other for dominance and would continue to do so until the end of time. One city was human—material, fleshly, downward-turning. The other city was divine—spiritual, turning upward toward the Creator of all things.

According to Augustine, the Pax Romana could only be the City of Man. If not a wilderness, as Tacitus had suggested, it must be a desert of the spirit. It did not matter whether Christianity was the state religion. The state itself could not be holy. Christ had warned Peter to remember the difference between what belonged to Caesar and what belonged to God. Now Augustine emphasized this famous distinction, which he deepened beyond what others had seen in it.

An individual thinking being, Augustine said, does not make the truth, he finds it. He discovers it within himself as he listens to the teachings of the *magister interiore*, the "inward teacher," who is Christ, the revealing Word of God. The City of God, therefore, is not an earthly city. It is within the heart and soul of every true Christian. It goes where he goes—it is not at Rome or any other "place"—and it cannot be conquered by the enemy.

Earthly power and glory were nothing compared to the glory of the spiritual inward city, which could exist as well in a beggar as in an emperor. In a sense, Augustine was saying, the Heavenly City was born out of the ashes of the fall of Rome, as the phoenix is born out of the ashes of the fire. As the Earthly City went down in flames before the barbarian onslaught, the City of God would become clear. And the city of the heart and the soul would live forever, because it had been ordained and given by God.

The City of God of St. Augustine was deeply influenced by the Greek thought of Plato, as filtered through the intellectual mysticism of Plotinus. But Augustine proclaimed that the City of God had also been promised by Christ in the Gospels. The Beatitudes of the Sermon on the Mount are the constitution of the Heavenly City, as Augustine foresaw it. Thus Christianity fulfilled the ancient promise of the empire, which it could never have realized on its own. The new wine of Christ's message, with its vigorous life, broke the old bottles into which it had been poured, the old institutions that could not change fast or completely enough. The broken bottles fell away, and lo! the message stood by itself.

Rome survived the defeat of 410. The empire of the West lasted until 476, when an Ostrogothic king began to rule over Italy and its remaining dominions. But the barbarian incursions continued, as we have seen. A Vandal army was at the gates of Hippo when Augustine died there in 430.

He died believing that he had been right. Christianity, in order to survive, had to renounce earthly glory and be willing to live on in small, isolated, lonely places where the glory of the Heavenly City would shine forth and be more easily seen. Christians, St. Augustine believed, were seeking another kind of triumph from the Roman triumph. The defeat of Rome, of New Carthage, or even of Hippo, did not really seem important, no matter how much misery they might produce. The goal of Christians was in another life, and their city was not of this world.

After the Fall

The later Roman empire had been dedicated to power, wealth, and worldly success. It had been a long time since anyone had paid much attention to the warnings of men like Cato the Censor, who had lived in a republic based on moral virtue that seemed utterly unreal to modern Romans. These moderns, by and large, lived more luxuriously than any peoples before them, enjoying all that the world could provide and paying little heed to the demands of Christianity even though it was the official religion of the state.

Many Christians had fought hard to defend Rome and the empire, because, after all, there was a certain virtue in doing so. But after the barbarians destroyed the old society and replaced it with a brutal and primitive feudalism based on force alone, Christians began to see more clearly the allure of Augustine's City of God. It was that city which they tried to build during the five centuries that are still called dark, instead of trying to rebuild the triumphant Roman City of Man, which had never meant much to them and now meant almost nothing at all.

Christians throughout the empire of the West, in Italy, in Gaul (we shall have to begin calling it France), in Germany, in Spain, along the coast of North Africa, in the British Isles—all embraced a new way of life. They did not seem to regret what they had lost; they hardly seemed to remember it. Despite their poverty and fear, Christians looked forward to something they had never been able to see clearly before, because its light had been obscured by the blaze of Roman greatness.

We live today in a world that is as deeply devoted to material things as was the late Roman world. For example, the Romans of the fourth century were obsessed by health, diet, and exercise. They spent more time in baths and health clubs than in churches, temples, libraries, and law courts. They were devoted to consumption. A man could make a reputation by spending more than his neighbor, even if he had to borrow the money to do it. And if he never paid back his creditors, he was honored for having made a noble attempt to cut a fine figure in the world.

They were excited by travel, news, and entertainment. The most important cultural productions of late Roman times, from books to extravaganzas in the theaters and circuses that occupied a central place in every Roman city or town, dealt with amusing fictions about faraway peoples and with a fantasy peace and happiness that did not exist in their real lives. They were fascinated by fame and did not care how it was acquired. If you were famous enough, the fact that you might be a rascal or worse was ignored or forgiven.

Romans cared most about success, which they interpreted as being ahead for today, and let tomorrow take care of itself. They were proud, greedy, and vain. In short, they were much like ourselves.

The new kind of Christians, after the fall, had little interest in their bodies as such. They cared about the health of their souls. They had no interest in consumption. They could lose reputation rather than gain it for possessing wealth in a society where poverty was next to godliness.

Their travels were in the mind, as their spirits soared upward toward God. Their news was the Gospels, the news of the life of Christ and of his promised second coming. Their entertainment consisted of hearing that good news proclaimed in churches and by itinerant preachers in town squares and at country crossroads. They cared nothing for fame in this world, for they believed that only if they lost their earthly lives would they gain eternal life and the fame of those who were saved.

Where wealth had been the measure of a Roman, now poverty became the measure of a Christian. In later centuries the Church would become as rich and powerful as the empire had been, and probably as corrupt. But in those early days the Church remained poor, or tried to, or meant to.

St. Benedict, for example, went to Rome around 500 AD to study at one of the few remaining Roman schools. He was shocked by the wealth and luxury (although it must have been a far cry from the luxury of the imperial days) and retired to live for the rest of his days in the somber monastery that he founded at Monte Cassino at the beginning of the sixth century. In so doing he laid down a pattern and a rule of life that was imitated everywhere in the West.

For centuries the Benedictines were devoted to poverty, prayer, and good works, following the rule of their founder and spiritual father. Eventually even the Benedictines became rich, powerful, and corrupt, but for half a millennium they managed to stay poor, as they never ceased to believe they ought to be.

For a while, they understood that the rich are never rich enough, and that to have enough is simply to be content with what you have rather than to have what you want. When wanting comes first, you can never have enough. If contentment is placed first, it does not matter how much you have.

Socrates, in his ancient fable of the City of Pigs, had proclaimed that the greatest pleasure of the citizens of his simple community was to recline on beds of myrtle and to praise the gods. The Christians of the Dark Ages also felt that the greatest of human pleasures was to praise the Creator, in all the ways that could be found to praise him. Simple meals, a simple life, time to contemplate eternity, and a voice free to praise God—what more could man want?

From our modern point of view those centuries that we still call dark were the nadir of Western civilization. Our ancestors did not feel that way about their time.

They did become frightened and nervous as the year 1000 AD approached, as we are nervous about the coming end of the second millennium. They were like children, afraid of the unknown. They feared the world might come to an end at the close of the year 999. When nothing terrible happened, they drew a collective sigh of relief and set about rebuilding their new version of the old Roman empire. We live in it today.

5

The Middle Ages: The Great Experiment

As we have seen, life during the centuries of the early Middle Ages was hard for almost all Europeans, the survivors and descendants of the fallen Roman empire. Because of the devastation wrought by the barbarian invasions of the fifth and sixth centuries AD, they faced three major challenges.

The Struggle for Subsistence

The first challenge was simply to survive. There is a level of economic life below which it is difficult, even impossible, for communities of human beings to persist. For centuries the human race, at least in the civilized part of the world, had lived well above that critical level. Now, with their world in ruins, many communities came dangerously close to abject poverty and even starvation and death. As a result, large areas became desert and wasteland, the habitat of the fierce predators that had previously been brought close to extinction, as well as the wild men and outlaws who lived like the beasts that surrounded them in the dark forests.

Even those communities that survived, at much reduced levels of population, did so with few comforts. Both men and women worked hard just to have something—hardly ever enough—to eat. Dwellings were primitive, often no more than caves cut into the hillsides. The people dressed in homespun clothing which they did not change from year to year. They were cold in winter, hot in summer. After dark, the only light came from their smoky fires.

A World of Enemies

Their lives were also filled with danger. Living in small, self-contained communities, lacking a powerful central authority or civil police, they were constantly attacked by pirates and marauding criminals. Being attacked by outlaws, the leading social disease of the time, was probably the main cause of death of medieval people.

It is very difficult for ordinary people to protect themselves from outlaws. Protection has always been a highly specialized occupation, and in fact it is the oldest profession.

Protection is a full-time job, and the people whose job it is must receive their sustenance from those they are protecting. In the absence of central authority and respect for law, provision for protection becomes even more expensive. The protectors have to have weapons. The provisions they receive must often come at the expense of the providers. Finally, they must be paid whatever they desire, even beyond what they may need. For since they have been given a monopoly of force in the community, they can often name their own price.

During the Dark Ages the price of protection was extremely high, as much as three-quarters of the income of those who were being protected. One cause of this very high cost (compared to the cost of protection and security today) lay in the fact that medieval protection soon became institutionalized, in a hierarchy that provided no more safety but did support many more protectors.

Local armed men and soldiers stood at the lowest level. It was hoped they would keep enemies and robbers out of the fields and homes. These men required protection, too, from other local soldiers as well as outlaws, and this was provided at a higher level by a lord, who organized protection for a fairly large region.

Eventually, within a defensible geographic area (which might be small or very large), only the king was truly autonomous, since he owed allegiance to no one as long as he kept the lower levels of protectors satisfied and was able to defend his borders from other rulers.

According to tradition, there were also knights-errant, who rode about seeking special persons, such as damsels in distress, to help and succor. For the most part such chivalrous figures existed only in fiction.

It was an expensive and inefficient system for maintaining some sort of civil peace. We call the system feudalism. But as long as the most intelligent, creative, and energetic persons in medieval society were concerned with something else besides brute survival, there was probably no alternative.

The Problem of God

God was the last of the three great medieval challenges, and the most important. Human beings had always been interested in God and had attempted to understand his ways. But the Greeks, and especially the Romans, had kept this interest under control. Only seldom, and on ritual occasions, had they allowed the divine frenzy to overcome them.

In the early Middle Ages it overcame the best and brightest among Europeans. It can almost be said that they became obsessed with God. They thought about God, they studied God, they tried to ascertain his will and to obey it, and they tried to discover God's purposes in the world and to advance them.

Their lives became more God-centered than ever before in Western history. Mathematics and philosophy headed the list of Greek studies, and politics and law the Roman; now theology became the queen of the sciences. It would remain so for nearly a thousand years.

The Science of Theology

Today, theology survives as just one of the humanities, with few students and even fewer passionate devotees. The humanities themselves, that group of sciences that once stood at the top of the academic heap, have fallen on evil days. Another kind of science, to which we shall have to devote much attention in later chapters, has taken their place. Furthermore, that science has scored great triumphs. We are right to worship it. But we should not forget that theology also scored triumphs in its day, and that its day was long.

What does it mean, to "study" God? How can there be a "science" of God? The very fact that these questions can be asked shows how far we have come, and how much we have changed, from the medieval worldview.

The City of God was different from the City of Man. Augustine had said so. It was also obvious. But how was it different? What was the "constitution" of the City of God? What was its polity, its justice, its peace? All of these things must be different from what they were in the City of Man.

Take peace, for example. Civil peace in the City of Man is a complex idea, which both Greeks and Romans had struggled to understand. It involves a balance of forces, a willingness to compromise, an acceptance of just authority, the establishment of lines of authority, the acknowledgment of a private domain beyond authority's reach, and many other things. It is probably the hardest condition to achieve in a civil state and the most valuable.

The peace of the City of God also involved complex relations with authority, but this time the authority was God, or the will of God. In the *Divine Comedy*, Dante has one of the Blessed say: "His will is our peace."

E la sua voluntade è nostra pace.

Only if our desire is entirely in accord with God's desire for us are we at peace.

Are we still free, then, or are we enslaved? We are free, because we freely choose what God chooses for us. To choose otherwise would mean to become enslaved by our own desires. If we are free from all wrong and misguided impulses, then God is what we naturally choose, and thus we are free in that sense too.

Do we acknowledge a private domain where God cannot, does not, or should not reach, a domain in which there is another kind of freedom? This domain exists and is acknowledged and protected in the City of Man, but in the City of God we can afford—we desire with all our heart—to open our being entirely to God, to conceal nothing from him. Any concealment is a kind of shame, and a kind of slavery.

And so, the line of theological reasoning went, we achieve a higher peace and a higher freedom by giving ourselves and our will to God. In return for that gift, which is the greatest of human acts, God rewards us with eternal peace.

That was the kind of knowledge sought by students of the Heavenly City. Its two basic textbooks were the Old and the New Testaments. But those two textbooks are not always easy to comprehend. Is everything they say to be taken literally, for instance, or is an allegorical reading of some texts required by God? Once that initial question is answered, in the affirmative, other difficulties arise.

In fact, every sentence of the sacred books requires interpretation, which is to say understanding and application to man's life and to his search for God. Are there sentences that contradict one another? This seems impossible, since for God to contradict himself would drive us from him, and according to his promise to Noah, a promise that is confirmed by the sacrifice of his only begotten son, he *will* not do it. When God *seems* to contradict himself in his acts, as for example when he allows bad things to happen to good people (as we understand bad and good), we must assume that we have misunderstood him, for if there is anything in the world that may be trusted, it is the goodness of God's will, toward others as well as toward ourselves.

For centuries the most intelligent, imaginative, and hardworking minds of western Christendom struggled with these questions and scores of others like them. They arrived at answers, then questioned and disputed the answers, in schools and universities. They contemplated them in silence and in monasteries everywhere. It was generally held that contemplation, which, strictly speaking, is different from theology, was the highest service to God, higher even than study and preaching, and so the very best men and women gave themselves up to it, and were silent to the world.

We do not know what they discovered in their silent, passionate thinking about the problems of God, because they did not write it down, they did not tell others, they did not care if we knew. There were no Nobel Prizes for theology, and no earthly reward or fame for the greatest discoveries. The rewards were in the discoveries themselves, in their hot, immediate truth. And in the peace that followed, forevermore.

Theology in Other Religions

Christians were far from being the only theologians in those centuries of the Middle Ages. Almost everyone seemed to be God-obsessed. The eastern, or Greek, Christians were impressive theologians, although they kept their heads about them and also kept their empire flourishing.

The Jews were God-obsessed and always had been. The first of the many waves of Semites to emerge from the Arabian Peninsula, in the second millennium before the Christian Era, the Jews moved and were driven westward until they settled in Jerusalem as their spiritual center and home. There for hundreds of years they nursed their unique monotheism and proclaimed to all who would listen the conclusions of their moral speculations about their Hidden God.

The Romans conquered the Jews in 63 BC. The Jews rose up again a hundred years later only to see their temple destroyed by Roman soldiers. There ensued what some feel was the greatest era of Jewish history, when Jews were dispersed throughout the Roman empire and may have made up as much as ten percent of its total population. In North Africa, Spain, Italy, Greece, and Egypt, as well as in Palestine and its surroundings, Jewish communities spoke the same language, obeyed the same laws (including commercial law), and traded with one another to the great benefit of the Romans as well as themselves.

Everywhere, too, Jewish scholars and rabbis not only studied and codified Jewish history and law but also studied and codified Hellenistic learning. Working together with Greeks and other Christians, the Jews of Alexandria contributed greatly to the compilation of the classical tradition that would re-emerge in the West after the fall of Byzantium in 1453.

No less God-obsessed than the western Christians were the millions of followers of Muhammed, who, after the Prophet's death in 632, quickly conquered all of Arabia, the Middle East, Persia, North Africa, and Spain. The westward spread of Islam was stopped by the Franks at Poitiers in 732, and Islam withdrew behind the Pyrenees. But the eastward expansion continued until, by the tenth century, there were Muslim outposts in many areas of Africa south of the Sahara, throughout the Indian subcontinent, and in the islands of the South China Sea (Sumatra, Java, Celebes, Mindanao, and elsewhere).

Initially Islam was not a proselytizing religion, although it made many converts nonetheless. Its message, taken from the Koran, of compassion and mercy inspired downtrodden peoples everywhere and still does. Arab and, eventually, Muslim traders generally brought with them not only zeal and integrity but also news of a new, desirable world. Then, of course, it was convenient to convert to the religion of your business associates if you had no particular religion of your own. Most Christians and Jews refused to convert to Islam, but pagans often succumbed.

The second caliph (that is, successor of Muhammed), Omar, conquered Alexandria, capital of the world of scholarship, in 642 AD. It was in Alexandria that the Arab Muslims first came into close contact with Greek culture. They fell under its spell at once. They soon became noted mathematicians, astronomers, and physicists, and they continued the work begun even before the fall of Rome of codifying and interpreting Greek scientific thought. Like everyone else, the Arab Muslims found themselves caught up in the frenzy of theological study and speculation that was sweeping the West.

Principles of Theocracy

In a democracy (from the Greek words *demos*, "people," and *kratos*, "power") the people rule, either directly or through representatives chosen by the people at stated intervals and according to agreed rules. Other words are also formed from the Greek suffix *-cracy*, denoting different types of rule: for example, mobocracy, aristocracy, technocracy. In a theocracy (from the Greek *theos*, "god"), God rules.

That is a difficult idea to understand. "The people" is an abstraction, but you can nevertheless feel that you are a part of the people, and therefore have a role to play, if only on Election Day, in the government that you help to choose to rule. "Aristocracy" is also understandable. It is the government of "the best," which is theoretically possible even though no system of choosing the best to rule over the rest has ever been found to be infallible. Also comprehensible are such constructs as "mobocracy," the rule of the mob (this is a kind of perversion of democracy), and "technocracy," a social and economic system that is ruled by technocrats, or experts. But what does it mean to say that God rules? What is God? How does God manifest his rule?

For millennia, all over the ancient world, kings, emperors, and pharaohs had claimed to be gods, that is, to be divine as well as secular rulers of their peoples. All the Roman emperors from Augustus on were worshiped as gods. But when Constantine adopted Christianity as the Roman state religion, he did not claim to be the Christian God. The Christian (as well as the Jewish and Muslim) God was not just one of many gods. He was God, alone, almighty, omnipresent, all-knowing. What did it mean to say that he ruled the world, in a practical sense?

For Jews and Muslims it was relatively easy to answer these questions. God had given the law to Moses and the prophets, and Jews had only to obey it. Men learned in the law, the rabbis, or teachers, could instruct you when you were in doubt. God had also dictated the Koran to his prophet Muhammad, and the Koran was understood to be not just the sacred book of Islam but its entire code of law. Again, learned Muslims, headed by the imam, might be needed for instruction and to resolve doubtful points.

Could a similar situation exist with Christianity? There seemed to be difficulties, for the New Testament is notably lacking in rules of practical behavior, even if its mysterious parables can be interpreted as a way of life. The greatest difficulty was posed in the question: Who could interpret for all Christians, and with what authority?

In other words, if the Roman empire had fallen and no longer existed, what could replace it as the temporal ruler?

The answer existed in the Christian Church, which though not founded by Christ as a secular institution, had nevertheless developed that role, since the Church alone possessed the authority to interpret the will of God.

Here there were further difficulties, for the Eastern empire, with its capital at Byzantium, claimed hegemony over the remains of the Roman empire in the West. Its claim was based on tradition and, even more important, upon explicit decrees and recorded acts of Constantine, who had established Byzantium (Constantinople) as the center of the empire. Therefore it seemed necessary to discover or to create some bridge between Constantine and the Church that would confer the needed authority upon the latter.

Such a bridge did not exist, so it was constructed. During the ninth or perhaps the tenth century, a person or persons unknown who were familiar with the operations of the Roman curia forged a document purporting to show that Constantine the Great had granted to Pope Sylvester I (314–335) and his successors spiritual supremacy over all matters of faith and worship and temporal dominion over Rome and the entire Western empire. It is now universally accepted that this document was a fake and that no such "Donation of Constantine" ever occurred. For hundreds of years no one questioned the edict. The supposed grant of dominion actually satisfied a deep need: it solved the problem of how God had arranged for his rule to be manifested among men.

At the same time, it was profoundly important that the arrangement was based upon a lie. Probably it had to be. A theocratic form of government may be feasible in small communities like monasteries or cloisters, or in such groups as the Plymouth Plantation in early Massachusetts. Can theocracy ever really work where large numbers of men and women, spread over a large area, are concerned? I doubt it. I recognize that good men disagree. However, they must point to an actually existing example of a working theocracy in order to make a convincing argument.

Empire and Papacy

The pope might claim temporal power over all Christians, but how was he to exercise it? An elected official, the pope was often an elderly man who did not live long in his office. His background did not qualify him as a temporal leader since at the time this inevitably meant military leadership. Consequently, the pope clearly needed to establish and perpetuate a temporal institution, headed by a man who would obey him, the pope, while at the same time he exerted military control over the far-flung communities of Christendom.

It was easier to establish such an institution than to perpetuate and, especially, to control it in turn. In fact, the institution practically instituted itself, under the name of the Holy Roman Emperor, a title claimed by various persons at various times. The most famous of them was Charlemagne, who, in a ceremony that was seen as highly significant, was crowned by the pope on Christmas Day of the year 800.

Charlemagne (742–814), or Charles I the Great, king of the Franks (768–814) and king of the Lombards (774–814), had long been the most powerful man in Europe before Leo III placed the crown upon his head in the basilica of St. Peter's at Rome and proclaimed him emperor and the heir of Augustus. Charlemagne gained no new power by this act. He did gain a kind of legitimacy that he and his successors held to be of considerable importance. And the papacy also gained another kind of legitimacy. From that time forth, popes continued to claim temporal superiority over the emperors.

However, the same question still had to be answered. How was the pope to exercise control over the emperor, who had most of the soldiers at his beck and call? Thus that symbolic act in St. Peter's in 800 was and remained supremely ambiguous. The emperor ruled by the will of the pope, so the pope said, and the emperor did not explicitly disagree. But the pope also ruled by the will of the emperor, for the emperor had many soldiers, and the pope had few.

Given the essentially ambiguous idea of theocracy, upon which the system was constructed, it is not surprising that this ambiguity survived in practice for many centuries. Why was the ambiguity not pointed out and objected to? Because, with all its defects, the system of pope and emperor satisfied an essential need. No other legitimation of governance could be imagined.

The relative power of the empire and the papacy rose and fell during the centuries after 800. Sometimes the pope really did seem to have the supreme power. Other times, the pope had to bargain away so much of his power that he was seen as a mere puppet whose strings were held and controlled by the emperor. Nevertheless, the system endured for five hundred years, until the outrageous scandal of the "Babylonian Captivity" saw the popes leave Rome and take up residence in Avignon, under the wing of the king of France, from 1309 to 1377. Never again would the popes possess the temporal power that they had always claimed and sometimes actually had. Nor, indeed, would the Holy Roman Empire survive as a viable institution when national states, like France, England, Spain, and the empire's successor, Germany, came to the fore and assumed political control of Europe in the sixteenth century. These new nation-states were headed by kings who ruled "by the grace of God," but that was a new idea and very different from the theocracy that held sway for ten centuries after the fall of Rome.

Monasticism

The empire and the papacy, powerful and wide-reaching as they were, still failed to rule theocratic Europe effectively in the eight centuries, from 500 to 1300 AD, which we call the Middle Ages. Something else was needed: an institution that would mediate between man and God, that would bring down to the human level the laws and commands of Christ and his vicar upon earth, the pope at Rome.

This role should have been filled by the Church, if the Church had ever been what Christ probably wanted it to be (if in fact Christ ever founded a church, which is somewhat doubtful). The Church's bishops did provide a semblance of law and order, and its priests did confer a certain spiritual comfort. But both priests and bishops were busy with their own concerns. Something more simple, and more humble, was required. The first to see this need, and to satisfy it, was Benedict of Nursia.

Born about 450 AD at Norcia, in central Italy, Benedict was sent to Roman schools. Shocked by the licentiousness of the decaying city, he retired to a cave in the rocks near the ruins of Nero's palace above

Subiaco, forty miles east of Rome. There he lived as a hermit for three years, until he became famous for his sanctity, when he was persuaded to serve as abbot of a nearby monastery. His zeal was resisted, and rebellious monks under his care tried to poison him. He resigned his post, but once again disciples gathered about him, and with their help he founded twelve new monasteries. Again there were conspiracies against his rule.

Saddened and disgusted, he left the area and wandered south to a hill rising sharply above Cassino, halfway between Rome and Naples. The region was still mostly pagan, but he converted the inhabitants by his fervent preaching and established the monastery of Monte Cassino, the founding house of the Benedictine order.

For many years he had considered the question of how a community of monks should live together. He wrote down a set of rules and standards of communal life that became famous as the Rule of St. Benedict. The compassionate, humble, and moderate character of the Rule, which carefully balanced prayer, work, and study, has become part of the spiritual treasure of the Church. Benedict died, probably at Cassino, around 547. The Benedictines are still a monastic order today, after nearly fifteen hundred years.

According to scholastic tradition, the monastery of Monte Cassino was founded in the year 529. The same year saw the issuance of a decree by the Christian emperor Justinian closing the Platonic Academy at Athens. The symbolism of this double event was long regarded as profoundly important. The closing of the Academy, which had survived for nearly a thousand years after its founding by the philosopher Plato, meant the end of Greek higher education in the West. (Greek academies remained in Byzantium for hundreds of years.) At the same time, it signified the beginning of a new and different kind of educational and scholastic institution. From that time forward, "no plant would thrive except one that germinated and grew in the cloister."

Benedictine monasteries arose all over Italy and elsewhere in Europe. They undertook the task of organizing, sorting, classifying, and copying classical materials handed down from the glorious Greek and Roman past, and to them we owe almost every surviving text. But the Benedictine monks did not confine themselves to crouching over worn lecterns and copying texts that, in many cases, they must not have fully understood. They also undertook an active role in the world. It was Benedictine monks who carried the message of Christianity to the farthest corners of the old empire, in Britain, northern Germany, and western Spain, as well as the pagan regions of Italy, like Cassino, that held out for the old religion for more than a thousand years after the death of Christ.

The simple humility of St. Benedict was remembered for centuries, and it continued to give the order that bore his name a reputation for sanctity and Christian zeal. But in time the monasteries, like the Church itself, grew rich. Great wealth is an obstacle to salvation, as Christ knew (it is harder for a rich man to attain the kingdom of heaven than for a camel to pass through the eye of a needle). This axiom applied as well to institutions as to individual men. Thus, by the twelfth century, all of the existing monastic orders had become corrupt.

A new view of the world swept over Christendom during the twelfth and thirteenth centuries, when two orders were established, the Franciscans and the Dominicans. Francis of Assisi (1181/2–1226), the tiny, haunted man who founded the Franciscans around 1210, was an altogether extraordinary figure of the later Middle Ages. Taking as the aim of his new life "to follow the teachings of our Lord Jesus Christ and to walk in his footsteps," Francis demanded that his followers subsist entirely on what they could beg as they walked through the world, preaching their message to all who would listen. His new order, and that of the Dominicans, founded about the same time by the Spaniard Domingo de Guzmán (c.1170–1221), were called mendicants, for they abjured great abbeys and cloisters in favor of a life of utmost simplicity and poverty.

In later years even the Dominicans and Franciscans were tempted by the riches that were forced upon them by those who hoped to purchase salvation for themselves by giving their wealth to holy men and women. Throughout the thirteenth century, however, monasticism rose to heights of piety and service to mankind that it had never reached before, and has never reached since.

No dependable statistics exist on the numbers of persons who belonged to monastic orders during the first century of the Benedictines, or the age of the Cluniac reform in the twelfth century, or the thirteenth century, when Franciscan friars and Dominican scholar-preachers tramped the roads of Europe. Perhaps, numerically, the orders were never very large. But they attracted a high proportion of the most intelligent and creative men and women of their times.

Often brilliant, always dedicated, these men and women removed themselves from the general secular life of the age when they entered a monastery or cloister. They made no further contribution to the economy or to the society. They believed they made another kind of contribution: they prayed for mankind, they preserved the treasures of the past, they taught their fellow men what they knew about the road to salvation, but in another life, not this one, and they tried to sacrifice their own immediate good to a greater good in a practically indefinable future.

Such sacrifices and offerings cannot be judged as insignificant. We do not know enough about the way the world works to prove that the prayers of holy men and women have not made a better world. Maybe they have even saved the world. But we also do not know that to be true. What we do know is that the secular Middle Ages had to do without the intelligence, imagination, and creativity of a significant proportion of its best human beings. We cannot measure the cost of that loss.

Crusaders

It would not be true to say that the pope and the Church lacked soldiers altogether. From time to time, mercenaries paid by the pope fought battles and sometimes won them against imperial and other armies. A notorious example concerned the papal army headed by Cesare Borgia at the end of the fifteenth century in Italy. The bastard son of Pope Alexander VI, Cesare and his father hoped not only to carve out a huge Italian estate for their family but also to unify the entire country and thus save it from the depredations of both the French king and the German (i.e., Holy Roman) emperor. But when his father died and Pope Julius II succeeded him, Cesare could not survive. He was killed in 1507, at the age of thirty-two, and the hopes of his family died with him, as did the dream of the historian Niccolò Macchiavelli (1469–1527), who had seen in the unique combination of a powerful pope and a brilliant young commander the prospect of an Italy free of foreign control.

Few popes had the advantages conferred upon Alexander VI by his natural son Cesare. But they did have another weapon that could be used to raise armies: the religious zeal they could help to implant among the great military leaders of Europe. During the eleventh century burgeoning European commerce led to trading expeditions as well as pilgrimages to Jerusalem and other holy places in the East. At the same time the Byzantine empire came under attack from the Seljuk Turks. Here was both an opportunity and a need, as Pope Urban II was quick to see. In 1095 he called for a Christian army to defeat the Turks and recapture the Holy Sepulchre from the Muslims. On July 15, 1099, Jerusalem fell to a motley army of crusaders, who exhibited their Christian charity by slaughtering the Jewish and Muslim inhabitants, including the women and children. During the next few decades crusaders of various stripe gained control of a narrow strip of land along the Palestine coast, which caused much jubilation back home.

The Saracens recaptured the crusader castles in 1144, leading to the Second (1140), Third (1189), and Fourth (1198) crusades, all of which ended in humiliating failure, with the result that all of the Christian outposts were lost, together with the lives and fortunes of tens of thousands of Christian men, many of them from the highest nobility. But the crusading fervor continued to reach an ever greater pitch.

In the spring of 1212 a shepherd boy named Stephen had a vision in which Jesus appeared to him disguised as a pilgrim and gave him a letter for the king of France. Stephen, who lived in a little French town, Cloyes-sur-le-Loir, set out to deliver the letter. As he walked along in the bright spring sunlight, he told everyone he met of his mission. Soon he had gathered around him a crowd of other children, determined to follow him wherever he was called to go. Eventually there were more than thirty thousand who decided to go to Marseilles, whence they hoped to travel by ship to the Holy Land. There they confidently expected to be able to conquer the paynim by love instead of force of arms.

Arriving in Marseilles, they were taken under the care of merchants who, seeing an opportunity for enormous profits, promised to carry them to Jerusalem, but instead shipped them to North Africa, where they were sold as slaves in the Muslim markets that did a large business in the buying and selling of human beings. Few if any ever returned. None reached the Holy Land.

A ten-year-old boy from Cologne, named Nicholas, then gathered a second group, preached a Children's Crusade in the Rhineland and finally attracted another twenty thousand boys and girls. After crossing the Alps into Italy, they met various fates, none of them good. As before, a large number were shipped to Africa and sold as slaves.

Four more crusades followed during the thirteenth century. The eighth and last, led by King Louis VII of France (St. Louis), was in some respects even more pathetic and sad than the Children's Crusade. Called by King Louis in 1270, it started with high hopes, but a vast army that landed at Tunis in July 1270 was soon decimated by plague. Louis was one of the first to die, but many followed him into death as his body was carried back to France.

The eight crusades, organized over a period of nearly two centuries, accomplished almost nothing concrete and cost a vast amount in life, treasure, and blasted hopes. But perhaps they were a necessary, even an inevitable result of the great experiment undertaken during the Middle Ages in theocratic governance.

Millennial Fears, Postmillennial Achievements

The number one thousand had always fascinated Christians. They feared the coming millennium for many reasons, not least because of the prediction laid down in the twentieth chapter of the Book of Revelation, in which it was said that "an angel come down from heaven . . . laid hold on the dragon, that old serpent, which is the Devil . . . and bound him a thousand years . . . : and after that he must be loosed a little season."

The prospect of a world in which the Devil prospered proved terrifying, even if only for a little while. Life seemed bad enough during these thousand years, even with the Devil bound in the bottomless pit. How much worse might life be once the Devil was allowed to do his malicious deeds unimpeded? And how long, or short, was "the little season" after which Christ would return to judge the quick and the dead?

Hundreds of thousands of persons throughout Europe trembled as the year 1000 approached (or was the fateful epoch to begin with the year 999?). During the later 990s most business simply stopped, as people decided not to undertake anything but the most temporary enterprises, and the devout surged through the streets, whipping themselves into a bloody frenzy of remorse for sin and hope for imminent salvation.

It is important to remember that not all of the persons even in Europe, to say nothing of surrounding regions, counted in the same way as Christians of that time. The world was a great deal older than a thousand years for the Jews, who dated their calendar from the supposed year of the Creation, which we now name 3761 BC. And for the Muslims, who dated their calendar from the year 622 AD, it was much younger.

At any rate, the year 1000 (or 999) passed without anything epochal occurring. The relief felt by Christians at this happy resolution was translated into a new outburst of energy, and the next three centuries, from about 1000 to about 1300, became one of the most optimistic, prosperous, and progressive periods in European history.

Under Henry III (1036–1056) the eleventh century saw the medieval empire at its peak of power and influence. The empire reached from Hamburg and Bremen in the north to the instep of Italy in the south, and from Burgundy in the west to Bohemia, Hungary, and Poland in the east. As the empire rose, the papacy fell. In 1046 no fewer than three men claimed the throne of St. Peter. Henry intervened, and at the Synod of Sutri in that year, he deposed all three and saw that his own nominee, Clement II, was elected. On the same day Clement returned the favor by crowning Henry and his wife emperor and empress.

It was not long before the pendulum swung in the other direction. By the end of the twelfth century, under Pope Innocent III (1198–1216), the papacy had reached its own acme of prestige and power, and Christian Europe came the closest it ever has to being a unified theocracy with no internal contradictions. But the ambiguous contradictions existed still, rising to the surface soon after the death of Innocent, when Frederick II, emperor from 1215 to 1250, renewed the struggle with the papacy. Both sides ultimately emerged exhausted from the conflict.

The ensuing political turmoil did not affect the rise in the general standard of living that was characteristic of these centuries. The emergence of a new class of urban merchants and traders contributed greatly to the new prosperity, the class that Karl Marx was to dub the bourgeoisie. As Marx declared, "the bourgeoisie has played a most revolutionary part in history," and at no time was this more evident than during the eleventh and twelfth centuries, during which hundreds of new towns, styling themselves communes, rose to prominence in Italy, Germany, and Flanders. They demanded and won self-government from their previous feudal masters.

Innovative bourgeois not only created new wealth with their trade and commerce but also subsidized the inventions of ingenious entrepreneurs in alchemy (the ancestor of modern chemistry), energy conversion, transportation, and metallurgy. The use of iron became common, even in the houses of the poor. Windmills and water mills were set up everywhere to convert the power of natural forces to useful work. A new kind of harness allowed horses to be used for the first time to draw carts and plows. And in Bohemia, Sweden, and Cornwall new mining techniques permitted the digging of the first deep shafts to richer deposits of iron, copper, tin, and lead.

Perhaps most important, the new urban class became employers of the surplus labor that a growing agricultural population produced, while peasants and farmers themselves increased their own efficiency through new inventions. As a result, farm workers' income rose as new wealth was created in the towns.

All of these changes constituted a danger to the medieval theocratic ideal. Primitive capitalism was inherently destabilizing, as capitalism has always been (Marx was the first to see that, too). Feudal theocracy, or theocratic feudalism, had too many instabilities of its own to long survive the creative muddle of the times. But this is easier for us to see than for the medieval folk. Their prime concern remained, as it had been for so long, theological study and speculation. Even in the new world that was being born, the oldest questions—concerning the conflicting claims of faith and reason, the will of God, and the nature of truth—held their ancient fascination and overshadowed everything else that happened.

The Dispute about Truth

One single question stood at the center of Christian theological study and disputation during the centuries of the Middle Ages. First posed by implication in Augustine's *City of God*, and first defined soon after the fall of Rome, it continued to be a leading subject of speculation for nearly a thousand years.

Simply put: accepting as true Augustine's doctrine of the two cities, is there one truth for both, or do they have separate and different truths? If something is true in one city, must it also be true in the other? Or, if there are two distinct truths, is one truth more important than the other? Consequently, must a person choose between them?

The question may seem unimportant or irrelevant now, for we have long since arrived at the answer and therefore no longer speculate about it. But medieval men did not find it an easy question to answer. And they saw, perhaps more clearly than we do, how fraught with consequences, both theoretical and practical, were all the possible answers.

Let us consider the views of seven great medieval thinkers on this question of the two truths, as it came to be called.

Boethius

Boethius was born in Rome around 480 AD, the son of an aristocratic family. He was well educated and evidently bilingual in Greek and Latin. Around 510 he began the major work of his life: the translation of the works of Aristotle from Greek into Latin so that future ages would know the best of classical thought. Boethius also acquired an important post under the Ostrogoth king Theodoric, and for a time enjoyed power and influence. But he fell into disfavor after 520; he was imprisoned, and executed in 524 after frightful tortures. While in prison he wrote his famous book *The Consolation of Philosophy*.

As far as his life's task was concerned, Boethius completed only a small part of it; that is, instead of translating all the works of Aristotle, he translated only the *Organon*, or works on logic. These translations, however, were used in schools for more than seven hundred years and made Boethius's name revered.

He also wrote treatises on theological subjects, remarkable for the fact that there is not a single mention in them of the Sacred Scriptures. However, Boethius was a Christian, as a contemporary biography makes clear. How could this be? The solution of the puzzle is found in a sentence that concludes his treatise on the Trinity, written about 515. The sentence was quoted innumerable times in the following centuries.

> As far as you are able, join faith to reason.

The Middle Ages believed that this, as clear as could be done in so few words, stated one of the great polar theological positions. Combined with the fact that the Bible found no place in the theology of Boethius, it implied that the nature of God could be comprehended by human reason; the truths of faith and of reason were the same.

Pseudo-Dionysius

Dionysius the Areopagite lived during the first century AD. Converted to Christianity by St. Paul, he was held (in later ages) to have been the first bishop of Athens. Around 500 AD, probably in Syria, a monk who used the pseudonym Dionysius the Areopagite published writings that exerted a great influence on the future history of theology in the West. The most important of these was a book, in Greek, *The Names of God.* The work exemplified a kind of "negative theology" in that it implied that theology, as conceived by a writer like Boethius, was both impossible and illegitimate.

The author now known as Pseudo-Dionysius began by stating that no name can be given to God that God does not give himself, through revelation. He went on to show that even the revealed names, which (since they are names) must be comprehensible to the human mind, cannot express the true nature of God, since God cannot be comprehended (encompassed) by the finite human understanding. The theologian may not even call God "real" or "being," because his understanding of those terms derives from his knowledge and experience of the world that was created; but the Creator cannot be understood in terms of his Creation.

Pseudo-Dionysius therefore placed himself in direct opposition to Boethius. According to Boethius, the City of God could be comprehended by human reason. According to Pseudo-Dionysius, the City of God could never be reduced to the City of Man.

For Boethius, the great authority was Aristotle. He had not been a Christian, of course, but in some of his treatises he had written in a way that Boethius and others could interpret as at least pre-Christian. And he was the apostle of reason. Boethius thought no one had ever known more about the natural world, and this was knowledge that could not contradict Scripture, because what was true in one realm must be true in the other.

The great authority for Pseudo-Dionysius was St. Augustine. Augustine's Neoplatonic roots in Plotinus and others he had read in his youth—together with his fervent reading of the Scriptures—had led him to emphasize the mystical vision of God. Only faith, in his view, could give the certainty that others claimed to find in the intellect. Thus the only truth that mattered was the truth of faith, given to man by the grace of God.

Avicenna

Avicenna became the most influential of all Muslim philosopher-scientists. He was born in Bukhara in 980 and soon showed himself the possessor of an exceptional mind. He had memorized the Koran by age ten. He soon outdistanced all his teachers and by eighteen was honored as an outstanding autodidact, and by twenty-one he was already a famous physician. At this time political upheavals in Persia and Afghanistan, where he spent most of his years, led to his embarking on a wandering, tumultuous life. Despite his troubles, he became the most productive of all Arabic writers.

Avicenna wrote two very large works, as well as many shorter ones. The first, *The Book of Healing*, is a vast philosophical and scientific encyclopedia, said to be the most comprehensive work of its kind ever composed by a single person. An encyclopedia of the medical knowledge of his time, *The Canon of Medicine*, became one of the famous books of medicine.

Both works were based on classical models. *The Book of Healing*, in particular, was laced with Aristotelian doctrine on all subjects except ethics and politics, which Avicenna did not discuss, perhaps a course he took for his own political reasons.

Both works were translated into Latin and exerted a great influence on Scholastics in the West, who were beginning to awaken to the realization that there might be more to knowledge than the interpretation and reinterpretation of the Scriptures, Augustine's *City of God*, and Boethius's translation of the *Organon*. They thirsted after the information that Avicenna gave them about Aristotle and Greek thought generally. Evidently the Greeks had been stalwart defenders of the claims of reason to provide real and valuable truths. But the Scholastics still could not read Aristotle himself, for there were no texts available in the West for a century after Avicenna's death in 1037.

Peter Abelard

No medieval scholar is better known than this brilliant, star-crossed teacher, whose fateful love affair with Heloïse has been the subject of many books and plays.

Born in Britanny in 1079, Peter Abelard was the son of a knight. He gave up his inheritance and a military career to study philosophy, particularly logic, of which he became the most proficient practitioner and teacher of his time.

It was an era for great teachers and logicians. Paris had become a petri dish of theological controversy, with students flocking from one teacher to another and rioting in the streets over logical points and questions of scriptural interpretation. Abelard threw himself into these controversies, partly for the excitement of it. He also took a few private pupils, including Heloïse (c.1098–1164), the brilliant and beautiful seventeen-year-old niece of Canon Fulbert (c.960–1028) of the Cathedral of Notre Dame de Paris.

Abelard seduced Heloïse, or perhaps Heloïse seduced Abelard; they had a son, and later they were secretly married. Canon Fulbert was furious, mainly because of the secrecy. Both Abelard and Heloïse feared that news of their marriage would put an end to Abelard's academic career. In any event, Fulbert hired gangsters, who waylaid and castrated Abelard. He spent the rest of his life in a torment of bitterness about his lost hopes. For a *castrato* could have no great church career.

Heloïse did not desert him, nor did he desert her. He continued to act as her spiritual advisor as she gained important ecclesiastical posts. Together they published a collection of their love letters, one of the most beautiful and revealing medieval books. Abelard need hardly have feared for his career. Even as a eunuch he attracted hordes of students, and the problem was to find time for his own work.

His most famous theological work, *Sic et Non* (Yes and No), consisted of a collection of apparent contradictions drawn from various sources, together with commentaries showing how to resolve the contradictions and providing rules for resolving others. In a fiercely disputacious age, marked by logical battles between students and between students and teachers, the book soon became very popular. Abelard also wrote a shorter work, *Scito te ipsum* (Know Thyself), which advanced the notion that sin consists not in deeds, which in themselves are neither good nor bad, but only in intentions. Sin is not the thing done, it is the consent of the mind to what it knows is wrong.

Abelard was chastised by the authorities, partly for his way of life, partly for his doctrines. He maintained a superficial appearance of orthodoxy, but underlying everything he wrote was a clear preference for reason over faith. His work and life alike challenged the dominant Augustinism of his time—and implicitly appealed to the Aristotelians to advance the cause of reason against the mysticism of the old way.

Abelard has often been considered a martyr to the future. He suffered castration, condemnation, silencing, and finally death (in 1142) to keep alive the mind of the West and to pave the way for the triumph of reason. This view romanticizes his life, which was not romantic in a modern way. But it does emphasize the role he played in the opposition between the two polar theological positions. Abelard was a Boethius man, and one of the greatest.

Bernard of Clairvaux

Abelard's major foe was this medieval Benedictine and saint, known as *doctor mellifluus* (for the honeyed sweetness of his style). Bernard, born in 1090 of a noble Burgundian family, entered the Benedictine order at Citeaux while still a young man. In love with God, and especially with the Virgin Mary, he soon threw himself into his monastic duties with such passionate intensity that he ruined his health. Despite his excesses of austerity (to mortify his pride he lived for years in a tiny stone cell that was flooded by two feet of water when it rained), he lived to the age of sixty-three.

Bernard had a simple favorite prayer: "Whence arises the love of God? From God. And what is the nature of this love? To love without measure." Such statements, by no means unprecedented, puzzled and perhaps infuriated Abelard, who believed in rational measure and could hardly conceive of a God who did not.

Bernard, the confidant, advisor, and severe critic of five popes, saw immediately how things stood. "This man," he said of Abelard, "presumes to be able to comprehend by human reason the entirety of God." Thus it was Bernard who got the pope to silence Abelard, to reduce him to a meager life in the monastery at Cluny, and who probably broke his heart. Bernard was one of the greatest Augustinians, and the supporters of Aristotle still had a long and weary road to travel.

Averroës

Until the time of this Arabic philosopher and commentator, Aristotle's actual doctrines remained rather dark and confusing to scholars of the West. But Averroës not only wrote about Aristotle in works that earned him the sobriquet of "The Commentator," he also included portions of the original texts of such books as the *Ethics*, the *Metaphysics*, and *On the Heavens* (or rather, Arabic translations of the original Greek, which in turn were translated into Latin so that men like Albertus Magnus and Thomas Aquinas could read them). The effects were explosive.

Averroës was born in 1126 in Córdoba, in Moorish Spain, at the time the greatest city of the West. Well educated, he soon acquired a reputation for learning and served a succession of caliphs as advisor, judge, and physician. Between 1169 and 1195 he published a series of commentaries on most of Aristotle's works (except the *Politics*, which may or may not have been available to him).

Averroës aimed to raise philosophy to what he believed was its rightful place in Islam. He failed to achieve this goal, for Islam had become as God-obsessed as Christianity. It was not an age when Muslims could feel free to speculate about religious matters.

Nevertheless, Averroës continued his critical commentaries, which included a major reinterpretation of Plato's *Republic*, in which he concluded that the Republic was the ideal state, lacking only a notion of Muhammed and the One God he had prophesized. Among other things, Averroës lamented the fact that Islam had not adopted Plato's view of women as the equal of men and had thus failed to give them civic equality. Such treatment, he thought, would have improved the economy.

Averroës had little or no effect on Islamic thought, but he was very influential in the West. His influence was not due to any particular views he held but because he revealed to scholars in the Christian world Aristotle's attitude toward nature.

Augustine had interpreted Plato and the Neoplatonists as holding that the natural world—"reality"—was a mere shadow of a greater reality which was, in some sense, the mind of God. It was now becoming apparent that Aristotle had not agreed. For Aristotle, nature possessed a hard substantiality, and he had known a lot about it. Moreover, he had believed it was philosophy's task to know about nature. He considered it an endeavor of great import for mankind.

It may be difficult today to comprehend why such views were so revolutionary, since we have long since accepted them. But the thinkers of the Middle Ages had doubted and even ignored them for centuries. It had been so long since anyone with intellectual authority, certainly with the kind of authority that Aristotle possessed, had advanced such ideas that at first it was hard to take them in.

Aristotle's *Organon* had been known through the translations of Boethius. But the *Organon* dealt with the laws of thought, with logic, and with philosophical method. The science of logic is at a remove from nature. Aristotle's *Physics*, his short treatises on such subjects as memory, dreams, longevity, and so forth, his *History of Animals*, the *Parts of Animals*, the *Generation of Animals*, to say nothing of the *Rhetoric* and *Poetics*, revealed a mind that was as interested in ordinary as in divine things, and was obviously not prejudiced against the study of these down-to-earth subjects because doing so would not necessarily lead to the mind of God.

In fact, a perusal of Averroës's commentaries could lead one to suspect that Aristotle, who had little to say about God but a lot to say about modest matters like worms and insects, the copulation of cattle, the weather, and flatulence, might even have been more interested in them than in theology. Which was a thoroughly revolutionary, not to say dangerous notion.

Averroës was a devout Muslim. Seeing the danger, he never ceased to insist that, whatever Aristotle might seem to suggest, there was in fact only one truth, contained in the Koran. What might seem like truth in the natural sphere was but the shadow of a higher truth. But this was rather like warning children not to put beans up their noses. The temptation to do such a surprising thing soon becomes irresistible.

People wondered. Why was Averroës so insistent that there was only one truth, and that the truth of religion? Was it perhaps because there was another and a different truth, the truth of nature, of the lower world; and if so, was this truth merely a shadow, or did it have a separate reality?

Thus the idea grew in the West that Averroës had advanced the doctrine of two truths, the one of God, the other of nature, with two different logics, and two different methods. It was, moreover, believed that Averroës thought the truth of nature was equally honorable. He did not think those things. But it was enough that western Christians believed he did.

This was the most serious challenge that Augustinians had so far faced. And the challenge was not easily overcome. By now the Augustinian tradition had devoted some seven hundred years to the study of theology, thus exhausting itself. Young men in the schools of Paris found it impossible not to be fascinated by the new notion that the natural world, the City of Man, was as worthy of study as the City of God. What Averroës, who died in 1198, had tried to avoid—the splitting of truth into two—seemed inevitable.

Thomas Aquinas

This famous priest, Doctor of the Church, and future saint, the immortal hero of the Dominican order, was as fat as he was indefatigable in his researches and writings. It is said that a special altar was constructed for him, with a large half-moon cut out of it, so that he could reach the Host with his short arms while saying mass. During his lifetime Thomas Aquinas possessed a degree of fame seldom enjoyed by mere human beings.

Thomas was born in Aquino, on the road between Rome and Naples, in 1224 or 1225. He enrolled in the monastery of Monte Cassino in the hope that he might become abbot of this powerful institution, to the great benefit of his family. After nine years as a pupil of the Benedictines, when Emperor Frederic II temporarily disbanded the monks at Cassino, Thomas went to Naples to continue his studies at the university. He also became a member of the Dominicans, then a newly founded order of mendicants who emphasized preaching and teaching.

In 1244 his new superiors ordered him to Paris, where they hoped he could escape the control of his family. But his family kidnapped him on the road and kept him prisoner in their house for a year. Thomas stubbornly refused to give in and finally obtained his freedom. He arrived in Paris in 1245, where he took up residence in the convent of Saint-Jacques, the university center of the Dominicans.

Enrolled as a student of Albertus Magnus, the greatest teacher of the era, Thomas spent seven more years studying theology, philosophy, and history before finally obtaining his degree as master of theology, but he did not receive his license to teach until 1256. He was now over thirty and would have fewer than twenty years to live.

Paris was the most exciting place in the world for a man of Thomas's bent in those middle years of the thirteenth century. Everyone was a theologian, either amateur or professional. Points of doctrine were argued on street corners and at breakfast and dinner. Two overarching controversies beset the times. Of course, Thomas threw himself with all his energy into both.

One involved the doctrine of universals. The question of universals is of no importance today; in 1250 it was a killing matter. When I use words like "red," "human," and "good," what do I mean by those universal terms? Obviously, in saying that something is red, I mean to suggest that it shares a quality with all other red things. But is "red" the name of something that separately exists? Is there something I can call "redness" (or "humanness" or "goodness") which exists apart from red things (or human or good things)?

Plato, the Neoplatonists, and, following them, Augustine, tended to believe in the real existence of universals. In fact, they seemed to hold that universals were the only things that did exist, and that red, human, and good things were but shadows of reality. According to Plato, the philosopher breaks through the fog and confusion of the apparently real and, by the light of the intellect, discerns the ultimate reality, which is clear, mathematical, and incorporeal. According to Augustine, the theologian, by his abstention from the pleasures of the senses and contempt for the world's goods, manages to rise up from the City of Man, heavy with dust and sin, to the mystical glory of the City of God.

Those who believed in the real existence of universals were called Realists. In opposition to them were philosophers who thought that the only real things were *things*, while general terms like "red," "human," and "good" were mere names. They were called Nominalists.

Aristotle had taken a position somewhere in between the Realists and the Nominalists and was therefore called a Modified Realist. The world is full of things. Every existing thing (like a red cow, a human being, or a good deed) requires two elements for it to exist: its form and its matter.

The form of a human being is his or her humanness. It is that element in the individual existing person that allows us to recognize him or her as human. It is a universal term, for all human beings are human in the same way, although they may be different in every other respect. The matter of an individual person is his or her individuality, his or her potentiality, his or her difference from all other human beings. It is our humanness that makes us *human* beings, and not some *other* kind of being. It is our matter that makes us Tom, Dick, or Mary.

So far, so good. But there were serious difficulties hidden in this Aristotelian formulation of the problem of universals. First of all, what about the crucial distinction between the soul and the body? Was the form of an individual human being his or her soul, or spirit? Did the form exist separately from its incorporation in a living, breathing human being?

If the form was the soul, then surely it must exist separately, for as every Christian knew, the soul was eternal, whereas the body was not. But was the soul individual, or was it just the form, humanness? Was it humanness that was eternal, or was there something about Tom, Dick, or Mary that endured forever, recognizably as Tom, Dick, or Mary? If so, that individual something seemed to be rather like Aristotle's matter. But the soul was not material.

Obviously, there were traps for the unwary in these discussions of the problem of universals, and one could die at the stake for supporting erroneous solutions. Errors were unlikely for Realists. They could view the living, breathing human being as merely a way station on the long journey of the soul to eternal damnation or bliss. An individual spent an instant as Tom, Dick, or Mary and then spent the rest of eternity enjoying, or regretting, how he or she had lived. The important thing was to reject the blandishments of the Earthly City, to have contempt for the world, to mortify the flesh, and to remember that one must die, while at the same time, and with all one's heart, striving to achieve the mystical vision of God that would sustain a person in this life and the next.

For the Nominalists, and especially for Thomas Aquinas, matters seemed not so simple. For one, the Nominalists and Aquinas had to consider the crucial importance of an individual's behavior (both physical and mental) during a lifetime, however short, however introductory. And there was the compelling reality of that life, and of nature as a whole. Human beings were placed here by a loving God on an earth teeming with beings and full of intellectual puzzles, equipped with a superb mental apparatus (especially if you were Thomas Aquinas) for dealing with those puzzles. Had God really not meant for man to think? Had he intended man to pass through the Earthly City with blinders, and with his eyes on another existence in the future?

The second great controversy that roiled the schools of Paris involved Aristotle's notion of nature itself, and how it was to be viewed and understood. Aristotle, as Averroës had shown, had been profoundly interested in the natural world. He had seen nothing wrong or ignoble in this interest, nothing that placed the soul in danger of damnation.

It was true that Aristotle had not been a Christian, but he was *the* Philosopher. Could he have been so totally wrong about nature as to view it in direct opposition to the way God wanted man to view it?

Man, said Thomas Aquinas, joins together, for better or worse, the two cities, that of God and that of Man. As far as his being goes, he is situated at the juncture of two universes, "like a horizon of the corporeal and the spiritual." One of these may rise and the other fall, but as long as man is man (and not a mere spirit), both are present, and both must be dealt with and understood for the sake of salvation.

It was one thing to condemn the world, but to be ignorant of its power and meaning was surely a mistake. How many men and women had been damned because they had misjudged the strength of the temptations offered by the world? Perhaps only Jesus Christ had been immune to temptation. But no mere human being could afford to be ignorant of what he had to face—or why did the Church preach to men and warn them?

In man, Thomas said, there is not only a distinction between spirit and nature (form and matter, soul and body), there is also a strange unity. Look in the mirror: where does the body stop and the soul begin? Look into the mind. The same question has no easier answer.

For threescore years and ten, body and spirit comprise a seamless garment, a miracle of the joining together of apparent opposites. And because the two are joined, there cannot be two truths, the one of the spirit, the other of the body; of religion and of nature; of the Earthly City and the Heavenly. It does not matter how short or long is seventy years as measured against eternity; eternity is not measured in years, it is a mere instant, it is no time at all. Besides, we know so much about those seventy years and so little about eternity.

That view proved *very* dangerous. In January 1274 Thomas was summoned before a council at Lyons to answer for his opinions, and publicly chastised, although not condemned, as Abelard had been. His defense was different from Abelard's. He said what everyone knew, that he was a true believing Catholic Christian, and that his sincere faith included a certain belief in the mystical godhead and in his own inability to comprehend it without God's help. But he did not disavow the unity of truth, and they did not make him do so.

What Thomas Aquinas had tried to do was to resolve once and for all the question of the two cities, the one of God and the other of Man, which had lain at the heart of theological speculation for a thousand years. Augustine had viewed them as in eternal conflict. Thomas tried to bring them together in peace. In effect, he tried to write a single constitution for both cities that contained no internal contradictions. He tried harder than anyone ever had, and he was the greatest thinker to do so. But he failed, as the next century decided.

The Pyrrhic Victory of Faith over Reason

Two intellectual parties opposed him in his attempt. On the one hand, there were the religious enthusiasts who considered—and who still believe today—that reason, the light of the natural intellect, is a kind of intruder in the realm of mystical communion between God and man. The heart has its reasons, as the mystic Blaise Pascal (1623–1662) would affirm, that reason does not comprehend. The heart is overcome by the ecstasy of sudden belief, and what matter then all the long arguments? Such thinkers were, and are, impatient with the efforts of St. Thomas Aquinas to bring them to God along a reasonable road.

On the other hand, a minority existed even in the thirteenth century who did not see why natural reason had to bow down before the ruler of the City of God, whoever and whatever he might be. Where was the evidence that he existed and that he demanded obedience? It was lacking. However, much evidence existed that the world was real and demanded understanding. The thirteenth century in which Thomas Aquinas lived was an age of prosperity and technological progress, when a previously primitive agricultural economy was changing to a mercantile, urban society. Every day men learned new things that made life better. It was unthinkable to reject history and return to the darkness of ages past.

The opposing parties agreed on one thing, namely, on the doctrine of two truths. For the religious enthusiasts, there was the crucial truth of the City of God and the trifling truth of the City of Man. For the naturalists, the emphasis went the other way. Their combined weight proved too much for Thomas Aquinas, despite his brilliance and fame. And perhaps he died in 1274 knowing he had failed to bring together the two cities under one immortal polity as well as in his attempt to end what he considered to be the vicious error of the two truths.

The triumph of the two truths was heralded by the "subtle doctor," the Franciscan Duns Scotus (1265–1308), who wrote at the turn of the fourteenth century. God is absolutely free, proclaimed Duns Scotus, and absolute freedom means being free of reason's necessity, as well as of all else. What is logically necessary must necessarily be so, Thomas had said; no, said Duns Scotus, God is not circumscribed in any way whatsoever, least of all by the human mind, with its reasons that cannot determine God.

William of Ockham (1300–1349), another Franciscan, went even further. He said the only real things are singular entities like an apple or a man. Universals have no existence whatever; they are mere names. Nature, moreover, consists only of things, and the human reason only permits man to "encounter" them. Nothing that man deduces about things has validity, and particularly what he deduces about the divine; faith and reason, therefore, have nothing whatever in common. Each has its own truth, but the one is vastly more important than the other, with the one determining salvation, the other the mere comfort of the body during this life.

Thus ended the great controversy, with a whimper instead of a bang. For another three centuries theology would retain intellectual dominion. But it had built a wall to protect itself from human reason, and reason was no longer on its side. As with all walls, this one had the opposite effect from what was intended.

Beyond the wall, the proponents of reason and study of the natural world were free to build up their strength, unimpeded, even unobserved. Finally, they would burst through the defenses and sweep all before them. And our modern world, forgetting Thomas Aquinas's warning, would completely discard the City of God and erect a new City of Man on the ruins of the spiritual world. Only one truth would exist. It would be the truth of nature, and faith would be an exile from it.

Dante's Dance

When did the Middle Ages end? There were medieval vestiges in Europe as late as the eighteenth century. On the other hand, eleventh-century men like Abelard and Roger Bacon were modern. The ending came somewhere in between.

Dante chose 1300, a Jubilee Year, as the symbolic moment of his great poem, *The Divine Comedy*. The date is as appropriate as any other, and more accurate than most, for marking the end of the Middle Ages and the beginning of the Renaissance.

The life of Dante Alighieri is as well known as his poem. Born in Florence in 1265, he fell into evil ways as a young man, whereupon he met Beatrice (she was only seven when he first saw her), who by her example and, especially, her glorious smile of greeting drew him back to the right way. She married another man and died young, while he lived on, to die in Ravenna in 1321, but he never forgot her or her smile. He dedicated the *Commedia* to Beatrice, proclaiming that in it he had said of her "what no man had ever said of a woman." She played a starring part in his cosmic drama, leading his soul to God and to the mystical vision with which the poem ends.

The *Comedy* is divided into three parts, Hell, Purgatory, and Heaven. Many people read only Hell, partly because Hell is more interesting than Heaven, since it is more like the world they know. Dante's Heaven, or *Paradiso*, interests us because many of the persons we have mentioned in this chapter are characters in it, and some of them play major roles. It is St. Bernard, in fact, who introduces Dante to the Virgin Mary, who in turn helps him take the final step to God.

In the tenth canto of the *Paradiso*, Dante, who has traveled through Hell and Purgatory under the guidance of the poet Virgil and has now reached Heaven with Beatrice as his guide, enters the sphere of the Sun. Here, in the brilliant light of the intellect, he discerns a number of still brighter points of light, dazzling to his eyes. The lights move, making a circle around him and Beatrice, and performing a slow, graceful dance. The lights circle them thrice, and then the circle stops, breathless, waiting, "like ladies not freed from the dance, but pausing in silence until they have caught the next strain."

One of the lights speaks, and Dante hears through his inner, mental ear. The spirit introduces himself as Thomas of Aquino, and points out, round him in the circle, Albertus Magnus, Peter Lombard, Solomon, Pseudo-Dionysius, Boethius, and others.

These are all the great theologians, and with several of them Thomas has had more or less violent differences on theological questions, but now all their conflicts are resolved. Dante makes us hear in our own mind's ear the chiming of the little bell that wakes the monasteries at dawn and calls the faithful to the first prayer of the day, their souls swelling with love. Whereupon, with the majesty and grace that befit the greatest theologians, the wheel of lights begins to circle once more, "with harmony and sweetness that cannot be known but there where joy becomes eternal."

Dante spent his last twenty-five years as an exile, banished from Florence and condemned by it to death for the crime of being on the wrong side in one of the periodic political paroxisms that rent his city. He had seen little or no harmony and sweetness in his own life.

Yet his wish that we accept the harmony and peace of Heaven is so deep and fervent that we do accept it, or almost do, at least as long as we are reading him. It was a noble desire, in that Holy Year of 1300, with Christians everywhere celebrating the anniversary of the birth of Jesus Christ and the much more recent transformation, in the public consciousness, of his mother from just a woman to almost a member of the Trinity. And in poetry it could happen, if in real life it could not.

Thus the Middle Ages ended in splendor and in abject failure. Dante was the culmination of everything that a thousand years of obsession with God could produce. Allegorically, symbolically, mystically, his vision of a universe structured by reason and unified by faith came together and worked.

But in the teeming life of the new fourteenth century, nothing came together and worked. By the year of Dante's death his vision had already begun to fade, although the memory of it would inspire men and women for centuries.

Like any utopia, what the Middle Ages had attempted was a noble experiment, but one that human beings were not equipped to make succeed. One can only wonder that the theocratic state, based on divine harmony and the peace of God, lasted as long as it did. The experiment was undertaken at a rare moment in human history which may never come again, short of another cataclysm like the fall of the Roman empire. But the memory of that great, failed experiment, based on the assumption that God ruled the world for the real and continuing benefit of mankind, haunts us to this day. Some, perhaps many, are almost seduced by the temptation to try the experiment again.

6

What Was Reborn in the Renaissance?

IN THE TENTH CANTO of the *Purgatorio*, Dante, guided by Virgil, enters the circle of the Proud. There, those who sinned during their lives because of their pride are absolved by seeing examples of humility all around them. As they patiently circle the mountain that they must climb, they repeatedly pass by didactic reliefs carved in a wall of rock.

Four of these reliefs are described by Dante in detail. First, the Angel Gabriel, who, obedient to God's command and in the adoration of his heart, hails the Virgin with the famous greeting: "Hail, Mary, full of grace!" Second, the Virgin herself, who responds in those words that are the symbol of humility: "*Ecce ancilla dei!* Behold the handmaiden of the Lord!" Third, King David humbly dances before the Ark, legs bared, while his proud wife, Michal, looks down scornfully from her high window. Fourth, the Roman emperor Trajan humbly accedes to the plea of a poor widow, who grasps his bridle and begs him to serve her need before he serves his own.

The symbolism is clear enough. But Dante adds some art criticism to his moral lesson. The carvings were "such," he says, "that not only Polyclitus but nature would be put to shame there." Polyclitus was the Greek sculptor whom Dante knew (by reputation only) as the greatest classical artist. The works he sees carved in the wall are more splendid than those Polyclitus composed. They are even greater than what nature can do. They are more real than real.

Dante lived around the turn of the fourteenth century. At that time the influence of Gothic sculpture descended into Italy from northern Europe and revivified all the arts. Gothic sculptors emphasized realism in their carvings of religious subjects, and this new realistic bent soon overcame the abstract, symbolic Byzantine style that had previously been dominant in most of Italy.

Pisan and Florentine sculptors began to imitate the Gothic style. Dante's friend and fellow Florentine, Giotto (c.1270–1317), painted frescoes that had a new realism and vitality. Dante himself excelled in the *dolce stil nuovo*, the "sweet new style" of writing verse that focused on the experiences of real, even ordinary, people. (In the *Purgatorio* Dante says of Giotto, "In painting Cimabue thought to hold the field and now Giotto has the cry, so that the other's fame is dim.")

The New Style in Painting: Perspective

Realistic portrayals of the lives and acts of ordinary people are not the only thing that art can do, and it is not what art traditionally had accomplished throughout the centuries leading up to Dante's time. And even during the fourteenth century, there were artists who held out against the new style. The painters of the Sienese school, in particular, continued to produce works that were notably Byzantine in style, with their quiet, stylized faces and forms and their obvious religious symbolism. For this reason we usually do not think of the fourteenth-century Sienese painters, great as they were, as being part of the Italian Renaissance. They were great painters, but they were not Renaissance artists.

As the Renaissance spread throughout Europe, it everywhere produced a new style in art that emphasized realism, naturalness, and verisimilitude. The subjects often remained the same as in the old Byzantine symbolic style: the Annunciation, the Crucifixion, the Deposition, the Marriage at Cana, and the like. But now the people depicted reflected the viewer's world, expressed feelings like his own, and moved him, as a consequence, in an entirely new way.

Giotto, though a master, was not a wholly Renaissance painter, in that he did not experiment with perspective as the Florentine artists of the fifteenth century did (the quattrocento, as Italians say). The discovery of the possibilities of perspective helped to produce works of art that are decidedly more familiar to us than those of Giotto (to say nothing of Cimabue), and more "Renaissance-looking." Perspective provided the painters of the century after the death of Giotto and Dante with expanded opportunities to emphasize realism and to bring the viewer into the picture.

Again, the Sienese resisted, refusing to employ perspective for a century. By the time they finally gave in, the Italian (more precisely, the Florentine) Renaissance style had become totally dominant, and indeed it dominated European painting for three hundred years thereafter, until in France in the late nineteenth century painters began to experiment with another new style that was as innovative as the Renaissance style had been.

Let us be sure that we understand the meaning of perspective. In such a painting straight lines (often imaginary) converge in what is called a vanishing point, located somewhere in the background (often at the center of the horizon). This gives the impression of a real scene that is visible to the viewer.

In fact, however, the effect is obtained by making the eye of the viewer the vanishing, or gathering, point of the lines of perspective. Thus light flows from his eye onto the objects that he sees, as from a centrally located lamp (or the sun). It is his vision, uniquely, that constitutes the image that is the painting.

This approach had never been used before, in any art, and it has not been done since in any other art beside that of the West (or art so deeply influenced by western art that it has lost its own special character). Even in western art it is often no longer done. The Fauvist painters in France broke the perspective pattern around 1900, the Cubists shattered it into tiny pieces, and it has seldom been put back together again except in derivative imitations of traditional styles.

Modern works of art call in question whether Renaissance works employing perspective really did produce a greater sense of realism and verisimilitude, despite what Dante said. At any rate, the camera does this better than perspective-trained artists. But although the camera creates a certain kind of realism, it does not do other things that painting can achieve (and that Renaissance painting could accomplish).

Man in the Cosmos

The new art of perspective said something radically different and new about the position and role of human beings in the cosmos, in the world picture, as we might say (using a term from a later age). In pre-Renaissance art, the scene depicted is seen not from the viewpoint of the beholder, an ordinary human, but from the viewpoint of God, from a point at infinity, so to speak, from which both space and time are reduced to relative nothingness as compared to the religious image, icon, or idea, which is an internal rather than an external vision.

The Sienese chose not to adopt perspective, because they wanted to retain this inward vision, or rather, because they did not wish to lose it, as they thought the Florentines were doing. The Florentines were willing to give up the inward vision because they wanted their art to say something else about the role of man in the world, and that inevitably meant saying something else about the role of religion in the world.

One of the greatest quattrocento paintings, by one of its greatest painters, Piero della Francesca (1420–1492), exemplified this new vision. Though born in Borgo Sansepolcro, Piero was trained in Florence in the 1440s and was Florentine in spirit. In Urbino, under the patronage of Federico da Montefeltro, he produced some of the best of his mature works, among them the famous *Flagellation* that has taunted and frustrated critics for nearly five hundred years.

Among other things, the painting is a study in perspective, as was every painting of Piero's. (He was a master geometer and wrote treatises on the subject.) It is divided into two parts. On the left, in the background, near the vanishing point of the perspective, Christ, a small, forlorn figure, stands bound to a column, while Roman soldiers raise their whips to torture him. On the right, in the foreground, depicted in vibrant colors, stand three Renaissance dandies, conversing with one another (about what? money? women?). They pay no attention to the drama that is taking place behind them. Their eyes are turned away from the suffering of the Son of God, and they evidently do not hear his moans or the whistle of the scourges as they fall.

Piero was not a skeptic or an unbeliever. He seems to have been a good Christian till his death. His *Resurrection*, in Borgo Sansepolcro, is one of the most ardent depictions of that subject in all painting. Thus he cannot be interpreted as casually depicting, in the *Flagellation* of Urbino, a state of things that he believed *ought* to obtain, in which religion has been pushed into the background, while more mundane subjects come to the fore.

Nevertheless, the painting does reveal a world in which earthly matters are more highly valued. Christ's suffering, though not forgotten, has become almost absurdly unimportant. Significant now are youth, good looks, fine clothes, money, and worldly success (according to the viewer's notion). And this belief, more than realism, naturalism, or verisimilitude, lay at the very center of the Renaissance style in art.

The Romans, and especially the Greeks before them, had viewed the world this way. They, too, had loved youth and good looks, health and money. The Middle Ages had shifted the focus. Now it was turning back to the old central concerns. The Renaissance was the rebirth of many things, but these values lay at the heart of them.

The Revival of Classical Learning: Petrarch

If a precise date is needed for the beginning of the Renaissance, it might well be July 20, 1304, the birth date of Francesco Petrarch, who first saw the light in Arezzo but who preferred to think of himself, in later years, as a Florentine, an Italian, and a man of the world. Educated at Avignon, where his father moved to be closer to the papal court, Petrarch was an autodidact who never stopped studying until his death. He was found dead on the morning of July 19, 1374, with his head resting on an edition of Virgil, on which he had been writing a commentary.

According to Petrarch's account, the most important event of his life occurred when he met a woman known only as Laura in a church at Avignon on April 6, 1327. He was twenty-two. His love for Laura, with whom he apparently did not have an affair, persisted until his death. He wrote his finest poems about her beauty and loveliness; about his love for her, which inspired him; and about his later recognition that he had loved her wrongly, placing her person ahead of her spirit. Laura supposedly died of plague on April 6, 1348, the twenty-first anniversary of their first meeting.

Numerous attempts have been made to identity a real woman (who may or may not have been named Laura, a word that in Latin can mean "fame") whom Petrarch loved, but without success, and there is some doubt that such a woman actually existed. Petrarch was aware of the power of Dante's love for Beatrice (who *was* a real woman), of how she had inspired him to write immortal verse. He was capable of creating Laura out of whole cloth and of falling in love (as a muse, at least) with his creation.

It is perhaps unjust to accuse Petrarch, after all these centuries, of making up Laura as a kind of publicity stunt, and then of spending the rest of his life pining for her in a literary way. And one does not have to accuse him of that. It is important to recognize that he was capable of creating such a vision, for he was a very skilled promoter, of himself and of greater things, and if he had desired to offer himself as the heir of Dante, inventing Laura would have been one good way to do it.

Petrarch also wished to be seen as the heir of mankind's first majestic flowering. As a youth he fell in love with the classics, with Greece and Rome and the civilization that had crumbled away a thousand years before. So far as he could, he devoted his life to attempting to revive and recreate that civilization. Thus he preferred to perceive himself as an ancient Roman, come to life once more, his greatest desire to promote a rebirth of Greece and Rome.

By the time he turned thirty-five, Petrarch was already one of the most famous scholars in Europe, mostly due to his great learning, partly because of his uncanny ability to bring his talents and achievements to the attention of the right people. In 1340 he found himself in the position of being able to choose between two invitations: to be crowned poet laureate in Paris, or in Rome. He had arranged for the invitations himself, and he chose Rome. He was crowned on the Capitol on April 8, 1341. (He would have preferred April 6, the anniversary date of his meeting with Laura, but events delayed the ceremony.) Afterward he placed his laurel crown on the tomb of the Apostle in St. Peter's Basilica, to make the occasion even more memorable and to emphasize that in becoming an ancient Roman reborn he was not thereby unchristian.

Inventing the Renaissance: Boccaccio

Giovanni Boccaccio was born in Paris in 1313, although the fact that his father was a Florentine allowed him in later years to call himself one, too. Like Petrarch, he was destined by his family for a career in business or law. Also like Petrarch, he managed to educate himself and to become a successful author.

He spent a number of years in Naples, one of the centers of courtly poetry. He, too, embarked on a hopeless love affair, this time with a young woman whom he called Fiammetta ("Little Flame"), who almost surely did not exist. In 1348 he retired from plague-stricken Florence, and in a country residence began to write the *Decameron*, a wonderful cycle of stories.

For our purposes, the great event of Boccaccio's life was also one of the great events of Petrarch's—their meeting in Florence in 1350. Petrarch was forty-six, Boccaccio thirty-seven. Boccaccio had already written an admiring book about Petrarch, but it was the likeness of their spirits that drew them together, made them fast friends, and engaged them in the joint work, which occupied them until Petrarch's death twenty-four years later, of creating the Renaissance.

In order to bring about a rebirth of the classics, both Petrarch and Boccaccio realized, they had to be able to read them. They had little difficulty understanding classical Latin; the problem was to find the texts, many of which existed only by reputation. Petrarch was certain, and he convinced Boccaccio, that the texts of many famous works must lie hidden away, perhaps even forgotten, in monastic libraries. They traveled about southern Europe, poking through archives, turning over the pages of ancient books. In this way Petrarch discovered a number of Cicero's letters. Supposedly they had been lost forever.

Classical Greek was another matter. Petrarch knew of no one who could read it, and his efforts to learn it by himself came to nothing. He admitted this sore point to Boccaccio, who consequently threw himself into the study of classical Greek with the help of a man named Leonzio Pilato, who at Boccaccio's instigation was named Reader in Greek at the University of Florence.

Pilato had spent some time in Byzantium, where many persons could still read classical Greek and where copies of the works of Homer and other ancient Greek authors could still be found. Pilato knew enough Greek to make rough translations of the *Iliad* and *Odyssey* into Latin. They were the first such translations of those two epics, known by reputation (and from an ancient Latin synopsis) as the greatest of all literary works.

Boccaccio learned a little Greek, and when he brought Pilato and his translation of the *Iliad* to Petrarch, the latter knelt down before his two visitors, much inferior to him in living fame, and thanked them for their great gift. Thus began, in the year 1361, the Greek studies by the Human-. ists that were to continue for more than three centuries.

Petrarch, as befitted an ancient Roman, wrote several of his works in Latin. A fine Latin it was, too, though not as elegant as the Latin written by later Humanists, who had had more opportunity to study the classical Latin authors. But Petrarch's *Rime*, or lyrics, most of them about his love for Laura, were in Italian.

There were two reasons for his choice of the common, or vulgar, native tongue. First, Dante had written his *Vita Nuova*, a collection of lyrics about Beatrice, in Italian. He had also composed the *Divine Comedy* in Italian. Second, Petrarch's desire to revive classical learning did not necessarily entail writing in the classical languages. Reading was one thing, writing another, and Petrarch knew that to attract a wide audience he would have to write in the vernacular. He also wished to raise the language of everyday life (that is, Italian) to a level of excellence that could be compared to the standard of the Latin of the Golden Age. For the same reason, Boccaccio wrote all of his major works in Italian, including *Il Filostrato* (the source of Chaucer's *Troilus and Criseyde*) and the *Decameron*; the latter was narrated in racy Italian prose.

At their meetings Petrarch and Boccaccio talked about a rebirth of learning and plotted its success. They urged their idea on all who would listen, including the popes, who, from time to time, employed both of them on diplomatic missions and thus provided them with much of their income. And they managed to win the attention of a lot of people.

Not everyone, however. It was harder to revive ancient learning than they had thought. In October 1373 Boccaccio began a course of public readings of the *Divine Comedy* in the church of Santo Stefano in Florence. He accompanied the readings with commentaries, explaining to his largely illiterate audience of common people the meaning and relevance of what Dante had written.

The revised text of the commentaries has survived. It breaks off after the seventeenth canto of the *Inferno*, at a point where, early in 1374, Boccaccio ended the course because of ill health. But it was not only his weakened state that stopped him. Boccaccio was also dispirited by the raging attacks of the learned against his program of bringing Dante to the attention and understanding of ordinary people. His heart broke only a few months afterward when Petrarch died. Boccaccio himself died just eighteen months later at his home in Certaldo. Those who had loved him and Petrarch, and who had understood what they desired to do, expressed their great dismay and said that now all poetry had become extinct.

The Renaissance Man

The term *Renaissance man* suggests a person, either man or woman, of many accomplishments. A Renaissance man is neither an expert nor a specialist. He or she knows more than just a little about "everything" instead of knowing "everything" about a small part of the entire spectrum of modern knowledge. The term is essentially ironic, for it is universally believed that no one really can be a Renaissance man in the true meaning of the term, since knowledge has become so complex that no human mind is capable of grasping all, or even a large part, of it.

Was there ever a Renaissance man, even during the Renaissance, in that sense of the term? The answer is no. The reason may seem surprising. Knowledge is no more complex today than it was in the fifteenth century. That is, it was just as complex then as it is now. It was no more possible for any human being to know everything about everything then than it is now.

This does not mean that everything we know was known by the men and women of Renaissance times. Obviously, we know many things they did not know. On the other hand, they knew many things we do not. They were much more knowledgeable about theology, for example, a science they took infinitely more seriously than do we. On the whole, they were better philosophers, for again they prized philosophy more highly than we do. Their knowledge of philology was, if not greater than ours, then very different. Those were general fields in which they thought it desirable to specialize, and to them the greatest thinkers devoted their best efforts.

In one general field we are far ahead of Renaissance men. We know vastly more about the way nature works than they did. People of the Renaissance had only just begun to recognize this field of knowledge as both respectable and important. We have concentrated on it, almost to the exclusion of everything else, for nearly five centuries. It is no wonder that we are far ahead of them. It is also no surprise that we remain far behind them with respect to other disciplines they thought more important than natural science.

These remarks are not made in support of their sense of priorities. Like every modern person, I am inclined to believe that our bias toward natural science and away from divine science (if I may make the distinction so simply) is correct. On the whole, we live better today than Renaissance men and women lived, longer, more healthfully, more comfortably, because of our emphasis on natural science.

The point is to correct a fundamental misunderstanding about what was meant by the idea of the "Renaissance man" *in the Renaissance*. As I have said, there never was a Renaissance man in the distorted sense we use today. But there were examples of such remarkable persons in another sense of that term, not only in the Renaissance, but also in classical antiquity and perhaps also in recent times. We shall even have to examine the question whether it is not possible for Renaissance men in the true sense to exist today.

As with so many ideas, this one can be traced back to Aristotle. It is addressed at the beginning of his treatise *On the Parts of Animals*, when he discourses on the method that he will employ in what follows. What he says is both simple and profound:

> Every systematic science, the humblest and the noblest alike, seems to admit of two distinct kinds of proficiency; one of which may be properly called scientific knowledge of the subject, while the other is a kind of educational acquaintance with it. For an educated man should be able to form a fair off-hand judgment as to the goodness or badness of the method used by a professor in his exposition. To be educated is in fact to be able to do this; and even the man of universal education we deem to be such in virtue of his having this ability. It will, however, of course, be understood that we only ascribe universal education to one who in his own individual person is thus critical in all or nearly all branches of knowledge, and not to one who has a like ability merely in some special subject. For it is possible for a man to have this competence in some one branch of knowledge without having it in all.

This famous passage, so full of meaning and usefulness for our own time as well as the Renaissance, may require some comment to be fully comprehensible. First, to the distinction between having "scientific knowledge" of a subject and "educational acquaintance" with it. "Scientific knowledge," here, is the knowledge possessed by a specialist in a given field, which entails knowing not just the general principles and conclusions of the field but also all the detailed findings included therein. As the ancient physician Hippocrates said, "Life is short and the Art long." That is, no individual in the short span of human life can hope to acquire "scientific knowledge" in the sense of knowing everything there is to be known in all fields or branches of knowledge. That was true in Aristotle's day, as he clearly implies, as of course it is true today.

What does Aristotle mean by an "educational acquaintance" with a subject? It is what a man or woman possesses who has been educated in the method of the subject, not just its details and its particular findings and conclusions. Such a person is "critical" in that field. That is, he is able to tell the difference between sense and nonsense, as we might say using modern terms, about the field. A "professor" of the field is an expert, a specialist. But Aristotle recognizes that such a "professor" might be less genuine than he would like you to believe. A person with an "educated acquaintance" with the field would be able to tell if that were so.

"To be educated," says Aristotle, "is in fact to be able to do this." That is, a person can only claim to be educated if he is able to be "critical" in a wide range of scientific knowledge—if he is able to distinguish between sense and nonsense even when he is not a specialist in any one area of knowledge. What an extraordinary claim! And how far it is from our current notion of what being educated means!

Finally, a man of "universal education"—who is none other than our Renaissance man—is one who is "critical" in all or nearly all branches of knowledge. Such a person does not have the "critical" ability in some special subject only. He has it in all, or nearly all.

In the paragraphs that follow the passage quoted above, Aristotle lays down some general methodological principles of what today we would call biology or zoology, the study of the anatomy, reproduction, and general behavior of animals. Following that exposition, he gives us the results of particular investigations he and others have made into the behavior of various species of animals. Much of what he says in this last area is true, but much of it is also suspect. We no longer believe, for example, that "the brain has no continuity with the organs of sense" or that the role of the brain is to "temper the heat and seething of the heart." Aristotle comes to these conclusions because of certain assumptions that he makes about animal life in general, assumptions which are incorrect and which he might have been less inclined to believe if he had understood scientific method better. Nevertheless, his earlier discussion of the principles of scientific methodology is for the most part still correct.

Because he understood how science is (or was) conducted, he could thus claim to be "critical" in all branches of science, that is, able to tell whether a "professor" of a particular branch of science was drawing "likely" conclusions from the phenomena with which he dealt. He was thus "educated" in a large area of knowledge. Aristotle was also well acquainted with the principles of many other fields, from ethics to politics, from rhetoric to poetics, from physics to metaphysics. He could reasonably claim to have an "educated acquaintance" with all or most of the branches of knowledge of his day. He was not, however, an expert or specialist or "professor" in many of them. Perhaps only in the sciences of logic and what he called metaphysics or "first philosophy" could he be viewed as such an expert.

Nevertheless, Aristotle was certainly a Renaissance man. Nor should the title be withheld from several other Greek thinkers, among them

Democritus and Plato, who was not only the premier philosopher of his time but also the premier mathematician.

Renaissance Men: Leonardo, Pico, Bacon

Leonardo da Vinci (1452-1519) was born in Vinci, a small town near Florence, the illegitimate son of a wealthy Florentine and a young peasant girl who was shortly married off to an artisan. Brought up in his father's household, Leonardo was apprenticed to the painters Verrocchio and Antonio Pollaiuolo and was accepted into the Florentine painters' guild when he was twenty. His great reputation as a painter is based on an astonishingly small body of work. Only seventeen surviving paintings can be attributed to him, and several of those are unfinished. Two or three, however, are among the most famous paintings in the world: *The Last Supper* in Milan, *Mona Lisa* and *The Virgin and Child with St. Anne* in the Louvre. Even his unfinished works had enormous influence on his contemporaries and on other great painters during the next two centuries, like Rembrandt and Rubens. He could not pick up a paintbrush or a pencil without making something utterly surprising and new, and he always worked surrounded by pupils.

But painting, although it consumed him, was not the focus of his extraordinarily abundant energies. Painting was only one of the ways in which Leonardo tried to express his immense knowledge of the world. acquired, as he said, simply by looking at things. The secret, he said, was *saper vedere*, "to know how to see." The exhaustiveness and the intensity of his vision are incomparable. He left thousands of closely written pages lavishly illustrated with sketches of every conceivable subject, from anatomy to architecture, from animals to angels, culminating in his final "Visions of the End of the World," a sketchbook in which he tried to depict his sense of the forces of nature, which in his imagination he conceived of as possessing a unity that no one had ever seen before.

Yet almost every one of his vast list of projects remained unfinished at his death, despite his nearly seventy years, his unexampled opportunities, and his habit of working incessantly. Critics have blamed him for a frenzied fragmentation of his thoughts.

I do not think that was Leonardo's problem. Rather, he had misconstrued the Aristotelian idea of the educated man. He sought to be not just educationally acquainted with every subject, but an expert in all of them. His mind brimmed with architectural and engineering plans, with projects for diverting the Arno, casting the largest equestrian statue ever made, constructing a flying machine. Never content with the principles of things, he wished to make everything that he imagined, and was frustrated because he could not do more than draw everything. This frustration was a constant spur to his imagination.

Only recently has the fundamental unity of his thought become apparent, as more and more of his notebooks and manuscripts have been discovered hidden in libraries throughout Europe. Leonardo, although imbued with Scholastic learning and much under the influence of the Aristotelians and their understanding of nature, had also discovered some things the Aristotelians never knew. Stasis, or rest, he realized, was not the supreme principle of the cosmos; restlessness and force were. Any thing could be understood if a person knew what forces had been and were being brought to bear upon it: the forms of animal and human bodies, the shapes of trees and of women's faces, the structures of buildings and mountains, the courses of rivers and the contours of the seacoasts.

Leonardo did not know enough about force or energy to carry his vision to completion. Yet he was evidently seeking a culminating synthesis when he died. He left behind him a host of unfinished work. He was a new kind of Renaissance man, a kind of failed Aristotle of a new world.

Pico della Mirandola's life was short. He was born in the duchy of Ferrara in 1463, eleven years after the birth of Leonardo, and died in Florence at the age of thirty-one. Yet he exhibited an immoderate ambition to study and know everything that has helped to define the term we are examining here. Pico was the Renaissance man *par excellence*; yet ultimately he failed.

Pico received a humanistic education at his father's home. He studied Aristotelian philosophy at Padua and canon law—the law of the Church—at Bologna, and learned Hebrew, Aramaic, and Arabic before he was twenty. He was drawn into "Plato's honey head," as Herman Melville described the sensuous wiles of that magician among philosophers, by the Renaissance Platonist Marsilio Ficino, but he also became acquainted with the Hebrew Kabbala and was the first to use cabalistic doctrine to support Christian theology.

By age twenty-three Pico believed himself the equal in learning of any man alive. In a daunting challenge, perhaps unequaled in history, he proposed in 1486 to defend a list of nine hundred theses drawn from various Greek, Latin, Hebrew, and Arabic authors, and he invited scholars from all of Europe to come to Rome to dispute with him publicly.

The public battle of minds never happened. Unfortunately for Pico, and perhaps for posterity, Pico's list of topics came to the attention of the Vatican, which declared thirteen of them heretical. Pico, stunned, issued an immediate recantation. This was insufficient to keep him out of prison, where he stayed briefly. After that he lived in Florence, nursing his intellectual pride and composing a remarkable document later published as *On the Dignity of Man*. This short, impassioned treatise is an extended commentary on the ancient Protagorean text: "Man is the measure of all things." Man, Pico implied, is the spiritual center of the universe, or perhaps he is one focus and God the other. This would have been sheer heresy a century before, but in those times it passed without notice, and Pico was absolved of heresy in the remarkable year of 1492.

Could Pico have defended all of his theses? Probably not, any more than any person could today (even if the theses were very different, which of course they would be). But Pico dared to try, and to challenge the world of learning. It was the arrogant action of a twenty-three-year-old. It was also the kind of thing that a Renaissance man would never hesitate to do, even if he should inevitably fail.

Poor Pico died in 1494. Francis Bacon was born in London only sixty-seven years later, in January 1561. By this time the Renaissance born in Italy had spread inexorably to northern Europe. Though still a bulwark of Aristotelean Scholasticism, Cambridge, where Bacon was educated, also contained hints and whispers of a new kind of philosophy of nature that fascinated him for the rest of his life.

Bacon was a politician, and he made his living in the service first of Queen Elizabeth and then King James I. He was indefatigable in his labors for his monarch. Posterity has decided he was also unscrupulous to a degree rather rare even in those hard times. His enemies finally caught up with him in 1621. He was accused of taking bribes in his office of lord chancellor, convicted, and sentenced to a large fine and imprisonment. He was soon released from the Tower of London, but he never again held office. It is to this period of withdrawal from public affairs that we owe many of the intellectual productions of his last years.

His *Essays*, written throughout his life and full of pithy wisdom and homely charm, are his most popular work, but it was his *Advancement of Learning* (first edition in English, 1605; second edition in Latin, 1623) and his *Novum Organon* (1620) that constitute his most important contribution to knowledge. They reveal, in all its flawed splendor, the mind of a Renaissance man.

Bacon's famous boast, "I take all knowledge for my province," on the face of it confirms his nomination as a Renaissance man. What did he mean? The boast was essentially Aristotelian; that is, Bacon, not an expert in any science (although he was a consummate politician), nevertheless felt he understood how any scientific investigation ought to be conducted, thus supporting his claim to have an "educated acquaintance" with all branches of the knowledge of his time. But he also fervently opposed Aristotle's method of scientific reasoning, holding that the so-called deductive method was a dead end. He much preferred his own inductive method.

The distinction is no longer widely held to be useful, but it remains interesting, at least. The deductive method, according to Bacon, failed because the seeker after knowledge deduced from certain intuitive assumptions conclusions about the real world that might have been logically correct but were not true to nature. The inductive method succeeded because the student of nature ascended by what Bacon called a "ladder of the intellect" from the most careful and indeed humble observations to general conclusions that had to be true because their foundation was experience.

It is now recognized that scientific method has to combine deduction and induction. The scientist cannot proceed without some sort of hypotheses. But he is also doomed to error if he fails to check his reasoning against nature itself, the final arbiter of the truth of formal statements. Bacon's analysis was useful, if only because it revealed the error of dependence on either mode of reasoning to the exclusion of the other. And his emphasis on experience, on getting your hands dirty in the investigation of nature, was important at a time when many experts shied away from such efforts.

It is thus ironic that Bacon's death was caused by a humble experiment. In March 1626 he was driving through Highgate and suddenly decided to test his idea that cold might delay the putrefaction of meat. He descended from his carriage, bought a chicken, and stuffed it with snow. The fate of the experiment is unknown (although of course the conjecture was right), but Bacon caught a severe chill and died a few weeks later.

Bacon, like Leonardo, failed to complete most of his grandiose projects, and, I think, for the same reason. He was not content merely to know things in a general sense, but desired to be an expert in everything. Nevertheless, his understanding of the nature of knowledge, and especially of the obstacles to its advancement, was profound. It is exemplified in his famous analysis of the so-called idols of the mind.

Bacon's invention of "idols" to explain the existence of human error is itself instructive. Mankind, if not led astray by idolatry, is capable of attaining to much more truth than is ordinarily the case. Bacon identified four different idols, all of them operative in his time and in ours.

The first were the idols of the tribe, certain intellectual faults that are common to all human beings, for example, a universal tendency to oversimplify, which often manifests itself as the assumption of more order in a given body of phenomena than actually exists, and a tendency to be struck by novelty. The latest theory always seems the truest, until the next theory comes along.

Idols of the cave are errors caused by individual idiosyncrasies. One person may concentrate on the likenesses between things, another on the differences. Such habits of thought can only be countered by gathering a large number of persons together in the search for truth so that the idiosyncrasies cancel each other.

Idols of the marketplace are caused by language itself. Bernard Shaw was only half joking when he once remarked that "the English and the Americans have everything in common except language." Different languages cause even greater problems, of course, which is why scientists prefer to communicate with one another in mathematical terms. But a universal language such as mathematics will ultimately fail because the greatest truths cannot become truly useful to the race until they are translated into the language of every man. But every man understands words in a slightly different way from every other, which leads to distortions and flaws in knowledge that are, perhaps, ineradicable.

Finally, Bacon identified what he called idols of the theater, which were philosophical systems that stood in the way of the patient, humble search for truth. Such systems do not have to be philosophical. In the twentieth century different systems of political thought have kept Marxists and democrats from understanding one another. The words may be intelligible, but the ideas behind them conceal their meaning.

The Renaissance Man and the Idea of Liberal Education

The Aristotelean ideal of the educated person, "critical" in all or almost all branches of knowledge, survived for centuries as the aim of a liberal education. Originally, the student would be taught seven arts or skills, consisting of the trivium (grammar, rhetoric, and logic) and the quadrivium (arithmetic, geometry, astronomy, and music). The names are antique, but the seven "subjects" were comparable to a modern liberal curriculum of languages, philosophy, mathematics, history, and science. The arts or skills were "liberal" because they were liberating. That is, they freed their possessor from the ignorance that bound the uneducated.

The twentieth century has seen radical change in this traditional scheme of education. The failure of the Renaissance to produce successful "Renaissance men" did not go unnoticed. If such men as Leonardo, Pico, Bacon, and many others almost as famous could not succeed in their presumed dream of knowing all there was to know about everything, then lesser men should not presume to try. The alternative became self-evident: achieve expertise in one field while others attained expertise in theirs. Much easier to accomplish, this course led to a more comfortable academic community. Now an authority in one field need compete only with experts in his field.

The convenient device for accomplishing the change consisted of a divided and subdivided university, with separate departments, like armed feudalities, facing one another across a gulf of mutual ignorance. The remaining competition involved the use of university funds, which were soon distributed according to principles that had little to do with academic values or knowledge as such. The original belief that an educated person should be "critical" in more fields than his own no longer existed. Eventually, as C. P. Snow (1905–1980) pointed out, the university's separate worlds ceased to talk to one another. The "uni" in the university also became meaningless as the institution, possessing more and more power as government funds were pumped into it for research, turned into a loose confederation of disconnected mini-states, instead of an organization devoted to the joint search for knowledge and truth.

Until World War II, undergraduate colleges, at least, hewed to the liberal ideal, without always doing so enthusiastically. After the war, the liberal curriculum was discarded almost everywhere, and the departmental organization of the educational establishment was installed at all levels below the university, even in many elementary schools.

All that remained, in the popular consciousness, was the sometimes admiring, sometimes ironic, and sometimes contemptuous phrase "Renaissance man," which was applied to almost anyone who manifested an ability to do more than one thing well. Even then, the phrase was never used in its original, Aristotelian sense. That ideal and idea have been lost completely.

Renaissance Humanism

The death of Dante, followed by the passing of Petrarch and Boccaccio, who died within less than two years of one another, meant that Italian literature would never again reach such a high level of greatness. Their demise did not mean the end of their dream of creating a new literature dealing with popular subjects in a high style, and written in the vernacular so that almost everyone might read it. Instead, the dream lived and prospered, undoubtedly beyond even their fondest hopes.

For a while, however, it might have been hard for an observer to foresee the ultimate triumph of this part of their Renaissance program, which was not widely understood. It was the emphasis of Petrarch and Boccaccio on the rediscovery of the great works of classical literature that caught other men's imaginations at first. Neither Petrarch nor Boccaccio was really fluent in classical Latin, and neither could read much Greek. Those who followed them advanced the study of the classical languages to ever higher levels of proficiency, especially after the fall of Byzantium to the Ottoman Turks in 1453, which brought many Greek-speaking refugees to Italy. These persons not only could read classical Greek, but they also carried with them numerous manuscripts of classical works.

By the sixteenth century, classical Latin, not medieval Latin, had become the language of European diplomacy and was read, spoken, and written by all the learned of the world. As late as 1650, the English poet

John Milton (1608–1674) still planned to write a great epic in Latin, because he believed that only if he wrote it in that language could he hope to achieve the universal fame that he so much desired.

As time went on, however, the efforts of Dante, Petrarch, and Boccaccio to advance the reputation of Italian rather than Latin became a compelling example for the rest of Europe. The use of the vernacular languages as literary languages became more evident as literacy everywhere increased because of the spate of printed books produced by Gutenberg's invention of movable type. (See below for a discussion of the Gutenberg revolution.)

During the first half century of printing, from 1450 to 1500, the majority of printed books were renderings of Greek and Latin works, previously available only in manuscripts. By the end of the century, most classical works had been printed, and publishers began aggressively to seek vernacular books. From 1500 on, published works in the national languages—Italian, French, English, Spanish, German, and others—were in the majority.

The Renaissance slowly spread throughout Europe, moving from its initial Italian base to France, England, Spain, and Germany. By about 1600, the first wave produced an inspired flowering of poetry and prose in the vernacular. The heroes of the first wave were writers like Clement Marot (1496?–1544) and François Rabelais (1483?–1533) in French, and Geoffrey Chaucer (1342/3–1400) in English. This first wave was usually followed, as it had been in Italy, by a profusion of works in classical Latin. In turn the use of Latin texts brought about a reaction in favor of the vernacular, which in every European country soon became the standard of high literature. Thus in France it was the influence of Pierre de Ronsard (1524–1585) in verse and of Montaigne in prose that established French, not Latin, as the language in which serious literary artists (although not, for a time, divines) would compose their most important works. After a similar hiatus following the death of Chaucer, the English works of Edmund Spenser (1552–1599) and Shakespeare helped to establish the form of modern English as we know it in the British Isles. Thus Milton finally decided to write *Paradise Lost* in English instead of Latin, to our benefit.

Moreover, Petrarch's and Boccaccio's belief that the greatest literature could be rooted in popular subjects, such as love, chivalry, and adventure, was adopted everywhere. Even when Humanists composed in Latin, as Erasmus did, in producing *In Praise of Folly*, they wrote in a more popular style and for a wider audience than had been the case in classical times.

And, as with the great painters, the great authors did not hide man's light under the bushel of religious piety. Much was written about religion during the years of the later Renaissance (from 1500 to 1650, say). Probably the majority of all published works, even in the vernacular, were religious in tone if not in intent. But the greatest writers wrote about man, not God, placing man in the center foreground, exalting him, praising him, questioning him, criticizing him, but not despising him and his worldly city as the Augustinians had been doing for a thousand years.

Montaigne

Michel de Montaigne, born near Bordeaux, France, in 1533, was brought up by his father in an odd and lovely way. Wakened every morning by music, the boy was given peasants for godfather, godmother, and nurse (so that he would take in the wisdom of peasants, his father said, with his milk), and taught Latin by a German tutor who spoke not a word of French. As a result Montaigne himself spoke little French until he was six, and Latin always remained his "mother tongue."

After a lifetime of political service demanded by his friend, the king Henry IV, Montaigne began in earnest to write the essays that made him famous. Because of his exposure to ordinary folk, he was able to compose, almost to invent, an easy, seemingly artless French prose that helped to establish the high standards of the language.

The *Essays* are more than a linguistic tour de force. In a way they are the quintessential Renaissance book. Besides being the first essays (as we conceive them) ever written, they are also the first book whose main aim is to reveal with utter honesty and frankness the author's mind and heart. Montaigne makes no attempt to conceal his faults, but he does not beat his breast, either, and demand forgiveness. He is content to report what he is, what he thinks, what he feels, in the expectation that he will be sufficiently like his reader—any reader—that his account will be interesting. And so it is.

St. Augustine, writing his *Confessions* more than a thousand years before the *Essays*, had revealed his mind and heart, too. But the intent of the great Christian apologist had been relentlessly didactic. In confessing his sins, and describing his conversion to the true faith, he had told the story of a wicked sinner saved by God's grace. If this could happen to me, he was saying, it can happen to you. Montaigne, however, is not so much interested in what has happened to him as in what he is, which is what any ordinary human being is.

In short, the book, if it is about anything other than itself, is about self-knowledge. Socrates, Montaigne's hero and exemplar, had said that knowing oneself was both hard and crucially important. Montaigne was aware of how difficult it is. To some extent, everyone refuses to know himself, which means admitting to himself that he is no more or no better than he actually is. All of us sometimes, and most of us always, are steeped in a brew of illusions. Montaigne sought to reach beyond his own illusions, to see himself as he really was, which is not just the way others saw him.

The Renaissance, in all of its manifestations, had placed man at the center of things. There was a coldness and a distance about the reorienting of man that may have irritated Montaigne. Who is to speak for man in the abstract? Montaigne, at least, could speak for himself. He could say what he was, what he wanted, what he feared (which was very little), what hurt him, what amused and pleased him, what struck him as vain and foolish in other men. Thus he placed himself at the center of things, believing that even if this attention might seem self-centered to some people, nothing would prove more interesting.

The *Essays* are supremely interesting. They also set a precedent, opening the way to a new kind of literary work that has become the most important of all in the subsequent centuries. A hundred writers, among them the greatest of those centuries, have tried to reveal themselves with a frankness and honesty that have even surpassed Montaigne's. Rousseau and Goethe. Wordsworth and George Eliot. Baudelaire and Dostoevski. John Berryman and Philip Roth. These and scores of others have poured out the health and the sickness of their souls, confident that both would be as interesting to others as to themselves.

Today a return to a literature of concealment, instead of disclosure, is impossible, short of a universal cataclysm that is accompanied by an everlasting iron censorship. We owe this achievement to Montaigne, more than anyone else. Montaigne, in "Of Experience," writes:

We are great fools. "He has spent his life in idleness," we say; "I have done nothing today." What, have you not lived? That is not only the fundamental but the most illustrious of your occupations. "If I had been placed in a position to manage great affairs, I would have shown what I could do." Have you been able to think out and manage your own life? You have done the greatest task of all. To show and exploit her resources Nature has no need of fortune; she shows herself equally on all levels and behind a curtain as well as without one. To compose our character is our duty, not to compose books, and to win, not battles and provinces, but order and tranquility in our conduct. Our great and glorious masterpiece is to live appropriately. All other things, ruling, hoarding, building, are only little appendages and props, at most.

It is an absolute perfection and virtually divine to know how to enjoy our being lawfully. We seek other conditions because we do not understand the use of our own, and go outside of ourselves because we do not know what it is like inside. Yet there is no use our mounting on stilts, for on stilts we must still walk on our own legs. And on the loftiest throne in the world we are still sitting on our own behind.

Shakespeare

I confess at the outset to some doubts about the authorship of Shakespeare's plays. The Stratford actor may have written them; the Earl of Oxford perhaps wrote them; perhaps it was someone else. After five centuries, the question whether "Shakespeare" is the real name or a pseudonym of an author otherwise unknown is of no importance, except to explain why I can make no attempt to compose a biography.

It is enough to say that the author of the plays was born in England around the middle of the sixteenth century and probably lived until about 1615. He wrote some thirty-five plays, all of which were apparently produced, sometimes more than one in a year. He was a great success as a playwright in his own time as well as all subsequent times.

When he (let us call him Shakespeare, even if we admit to not knowing to whom the name really refers) began to write, he had little to go on in the way of good dramatic examples. The great Greek tragedians were unknown to him; he had only Seneca and a handful of dreadful contemporary Senecan tragedies; Plautus and Terence, old Romans; and a few imitations of their classic though banal comedies. Thus he literally created English dramaturgy. In itself that is a signal achievement. But it is only the beginning of what Shakespeare did.

If Shakespeare's plays did not exist, we would not know how marvelous the drama can be. More than that, we would not know how deeply literature can reach into the human soul.

Man and woman are always the focus of the plays. The medieval world picture that Shakespeare inherited fades into the background, and humankind emerges, naked and unadorned with vestments or protected by canon law. The plays are hardly even Christian, to say nothing of being orthodox. Nor are they existentialist, although they do pit men and women against the universe, and then measure their performance in that unequal contest.

Shakespeare's genius was unique, for he was as skillful in comedy as in tragedy, and he even knew how to mix the two, using comedy to draw out the tragedy, and tragedy to sharpen the comic touch. Life does that, too, recognizing no prejudice in favor of tragedy or comedy, and the plays are thus as close to a satisfactory imitation of human life as any author has ever managed to achieve.

Greek tragedy, which Shakespeare did not know, had dealt with family problems, but on a heroic, superhuman scale. It is hard for any father or husband to recognize himself in Oedipus, for any wife or mother to see herself in Clytemestra, Agamemnon's tortured queen. It is one of the most precious contributions of Shakespeare that he invaded the life of ordinary families in his plays, revealing to us what we had always known but never faced. Every one of the famous tragedies is a family tragedy, whatever else it is; Lear and his daughters, Hamlet and his mother and stepfather, Othello and his young bride, Macbeth and his bloodthirsty, old, ambitious wife. Two warring families kill the darling young lovers in *Romeo and Juliet*, and Antony and Cleopatra, although not married—perhaps *because* they were not married—are as passionately in love after twenty years as they were when they were young.

Plautus and Terence had invented a stageful of stock comedy figures: the boastful soldier-lover; the naive, deliciously attractive daughter; the foolish father born to be tricked out of his jewel; the sly servant pulling all the strings—all of them posed in mock-familial situations that imitated real life. Shakespeare, inheriting these figures, turned them into real men and women in his incomparable comedies. Apart from the mandatory lovers, who more often than not make fun of love itself, these plays contain pairs of fathers and daughters so true and real they possess the power to break the heart. And then Shylock, a masterstroke, a tragic figure dropped into the center of a comedy, whose own heart breaks amidst the surrounding laughter, including the laughter of his daughter.

The French language inherited from Rabelais proved inadequate to Montaigne's needs, and as a result he had to invent a new prose. The English that Shakespeare would employ in his last masterworks hardly existed when he began to write his earliest works, and he, too, had almost to invent a language. Dante, Petrarch, and Boccaccio had performed similar magic for Italian, and Cervantes would perform it for Spanish, Lessing and Goethe for German. As in everything else, Shakespeare was the greatest of these linguistic creators. Inexhaustible in his imagination, he was also inexhaustible in his inventiveness. We compliment ourselves when we claim that ours is the language that Shakespeare spoke. Would that we spoke or wrote it so well.

HAMLET:

What a piece of work is man! how noble in reason! how infinite in faculty! in form and moving how express! how admirable in action! how like an angel in apprehension! how like a god! the beauty of the world! the paragon of animals! And yet, to me, what is this quintessence of dust?

Hamlet

GLOUCESTER:

Like flies to wanton boys, are we to the gods.
They kill us for their sport.

King Lear

PROSPERO:

Our revels now are ended. These our actors,
As I foretold you, were all spirits and
Are melted into air, into thin air:
And, like the baseless fabric of this vision,
The cloud-capp'd towers, the gorgeous palaces,
The solemn temples, the great globe itself,
Yea, all which it inherit, shall dissolve
And, like this insubstantial pageant faded,
Leave not a rack behind. We are such stuff
As dreams are made on, and our little life
Is rounded with a sleep.

The Tempest

Cervantes

Miguel de Cervantes Saavedra was born probably on September 29, 1547, at Alcalá de Henares, near Madrid. He died most probably on April 22, 1616, but lovers of literature prefer the traditional date, April 23, because that is also the day on which Shakespeare is supposed to have departed. The idea that those two fine old gentlemen died on the same day and went to heaven together—if they did not go to heaven, then what's a heaven for?—is such an alluring and delightful idea that the facts, whatever they may be, should not stand in the way of it.

Cervantes was first a soldier, then a writer. As a soldier he became a considerable success, so much so that when he was captured by Barbary pirates in 1575, they thought he was an important man and demanded a high ransom. This perception may have saved his life, for he continued to be well treated despite several attempts to escape. It also cost him five years of slavery, for his family could not raise the money until 1580, when they managed to free him. But they paid a great price, for in doing so they impoverished themselves and him for the rest of his life.

Cervantes wanted to be a writer, and he wrote every kind of work he thought might bring him in a little money: plays, stories, a pastoral romance in the then-modern style. Nothing he did succeeded. He had always loved reading, especially the chivalric romances of the previous century. So, perhaps in despair, he dreamed up a story about an old gentleman of La Mancha, where he was then living, who had read so many such tales that he went out of his mind and believed those stories to be true. He thereupon decided to become a knight-errant himself and set out, with rusty sword and battered shield on his gaunt nag Rosinante to see the world and conquer dragons wherever he discovered them. As everyone knows, he found nothing to conquer but herds of sheep and giant windmills, which dot the empty plain of La Mancha to this day. Instead of unseating the windmills, which he thought were armed knights, he was himself unseated by the mechanical sails that turned inexorably in the wind that parched the plain. So Don Quixote was brought home in a cage and deposited in front of his own house.

Cervantes told the story in twenty pages. He must have read it to the four or five women relatives who shared the two rooms of his little house at Esquivias, where he wrote in the kitchen while the women stepped over him. They liked it, and he decided to write more.

Don Quixote needed a companion, a squire, as he liked to call him, and Cervantes invented him, too, imagining the round, practical peasant Sancho Panza, who thenceforth accompanied the would-be knight as they rode the crooked highways of a vanished Spain, though it is a Spain more real, for most Spaniards, than their modern nation. Don Quixote had many adventures, in almost all of which he was tricked, cheated, and betrayed, and Sancho felt himself drawn into his master's imagination, so that he, too, began to have adventures and think he was truly a squire of a true knight. But what they did most of the time was talk, and their talk has come down to us as the best that is to be found in any book.

Ah, but says *Sancho*, your strolling Emperor's Crowns and Sceptres are not of pure Gold, but Tinsel and Copper. I grant it, said Don *Quixote*; nor is it fit the Decorations of the Stage should be real, but rather Imitations, and the Resemblance of Realities, as the Plays themselves must be; which, by the way, I wou'd have you love and esteem, *Sancho*, and consequently those that write, and also those that act 'em; for they are all instrumental to the Good of the Commonwealth, and set before our Eyes those Looking-glasses that reflect a lively Representation of human Life; nothing being able to give us a more just Idea of Nature, and what we are or ought to be, than Comedians and Comedies. Prithee tell me, Hast thou never seen a Play acted, where Kings, Emperors, Prelates, Knights, Ladies, and other Characters, are introduced on the Stage? One acts a Ruffian, another a Soldier; this Man a Cheat, and that a Merchant; one plays a designing Fool, and another a foolish Lover: But the Play done, and the Actors undress'd, they are all equal, and as they were before. All this I have seen, quoth *Sancho*. Just such a Comedy, said Don *Quixote*, is acted on the great Stage of the World, where some play the Emperors, others the Prelates, and, in short, all the Parts that can be brought into a Dramatick Piece; till Death, which is the Catastrophe and End of the Action, strips the Actors of all their Marks of Distinction, and levels their Quality in the Grave. A rare Comparison, quoth *Sancho*, though not so new, but that I have heard it over and over. Just such another is that of a Game of Chess, where while the Play lasts, every Piece has its particular Office; but when the Game's over, they are all mingled and huddled together, and clapp'd into a Bag, just as when Life's ended we are laid up in the Grave. Truly *Sancho*, said Don *Quixote*, thy Simplicity lessens, and thy Sense improves every Day.

Because the tall, gaunt knight and his rotund squire immediately and forevermore captured everyone's imagination, their image is the best known of any fictional characters in the literature of the world. In due course, *Don Quixote* was published and republished, translated into all the languages of Europe, and made its author nearly as famous as his characters. Still, he did not make any money to speak of. In any case he had been mistaken in believing that literature was a road to riches.

If the *Essays* of Montaigne are not the quintessential Renaissance book, then surely Cervantes's *Don Quixote* deserves that title. For what better way is there to usher in a new world than to mock the old and start everyone laughing at it? The medieval world picture had included a belief in chivalry, which was a necessary part of the fictitious entity that was the theocratic state. Knights-errant were the ombudsmen of God's kingdom on earth, sowing justice as they rode through the fields and into the little villages of countries that existed only in men's minds: Avalon, Arcadia, and the like. Pure in their morals and their religious piety, they served a heavenly king and a matchless maiden, a virgin mother, up to and beyond death.

The ideal had been so beautiful that it had lasted for centuries, and it was not surprising that it mesmerized Don Quixote. But it is not surprising, either, that it drove him mad, for the conflict between beautiful ideals and things like real, endlessly whirling windmills is savage enough to wither the wits of anyone not very quick on his feet. In any event, the future belonged to the windmills, and all their technological successors. But does that mean romance had died? Or was there a way to enjoy both romance and progress?

The true greatness of Cervantes lay in his discovery of the way. Don Quixote and his friend Sancho Panza seek what a modern poet has called an impossible dream, a dream of justice in an earthly paradise, a contradiction in terms, as practical men have always known. What matter that the dream existed only in their minds? Where else should a dream be? Meanwhile the real world could go about its deadly, inexorable purpose.

Cervantes's two heroes are not exactly at the center foreground of the stage. They are just a little above it, for their feet are not on the ground. Cervantes was the first to see that the new world coming into being needed such heroes; otherwise, it would go mad. Most of the enduring literature of the last four hundred years has taken up his idea, either inventing new kinds of heroes with their heads in the air or showing how mad the world has become when it lacks them.

The Black Death

It is strange to think that a terrible plague should be the propagator of culture and conduce to the spread of the Renaissance idea, but so it proved to be. It brought together two elements crucial to the spread of knowledge: the technology of paper and printing, on the one hand, and the indispensable word—the manuscripts that were turned into books—on the other.

Plague is primarily a disease of rodents, usually rats. It is carried from one rat to another by the rat flea, but human beings can catch the disease if they become infested by fleas. In the crowded conditions of medieval cities whole populations commonly did just that. In times of extreme stress, during sieges or famines, city dwellers were especially at risk. If plague became epidemic, as often happened, the death toll was terrible, for there was no known cure. (Only modern antibiotics can control the disease.)

In early 1347 a Genoese trading post in the Crimea was being besieged by an army containing Kipchaks from Hungary and Mongols from several lands of the East. The latter brought with them a new form of plague, and in the conditions of the siege, it flared up and killed a number of soldiers. It occurred to the Kipchak commander that he might be able to take advantage of his bad fortune, and he catapulted several infected corpses into the Genoese town.

The Genoese had no immunity, and soon many of the occupants of the settlement died. One of their ships managed to escape the blockade, sailing through the Dardanelles, around the coast of Anatolia, and across the Mediterranean to Messina, in Sicily, where it arrived in the summer of 1347. It brought a cargo of terrified refugees and gold, and it brought plague.

From this time forth the disease became epidemic. It wiped out one-half of the population in Messina in two months, and it soon spread to other Sicilian towns. It crossed the straits into Italy that fall and moved up the peninsula at a fairly steady rate of about seven miles a day. The deaths began in the prosperous towns of northern Italy early in 1348, as well as in North Africa, to which other ships had carried the infection. France and Spain became involved later in 1348; Austria, Hungary, Switzerland,

Germany, the Low Countries, and England in 1349; Scandinavia and the Baltic region in 1350.

Estimates vary as to the fraction in Europe that died in this plague that has entered history as the Black Death. There is no doubt that it was at least one-quarter and perhaps one-half or even more; one-third is probably a safe minimum figure. Deaths therefore numbered between twenty-five and forty million persons. Nor did the epidemic end in 1350. There were lesser outbreaks in many cities for the next twenty years.

The disease left an indelible impression on the minds of the survivors, although Petrarch, for example, stated that he did not think future generations would believe what had happened. In terms of the sheer numbers of persons who died, the Black Death was one of the worst disasters in history. In terms of the percentage that died, it was possibly the worst— worse than any other epidemic, any war—anything.

It is an ill wind that blows nobody good. Perhaps one-half of all European agricultural laborers died. Those who survived experienced a large increase in their real wages, as they were now able to bargain for their services with the inhabitants of the towns, who desperately needed the food that the serfs alone could produce. However, within about a hundred years the population of serfs had caught up, and inflation had wiped out their economic gains.

The disease killed people, but it did not harm property. And it struck rich and poor indiscriminately. Now everything the dead had owned belonged to someone else. The newfound wealth of the survivors sent them on one of history's great spending sprees. The last quarter of the fourteenth century was therefore an epoch of burgeoning prosperity. The rampant consumerism was fueled by a general relaxation of morals that followed the epidemic. When you are surrounded by death, it is not so easy to impose strict rules on your family, neighbors, or subjects.

Survivors of the plague did not only inherit money, lands, and buildings. They also inherited clothes, bed furnishings, and other articles made of cloth. But a person can wear only so many suits or dresses, make up only so many beds. Hundreds of millions of garments were suddenly useless. Toward the end of the fourteenth century a new use was discovered for all these discarded articles: manufacturing rag paper. The new material was valuable for many purposes, but by 1450 there was a large surplus of it, and its price had fallen to a low level.

The Black Death had another special effect on the new Renaissance that Petrarch and Boccaccio had inaugurated. Byzantium became one of the first cities to suffer from the devastating epidemic. The Holy Roman Empire of the East would endure for a century, until it fell to the Muslim Turks in 1453, but from 1355 on, the flight of educated and cultured persons from Byzantium to the West was steady.

Their coming fed the hunger for news, information, and genuine knowledge of the classical tradition that Byzantium had preserved. The main cohort of scholars did not arrive in Italy until the fifteenth century, but each year saw some arrivals, and they had a cumulative effect. By the year 1450 the urge to read and study Greek and Roman texts had expanded enormously. But there was as yet no practical way to satisfy it.

Gutenberg's Achievement

Remarkably little is known about the life of the man whose inventions exploited all of these consequences, in themselves often dire, of the Black Death. Born during the last decade of the fourteenth century in Mainz, Germany, Johann Gutenberg spent his life in secret activities that he managed to conceal, for the most part, even from the partners who lent him large sums to pay for them. His secrecy and, perhaps, some other character flaw finally led to his ruin. One of his creditors brought a lawsuit and, after winning a judgment in court, received all of Gutenberg's materials and machines. The inventor was left a pauper.

Gutenberg died, a broken, desolate man, around 1468. By that time the famous Bible that is now called by his name had been printed and was an acknowledged masterpiece. In this first book to be printed from movable metal type, Gutenberg evidently was trying to reproduce medieval liturgical manuscripts by mechanical means without losing any of their beautiful color or design. To this end, which was far from the aim of most of his successors, he invented four basic devices, all of them used in printing until the twentieth century.

One was a stamping mold for casting type precisely and in large quantities. Movable type had previously been either engraved in metal or carved in wood. Both processes were laborious and slow. Wooden type soon deteriorated. Engraved type lasted a long time, but each engraved letter was subtly different from every other in size and shape. Gutenberg's molds produced many copies of a given letter that were both durable and exactly the same.

The second invention consisted of an alloy of lead, tin, and antimony out of which the cast letters were made. Lead alone would have oxidized rapidly, with a consequent deterioration of the form, or matrix, in which the type was held. Antimony was needed to make the type hard so that it would withstand the making of a number of impressions. The mixture of lead, tin, and antimony was used until very recently to make type.

The third invention was the printing press itself. Previous printing from wood-block type had utilized light, wooden presses. However, when books were bound, a heavy, metal press was used. A large screw, similar to that employed to press olives and grapes, supplied the much greater pressures needed. Gutenberg's printing press was an adaptation of the binding press. It would have soon destroyed the carved wooden type used previously, but the new, durable metal type stood up to the higher pressures and produced a clean, precise impression.

Finally, Gutenberg, after much experimenting, produced a printing ink with an oil base. The ink could be colored in various ways, which allowed the printing of such beautiful books as the Gutenberg Bible.

A certain Ts'ai Lun, a Chinese government official, is credited with the discovery of paper. The traditional date is 105 AD. By the end of the second century AD the Chinese were printing books on rag paper using wooden type. The secret of papermaking was discovered by the Arabs during the eighth century and brought to Egypt and Spain. For some reason it did not interest Europeans for a long time thereafter. Not until the end of the fourteenth century did the principles of production of rag paper become widely known in the West. Then, papermaking, employing the vast number of rags made available by the Black Death, became an important industry. Rag paper was much preferable to parchment or vellum, both made of animal skins, for many purposes. Paper lay flatter and could be folded more easily. It was thinner, so it could be bound together in sheets to make a more compact book. Most important, it received a much cleaner and more distinct impression when printed.

The first books composed with movable metal type were printed by Gutenberg around 1450. Not surprisingly, they were printed on rag paper, whose low price, owing to the surplus of rags, made it an obvious choice. Soon thousands of copies of books were being printed on paper, Gutenberg's constellation of inventions being a splendid new use for this now widely available material.

Gutenberg's inventions soon reached Italy. In Venice and other northern cities, the hunger for the classics proved insatiable. Within fifty years nearly every important Greek and Roman work had been printed and distributed all over the learned world. The books were sold at the much lower prices made possible by the new technology. Many of the original texts had been brought in manuscript from Byzantium by refugees fleeing the takeover of the city by the Ottoman Turks in 1453.

Gutenberg, who had had no such intention, thus secured the triumph of Petrarch's and Boccaccio's Renaissance. With the classics available in relatively cheap editions, the work of studying the ancient languages and cultures could proceed. Once only the rich had been able to buy handwritten manuscripts. Suddenly, any scholar could own books.

In addition to furthering the efforts of classical philology, the ancient books that any literate person could now afford to own were filled with ideas that had been forgotten, ignored, or suppressed for centuries. Also, many people wrote books of their own about their current interests and concerns, in the hope of making converts to their views, often in far-off places and among strangers. That most subversive of inventions, the printed book, could be used to change and overturn all kinds of ancient institutions.

Petrarch and Boccaccio had appreciated the potentialities of the crafty promotion of an idea. They had advanced that concept farther than any individuals had ever managed in the past. Now it was no longer necessary to be a genius to make an impact. It was enough to have a new idea, not necessarily a good one, and write a book about it. Publishers were eager for new titles. Who knew what would happen then?

It was a remarkable conjunction of events—the new availability of rag paper, the invention of printing with movable metal type, and the sudden appearance of a large number of excellent manuscripts crying out for publication—that propagated the Renaissance. Without these elements, the dream of Petrarch and Boccaccio would have turned out to be very different indeed.

Renaissance Cities

The city-state was one of the great Greek inventions. Aristotle described what happens. The state comes into existence for the sake of life, he said; that is, it is an important survival mechanism. But it *continues* in existence for the sake of a *good* life. Human beings, having formed some kind of state, soon realize how much more enduring, secure, and enjoyable communal life is than the life of any single person or family.

City-states sprang up all over Greece and in the Greek colonies. The basic principle was economic: they were communities of men, women, children, and slaves, joined together so that the community's inhabitants could enjoy better and richer lives. The city-states flourished and by ancient standards enjoyed much freedom. As a result, some men (but few women or children, and hardly any slaves) were able to live extremely well, exercising in the palestra, discussing philosophy, and seeking the meaning of virtue.

Alexander the Great tried to establish city-states in the lands he conquered at the end of the fourth century BC. But the idea proved foreign and did not take hold. His imperial cities, like Alexandria and Babylon, were devoted more to administration than to culture and commerce, while Athens continued as a sort of glorious fossil. The Romans, who adopted so many other Greek ideas, did not adopt the concept of the city-state, for the imperial city appealed to them more than did the busy, crowded, innovative Greek towns. With the barbarian invasions, civilization retreated within monastic walls. Even the imperial Aix of Charlemagne was far from being a city in the Greek sense.

But the Greek idea of the city-state did not die. It revived in the eleventh and twelfth centuries, when Italian communes like Milan, Pisa, and Florence grappled with their feudal overlords, overthrew their ancient masters, and grasped the power themselves.

The medieval Italian commune, like the ancient Greek city-state, was first of all a commercial entity and enterprise. The freedom enjoyed by a new class of urban merchants and traders was employed to produce new fortunes and widespread wealth. By the year 1300 the little city of Florence had become the banker of Europe. Its coin, the florin, became the first international currency. But Florence was more than just a business corporation. Its citizens also sought a kind of glory not dreamed of since fifth-century Athens: a splendor of art and architecture belonging to all the people that would make their city the envy of people everywhere and would produce in the hearts of Florentines a satisfaction and civic pride unknown for centuries.

The revived idea of a city-state ruled by the people spread throughout Europe. In fact, communes were rising in Germany when the Italian city-state was already dying, destroyed by the vicious infighting of the twelfth century that spoiled freedom in every town and brought in foreign mercenaries to keep the peace. These soldiers almost always stayed longer than they were wanted and ended up controlling most of Italy.

Florence lost its political independence, although not its prosperity and artistic leadership, at the end of the fifteenth century. At the same time, Rome was rising from the ashes of its fall a thousand years before, but not as a city-state. It too became an imperial city, with great power and splendor but little communal life. The Medici, the leading family of Florence during its greatest days, had been able to walk unguarded through the streets, granting audiences to rich and poor alike. In Renaissance Rome, which means Rome after about 1500, the popes ruled from behind high walls. With their wealth they were able to buy the best Florentine artists, but the great new buildings, ornamented as never before, no longer belonged to the people of Rome.

Nation-States

The small Italian communes had helped to free Europe from the vise of feudal rule. But they did not endure. They fell prey to larger city-states, and those communities were unable to avoid constant civil conflict. A new political idea was needed.

No one has ever been able to define the word *nation* exactly, but it had, and still has, something to do with a commonalty of things like language and traditions, and an ability to defend itself against all enemies. A nation that could not defend itself did not long endure, and princes made sure

their subjects appreciated this fact and therefore did not object too strenu-
ously to the taxes required to pay for defense. Then as now, the best
defense was often attack, and so wars were frequent. To put the best face
on them, these wars were usually waged for the sake of peace. Bigness
proved an advantage, and so the nations grew in size, absorbing their less
fortunate neighbors into larger and larger political units. For the sake of
efficiency, central economies seemed desirable as well. So more and more
economic power was concentrated in fewer hands.

War was not incessant, and diplomacy filled the interludes of peace. It
became traditional for diplomacy to be conducted in elegant Latin, for
Latin was the only language shared by the warring potentates. Renaissance Humanists were the best Latinists, and so they found employment
serving the aims of princes, which were always to grow bigger and more
prosperous. Thus the heirs of Dante, Petrarch, and Boccaccio soon found
themselves employed by vain monarchs, imitation emperors who called
themselves Roman, and impious popes. The artists were employed to
decorate their throne rooms.

The history of the European Renaissance illustrates the adage that
nothing fails like success. By 1700 most of the original characteristics of
the Renaissance had been distorted beyond recognition by rich, powerful,
and unscrupulous men who saw ways to use them, and worse, by exquisitely cunning practitioners of all the arts who invented means to sell
them.

Despite this sad but inevitable result, the political achievements of the
Renaissance proved significant. More than a century was needed for the
population lost in the Black Death to be replaced. By 1500 the total
population of Europe exceeded what it had been in 1350 and grew rapidly,
as conditions of life everywhere improved. Because of the decimation of
rural communities by the plague, arable land had turned back to forest.
Now it was reclaimed, and indeed the "inexhaustible" forests of Europe
were already beginning to prove inadequate for the increase in shipbuild-
ing brought on by naval wars.

By 1500, too, political institutions throughout Europe were capable of
dealing with challenges that would have overcome and brought to ruin the
small, independent, and ungovernable communes that had flourished two
hundred years before. The new institutions were on a much larger scale
than had been seen in the West since the fall of Rome.

The new nations were everywhere despotic, but their subjects could be
persuaded that, at least most of the time, their rulers seemed benevolent,
and in any case no alternative existed to being ruled by a single monarch.
Whether or not the kings proved benevolent, they performed useful functions, or saw that their ministers did. New roads were built, new and
larger ships plied the seas and the inland waters, some kind of postal

service operated in most countries, commerce was reasonably well protected (although usually cruelly taxed, since no one yet understood the
idea of free trade), taxes were as unjust as ever but not as arbitrary, news
was available and sometimes could be depended on. In short, modern life,
after two centuries of the Renaissance, was a far cry from what it had been
during the Dark Ages.

There was a sense of progress, that life was growing better and would
continue to improve. This belief grew by what it fed on; nothing is more
conducive to progress than the widespread belief that it can occur. Nevertheless, some great problems remained to be solved.

The Crisis of the Theocratic State

The most vexing problem concerned religious schism. There was no
avoiding the challenge that Renaissance ideas posed to the theocratic
state. This challenge was first felt most poignantly by the Church, to the
benefit of the new nation-states. But it would not be long before the
despotic monarchies that had replaced the earlier communes would also
lose their power, beset and overthrown by the new image of man, and not
God, as residing at the center of things.

The Church was always ambivalent about the Renaissance. On the one
hand, many great churchmen might as well have been Renaissance
princes for all the piety they felt or exhibited. At the same time, other
churchmen were revolted by the growing worldliness of their peers.
Around 1500 there began to be talk of reform. There had been reform
movements in the past, but now the need was widely perceived as critical.

The Church had taken on new political responsibilities as managers of
temporal estates. That cost a great deal of money. It was all very well to
admire the poverty of the early Church. But how could the modern
Church become poor again without destroying itself or being destroyed by
its enemies? The new despots, the kings of France and England, the
German emperor, even the king of Spain, despite his protestations of
unswerving loyalty to Rome, sought increasing independence. But at what
cost in lost souls drawn away to damnation? Reform was needed, true, but
could the Church afford to admit it publicly?

For too long nothing was done. Finally, the new means of promoting
change—printing—opened the way to reform. The religious reform
rocked Europe socially and politically for two centuries.

The careers of four famous men, all born during the last half of the
fifteenth century, reveal the depths of the religious chasm that divided
peoples and nations in those times. The men were well known to one
another, and two of them were close friends.

Erasmus

Desiderius Erasmus was born in Rotterdam in 1466. His parents were not married, his father being a priest and his mother the daughter of a physician and a widow. His illegitimate birth seems not to have impeded his career. If medicine is taken as the representative of scientific knowledge, then this cross of two kinds of knowledge, the one secular, the other sacred, symbolizes the life of the man.

Erasmus became a priest and eventually a monk. Always a reasonably devout Catholic, his greatest love was learning, especially the science he and others placed on the highest rung, namely, philology: the study of the ancient languages, of Latin and Greek, in which, he thought, practically everything worth reading had been written. His Latin style was said to be the equal of Cicero's, and his knowledge of Greek was unsurpassed in his time. Hence his translations of Greek classics into Latin were both admired and widely read.

By 1500 Erasmus had become famous as a scholar and diplomatist, as most Humanists had to be to gain a living. At that point in his life, he became interested in the Greek text of the New Testament. The more he studied it, the more he came to doubt the accuracy of the Vulgate, St. Jerome's translation into Latin, dating from around 400.

In England, Erasmus began the task of providing the best possible text of the New Testament by copying manuscripts found in monasteries and given to him by his friend Thomas More. Returning to the Continent, he began a Latin translation. It appeared, together with a commentary and an improved Greek text, in 1516. His work differed in many places from the Vulgate and was immediately recognized as the most accurate translation so far.

Erasmus wished to produce a completely accurate text of both testaments (although he did not like the Old Testament and never did much work on it) that could be published and widely distributed, studied by many different scholars, and as a result further refined. What now seems an obvious use of the new technology of the printing press was apparently Erasmus's invention, and of course the idea caught on. But it led to consequences that Erasmus did not desire.

When Erasmus turned fifty, Martin Luther threw down his famous challenge to the Roman Church (the origin of Protestantism), and by the time Erasmus died, there was a full-blown revolution under way. Erasmus at first tried to ignore both the content and implication of Luther's words. His personal piety was sincere, but fundamentally he did not wish to take religion (as opposed to religious scholarship) as seriously as Luther did. Erasmus wanted to be free to study, to read the great classic books, to write graceful, charming, and readable *Colloquies* (that is, "conversations") in Latin that could be used to teach pupils the elegant use of the language (and were so used until the twentieth century), and to drink good wine, eat good food, and laugh at the follies of the world.

In Praise of Folly is his most famous work, and deservedly so. In it Erasmus had the freedom to discourse, in the ironic style of Lucian (the Greek author whose works he translated), concerning all the foolishness and misguided pompousness of the world. In later ages his book was much loved. At the time, however, it made him more enemies than friends. Pompous, foolish men do not like being laughed at.

In the end, the friends of Erasmus forced him to choose between Luther and the pope, and of course he chose the pope, for he never wanted to be anything but a sincere, if nonaggressive, Catholic. When he wrote a piece critical of some of Luther's views, Luther answered it angrily and brilliantly, as he did everything, and Erasmus retired from the fray, feeling pompous and foolish himself. He died in 1536, a few months short of his seventieth birthday, in the knowledge that his Renaissance brand of gentle skepticism could not satisfy an angry new world.

Thomas More

Thomas More, the famous author, politician, and martyr, became Erasmus's best friend. In impeccable Latin, Erasmus called him *omnium horarum homo*, which is well translated as "a man for all seasons." Born in 1477 in London, Thomas More was brought up in the household of John Morton, archbishop of Canterbury and lord chancellor. After two years at Oxford he was brought back to London to study law. He first met Erasmus in 1499, when the latter visited England. Five years later, after More married, he set aside a suite of rooms for Erasmus, who became a frequent guest.

A busy, successful lawyer, More never stopped reading and writing. In 1516, he published *Utopia*, the "golden little book" that invented a literary world immune from the evils of Europe, where all citizens were equal and believed in a good and just God. A sort of primitive communism was the mark of More's Utopia (a word that he made up). Hence his name is listed in Red Square as one of the heroes of the Russian Revolution.

From 1518 on, Thomas More devoted himself exclusively to the king's service, rising to the post of lord chancellor in 1529 after the fall of Cardinal Wolsey. This made him the second greatest man in England, but his reign was brief, for he could not bring himself to accept, in good conscience, Henry VIII's divorce from Catherine of Aragon and his subsequent marriage to Anne Boleyn. The pope did not accept it either, and Henry consequently disowned the pope, as the pope excommunicated him, and declared himself the head of the exclusively English Church.

More could have accepted a royal adulterer, reluctantly, but he could not subscribe to an oath declaring the king of England supreme in religious matters. Henry proved relentless, although he respected More and might have loved him in other circumstances. Charges of treason were filed, More was tried and convicted, and sentenced to the traitor's death—to be drawn, hanged, and quartered—but the king commuted this sentence to beheading. More died on July 6, 1535.

In one of his colloquies Erasmus had written: "Kings make war, priests are zealous to increase their wealth, theologians invent syllogisms, monks roam through the world, the commons riot, Erasmus writes colloquies." There was a certain justice here: Erasmus, the most influential scholar in Europe, refused to exert his influence to quell the appalling tide of violence that afflicted his later years. Probably he was afraid to.

Thomas More, both knight and saint (he was canonized by Pope Pius XI in 1935), seemed without fear, but he lost his life because the conflict with his king was an unequal one. This was a time when matters of conscience almost inevitably led to violence.

Henry VIII

Henry Tudor, future king of England, was born at Greenwich in 1491. He was the second son of Henry VII, and only ascended to the throne because his older brother, Arthur, died in 1502. Henry became king in 1509, accompanied by the enthusiastic expectations of all Englishmen. Eighteen years old, six feet tall, and powerfully built, he was the very picture of a king, and he never after failed to impress his countrymen with his regal bearing, no matter how much he disappointed them with his policies. However, he usually had ministers to blame for those decisions even if they were really his.

Soon after his accession, Henry married Catherine of Aragon, his brother's widow, gaining at considerable expense papal acceptance of what many people viewed as an incestuous union. For a while he liked Catherine, but several of her children were stillborn, and the only survivor was a girl, Mary, the future queen. Disappointed and annoyed, and certain that the lack of a male heir could not be his fault, Henry turned for solace to Anne Boleyn, the sensuous sister of one of his earlier mistresses. Anne promised him a son as well as untold delights, but only if he would divorce Catherine and make her queen. Henry wanted both as much as she did, but he did not know how to go about it.

The problems were many. First, Catherine of Aragon was the aunt of Charles V, Holy Roman Emperor. On his election in 1519 Charles had immediately become the most powerful man in Europe, combining in his own person the crowns of Spain, Burgundy (together with the Netherlands), and Austria, as well as Germany. Charles had deep feelings of family loyalty and refused to see his kinswoman insulted. Henry applied for an annulment to the pope, Clement VII, but Clement was afraid of Charles, who actually imprisoned him for disobedience in 1527–1528. Besides, Henry had received a special dispensation to marry Catherine in the first place. All this took years. Meanwhile Anne sighed and Henry burned.

Henry demanded relief from his first minister, Cardinal Wolsey. Wolsey tried everything he could think of to move the pope to grant an annulment on the grounds of incest, but to no avail. Disgraced by his failure, he was charged with treason but died on the way to face the king. A new minister, Thomas Cromwell, soon presented the king with a better idea. The crown could disavow the pope and set itself up as the supreme authority in England, in spiritual as well as temporal matters. Henry could then divorce his queen, marry Anne Boleyn, and reform a separate English Church.

And this was done in 1532. Among the king's closest advisers, only his lord chancellor, Thomas More, objected to the new policy. Henry himself adopted it with enthusiasm. He was the Renaissance prince par excellence and considered himself, as king, at the very center of the world's stage. As he had sometimes said, no man on earth could be supreme over him, not Charles V, not the pope at Rome. Henry did not lack devoutness, but, as behooved a man of the Renaissance, his allegiance was to God alone, and not to the Church. Under a new law drafted by Cromwell, Henry was declared the supreme head of the English Church. In the eight years of Cromwell's rule over England, of course in Henry's name, the English Reformation proceeded apace. Among other things, Cromwell disbanded almost all the monasteries in the country, absorbing into the crown their vast wealth. He thereby more than doubled the wealth of the king.

Anne Boleyn proved less exciting as a wife than she had been as a mistress, and Henry soon tired of her. Besides, she, too, gave him only a daughter, the future Elizabeth I. For her failure, Anne died on the block. Her successor, Jane Seymour, died in childbirth. Cromwell then struggled for three years to find a suitable bride for a man who, though king, had begun to be seen as highly dangerous by prospective fathers-in-law. Cromwell's choice fell on Anne of Cleves, who might bring with her German alliances, but Henry hated her as soon as he saw her—at their wedding—and he divorced her, too. Catherine Howard pleased him for a while as his young fifth wife, but she was really promiscuous, even as queen, and she, too, lost her head. His sixth and last wife, Catherine Parr, dull and kindly, comforted his old age until he died in January 1547.

Henry's matrimonial adventures made him a laughingstock, and he was hated in his last years for his willful cruelty. Roman Catholics have never forgiven him for his legal rape of the Church's wealth. In fact, he was never an effective king, although he had effective ministers, whom he killed when they ceased to be useful to him. Nevertheless, he is the most famous of English kings, and one of the most famous of European monarchs. For he perfectly represented what a king should be in his times, when the Renaissance had given men everywhere new ideas about the theocratic state and the new nation-states that would replace it.

Henry considered himself to be a competent theologian, and he spent much of his last years in torturous efforts to interpret for his countrymen the new relationship between man and God that was symbolized by his role as a secular king who at the same time ruled over the Church of England. He never ceased to be troubled by the role he had played in bringing Protestantism to his people. If he had not been the lusty, vain, self-centered Renaissance man he was, he might not have done it, in which case England might still be a Catholic country.

Martin Luther

The great, God-tormented founder of Protestantism and fomenter of the Reformation and its wars was born in Eisleben, Germany, in 1483. Despite his father's wish that he become a lawyer, he entered the religious life and became an Augustinian monk, of the same order to which Erasmus belonged. His brilliance in theology was soon recognized. The University of Wittenberg made him professor of theology in 1510.

That same year he traveled to Rome on church business. Years later he could still vividly remember the shock he had felt upon discovering the laxity and worldliness of Roman prelates. Indeed, the year 1510 might be termed the high tide of the Renaissance in Italy, for Julius II was pope and with the help of Michelangelo and Raphael spent all his energies on plans to renew the ancient splendor of the Eternal City.

As a professor Luther was both challenging and compelling, and attracted brilliant pupils who later became his stalwart followers. But the years after 1510 were full of inward struggle, as he wrestled with questions about what St. Paul had called the righteousness of God. How could he love such a stern and merciless being, Luther asked.

Finally, he believed the justice of God was completed, for man, in the gift of faith, that man was therefore justified by faith, and faith alone. Thus, there was less need for the vast infrastructure of the Church, which seemed to him to be an obstacle, rather than an avenue, between man and God.

The Reformation began—few historical movements can be dated so precisely—on the evening of October 31, 1517, when Luther nailed his Ninety-five Theses to the door of All Saints' Church in Wittenberg. Many dealt with the subject of indulgences. His negative view was brought about by the visit of a Dominican indulgence salesman who had tried to sell salvation to some men Luther knew. Officially, the Church had always been careful to say that an indulgence, at whatever price, would not by itself avert damnation or guarantee salvation, but sales representatives then as now were not always so punctilious, and this one had made wild and shocking promises of more than he or any man—so Luther thought—could ever deliver.

All Saints' Church contained numerous valuable relics, each of them entailing indulgences, which would be revealed on All Saints' Day, the next morning. Hence a large crowd would see the theses, which were also implicit challenges to papal authority. Taking advantage of the new technology, Luther had the theses printed and sent copies to many friends and colleagues.

In the nearly five centuries since 1517, other rebels and reformers have nailed challenges to the doors of churches and other buildings or have read them over television, the modern equivalent. Few have experienced Luther's success.

The revolt started slowly, but it grew inexorably. Luther was a consummate politician. More important, his challenge to Rome found support. Germany, in particular, was ready for him, welcoming him with open arms.

The Church was adamantly opposed. Accused of heresy and formally excommunicated by the pope, he was called before an Imperial Diet in Worms in April 1521. He responded to his accusers in a brilliant speech that ended with the famous intransigent words: "Here I stand! I can do no other!" Absolved of the charges, Luther strode through the crowd of enemies to his friends, who surged around him, his arm raised in a gesture of relief—he had half expected to be condemned to the stake—and triumph.

The Reformation was a complex movement, as was the Counter-Reformation that rose up to meet its challenge. Both agreed that the Roman Church needed reform, and both demanded and brought it about. The easy-going, latitudinarian Christianity was no longer possible.

Reform became both an end in itself and a rationale for other purposes. Henry VIII proclaimed he wanted to reform the clergy, but he also sought a divorce and the riches stored in Catholic monasteries throughout England. The German princes who backed Luther desired reform, but they also wanted independence from Rome and a larger share of the taxes that church establishments collected within their dominions. And there were many other secular forces at work as well.

What charged the atmosphere most, however, was the Renaissance challenge hurled at the Church by Luther's theological lectures, and some of his theses: How shall a man be saved? By the intercession of priests and bishops, as the Church had always said, or by his own, private, individual faith? If faith was private and individual—and how could it not be?—then it was hard not to agree with Luther's position, and demand both national independence from Rome and individual independence from religious establishments.

Luther insisted that he had never meant to go that far, and churches survived, even if they were not Roman Catholic churches. Luther even went to his grave insisting on the efficacy of the Eucharist, saying—with his customary earthiness—that if the Lord asked him to eat crab apples and manure he would do so, and therefore why should he not believe in the sanctity of the body and blood of Christ, since the Lord told him to do so.

But the underlying spirit of this rock-hard, unsmiling man was revolutionary. Others understood this spirit and followed him wherever he led them. They avidly accepted his deep-nurtured conviction that you could kill other people if their beliefs about God were wrong.

Toleration and Intolerance

Luther did not single-handedly start the wars of religion of the sixteenth and seventeenth centuries. But as much as anyone he initiated and supported the intolerance that marked the epoch.

Protestants killed for their faith; the Church responded with a revived Inquisition. For a hundred years and more after Luther's death in 1546 a man's belief in small matters could be cause for murder. Jonathan Swift satirized these warring partisans, who he said would fight over which end of a boiled egg, the big or the little end, should be broken. For a time, indeed, the interdenominational conflict was almost as unhealthy as the Black Death.

The seventeenth century saw the theoretical resolution of the problem Luther had helped to create. No single compromise position regarding church rule, or the sacraments, or the role of bishops, or marriage of the clergy, could be found. The only solution was to have many Christian churches, not just one. The question then became, which church shall be ours, in this nation, in this city? That question produced mayhem long after the idea had been accepted in principle.

Finally, religious differences became in themselves intolerable. They had to change, in the view of reasonable men. The most eloquent proponent of this view was John Locke (1632–1704), whose letter on *Toleration* was published in 1689.

If you believe that you possess an immortal soul, that your stay on earth is short, and that the character of your faith will determine how you spend eternity—in torment or in bliss—then religion is very serious business, more serious than anything else you can do or think about. To die in your faith, if you believe that to do so is to gain eternal bliss, is obviously no loss whatever compared to living out of your faith, and losing heaven.

This belief approaches religion only from an individual's point of view. Two other views have to be considered. One involves a person whose faith differs from yours. During the two centuries prior to the letter on *Toleration*, it was easy for men to believe that their faith required them to torture, to kill, to burn at the stake others who disagreed with them, even though those differences were hard to discern. Furthermore, we now question and condemn the view that any difference of religious opinion is sufficient cause for torture and death. In Luther's time most people would have had difficulty even understanding the question.

Then there is Locke's view, which he claims is the same as God's. He asks, does the God of Mercy and Love approve the actions of those who, "out of a principle of charity, as they pretend, and love to men's souls . . . deprive [others] of their estates, maim them with corporal punishments, starve and torment them in noisome prisons, and in the end even take away their lives?" Locke's answer is strong and clear:

> That any man should think fit to cause another man—whose salvation he heartily desires—to expire in torments, and that even in an unconverted state, would, I confess, seem very strange to me, and I think, to any other also. But nobody, surely, will ever believe that such carriage can proceed from charity, love, or good will. If anyone maintain that men ought to be compelled by fire and sword to profess certain doctrines, and conform to this or that exterior worship, without regard had unto their morals; if any endeavour to convert those that are erroneous unto the faith, by forcing them to profess things that they do not believe and allowing them to practice things that the Gospel does not permit, it cannot be doubted indeed but such a one is desirous to have a numerous assembly joined in the same profession with himself; but that he principally intends by those means to compose a truly Christian Church, is altogether incredible.

The modern tone of those words, despite the antique flavor of the language, is a sign of how close to us in spirit were certain thinkers of the seventeenth century. The fact that Locke was savagely attacked for publishing them indicates that the era of the Reformation and Counter-Reformation and the century of religious wars were far removed from our view of these matters.

Man at the Center

We began this chapter by asking what great concept was reborn in the Renaissance. The answer: the ancient idea that man is the focus of human concern. As Protagoras said twenty-five centuries ago, man is the measure of all things.

The Protestant Reformation, with its emphasis on the individual need for grace, confirmed the answer. Everyone now had to be able to read the Bible so that he could determine its meanings for himself. The invention of printing made that practical; the translations of the Bible into all the European languages made it easier. Everyone was now his own theologian, and God had descended into the breast of every Christian.

The new self-centeredness had other effects, as modern historians have shown. The connection between Protestantism and the rise of capitalism seemed to German sociologist Max Weber (1864–1920) and English historian R. H. Tawney (1880–1962) to be especially close. The discipline that a man must exert once he has cast himself adrift from the support of an international church may be akin to the self-reliance needed for success in a capitalist economy. It may also be the character trait that makes good citizens in a democratic polity.

Whether or not those things are so, they were not yet known to the men and women of the European Renaissance. They may have had a very different idea of what was so interesting to them about the classical civilization they had rediscovered.

For a thousand years since the fall of Rome, men and women had turned over responsibility for their moral lives to surrogates of God on earth: the pope at Rome, his bishops, their parish priests or ministers. They had done this for very good reasons, primarily because they were convinced that if they did they would win salvation and eternal bliss.

Perhaps to their surprise, they discovered that the ancient Greeks and Romans, whom they admired for so many things, had by and large made no such bargain. The Romans especially had believed in God and tried to lead upright, moral lives, but they had accepted responsibility for the choice of how they lived. That responsibility had apparently been, in their estimation, inalienable.

The more the Renaissance pondered this belief, the more striking and courageous it seemed. Classical man had been responsible for himself, and had accepted the consequences of his errors if he made them. The risk he took proved great, as the Renaissance realized. Could the reward be equally great?

Renaissance men, and women, too, decided it was, and this became the most important reason for their collective decision to discard the theocratic state and replace it with a secular state and society for which they would henceforth take complete responsibility. They would depend on religious advisers for counsel, but not for leadership. We moderns inherit their decision and, with a very few exceptions (see Chapter 12), have adhered to this belief ever since.

7

Europe Reaches Out

A T THE BEGINNING of the Christian era the population of the world
totaled about 300 million people. In 1500 it was still only about 400
million, distributed roughly as follows:

China, Japan, and Korea	130 million
Europe (including Russia)	100 million
Indian subcontinent	70 million
Southeast Asia and Indonesia	40 million
Central and western Asia	25 million
Africa	20 million
The Americas	15 million

Between 1500 and 1800 world population more than doubled, and it
doubled again by 1900, to about 1,600 million. By 1960 it had doubled
once more, and it will have doubled again by the year 2000, when there
will be between six and seven billion human beings on the planet.

The spread of new agricultural discoveries and techniques around the
world was the primary cause of the population doubling between 1500
and 1800. Because so much more food had become available, many more
people could exist. In 1500 less than a quarter of the world's cultivable
land had been placed under the plow. The remainder was inhabited by
hunters and gatherers, nomadic pastoralists, or hand cultivators, such as
the Inca. Those primitive methods proved much less efficient than plow
cultivation. Furthermore, population was limited by recurrent famines
brought on by the failure of native crops and the refusal of peoples to eat
strange foods even if they should become available.

After 1500, the onset of a world economy was marked by the spread of
domesticated animals and food plants. Cattle, sheep, and horses were
introduced into the New World, where they eventually flourished. Wheat,

originating in the Near East, spread first throughout Asia and then spanned the globe. This staple was soon joined by bananas, yams, rice, and sugar cane, all from Asia, and by maize, potatoes, tomatoes, and many other foods from the Americas.

Something like a hundred thousand years were needed to bring the world's population to the level of four hundred million reached by the year 1500. During the five years from 1995 to 2000 the number of human inhabitants of the globe will increase by more than that number. More than just a change in agricultural practices is involved in the present explosive growth in population. But the explosion began to gather strength around 1500, which makes that period a watershed in human history.

Mongol Empires

Today, Mongolia is the sixth largest country in Asia but one of the most sparsely inhabited, with a population of fewer than two million persons. A bare, windswept region of desert and grassland, Mongolia has never been able to support many people. But those it has produced have had a major effect on the rest of the world.

We have seen how, in the third century AD, the Hsiung-nu, or Huns, broke through the Great Wall of China and initiated a movement of peoples that led, two hundred years later, to the destruction of the Roman empire. After that time Mongolia remained quiet for a millennium; that is, the Chinese kept the fire burning low by a combination of military force and diplomacy. However, at the beginning of the thirteenth century a new wave of fierce and ruthless horsemen burst out of Mongolia and soon created the largest empire that the world has ever seen.

The names of the Mongol leaders are among the most famous in history. Genghis Khan (1167–1227) unified the Mongol tribes by 1206 and during the next twenty years conquered northern China and all of Asia west to the Caucasus. The Great Khan Ogedei (d. 1241) completed the conquest of China and Korea and planned the western campaign that carried the Mongols all the way to the Adriatic. In April 1241, Ogedei's Mongol hordes routed armies of Poles, Germans, and Hungarians at Liegnitz and Mohi, within easy distance of Vienna. Only the death of Ogedei in December of that year saved Europe from these new barbarians.

Kublai Khan (1215–1294) founded the Yüan dynasty and, as the first Chinese emperor of his line, reunited China for the first time since the fall of the T'angs, in 907. Finally, Timur (1336–1405), who because of his lame leg was called Timur Lang, or Tamerlane, with unexampled barbarity conquered a vast empire that ranged from southern Russia to Mongolia and southward to India, Persia, and Mesopotamia, but after his death his empire fell apart.

Marco Polo

Marco Polo was born in Venice about 1254 and died there in 1324 after a lifetime of extraordinary adventures. His family had traded with the East for a long time, and had traveled to Asia from Constantinople starting in 1260, eventually arriving at the summer residence of the Great Khan, where they had met Kublai Khan himself. The name of the place was Shang-tu, Coleridge's Xanadu. Kublai sent Marco's father, Niccolo, back to Europe as an ambassador, carrying letters asking the pope to provide Kublai with one hundred intelligent men "acquainted with the Seven (liberal) Arts." Niccolo reached Venice in 1269, when he saw his son for the first time. Marco was then about fifteen.

The pope, Clement IV, had recently died, and Niccolo waited for a new one to be elected so he could obey Kublai's request. After two years a successor had still not been chosen. The Polos, father and son, started off on a new journey. In Palestine, the papal legate gave them letters for the Great Khan, and this introduction turned out to be just what they needed, as the legate was soon elected pope as Gregory X. The request for a hundred educated men could not be filled. The Polos left Acre at the end of 1271 with two friars, but these men, unaccustomed to the rigors of travel in Asia, soon turned back. Undaunted, the Polos continued on alone.

Many years later, when Marco returned to Venice, he wrote about their journey in *Il Milione*. A best-seller in his time, "The Travels of Marco Polo" is still one of the great travel books, even though many of Marco's contemporaries evidently considered the work to be a complete fabrication. Scholarly efforts in recent times have revealed the solid core of historical and geographical information in the volume.

It took the Polos about three years to travel from Acre to the Mongol summer capital of Shang-tu. Probably they were delayed by sickness (one or both of them may have contracted malaria), but they were also inveterate tourists who enjoyed making lengthy side tours to visit sights of which they had heard. Kublai Khan was happy to see Marco's father again, and to receive the vial of sacred oil that they had carried all the way from Jerusalem, together with the papal letters. Evidently the Khan was most pleased with the younger Polo, who delighted the great man with stories of strange peoples in distant lands.

Kublai adopted the young Venetian as a kind of roving ambassador without portfolio, and he sent him on numerous fact-finding missions to distant parts of the empire, from which Marco returned with some valuable information and, even better, good stories. Marco seems also to have been entrusted by Kublai with the administration of the salt trade and may even have been named governor of a small city.

Marco and his father remained at the court of the great Khan for at least fifteen years, during which they made a small fortune in trade and had many glorious adventures, fewer than half of which, Marco is supposed to have declared on his deathbed, could be included in his book. Around 1290 they evidently became impatient to return to Venice, and they told Kublai of their desire. At first he would not let Marco leave. For more than a year the Polos waited for an opportunity to turn their homeward journey into an advantage for the emperor. According to the traditional dating, it arose in 1292.

A Mongol princess was to be sent by sea to Persia to become the wife of Arghun Khan, the Mongol ruler of that country. Some six hundred courtiers would accompany the princess, but the Polos convinced Kublai that they should join the princess since they had previously traveled the route she would follow. In fact, since the princess planned to travel by sea around the Indian subcontinent, and the Polos had journeyed overland from Persia to China, they had no more experience of the route than she did.

Marco does not dwell in his book upon his parting from the Great Khan, but it must have been moving. The emperor, now nearing eighty, would have known that he would never see his young friend again, and Marco was probably certain that he would never return, since a change of regime might not be so welcoming to foreigners. Marco was now nearing forty himself, an advanced age for the times, and he was looking forward to spending his last years in his native Venice.

The journey from China to Persia took more than a year. When the princess's fleet arrived at its destination, she discovered that her intended had died a long time before. Arghun's son, Mahmud Ghazan, was now the ruler of Persia. He married the princess himself. The Polos joined in the celebration of the nuptials and then departed for Europe, laden with gifts.

At Trebizond, on the southern coast of the Black Sea, they left the Mongol sphere of influence and entered the Eurasian civilization where they had been born. They were welcomed in a gruesome manner by a band of robbers, who stripped them of most of their riches but spared their lives.

The event was more than merely ironic. From time immemorial it had been considered impossible for Europeans to travel overland to the Far East. In a kind of golden age, the Great Khans guaranteed safe passage from around 1200 to around 1400. Their power did not reach beyond Trebizond, but east of Trebizond travelers were secure.

Even in the East this security was only temporary. Tamerlane lost control of China proper in 1368, when a native Chinese regime, the Mings, took over the country. As the Mongol power decreased, the Mings grew in power and influence. At the beginning of the dynasty, the Chinese thrust was outward. Expeditions led by the great eunuch admiral Cheng Ho (1371–1435) explored the Indian Ocean. By 1431 a fleet of sixty-two ships with nearly thirty thousand men had reached the east coast of Africa. Within less than a half century the Chinese would have discovered Europe.

Then, in a sudden reversal of policy, the Ming emperors, for reasons not well understood, halted all voyages and began to foster an attitude of antiforeign conservatism. Science decayed. Trade became passive. The maritime discoveries were ignored or forgotten. China sealed itself off for nearly five hundred years. Soon it became an exploited rather than an expansive nation.

With the death of Tamerlane in 1405, and the withdrawal of the expeditionary fleets a generation later, the curtain fell once more between Europe and Asia. Travel practically ceased, and Kublai Khan lived on as a romantic legend that only a handful of Venetians believed. The Polo family knew that it was possible to reach the Far East, the source of the world's greatest riches, both by land and by sea, for they had followed both routes. But as time passed, and family legends became confused and distorted, the dangers of travel led other Europeans to fabricate obstacles where none existed. By the middle of the fifteenth century "common knowledge" fostered the view that no route existed for Europeans to reach the East. Even the hardiest traders feared the monsters, ghouls, and other infernal powers that were supposed to bar the way. At the same time, economic forces were gathering that were making it more and more necessary to discover such a route.

Voyages of Discovery

For centuries, husbandmen in northern Europe had been unable to keep more than a few cattle alive during the long, cold winters, and as a consequence most of the herds were slaughtered by their owners every fall. Without spices, especially pepper, to preserve the meat, it soon spoiled, and so pepper was more than just a delicacy. Provisioners, to avoid economic ruin, had to purchase pepper from the only known source, the Arab traders who brought it on their camels through the mysterious desert to Ormuz, Aden, and Alexandria. Unfortunately, the Arabs would take only one thing in exchange for it: gold. And in Europe gold was pitifully scarce.

Travelers who might not be trustworthy claimed that gold was plentiful south of the Sahara. But how to get there? Caravans crossed the desert, but Europeans were unwelcome. The only alternative was the ocean, outside the Pillars of Hercules, now the Straits of Gibraltar. But the oceans of the world were not navigable, as everyone knew. Great and dangerous wastes, they were inhabited by unspeakable beings that swallowed ships and men as a dog swallows a morsel.

There might be an alternative, as the Portuguese Prince Henry the Navigator (1394–1460) believed. Little Portugal was outside the Straits of Gibraltar to begin with, and her fishermen did not fear the Atlantic as much as inland peoples did. Furthermore, since 1420 Portuguese sailors and soldiers had been fighting the natives of the Canary Islands, islands lying eight hundred miles southwest of the southern tip of Portugal, and only a few miles off the African coast. Why not use the Canaries as a stepping-stone? From them ships could continue southward along the coast in the hope that they might discover good harbors and begin direct trade with those who possessed gold.

And so it was done. During Henry's life the coast was revealed to extend as far south as the great eastward curve of West Africa, at Sierra Leone. During the next twenty years, until 1480, the Portuguese explored the Gold Coast, so named because here plenty of gold could be found to buy pepper. In 1485 Diogo Cao continued south beyond Cape Palmas, beyond Cape St. Catherine, until he reached Cape Cross, at 22° south latitude. By then the burning question was not whether gold would be discovered, but whether a way might be found around the continent itself. Did Africa ever end? Could ships sail around it to India and the Spice Islands? If so, then it might be possible to trade directly with the spice merchants, eliminating the need to pay gold to the Arab middlemen.

Bartolomeu Dias (c.1450–1500) proved the route. He set out from Lisbon in August 1487, sailed south to the Cape Verde Islands, then continued down the coast, following a now familiar route. He passed Cape St. Mary, Cape St. Catherine, and Cape Cross, sailing ever southward along the eastward curving coastline. Early in January 1488 storms forced him out to sea. When the winds moderated, he traveled eastward again, seeking land. He found nothing. At first bewildered, he soon understood what had happened. He had passed the southern tip of Africa without seeing it. (He saw it and named it the Cape of Good Hope on his homeward journey later that year.) Turning north, he sighted land again on February 3, 1488. The coast here continued to the northeast. His men demanded that he return, and Dias did so after sailing north a few more days, until he reached the mouth of the Great Fish River, nearly five hundred miles east, near present-day Port Elizabeth. The coast did not turn southward again. The way to India seemed to be open at last. Africa could be circumnavigated.

Vasco da Gama (1462–1524) was the first to do that, sailing from Lisbon in July 1497 and, after many adventures, reaching Calicut, the chief Indian trading port, at 11° north latitude, in May of the next year. Da Gama soon came into conflict with the Muslim traders in the port, who did not appreciate him as a competitor and a Christian, and he returned to Lisbon swearing revenge. In 1502 he went back to Calicut, bombarded the town, burned a ship full of Arab men, women, and children because its captain had offended him, and demanded that the Muslims turn over the trade to the Portuguese. Within a generation his demands had been met, and his countrymen were the masters of the spice trade.

Columbus

The trade remained more complicated than the Portuguese liked, for Indian middlemen now ate up much of its profits. Could a way be found to the East Indies, the ultimate source of the spices, so that the fabulously valuable products could be bought direct from those who grew them, creating a monopoly of trade and profits? Muslim pirates infested the Indian Ocean. Hence, Portuguese and Spanish explorers began to dream of a westward route that might avoid all competition.

Christopher Columbus (1451–1506) realized the dream. Italy claims him as a native son, and indeed he was born on her soil, in Genoa, but in every other respect he was not Italian. He may have been the child of Spanish-Jewish parents exiled by the Inquisition. Whatever his descent, he arrived in Portugal on August 13, 1476, swimming ashore from a burning ship. This mythical appearance on the world scene was typical of the man, and he took it to be prophetic of his future greatness.

Columbus was surely brilliant. He was also probably mad. His brilliance was manifest in many ways. An excellent navigator and a capable, experienced seaman, he plotted a route to the "Indies" that was correct in every way, except that he made a number of miscalculations, based partly on ignorance and partly on the monomania that led him to believe true whatever he wanted to be true. His navigational skill, combined with his monomania, resulted in his absolutely certain belief that "India" (if not "Cathay," that is, China) lay about 3,900 miles west of the Canaries. That is not where India is, or China, but it is almost precisely where the Americas are found. Was this brilliance, madness, or fool luck?

Columbus's monomaniacal certainty that he was right about the things that were most important to him brought him much success, as well as tragic failure and loss. Within two years of his swim to shore he had persuaded a leading family of Portugal to permit him to marry one of their most eligible young women. Columbus thereupon began his long campaign to persuade some powerful Portuguese or Spaniard to sponsor his plan to sail westward to India and Cathay. His certainty was such that many were interested; they believed that a man so lacking in doubts must be right.

Columbus did not conceal from his backers that his certainty was not based on the ordinary foundations. Neither reason nor mathematics nor even maps underlay his decision to sail westward, he told King Ferdinand and Queen Isabella in 1502. His conviction came from certain passages in the Bible, for example, Isaiah 11:10–12 and II Esdras 3:18. These fanciful geographical sources were persuasive for the financial backers of those times, as they would not be today.

After years of negotiations, Columbus was finally permitted to make his proposal to the Spanish king and queen in 1490. They were stunned by his demands, which were extravagant, not to say scandalous. No explorer had ever asked to be made a noble, with his titles to remain in his family forever, and to receive a 10 percent permanent commission on all transactions that should occur in his domain. He was turned down, whereupon he left the Spanish court early in 1492, headed for France and England. Before he got far, friends at court persuaded Ferdinand and Isabella to recall him, and all his requests were met.

Columbus was an active not a passive genius, and his energy and sense of his own mission stood him in good stead as he oversaw the purchase and fitting out of his three vessels. He was greatly aided by his friend Martín Alonso Pinzón, who sailed on the *Pinta* and to whom more credit is owing for the whole enterprise than Columbus was ever willing to allow. The expedition was ready in a shorter time than anyone thought possible, and the *Santa Maria*, the *Pinta*, and the *Niña* left Palos, half an hour before sunrise, on August 3, 1492.

Columbus's crew had been hastily assembled and was as ignorant and superstitious as any group of seamen in those times. Columbus understood he faced a daunting task in having the men sail westward through an empty ocean day after day, week after week. At the same time, he wished to keep both his course and the distances sailed each day concealed from his crew, for fear that they might sell his secrets to other adventurers. This conflict led to contradictions, which are only partly resolved by a comparison of his official account of the voyage and his private journal. Further confusions were introduced by his shockingly bad measurements of the height of the North Star, which led to wide miscalculation of his ships' position at any given time.

In the end, how could he fail to find America if he only managed to keep going? South, Central, and North America, after all, form an impassable, 8,700-mile-long barrier all the way from about 57° south latitude to about 70° north latitude. To miss both continents and the land bridge connecting them, a ship sailing westward would have to swing south around Cape Horn or north through the nearly permanent ice sheet of the Arctic Circle. Neither would happen to Columbus. Thus, on the wings of his own mad certainty and geographical inevitability he discovered America, sighting land for the first time on October 12, 1492. It was a lovely little island, one of the Bahamas, which he named San Salvador. It is now called Guanahaní.

The marvelous irony is that Columbus never knew he had discovered a new world. In all he made four voyages to the West Indies, but he persisted in believing that he was in the East Indies, that Japan and China were nearby, that India was just over the horizon. He was certain of that. The Bible had told him so. But what did his error matter, except for Columbus's personal life? Others, after him, soon discovered where they actually were, and wherever they were there was much that was wonderful and strange, with gold and silver to be had for almost no trouble. There were also tobacco and cotton to carry back to Europe. They would change life in the Old World even more than gold.

Columbus's personal life turned out to be an abject failure despite his astounding success as a greatly mistaken but even more greatly fortunate navigator. A magnificent seamen, he was an abysmal administrator. Ferdinand and Isabella soon saw this. They had made him promises, and they never ceased to be generous and affectionate toward this strange, mad, wonderful man who had made them almost as famous as he was. But they could not endure his autocratic assurance that he was the king of the Western World, and they merely the Spanish viceroys.

In 1500, during Columbus's third sojourn, they sent an ambassador plenipotentiary to Santo Domingo, on Española, Columbus's name for the island that is now divided between Haiti and the Dominican Republic. Months of bitter negotiations ensued, but Columbus, who really was only a viceroy, could not win them, and he was finally arrested and returned to Spain in shackles. The queen ordered that he be released and that he appear before her. When he did so, this great man fell to his knees and burst into tears.

There is a sense in which Columbus did not discover America, for European fishermen had known about the existence of uncharted land in the Western Ocean for centuries before he ever got there. It had been in their interest to keep America secret, and they had done so since the Icelandic voyages of the tenth century, and perhaps for centuries prior to that. It was in Columbus's interest to make America public, to proclaim it to the world, even if he did not know it was America. He was even more successful at revealing the secret than the fisherman had been at keeping it. And once the secret was out, the world was never the same.

Sailing Around the World

The discovery of America by Christopher Columbus is probably the single greatest addition to human knowledge ever made by one man. But there was still much to know. Columbus had insisted that the earth was round, and that by sailing westward a sailor would eventually come back home. But was this really true? No one could be sure until someone had done it. And the West Indies, it had to be admitted, were not the East Indies. Rich and interesting as the new lands were, they were not the Spice Islands which Europeans had dreamed of gaining direct access to for so long.

The Portuguese navigator Ferdinand Magellan (c.1480–1521) was chosen by the Spaniards to resolve the problem. He was to seek a southwest route to the East Indies, around the tip of South America. Could a way be found? Where, in fact, was the tip of the continent? Magellan left Spain in September 1519 and after an easy voyage entered the bay of Rio de Janeiro in December. He spent the early months of 1520 probing the mouths of various rivers in search of a passage through the continent. He did not find one until November 1520. Then, traveling ever southward, he discovered and sailed through the Straits of Magellan and entered the "Sea of the South" on November 28. The fleet began the great crossing of the Pacific Ocean, so named because the seas were moderate, the wind fresh and steady at their backs, all the way from South America to the Philippines.

Despite the easy sailing, the voyage was a hard one. Until December 18 the fleet, now reduced from its original five ships to three, followed the Chilean coast northward to find the trade winds. Then Magellan struck out into the open sea to the northwest. Neither he nor any of his men had an accurate idea of the distance they would have to cover, but they soon realized they lacked enough water and food. Tortured by incessant thirst, decimated by scurvy, forced to eat rat-fouled biscuit and, finally, the leather off the yardarms, they nevertheless did not turn back, owing to Magellan's iron determination.

The fleet made its first landfall, after ninety-nine days at sea, on March 6, 1521, at the island of Guam in the Marianas. There they tasted their first fresh food and water in more than three months. Magellan, anxious to push onward, stayed only three days, leaving on March 9 to sail west-southwestward toward the islands that were later called the Philippines. He claimed the land for Spain and converted the ruler and his chief men to Christianity, but his triumph was short-lived. On April 27, 1521, only a month after arriving in the Philippines, Magellan was killed in a fight with natives on Mactan Island.

Without Magellan to drive them onward, the fleet suffered further reductions. Two ships reached the Moluccas. Only one returned to Spain, under the command of Juan Sebastián Elcano, a Basque navigator who had been Magellan's second in command. His ship, the *Vittoria*, limped home, leaking at every seam, but she was laden with spices, and she had sailed around the world. Elcano was rewarded with an augmentation to his coat of arms, a globe with the inscription *Primus circumdisti me*: "You were the first to encircle me."

The Birth of World Trade

All of the oceans were now proved to be connected, and no reasonable person could ever think again that the earth was anything but round. Since the oceans were open in every direction, they were theoretically free for all ships to sail around the world. But the passage through Magellan's narrow strait, possible only during the months of December through April (the southern summer), was difficult at best, and it could be guarded. For a century Spain and Portugal managed, by force and guile, to maintain a monopoly of the southern trade route between West and East. Frustrated, the English, French, and Dutch began to search for a northern route that would be free of harassment by Spanish and Portuguese men-of-war. The result was another surprise, the discovery of the continent of North America, whose vast potential riches were soon realized by all of Europe. And thus a new kind of trade was born that ultimately would bring the whole world together into one economic entity, no matter how many separate political units it might hold.

Within a century this trade no longer dealt primarily in luxury goods. Large profits were to be made in the bulk shipment of mundane things like cloth, sugar, and rum. It was a far cry from the old overland trade in small amounts of valuable spices and drugs that could be carried on a camel's back. No one complained about the change, for the riches to be gained were incomparably greater. Besides, the trade routes—sea routes—could be controlled by Europeans from one end to the other. No middlemen were needed, Arab or otherwise.

Soon, other bulky cargoes began to be carried, like tobacco and rice and even, in the nineteenth century, granite and ice, which started as ballast but ended up making the fortunes of New England captains. Shiploads of cheap Chinese porcelains were also brought from the Orient to America and Europe. These goods helped to define Western taste for generations.

In this new world sugar and slavery became inextricably linked. Prior to 1500 the world's sweet tooth had had to be satisfied by honey and by a few rare sweetmeats from exotic sources in the East. First the Spanish, then the English, established sugar plantations in the Caribbean islands and Central America. Portuguese adventurers founded their own sugar plantations in Brazil. Sugar became as plentiful as salt, and as profitable. But labor was always short in these plantations. The work was hard and killed men. Native populations, sparse to begin with, had been further reduced by the European onslaught, which brought not only cruel weapons but also strange diseases against which the natives did not possess immunity. The solution was African slavery. For three centuries, African slaves were the most valuable of all cargoes, even if only half of those shipped on vessels leaving the coast of West Africa ever reached the Americas alive. If any objected to this trade in human beings, Aristotle's doctrine of natural slavery could always be invoked to justify it. And who was more "naturally" a slave than a man or woman whose skin was black? Few questioned the "logic" of this argument until the nineteenth century.

Trade in Ideas

The ships that plied the oceans of the world during the three centuries after 1492 carried invisible cargoes in addition to the bulk cargoes that were visible to all. These were knowledge and ideas, together with religious beliefs, and they flowed in both directions, from West to East and from East to West. And in the interchange, ideas were transformed.

Gunpowder, invented in China around 1000 AD, is a good example of the change. The Chinese used gunpowder primarily to make fireworks and for other peaceful purposes. Arab mercenaries, obtaining gunpowder from the Chinese, made the first guns. The Europeans perfected them. More, they studied the art of using guns and cannon with a unique intensity. By 1500, European military strategy, both on sea and land, was based on the concept of acquiring and maintaining superior firepower. And to this day, in the West, the superiority of firepower over manpower and tactics has persisted as the central idea of military thinking.

Since Western military leaders have always agreed on the priority of this principle, almost all wars among Western powers have been won by the side possessing superiority in weapons and ammunition. Sometimes the weaker side has been able to put up a good fight, as for example in the American Civil War, when the South, lacking the foundries of the North and thus the capability of producing comparable armaments, made up for their disadvantage for close to four years with superior tactics. One must assume that the men, considered objectively, were equal, since brothers often fought on opposite sides in that war. Eventually, the greater weight of guns and armor that could be brought to bear by the North won the war, thus confirming the age-old prejudice.

Only in the twentieth century has the prejudice been successfully countered. In the Vietnam War, for example, the United States, possessing overwhelming superiority in firepower, was defeated by an army of irregulars armed with rifles and grenades instead of bombs and fireships, and whose men rode bicycles along jungle trails instead of tanks, which could only follow the roads. As a consequence, that war could turn out to be one of the most important in history, not only for its political reverberations but also because it may force a change in the way military men think.

However, it must be noted that this obvious lesson did not bring about a change in the thought of Soviet strategists, who, only a few years after the end of the Vietnam War, found themselves embroiled in a similar conflict in Afghanistan. Like the American generals in Vietnam, the Soviet generals in Afghanistan believed they could not fail to win because of their heavier tanks and their larger projectiles. They, too, were defeated.

The belief in the advantage of possessing superior firepower is not just a prejudice, of course. Other things being equal, the side having the bigger, faster-firing guns will almost always win. (The same went for the side having the sharper swords and the better armor, or the better arrows and the stronger horses, in another age.) And for centuries following that remarkable time when Europe reached out and discovered the rest of the world, other things *were* equal. Soldiers of the East were no better or worse than those of the West. Nor were the tactics of either side notably superior. Thus the fact that the West continued to possess the bigger guns meant that it almost always won its battles with Eastern foes.

In other words, Vasco da Gama's action in 1502 was not an accident. When he brutally set fire to an Arab ship with his heavier guns, he assured his victorious side a monopoly of trade. Such actions, and such consequences, were commonplace. Thus a myth grew up that the West was "irresistible." Since both East and West came to believe it, the myth was the most powerful of all weapons in the West's arsenal.

It could only be countered by another myth. The Europeans who visited China and India found both countries so vast that for a long time they could not grasp their complexity. The secrets of power, particularly in China, evaded Westerners. They could not understand why knowledge of a two-thousand-year-old text should confer supreme power on some old man and cause him to be obeyed as a representative of an emperor whom no European ever met. Thus Europeans did not know who ruled in China and how he, she, or they ruled, and since they could do business without this knowledge, Westerners did not seek to learn it. The myth of the "mysterious" East was born during those first meetings between East and West, and it persisted for many generations. And their presumed mystery was the only protection Easterners had against the big guns of the West.

There were two things that the West thought they knew about the East.

First, the East lacked any respectable religion, which meant any mono-theistic religion. Second, the East was incredibly rich. We will return to the matter of the "riches of the East" in a moment.

In trying to persuade Ferdinand and Isabella to support his venture, Columbus had always emphasized two points above all others. There was gold to be had for the taking in the New World. In return, Christianity could and should be brought to the natives, innocent pagans as they undoubtedly were. The promise of gold did not fall on deaf ears, although the king and queen, being truly pious, may have reacted even more strongly to the idea of helping to spread the gospel over the newly discovered lands.

Unfortunately for the reputation of Christianity in the East, that religion had just begun to split into warring factions when Columbus discovered the New World. Ferdinand and Isabella, for example, were certain that it was Roman Catholic Christianity that would benefit the innocent natives and bring them to salvation, if necessary at the point of a gun. A century later, in North America, the English and the Dutch brought Protestant divines to convert the Indians. The natives usually converted, for the firepower of the Europeans was irresistible. But the new converts watched in amazement as the apostles of peace fought each other over questions of doctrine that the innocent natives could not understand.

Apart from salvation, did the natives benefit from their new religion? Certainly yes. If it had not been for the missionaries who accompanied the soldiers and the traders, the natives would have fared even worse than they did. They did not fare well, for the missionaries were usually comparatively powerless. But they were not wholly without power, and more than once they were able to insist on better treatment of native peoples than they would otherwise have received.

Today, the countries that make up the Third World are generally perceived as extremely poor. During the first centuries after 1500 the same countries were generally perceived as enormously rich. Has their economic situation changed so radically? Relative to the West it has changed somewhat, but not enough to explain the change in perspective, which is owing to our having greater understanding today of wealth and poverty than our forefathers possessed.

The European sailors, soldiers, and merchants who first visited the East were too unsophisticated politically to realize that the East seemed rich because only a few persons among a great many possessed all of the wealth. Europeans did not even recognize the poverty in which most Easterners lived. Nor did they understand that this abject poverty was created by birth, maintained by custom, and mandated by law.

One reason they did not comprehend the poverty of the East was the extremes of wealth and poverty at home, from some of the same causes.

But in most European countries more mobility existed between economic classes, and besides, even as early as the middle of the sixteenth century, there were already ideas abroad about social and economic equality that colored everything Europeans thought. Those ideas did not exist in the East until Westerners began to export them to the rest of the world at the beginning of the nineteenth century after the French Revolution, which is to say three hundred years after Columbus discovered America.

In the end it would be ideas that dominated the trade between West and East. But no one knew this at the time.

Homage to Columbus

Try to imagine the world into which Columbus was born in 1451. Suppose you were a European, of any country. What would the world have looked like to you?

In the first place, it would not have looked round. The mathematical idea of a round earth goes all the way back to the ancient Greeks, but it was an abstraction for most people everywhere. (Sailors, who could see a ship disappear over the horizon, knew at least that the sea was not flat.)

The roundness of the earth is not an abstraction for us. We are quite certain that if we decide to travel around the globe, in any direction—east, west, north, south—we will sooner or later return to where we started. If we follow established routes, it need not take long at all, three or four days at the most. Furthermore, we know that, within the limits of political calm or turmoil, we will be just as safe anywhere on earth as we are at home. That is, we are certain that there are no monsters or other mystical barriers that would hinder us from circumnavigating the globe.

The world would not have looked round to you in 1450 because your mind, unless you were a genius like Columbus, could not have conceived it as round, which is to say, as we conceive it. Columbus changed the picture of the world that is in everybody's head. No one else who ever lived has done that so thoroughly.

Those were all great men, those explorers, those discoverers. Prince Henry the Navigator. Bartolomeu Dias. Vasco de Gama. Ferdinand Magellan. And so many others. They all took chances that stagger the mind. Most of them never returned home to enjoy the fruits of their great discoveries. Of the two hundred and seventy men who accompanied Magellan on his five ships when he left Spain in 1519, only eighteen returned two years later. A few had deserted, but most had died of starvation, illness, or wounds. The chance of surviving one of those early voyages, breathtaking in their scope and daring, was much slimmer than the dangers faced by Neil Armstrong when he went to the moon in 1969. And yet in the harbors of Spain and Portugal in the early years of the sixteenth century, and later in the English, French, and Dutch ports as well, the steady stream of ships that departed those places never lacked for sailors to man them and for captains to lead them.

They were not rash. Like Neil Armstrong and the other astronauts, they were convinced that they were supported by the best technological support available in the world. In other words, they believed they had the best chance possible. They went anyway, often marrying and fathering a child before they departed so that their names might survive, if not their physical being, and they seldom failed to write their wills. They went despite their fears, for nothing could stop them from going.

Why did they go? For many, the promise of great wealth, real or imagined, was enough to draw them from their homes and down to the sea in ships. For those who went after the first great discoveries had been made, the pursuit of wealth may often have been the greatest lure. But I do not think it was so for the discoverers themselves. And certainly it was not so for Columbus.

Brilliant as he may have been, and mad as well, Christopher Columbus was one of the most remarkable men who ever lived. He never turned aside from the opportunity of wealth, but wealth was not what he sought, what he was willing to give his life for. What he sought was eternal fame, for he knew, as perhaps no one else realized in his time, that the discovery of a new world would bring him that.

The overweening desire for honor or fame was called by the poet John Milton "that last infirmity of noble mind." The phrase is often misunderstood. Milton meant that of all the motives that drive men, there is only one that is greater than the desire for fame and honor. That is the wish for salvation, for Christian blessedness. The desire for fame possesses a high purity that is only exceeded by what the saints want or know. Columbus was not a saint, God knows; he was much too great a sinner for that. But if there are secular saints, men and women who possess a purity of heart and will that is just short of the saintly and the divine, then Columbus was one of those.

8

The Invention of Scientific Method

O F ALL THE KINDS of knowledge that the West has given to the world, the most valuable is a method of acquiring new knowledge. Called "scientific method," it was invented by a series of European thinkers from about 1550 to 1700.

The genesis of scientific method goes back to the classical Greeks. Like all their gifts, it bears watching. But even though scientific method sometimes seems as dangerous as it is beneficial, we could no longer live without it.

So far in this book, when we have used the word *knowledge* we have usually meant what *anyone* could know. In medieval Latin "knowledge" was *scientia,* and everyone could possess some or all of it. From the Latin comes our modern term *science.* But "science" no longer means the knowledge that anyone has or may have.

It does not mean a poet's knowledge, for instance, or a carpenter's, or even a philosopher's or a theologian's. Usually, it does not mean a mathematician's knowledge. "Science," today, is a special kind of knowledge possessed only by "scientists." Scientists are special people. They are not anybody.

The Meaning of Science

So much is probably obvious. Yet there are complexities in the meaning of "science" that are hard to unravel. Let us try using the word *science* in some sentences.

1. Science will never understand the secret of life.
2. Sooner or later, scientists will find a cure for AIDS.

3. Science and art have nothing in common.
4. I'm taking a science course, but I'm also going to study some history.
5. Mathematics is the language of science.
6. Scientists are trying to determine if Shakespeare actually wrote all the plays that are ascribed to him.
7. Literary criticism isn't really scientific because it isn't predictive.
8. Most poets glaze over when they come upon a mathematical formula; most scientists glaze over when they come upon a poem.
9. Being bilingual doesn't mean you know anything about language.
10. I know the answer, but I can't explain it.

All of those sentences are "real" in the sense that they were taken from published sources and were written by respectable authors (Sentences 4, 9, and 10 were recorded from oral communications by respectable speakers). What do I mean by "respectable"? I mean that the authors or speakers were reasonably well educated and seriously meant what they said; that is, they thought that what they said was both comprehensible and true. Furthermore, all of the sentences are modern in the sense that they were composed within the last ten years. They clearly represent some kind of modern consensus about the meaning of the word *science* (which does not appear in the last two sentences, but is implied in both of them; that is, it is hidden or imbedded in the word *know*).

Let us examine a few of the sentences. The first one, for example: "Science will never understand the secret of life." Is this true? Manifestly scientists have recently, and in some cases not so recently, discovered many of the "secrets" of life, among them the structure and evolution of cells, the operation of the immune system, the role of DNA in genetics, and a great deal more. And we can expect scientists to go on studying life, and finding out its secrets. But there is something about the word *secret* in that sentence that makes the sentence both true and incontrovertible. By definition science is not able to understand the kind of secret that the secret of life is supposed to be, which by implication has something to do with an unfathomable mystery. Some other kind of knowledge is evidently required to solve *that* mystery, no matter how much knowledge scientists have about life, now or in the future.

Or take Sentence 5: "Mathematics is the language of science." This clearly proclaims that mathematics and science have a close relation, but it just as clearly proclaims that they are not the same thing. Scientists may *use* mathematics, but they do not *do* mathematics; and mathematicians can be just as ignorant of scientific methods and results as ordinary laymen are. Albert Einstein was a great theoretician but not a great mathematician; when he got into a fix he would go to his mathematician friends, who would invent the mathematics to get him out of it. But his friends, with all their skill, could never have come up with the theory of relativity.

At the same time, the sentence seems to say that mathematics is a different kind of language from French or Chinese, or from the language of body movements or musical notation. All of those are languages of a sort, but none of them could ever be called *the* language of science, although scientists might study any one of them.

Sentence 7, "Literary criticism isn't really scientific because it isn't predictive," is very curious. It is an old chestnut that science is not science unless it is predictive; that is, you do not really know something about the way nature works unless you can predict how it is going to work under this or that circumstance. The curious thing is that one main function of literary criticism (as, for example, the book review in the daily paper) is to tell you whether you will like (or be interested in) a book. Of course, the predictions are not certain. But not all experiments turn out the way you expect them to, either. Nor is the judgment of the critic couched in mathematical formulas.

I would be the first to admit that literary criticism is not science, in the ordinary sense of the term. But I do not believe this is so because it fails to make predictions. Nevertheless, the sentence gets at a feeling we have about science, and contributes to the meaning of the word *science*.

Sentence 9, "Being bilingual doesn't mean you know anything about language," gets at another fundamental feeling that we have about science, whether or not we should have it. That is, it proclaims, by a wonderful indirection, that the kind of knowledge that anyone must have in order to do something consistently well, like speaking two languages, is not scientific knowledge. By implication, scientific knowledge, in itself, is not practical or useful. This sentence says nothing good about science. Most people would rather be bilingual than a scientific linguist. Bilingualism, in fact, is good for the brain (it makes it work better and faster), whereas knowing all about linguistics is of little use unless you want a job as a university teacher. The implication of the sentence is that often, if not always, the knowledge that scientists have is specialized and relatively useless for ordinary persons.

However, Sentence 2, "Sooner or later, scientists will find a cure for AIDS," expresses our deep faith in science, our sense that we have to and can depend on science to solve the really hard, pressing, practical problems that we face. The sentence also suggests our sense that only scientists can be expected to find a cure for AIDS. Poets, carpenters, and philosophers, we are sure, will not find any such cure. Nor will an ordinary person, just by thinking about it, intuit a cure. This is one of the most widely held notions that go with the word.

In our scientific age, most teachers, hearing a student say Sentence 10, "I know the answer, but I can't explain it," would be tempted to respond, "If you can't explain it, then you don't know it!" And to give the student an F for presumption. Knowledge that cannot be framed and communicated, mathematically or otherwise, is not knowledge, in other words, and is certainly not scientific knowledge, which is felt to be (perhaps preeminently) public knowledge in the sense that it can and must be statable so that other scientists can test and validate it.

But this is to rule out as science, which once meant all kinds of knowledge, as we have seen, a vast panoply of human mental states and acts that do not have the kind of inherent certainty that scientific knowledge is supposed to possess. The best detectives always have hunches they cannot explain but that nevertheless turn out to be right, at least in fiction. Great athletes have an inexplicable and inexpressible genius when it comes to knowing where or how to run or throw the ball. Soldiers who survive may often do so because of their sixth sense about danger. And saints are more certain than any scientist about what God has told them, or about what they know about God in some other way.

However, we are not trying to prove the sentence wrong, and in fact it is not wrong, for it expresses something we feel about science, namely, that it cannot be exclusively intuitive, although intuition may be somehow involved in any important scientific discovery or breakthrough.

Finally, Sentence 3, "Science and art have nothing in common," reveals what is perhaps our deepest prejudice about science—and about art—at the same time that it is manifestly not true, at least on the surface. That is, science and art have many things in common, for example, in that both are activities involving some of the most capable men and women, that both science and art enlighten us and give us surcease from pain, that both are immensely difficult and require every ounce of effort and intelligence to succeed in them, that only human beings do them, and so forth.

But the sentence is true in another sense, which is also suggested by Sentence 8. We are pretty sure that scientists and artists, even if many of the things they do are similar—think of a metallurgist and a sculptor in metal—see what they do in different ways and do it for different reasons. It is their different viewpoint that tells us most about what "science" means and what "scientists" do.

Three Characteristics of Science

Science, then, in our common everyday sense of the word, is a human activity characterized by three things. First, science is practiced by special people with a specific view of the world. Scientists try to be objective, unsentimental, unemotional. They do not let their feelings get in the way of their observations of real things, facts, as they call them. They often work in laboratories or in other areas where they can carefully control what they are working on. They do not just wander out onto the dock at sunset and look at the world with wonder, as a poet might. Ideally, they are also both honest and humble. They always try to report their findings so others can check them out and then utilize them in their own work. They do not claim more than they can prove, and often even less. But they are very proud of their calling and prefer to talk to other scientists rather than anybody else, especially poets, who tend to make them feel uncomfortable, to put them down. (Of course poets also feel scientists return the favor.)

Second, science deals almost exclusively with things, not ideas or feelings; and with the external world and its workings, not inner states and their workings, despite the effort of some psychologists to be or seem scientific. The human body is considered to be a part of the external world; the soul is not. Therefore, scientists work to understand the body but not the soul. Most scientists doubt the soul exists. The solar system and the universe are also part of the external world, although we have little enough direct evidence of their mode of existence. Scientists tend to assume the basic conditions of nature on earth are the same everywhere in the cosmos.

Mankind is only questionably part of the external world in this sense. Scientists are generally reluctant to deal with the behavior of large groups of men and women. Thus economists, for example, struggle to be considered scientists, but usually in vain. The external world of scientists contains some things, like quanta, quarks, and quasars, that are fully as mysterious as angels and normally as invisible. But this does not trouble them, as they believe they can deal effectively with the elementary particles that they cannot see and according to the uncertainty principle never can see, but not with angels, which will probably never appear to scientists because scientists do not believe in them.

When you come right down to it, the external world is anything that scientists can measure and describe in mathematical terms, and it excludes everything they cannot. This means the external world is a rather hazy notion, but the idea behind it is not hazy at all.

Third, science deals with whatever it deals with in a special way, employing special methods and a language for reporting results that is unique to it. The best known method, but not necessarily the most often employed, consists of experiment, which involves getting an idea—from where, most scientists do not question—framing it in a testable hypothesis, and then testing the hypothesis in a controlled environment to find out whether or not it is valid. The environment must be carefully controlled so that extraneous elements do not intrude to invalidate the experiment, and so that others can repeat the experiment in the hope of arriving at the same result, which is the best evidence of its reliability.

But it is the language in which results are reported and in which the work itself is done and with which it is controlled—namely, mathematics—that is perhaps the most distinctive characteristic of all. Most scientists would say that if you cannot describe what you are doing in mathematical terms, you are not doing science, and they prefer to report their results in mathematical terms because doing so is much easier and quicker (for them) and because scientists all around the world can understand them.

It is also important that the work itself is done mathematically, which means that the observations being studied must be transformed into—or reduced to—numbers in the first instance, so they can be studied in a rational manner. The old idea of the earliest Greek scientists—that the world is essentially intelligible because it is somehow conformed to the human mind—is thus converted into the Pythagorean view that the world, at least the external world that is the subject matter of science, is essentially mathematical and thus intelligible because the human mind is essentially mathematical, too.

Wherever mankind has been able to measure things, which means to transform or reduce them to numbers, it has indeed made great progress both in understanding and in controlling them. Where human beings have failed to find a way to measure, they have been much less successful, which partly explains the relative failure of psychology, economics, and literary criticism to acquire the status of science.

Science was the major discovery, or invention, of the seventeenth century. Men of that time learned—and it was a very great, revolutionary discovery—how to measure, explain, and manipulate natural phenomena in the way that today we call scientific. Since the seventeenth century, science has progressed a great deal and has discovered many truths, and conferred many benefits, that the seventeenth century did not know. But it has not found a new way to discover natural truths.* For this reason, the seventeenth century is possibly the most important century in human history. It instituted irrevocable change in the way human beings live on earth. We can never go back to living the way we lived in the Renaissance, for instance. We can only wonder whether the change was in all ways for the better.

---

*It may not be strictly correct that we have not discovered any new ways to discover truths. See Chapter 15.

Aristotelian Science: Matter

In order to invent scientific method, thinkers of the seventeenth century first had to overthrow the world view of the greatest scientist who had lived up until that time, Aristotle. To understand what happened we have to know something about the world as Aristotle saw and described it. Two aspects of that world, in particular, concern us: matter and motion.

Every material thing, said Aristotle, has both a material and a formal aspect. Matter, in one sense, is a thing's potentiality. Matter in this sense does not exist by itself. In another sense of matter, it is the stuff out of which things are made. It is the wax that is shaped by the imposition of the form, to use an old image that was often employed by Aristotelians.

In our sublunary world, the world below the moon, beyond which things are considerably different, there are four kinds of stuff out of which things are made. Four elements, as the Aristotelians preferred to say. They are Earth, Water, Air, and Fire. I give them capital letters because none of them exists purely in our imperfect world, but always in mixtures that are more or less earthy, more or less humid, more or less aerial, more or less fiery.

Heavy things are mostly, although never entirely, made of the Earth element. Lighter things have an admixture of Water, Air, or even Fire, which, like the other elements, joins with them in mixtures. Since the four elements never appear alone, in their essential purity, it is very hard to measure them. In a sense they are invisible. But it is obvious enough, the Aristotelians said, that a man has a good amount of Earth in him, which makes him heavy, contributes to the strength of his bones, etc.; a good amount of Water, which produces his blood and other internal fluids; of Air, which he breathes in and out; and of Fire, which gives him his heat and is in a sense the essence of the life in him. And so with other material things beneath the moon.

Above the moon, that is, in the sun and the planets, the fixed stars and the great spheres on which they all move, there is a fifth element, a Quintessence, as it was called. The sun and the other celestial bodies are made out of the Quintessence, which exists in them in a pure state. The moon is mostly made out of the Quintessence, although there is a small admixture of the sublunary elements in it because of its proximity to the earth, which is mostly made of Earth. The proof of this is the markings on the moon, which are like the ravages made by time upon a beautiful face. It is important to remember that the quintessential element of which the celestial bodies are made is still matter. It is not what angels are made of, for example, because angels are nonmaterial, as is God.

Aristotelian Motion

The fundamental fact for Aristotle, the basic, underlying assumption of his physics, which was well and consistently structured, is that the natural state of all sublunary things, material and immaterial, is rest. Motion, as a consequence, is always either violent and unnatural, or it is a natural correction of a previous state of imbalance, that is, a seeking, on the part of the body, for its place of rest. Once that place of rest is achieved, motion stops.

Earth, Water, and to a certain extent Air naturally seek a place that is downward, toward the center of the earth, which they would reach if they could, that is, if they were not stopped at some impermeable surface, like that of the earth itself. Fire seeks to fly upward to its natural place of rest, which is above us, but not infinitely far, that is, that place is well below the sphere of the moon. Air is often, perhaps always, mixed with Fire, as well as with the heavier elements, and so its behavior is flighty and unpredictable. It goes up, it goes down, its movements being highly perturbed because of the odd mixture of elements within it. If Air were pure, it would rest in its natural place around us, with Water and Earth below it, Fire above, and there would be no wind.

Before discarding this picture of the world, consider how sensible it seems, and what a stroke of genius it was to arrive at it. In our experience, everything *is* at rest, unless it is seeking that natural place where it can find rest, as the river seeks the sea, the flame its place above us, or is forced to move by something else. When we force something to move—say, throw a ball—it soon rolls to a stop and will stay in the place it has found until we pick it up and throw it again. So it is with all material things lacking souls. We have no direct sensory experience of anything—anything at all—that does not seem to "desire" to find a place where it may rest.

And what of things that have souls, like animals and men? They, too, seem to seek a natural place, a home, ultimately a grave. For is not the grave the end and goal of all striving? The body seeks that goal. But the human soul strives for something else, atonement with God, the peace that God alone can give. That is the highest and strongest desire of the soul, even if sometimes, as Dante explains in the sixteenth canto of the *Purgatorio*, the soul wills not aright.

"My love is my weight," said St. Augustine, a statement that is unintelligible unless one understands Aristotle's universe, and then it is obvious. My body seeks the earth, because it is earthy. The element Earth predominates in it. But my spirit seeks a higher resting place. That is what it loves. The weight of my body draws me downward. The weight of my spirit is light, lighter than Air, lighter than Fire, and its lightness snatches it upward to its natural resting place, while my body rests in its long home.

In the sublunary world, then, there are rest and two kinds of motion: motion that is natural because it results from the "weight" of a thing, which always seeks its proper place ("proper" means "own"); and motion that is unnatural or violent, as Aristotle said, because it is the result of a force being applied to a thing. But what of the world above the moon? There is motion there, too! The sun and the planets move, the fixed stars circle the world once every twenty-four hours. What kind of motion is that?

This was a hard question, for beneath the moon all motion is in straight lines, unless some violent force turns a body out of the right path. Above the moon, the sun, the planets, and the fixed stars apparently move in circles. Are they forced to do so? We cannot assume that, said Aristotle and his Christian followers, for the heavenly bodies are perfect, and it would be imperfect to be pushed. Their circular motion must, somehow, be a natural motion.

The solution followed easily: the natural motion of the Quintessence is uniform circular motion, which differs from the motions of sublunary things as the heavenly bodies differ from those things. Immediately, all is explained. The heavenly bodies, or rather the spheres on which they move, turn forever because that is their nature, and we see the result when we look up into the sky.

From time to time another theory was advanced, to the effect that angels drove the planets in their paths, effortlessly moving them forever in their appointed rounds. This theory, in fact, was widely accepted during the early Middle Ages. When Aristotle was rediscovered after 1000 it became clear how much better was his assumption of a natural quintessential motion that attached itself to a natural quintessential substance. The world made more sense that way. It was somehow more fitting, more beautiful, more perfect, and more the way God would obviously have made it. And so this theory that the planets moved in that way turned into dogma. To question this belief was to question God's design for the world.

The Revolt Against Aristotle

Galileo challenged Aristotle's theory of motion, thus producing the most famous moment in the history of science, but it was far from the first such event. The questioning had begun at least two centuries before Galileo was born.

Why did the questioning start? Aristotle's theory of motion explained the way things naturally fall and run downhill—a ball dropped from a tower, a river running to the sea—but it was much less successful at explaining what Aristotle called violent motion. This is the kind of motion that a body undergoes when it is thrown or hurled by some sort of machine like a catapult or a cannon. It was the invention and regular use of catapults, in fact, that may have led to such questioning. The traditional theory did not explain very well how they worked.

That may be difficult to understand, since we now have an entirely different theory of motion. But if you remember that Aristotle's law of inertia was based on the principle of rest, you will see the problem. Nothing moved, in his theory, unless it was pushed, or unless it was partaking of a natural motion, like the fall of an object toward the center of the earth, or the uniform circular motion of the heavenly bodies.

A projectile shot from a catapult was not moving naturally. While it was rising on the catapult's throwing end, it was obviously being pushed. But why did it keep moving once it left the catapult? It was no longer being pushed. Why did it not drop straight down to the ground as soon as it was free to do so?

Aristotelians had answers to these questions, but they were inadequate, indeed, rather lame. The splendidly commonsensical theory of inertial rest broke down when it came to violent motion. For example, it was said that the air in front of the projectile became disturbed and rushed around and behind the projectile in order to fill up the vacuum caused by its passage, since "Nature abhors a vacuum." This frantic effort on the part of the air to avoid a vacuum pushed the projectile forward. And there were even more fanciful explanations.

Many thinkers gave it up as a bad job. Violent motion was just hard to explain, they said, but the theory in general was so obviously right that this should not matter a great deal. But some eminent theologians at the University of Paris were more skeptical. Since they were recognized authorities in theology, they could question with impunity a part of Aristotelian theory, knowing as they did how to save the remainder. This is what Galileo, later, did not want or know how to do.

Jean Buridan (1300–1358) was one of those Parisian theologians. Nicholas of Oresme (c.1325–1382) was another. They saw the problem clearly, and they came up with a solution. The catapult, they said, imparts a certain *impetus* to the projectile, which continues to move on its own until the impetus is spent.

Violent motion, in other words, is inherent; like natural motion, its principle is in the body that moves. Once the impetus has been imparted to the projectile by a violent force, the projectile no longer needs to be pushed. It keeps on going until (in the case of a cannonball or a projectile from a catapult) it falls to earth.

This was good as far as it went, but it did not go far enough. The problem of uniform circular motion remained, and the theologians did not see how to apply their insight to that problem. Also, to do so might be treading on dangerous ground.

There were several serious problems about the way the heavenly bodies moved, or were supposed to move. First, did the assumption of uniform circular motion save the phenomena, as the saying went? Did it explain what astronomers observed when they looked at the sky? For Ptolemy, the great Alexandrian of twelve hundred years before, uniform circular motion had been adequate to explain what he had been able to observe, and what his predecessors could hand down to him in the way of observations. But now the heavens had been watched with scrupulous care by a horde of astronomers over the centuries, Arabs and Greeks, Indians and Italians. When their observations were pooled and collated, it began to look as if the theory of uniform circular motions, even when the motions were combined in ingenious ways, would *not* save the phenomena.

The combining of uniform circular motions had been necessary for some time. The ancient Greek astronomers had been able to see, for example, that the apparent path of Venus in the heavens is not a uniform circle around the earth. The phenomena could be explained if one assumed that an ideal point circled the earth uniformly, which point was the ideal position of Venus, while the planet itself circled uniformly around that ideal point. This view accounted for the observed fact that Venus appeared to move forward in its orbit faster at some times than at others, and in fact sometimes appeared to move backward in its orbit, to retrogress. The uniform circular motion of Venus around its ideal point was called the epicycle of Venus.

As more accurate observations continued to be made by astronomers over the centuries, more epicycles were needed to explain the observations. Eventually, every planet needed an epicycle. Mars needed two, for only if it were assumed that the planet uniformly circled a point on an epicycle that in turn uniformly circled the ideal point of Mars could the perturbations of the observed orbit of the planet be explained. Even so, the theory of epicycles did not work perfectly, as the accuracy of observations continued to be improved. Besides, epicycles were not elegant. It was unpleasant to have to think of the heavens cranking around in such an unaesthetic manner.

But if the planets did not move in uniform circles around the earth, how then did they move? Was there any other kind of simple motion that would explain the appearances and could be called "natural"? There did not appear to be such a motion. At least no one could imagine it.

As time went on, there were many other problems that had not been solved. For example, why did the heavenly bodies move in the first place, whether in uniform circles or in some other way? The answer that had once been universally acceptable—that God wished them to move, and so they moved—had begun to be troublesome to the most adventurous minds. The assumption of the Quintessence was also difficult to accept.

This was especially true of the quintessential motion itself. Many thinkers were beginning to be uncomfortable with a type of motion that is never observed on earth, where nothing ever moves naturally in a uniform circle. (On earth, if something moves in a circle it is because it is being *forced* to move in that way.) If angels or intelligences did not move the sun and the planets and the fixed stars—if they moved by themselves—then what was the cause of that motion?

In addition, there was the problem of the crystalline spheres on which the heavenly bodies were said to move. They could not move in empty space, because empty space, for several reasons—for example, that nature abhors a vacuum—was unthinkable. (Aristotle had quarreled with Democritus on this point.) These great spheres, which made heavenly, although inaudible, music as they turned, were invisible. That was all right. We certainly do not see them. But the epicycles, some on top of others, were also crystalline spheres, and it appeared as if some of the spheres had to intersect other spheres. But this was impossible, because the quintessential matter of which they were made was assumed to be impermeable, unchangeable, indestructible, and so forth.

Finally, there was a special problem about the fixed stars. They were supposed to move on a crystalline sphere outside the sphere of Saturn. (Beyond the fixed stars was the Empyrean, the abode of God.) Observations made since Ptolemy's time on stellar parallax had shown that this sphere, and all the stars on it, must be very far away. But if they were so far away, then the speed with which their sphere turned about the earth every twenty-four hours must be almost unimaginably great. In a sense, this was not a problem, as God could have arranged for it to turn as fast as he pleased. There was no limit on the divine power. Even so, the theory seemed difficult. And many men in several lands sought a simpler solution to the problem.

Copernicus

Nicolaus Copernicus was born in 1473 and lived most of his life in Poland. He received an excellent education in the universities of eastern Europe and by 1500 was already said to have mastered all the scientific knowledge of his time: medicine and law as well as mathematics and astronomy. He could have chosen any learned profession, but he selected astronomy.

The more he studied and thought about the reigning Ptolemaic-Aristotelian theory of the heavens, the more it troubled him. The theory seemed complicated. Was it unnecessarily so? For example, if the earth rotated, that would explain why the fixed stars revolved around the earth every day, and the problem of their rapid motion would be solved. They would not have to move at all. And if the earth revolved around the sun, instead of the sun around the earth, that would simplify the problem of explaining the planetary orbits.

Copernicus studied all the old Greek astronomical texts he could find. He discovered that a rotating earth and a heliocentric system had been proposed by more than one ancient Greek astronomer. Was it possible to make a small change in the assumptions, and obtain a major improvement? Copernicus began to think so.

He was timid, however, and he did not publish the book he was writing, *On the Revolutions of the Heavenly Orbs*. He delayed and delayed. In fact, he only permitted the book to go to the printer when he was on his deathbed. A copy of his great work was brought to him on the day he died in 1543.

He had been afraid of religious controversy and of what the orthodox Aristotelians would say about his ideas. In fact, they said surprisingly little, partly because an introduction to his book, written by a friend, emphasized that the theory was only a hypothesis, designed to simplify certain mathematical difficulties. Copernicus was not actually saying that the earth *did* rotate once a day and *did* revolve around the sun once a year, the introduction asserted, although careful readers of the book realized that Copernicus actually *was* saying that. And so the new theory did not produce the intellectual revolution that Copernicus may even have wished for, although he was afraid to bring it about during his lifetime.

Perhaps the main reason Copernicus did not carry out the so-called Copernican revolution is that he had been careful to retain two important features of the Aristotelian system. One involved uniform circular motion. The other was quintessential matter, for which such motion was said to be natural. Theologians, therefore, as well as some astronomers, could believe that nothing really important had changed.

Tycho Brahe

This great Danish astronomer knew much had changed. Born in 1546, Tycho was abducted by his childless, wealthy uncle at an early age; after the initial family shock had been overcome, the uncle raised the boy, saw that he received an excellent education, and made him his heir. Tycho disappointed his benefactor in one respect. Despite his uncle's wish that he become a lawyer, he instead insisted on a career in astronomy. Inheriting the estates of both his father and uncle before he was twenty-five, he became independently wealthy and able to do what he wished with his life.

Aided by further financial assistance from the king of Denmark, Tycho established his own observatory on an island near Copenhagen, where he set about doing what he considered his life's work, namely, to correct all of the existing astronomical records, which he knew were grossly inaccurate.

Perhaps the most dramatic event of his life was his discovery, in 1572, of a nova in the constellation of Cassiopeia. He observed the bright new star over a period of months and in 1573 published a monograph on it that made him instantly famous and instantly controversial.

New stars were not supposed to come into being in the Aristotelian and the Christian universe. The world below the moon was chaotic, imperfect, and unpredictably changeable. That was an acceptable although not a very desirable situation. Basically, it was the fault of the Devil, who had disturbed God's originally perfect world by tempting Eve and Adam into sin. Above the moon, however, the heavens did not change. They continued to reflect God's immutable love for the world and mankind. The theologians, therefore, after duly investigating Tycho's monograph, concluded that the paper and its author were in error. The new star was not really new. It simply had not been observed before.

Tycho was not surprised, nor was he terribly disappointed. He was personally wealthy, and Denmark was a Lutheran country. His king was a staunch Protestant and cared little more than did Tycho for the criticisms of Roman Catholic divines. In any case, Tycho continued to desire more than anything else to leave to posterity a collection of astronomical observations sufficiently accurate so that future generations would be able to depend on them.

After 1588 a new king provided Tycho less financial support, and he finally had to give up his beloved observatory and settle in Prague, where in much reduced circumstances he was able to complete his work with the assistance of a young student, Johannes Kepler, to whom, at his death in 1601, he left all of his astronomical data. What Kepler did with them we will learn in a moment.

Gilbert

William Gilbert, an Englishman, added a crucial piece of information to the growing body of knowledge that would eventually overthrow the fixed and unchanging Aristotelian world picture and replace it with another. Like his contemporary William Harvey (1578–1657), the discoverer of the way the heart works to pump blood through the arteries and veins of the body, Gilbert (1544–1603) was trained as a physician and practiced medicine with much success. But it was his scientific hobby that made him famous. He was fascinated by lodestone, the mineral now called magnetite that possesses natural magnetism and is found in many places throughout the world.

Gilbert studied lodestones of all kinds, shapes, and powers of magnetism. His most important discovery was that the earth itself is a magnet, which he deduced when he observed that a compass needle dips downward when it finds the magnetic north (in the northern hemisphere). Gilbert also suspected that the earth's gravity and its magnetism were connected in some way, but he never understood how.

England, like Denmark, was Protestant, and Gilbert was supported by another Protestant monarch, Queen Elizabeth I. He therefore was able to proclaim to the world his remarkably modern ideas. He argued forcefully for Copernicus's heliocentric picture of the solar system and concluded that not all of the fixed stars were the same distance away. But his most provocative idea suggested that the planets must be held in their orbits by some kind of magnetism. No one else understood the implications of this suggestion at the time; nor, in fact, did Gilbert himself understand very well what he was proposing.

Kepler

Johannes Kepler was born in Württemberg in 1571 and died in 1630. Although the son of poor (although noble) parents, he received an excellent and wide-ranging education in Lutheran schools and at the University of Tübingen. He hoped to follow a career in the church, but he wrote a paper on an astronomical subject that came to the attention of Tycho Brahe, now at Prague, and Tycho invited the young man to join him as his assistant. After much soul-searching, Kepler accepted, and when Tycho died the next year, in 1601, Kepler was appointed imperial mathematician in his place and inherited Tycho's large body of accurate astronomical observations.

Kepler evidently felt that he had inherited more than just data. He also began to view more positively Tycho's unorthodox views, some of which Kepler now recognized for the first time. Tycho had published papers disputing the theory of the crystalline spheres on which the planets were supposed to move. Kepler followed up his argument that the planets moved freely in space and incorporated it in his own works. Like Tycho, Kepler also came to view Copernicus's heliocentric theory as more than a mere hypothesis, and he published papers arguing that no description of the world with the earth instead of the sun at the center could be accepted. But his greatest contribution was a set of three laws of planetary motion that solved the problem of epicycles and eccentric orbits once and for all. The three laws are still valid and are called by his name.

The first of the new laws made a substantial change in the Aristotelian system, for it asserted that planetary motion is not uniformly circular. The planets do not travel in eccentric circles around the sun, but in ellipses, with the sun at one of the two foci of the ellipse. Kepler's ellipses were very close to circles, which explained why the previous assumption of circular orbits had adequately explained the phenomena as long as observations remained relatively inaccurate. The new assumption was correct within the limits of observational accuracy of the time and required no further adjustments, no eccentricities, no epicycles, no tricks of any kind.

Kepler's second law of planetary motion asserted that a radius vector joining a planet to the sun sweeps out equal areas in equal times. What this means is that in a certain time, a planet will travel more quickly along its orbit when it is closer to the sun than when it is farther away from it. This brilliant insight, a major inspiration to Newton, applies to all bodies moving in fields of force, not just planets. It explained most of the discrepancies between astronomical theory and observation. Unfortunately, the idea remained an intuition in Kepler's mind. He knew it was correct, and it is, but he did not really understand why.

The third law asserted a mathematical relation between the periods of revolution of the planets and their distance from the sun. Discovering this law was a remarkable achievement considering the primitive instruments Kepler had at his disposal.

Kepler spent many years not only advancing his ideas about these laws and preparing Tycho's tables of observations for publication, but also mulling over what he recognized as the great remaining unsolved problem of planetary motion: the motivation whereby the planets revolve around the sun. What holds the planets in their orbits, and what drives them ever forward?

He realized that the speculations of Gilbert about the earth as a magnet must have something to do with the answer to the question, but he never understood what it was. He discarded almost all of the Aristotelian celestial baggage, including the idea of intelligences that guided the planets in their eternal rounds. He was also able to accept the idea of a force acting at a distance upon the planets, with no physical entity between the sun and the planets that it controlled. But he could not discard one crucial Aristotelian assumption, that of inertial rest. He came so very close to discovering the secret that made Newton the premier scientist, but he missed it because he thought the planets would stop moving unless something kept pushing them, and he could not imagine anything doing that other than Gilbert's magnetic force. He was very slightly wrong on both counts, and so he is remembered as an important precursor to Newton, but no more.

Galileo

Galileo Galilei was born in Pisa in 1564 and died in Acetri, near Florence, in 1646. He was a Roman Catholic and he lived in a Catholic country. That was one major difference between him and Tycho, Gilbert, and Kepler.

He studied at Pisa and taught mathematics at Padua. He was the leading mathematical physicist of his age, not just because he was very good at geometry. He was also the first modern man to understand that mathematics can truly describe the physical world. "The Book of Nature," as he said, "is written in mathematics."

As a young man Galileo conducted elegant experiments showing the inadequacy of Aristotle's theory of violent motion. He accepted Buridan's impetus theory and proved that projectiles shot from guns follow parabolic paths as they fall to earth. He studied the pendulum and showed that it, like the planets, sweeps out equal areas in equal times. All of this was theoretical work, and it did not get him into trouble. His troubles began in Venice in the spring of 1609, when he learned of the recent invention of the telescope. Upon returning to Padua he made a telescope of his own and quickly improved it to the point where it was better than any existing instrument. During the summer and fall of 1609 and the winter of 1610, he undertook a series of observations.

The first thing Galileo looked at with his telescope was the moon. To his great wonder he discovered that the surface of the moon was not smooth. There were mountains and valleys corresponding to the features that had always been seen but never before understood. This was not so shocking, as it had always been supposed that the moon was not made entirely of quintessential matter. He looked at Jupiter, and discovered its moons. Jupiter, then, was a little solar system which in turn revolved around a larger body. Finally, he turned his telescope on the sun and discovered curious spots on the sun's surface. These dark areas were not constant. He could see them change shape and position from night to night, from month to month.

The heavens, therefore, were not immutable and indestructible. Mountains and valleys had been formed on the moon by processes that, Galileo concluded, must be similar to those that operate on the earth. Jupiter was a miniplanetary system, and there might be many more such systems that he could not see as yet with his primitive instrument. And the sun was a living thing that was subject to change and did so before his eyes.

In 1611 Galileo went to Rome to describe what he had seen to the pontifical court. He took his telescope with him. Many were impressed by his findings, the meaning of which they did not at first comprehend. But he demanded that they open their eyes to those consequences. Among other things, he said he could prove mathematically that the earth went around the sun and not the sun around the earth, that Ptolemy was wrong and Copernicus right. And, he insisted, his telescopic observations proved that the heavens were not basically different from the sublunary world. There was no such thing as the Quintessence. All matter, everywhere, must be the same, or at least very similar.

You can prove no such thing with your mathematics, said Cardinal Robert Bellarmine (1542–1621), chief theologian of the Roman Church. He reminded Galileo of the time-honored belief that mathematical hypotheses had nothing to do with physical reality. (It was this belief, held by the Church for centuries, that had protected Copernicus's work from oblivion.) Physical reality, the cardinal said, is explained not by mathematics but by the Scriptures and the Church Fathers.

Look through my telescope and see for yourself, said Galileo. Bellarmine looked, but he did not see.

Why were Cardinal Bellarmine and the Dominican preachers whose aid he enlisted in a campaign against Galileo unable to see what Galileo saw, and what we would see if we looked through that telescope? Their eyes were physically the same as ours, but they did not see as ours would.

They deeply believed in the Ptolemaic system and the Aristotelian world order. But not because they were physicists who thought that those theories better explained the phenomena. They knew little or nothing about the phenomena. They believed in the old theories because the theories supported even more deeply held beliefs. And to question those deepest beliefs was to bring their world crashing down around their heads. They could not face that possibility.

St. Augustine, more than a thousand years before, had described in *The City of God* the distinction between the two cities, the heavenly and the earthly, which could be said to define the life of man and the pilgrimage of his spirit. Augustine's distinction, certainly, had been allegorical only, that is, he had not thought that one could actually see, except with the mind's eye, either the City of Man or the City of God.

But over the centuries those great images had taken on a kind of reality that proved more powerful than what one might see before one's very eyes. The City of Man was here, beneath the moon. It was earthy, material, strong-tasting and strong-smelling. It was the ordinary life of man. But in the heavens, at night, the City of God became visible to those who had eyes to see it. It shone there, unchangeable, indestructible, always beautiful. It was the promise of God to the faithful, the ark of the Christian, not the Jewish, Covenant.

It was the loveliest, the most desirable thing in the universe. To call it in question, to destroy it, to bring it tumbling down, was unthinkable. Anyone who threatened to do so had to be stopped, and if necessary burned at the stake. Even if he should be the world's greatest scientist.

Galileo had little or no interest in the City of God of St. Augustine. He was a good Christian, but his faith was as simple as his mathematics was subtle and complex. He went to church, he took communion, and during the sermon he did computations in his head. He watched the hanging lanterns of the cathedral swinging lazily in the breeze and worked out theories about the pendulum. For him, too, the heavens possessed an extraordinary splendor, but it was very different from the splendor of Cardinal Bellarmine's divine city. The heavens held a promise for him, too, but the promise was different. They could be studied, understood, even controlled in some way. So Galileo dreamed.

Bellarmine was much at fault for not trying to understand Galileo, for not recognizing the kind of new man he was, who would never willingly harm the Church, a good Catholic who would not allow himself to be wooed by the Protestants, as Bellarmine feared. Another time-honored doctrine supported Galileo, to wit, when the Scriptures conflicted with scientific truth, the Scriptures had to be interpreted allegorically, to avoid "the terrible detriment for souls if people found themselves convinced by proof of something that it was made then a sin to believe." This sophisticated argument had probably been suggested to Galileo by one of his theologian friends. He would not have thought of it by himself. But Bellarmine ignored the argument, although it would have given him a good fallback position. He forged ahead, heedless of the political consequences of prosecuting and condemning Galileo, perhaps even to death.

Galileo was also much at fault for not trying to understand Bellarmine and those who thought like him. The dispute was not merely scientific, and it was certainly not about a particular scientific truth, such as whether the sun goes around the earth or the earth around the sun.

It was about science itself, about the role it ought to play in human life, and particularly about whether scientists should be permitted to speculate with absolute freedom about reality. Even more than that, it was about the City of God, which could never again be viewed in the same way if Galileo was right.

Or rather, if he were allowed to say he was right in the way he wanted to say it. Everyone knew he was right in a way; his hypotheses were much more satisfactory than anyone else's. But Galileo wanted to go beyond mere hypotheses. He insisted that what he could prove mathematically and by means of his observations was *true*, and that it could not be questioned by anyone except a better mathematician or a better observer.

The Church had no authority, he was saying, to describe physical reality. But then what authority would remain to the Church? If the Church could no longer say, in every sphere and not just that of the spirit, what is and what is not, would not the Church be reduced to a mere adviser of souls? And if that were to happen, the danger existed that millions of souls would cease to ask for the Church's advice. And would not most of them then, in all likelihood, go to hell?

So Cardinal Bellarmine argued. His understanding of the choice that mankind faced was clear. Galileo was condemned to be silent, and for the most part he was. Bellarmine became a saint. He was canonized in 1930.

But in the long run, of course, Galileo won. The Church has been reduced to an adviser of souls, in the Western world at least, and science has been elevated to the position of supreme authority.

Bellarmine failed because he was not a good enough theologian. He should have read Augustine better and seen that the two cities are only allegorical. They are not real in the same way as what one sees through a telescope. St. Augustine, and many who understand him better, had always been able to juggle two kinds of reality, which might be said to correspond to the two cities. Let Galileo be the authority in the City of Man. The Church could remain the authority in the City of God. Because the Church wanted both kinds of authority, it ended up with neither.

Now, when we look up at the stars on a clear, dark night, we see a splendid vision, but it is not the vision that mankind once saw there. We have both gained and lost because of that.

Descartes

René Descartes was born in La Haye, France (now called La Haye-Descartes) in 1596, and died in Sweden in 1650 from a severe cold brought on by the requirement that he conduct philosophy lessons at five o'clock in the morning during northern winters. He had always preferred to lie in bed, and, besides, he hated the cold, but his patron, Queen Cristina, insisted on philosophy at five, and he could not say her nay. Such ironies make the history of science an amusing subject of study.

Other ironies illuminate the biography of René Descartes. He possessed a deep Catholic faith, but his writings did more to undermine the authority of the Church than the words of any other person. He created a scientific methodology that would revolutionize not only science but also the way mankind lives in the world. But his own views of things were often wrong, and in some cases so disastrously conceived that they impeded French scientific progress for two centuries, since French thinkers tended to believe that they must follow Descartes, whether they understood him or not. Similarly, English insistence that Newton's terminology for the calculus was better than Leibnitz's—which was nonsense, despite the fact that Newton had certainly been the first to invent the calculus—set back English mathematics for more than a century. Most ironic of all, Descartes's search for certainty was based upon the principle that everything should be doubted. This was an odd idea, but in fact it worked.

Descartes received the finest Jesuit education that could be obtained in the Europe of his time, an education that included an exhaustive study of Aristotelian logic and physical science. But when he graduated, at the age of twenty, he was in despair, for he felt that he knew nothing with the certainty with which he desired to know everything. Or rather, he knew nothing with that certainty except some mathematical truths.

In mathematics, he felt, it was possible to know things, for you started from axioms that possessed the character of indubitable certainty, and built from there, by small steps, a structure that possessed the same character. Such certainty adhered to nothing else, he thought, not to any other science, not to history, not to philosophy, not even to theology, despite the claim of the last to the highest certainty available to man's mind.

By 1639, after wide travels, much reading, and a voluminous correspondence with the most progressive thinkers of Europe, Descartes was ready to write a kind of summa of his philosophy which would organize all knowledge into one great structure, based on a universal method that led to certainty. But in that year he learned of Galileo's condemnation, and he decided he had better not write *that* book. Instead, he wrote *The Discourse on Method*, which concentrated on the method only, and left to others the work of applying it to discover controversial new truths. Nevertheless, even the *Discourse* got Descartes into serious trouble.

It is an absolutely astonishing book. In it, in French that exemplified the clarity and distinctness of the author's thought, he recounted the history of his intellectual development, how he began to doubt whether what he had been taught was true, and continued to doubt until he arrived at the simple conclusion that all might be doubted except one thing, namely, that he, the doubter, existed *because* he doubted. (*Dubito ergo sum.* "I doubt; therefore I am.") He then proceeded to discover a method of achieving similar certainty in other realms, based on the reduction of all problems to a mathematical form and solution. Thereupon he proved the existence of God mathematically and at the same time showed how God had created a world that would run forever without his assistance, like a huge, complex, and ornate clock. And he managed to do all of this in twenty-five pages. An amazing performance.

The method itself was the important thing. To understand some phenomenon or set of phenomena, first rid your mind of all preconceptions. This is not easy, and Descartes was not always successful in doing it. Second, reduce the problem to mathematical form, and then employ the minimum number of axioms, or self-evident propositions, to shape it. Then, using analytic geometry, which Descartes invented for the purpose, further reduce the description of the phenomena to a set of numbers. Finally, applying the rules of algebra, solve the equations that result, and you will have the certain knowledge that you seek.

Galileo had said that the Book of Nature is written in mathematical characters. Descartes showed that these mathematical characters are simply numbers, for to every real point there can be attached a set of

Cartesian coordinates, as Leibinitz was to name them, and to every line, whether curved or straight, and to every body, whether simple or complex, corresponds a mathematical equation.

Human beings are not mathematical equations, admitted Descartes, but it is sufficient for many purposes to describe them as such. In the case of the machines that we call animals—they are machines, he said, because they lack souls—the equations are sufficient for any and every purpose. For all other machines, including that greatest of machines, the universe, the equations are certainly adequate. It only remains to solve them. That may be very difficult, but by definition it is possible.

The Cartesian worldview affected everyone, not least those who hated and condemned Descartes for it. Pascal could not forgive him for not needing God except to start the universe going, and the Catholic theologians, by now as desperate as Descartes had been on his graduation day, felt it necessary to condemn him for a dozen kinds of heresy and to place his *Discourse* on the Index of forbidden books. But even they coveted the certainty that Descartes and his method promised. If only theology could be reduced to geometrical form!

That cannot be, despite the effort of Spinoza to make it so, for theology deals with an immaterial world that mathematics cannot enter. This is the main characteristic of theology that had attracted the passionate interest of the best thinkers for a thousand years. Now, suddenly, it ceased to be attractive. The world of the immaterial, which had been supremely interesting, suddenly ceased to be interesting at all. It is one of the most radical changes in the history of thought.

There were major consequences. Descartes's triumph consisted of his invention of a method for effectively dealing with the material world. His disastrous failure came about because his method could effectively deal only with the material world. Thus, living as we do in the wake of his great invention, we inhabit a world that is resolutely material, and therefore in many respects a desert of the spirit.

Before Descartes, theology had been the queen of the sciences, mathematical physics a poor relation. After him, the hierarchy was practically reversed. Not for an instant had there been a balanced universe of knowledge. Is such a thing possible? That is an important question for the future to decide.

Newton

In addition to everything else, Descartes made Newton possible. Isaac Newton, the preeminent scientific genius of all time, was born in Woolsthorpe, Lincolnshire, England, on Christmas Day of 1642. He studied at Cambridge and, upon graduation, was offered the post of professor of mathematics. Isaac Barrow, his predecessor, who had been his teacher, resigned to make way for his extraordinary pupil.

Before graduating, Newton had discovered (that is, he stated it without proving it) the binomial theorem. That would have made the career of most other mathematicians. It was only the beginning for him. In 1666, when he was twenty-two, the plague that had decimated London attacked Cambridge, and he retired to his farm in the county. Farming did not interest him, and he equipped a room with instruments for experiments on light. Forty years later the revolutionary results that he discovered would be described in his *Opticks*. But this year held even more revolutionary thoughts for Newton.

All intellectual roads led to that room in Lincolnshire. Gilbert had performed his experiments on the lodestone and had hypothesized an earth exerting an attractive force, like a magnet. Galileo had not only seen the moons of Jupiter but had also studied falling objects and had accurately measured the force of gravity at sea level. Descartes had shown how to apply mathematical methods to physical problems. Kepler had described the elliptical paths of the planets, and had assumed a strange force, emanating from the sun, that drove them in their courses. And the Parisian theologians had proposed the impetus theory of violent motion, which called in question Aristotle's assumption of inertial rest. Looking back, it does not seem to have been difficult, what Newton did. One might think almost anyone could have done it, having all those pieces before him.

To say that is not to detract from the genius of Newton. For although all the pieces of the puzzle lay before him, so that he only had to put them together, it remains true that what was required was a mind entirely free of traditional prejudices and capable of seeing the universe in a new way. There have been few such minds, and in science, very few.

More was required than pushing around pieces of a puzzle. First, Newton had to be very well educated in the science of his time. Then, he had to be an accomplished experimenter and handler of instruments. Finally, like Descartes, he had to be an exceptional mathematician, capable of inventing the new mathematics needed to solve the problems he set for himself. Descartes's analytic geometry had been effective in dealing with a static universe. But the real world was constantly in motion. Newton invented the differential and integral calculus to deal with that phenomenon. Perhaps no other single gift to science has ever been more valued.

Gilbert plus Galileo plus Kepler plus Descartes add up to Newtonian mechanics. A new set of laws of motion was the first stage of the process. They are stated with consummate simplicity at the beginning of Newton's great book, *Mathematical Principles of Natural Philosophy* (*Newton's Principia*, for short). They define a universe utterly different from Aristotle's.

The first law asserts that every physical body continues in its state of rest, or of uniform motion in a straight line, unless it is compelled to change that state by a force or forces impressed upon it. A moving projectile continues to move in a straight line unless it is retarded by the resistance of the air or its path is curved downward by the force of gravity. A top, set spinning, continues to spin unless it is retarded by friction with the surface on which its point spins, or by the resistance of the air. The great bodies of the planets and comets, meeting with less resistance or perhaps no resistance in empty space, continue their motions, whether straight or curved, for a much longer time.

This law obliterated the Aristotelian concept of inertia. There is no such thing as the "natural state of rest" of a body. If a body is at rest, it will remain at rest forever unless it is moved. If a body is moving, it will continue to move forever unless it is stopped, or its movement is changed in speed or direction by some force impressed upon it. Thus, no motion is "natural" and opposed to some other kind of motion that is "violent." Nor does one kind of motion have to be explained differently from other kinds. It follows, of course, that there is no such thing as quintessential motion, "naturally uniform and circular." Uniform motion in a circle is possible, but it is no more nor less natural than any other motion. Like all motions, furthermore, it is explained in terms of the inertia of bodies and the forces impressed upon them.

Newton's second law of motion asserts that a change of motion is proportional to the force impressed upon the body and is made in the direction of the straight line in which the force is impressed. A greater force induces a greater change of motion, and multiple forces produce a change that is a combination of the different strengths and directions of the forces. Analysis of the composition of forces is always possible using ordinary Euclidean geometry.

Ordinary Euclidean geometry cannot explain how the continuous impression of a force upon a body moving in a straight line can make the body follow a curved path, for example, a circle or an ellipse. The example was of the first importance, for all orbits are curved in the solar system. Newton made the assumption that a curved orbit could be conceived mathematically as made up of an indefinitely large number of indefinitely short straight lines, joined to one another in a string around the center (or focus) of the orbit. In mathematical terms, the curved orbit could be considered the "limit" of a process of reduction or differentiation, in which the individual segments became each as small and as close to being mere points as desired, and of integration, in which the totality of all the segments came as close to being the smooth curve of the orbit as wished. That is the method of the calculus so far as it can be described in words and not mathematical symbols.

The third law of motion asserts that to every action there is always opposed an equal reaction. Or, the mutual actions of two bodies upon one another are always equal although directed in opposite directions. "If you press a stone with your finger," Newton says, "the finger is also pressed by the stone." And, by this third law, if you blast heated air out of the rear of a jet engine, the airplane to which the engine is attached will move forward in the opposite direction. Further, if one body revolves around a second body, then the second also revolves around the first; they revolve around each other. The velocities need not be equal; if one body is much bigger than the other, it will move very slowly, while the other moves relatively very quickly. But the total motions will be equal.

Curiously, this gave the final solution of the ancient puzzle: does the sun go around the earth, or the earth around the sun? They go around each other, and Ptolemy and Copernicus were both right, though for the wrong reasons.

Taking the three laws as given, then, let us suppose the planets in motion. They will remain in motion unless they are hindered by some force. The force need not stop them altogether. This force may only deflect them out of the straight line of their inertial paths. It may, indeed, deflect them into elliptical paths. By the traditional geometry of conic sections (going all the way back to Apollonius of Perga, in the third century BC; nothing new here) it *will* deflect them into elliptical paths (let us call them orbits henceforth) if the force is centripetal—that is, if the force attracts the planets *inward,* away from their inertial tendency to fly away from the center in straight lines—and if this centripetal force varies as the inverse of the square of the distance between the planets and the body exerting a force upon them.

Suppose that body to be the sun. What might that centripetal force be? Gilbert and Kepler had speculated that it must have something to do with the natural magnetism of the earth, but they were not in possession of Galileo's measurements of the force of gravity at sea level. Factor in those numbers, and the mysterious force is discovered. It is no other than gravitation, the force that holds the moon captive in its course around the earth, and allows the moon to control the ocean tides, that drives the solar system in its stately rounds, and that makes ripe apples fall to the ground or upon the head of an unsuspecting mathematician lying beneath the tree.

Newton claimed that he had understood all this while he was spending his enforced vacation in Lincolnshire in 1666. It seemed so simple to him, he said, that he told no one about it for twenty years. In the meantime he did other work that interested him more. When his *Principia* finally appeared in 1686, it made the world gasp. The greatest problem in the history of science up to that time, the problem of how and why the universe worked as it did, had been solved. The poet Alexander Pope wrote:

> Nature and Nature's Laws lay hid in Night;
> God said, Let Newton be: and all was Light.

Rules of Reason

Isaac Newton was by nature a humble man, although a crusty one who often got into battles with his scientific colleagues. He once said to a biographer, "I do not know what I may appear to the world, but to myself I seem to have been only a boy playing on the sea-shore, and diverting myself in now and then finding a smoother pebble or a prettier shell than ordinary, whilst the great ocean of truth lay all undiscovered before me."

The image is as famous as it is intriguing. And probably it is even more accurate than Newton knew. That is, he was correct in admitting that he did not know a great deal compared to what could be known, even if he knew more than any other man of his time. And he was also correct in judging himself comfortable in his ignorance. The great ocean of truth lay all before him, but he did not even wish to stick his toe into it, to say nothing of shoving off from the shore with the goal of reaching the other side.

Book Three of Newton's *Principia* bears the awesome title, "The System of the World." It opens with two pages headed "Rules of Reasoning in Philosophy." We are to understand, first, that by "philosophy" Newton means "science." We may also understand that here is Newton's response to Descartes, his great footnote, as it were, to the *Discourse on Method*.

What are these rules of reasoning in science? There are only four. The first is this: We are to admit no more causes of natural things than such as are both true and sufficient to explain the appearances. This is a restatement of the logical principle first enunciated by William of Ockham in the fourteenth century, and now known as Ockham's Razor: "What can be done with fewer is done in vain with more." Newton, waxing a bit poetical, explains it thus:

> To this purpose the philosophers say that Nature does nothing in vain, and more is in vain when less will serve; for Nature is pleased with simplicity, and affects not the pomp of superfluous causes.

The second rule asserts: Therefore to the same natural effects we must, as far as possible, assign the same causes. "As to respiration in a man and in a beast," Newton adds; "the descent of stones in Europe and in

America; the light of our culinary fire and of the Sun; the reflection of light in the Earth, and in the planets."

Rule three answers a query that had plagued Aristotelians for centuries. It asserts, the qualities of bodies which are found to belong to all bodies within the reach of our experiments, are to be esteemed the universal qualities of all bodies whatsoever. As an example, Newton says, if the force of gravitation may be found to operate within the solar system, as it seems that it does, then we can—in fact we must—"universally allow that all bodies whatsoever are endowed with a principle of mutual gravitation."

The fourth rule of reasoning is, in Newton's view, perhaps the most important of all. The entire rule should be quoted:

> In experimental philosophy [that is, science] we are to look upon propositions inferred by general induction from phenomena as accurately or very nearly true, notwithstanding any contrary hypotheses that may be imagined, till such time as other phenomena occur, by which they may either be made more accurate, or liable to exceptions.

Newton writes, "This rule we must follow that the argument of induction may not be evaded by hypotheses."

Newton loathed hypotheses. He saw in them all the egregious and harmful errors of the past. By "hypotheses" he meant the kind of explanations that the Scholastics had dreamed up to explain natural phenomena, the theory of the Elements, the assumption of the Quintessence, and the tortured explanations of so-called violent motion, which even the Parisian theologians had not been able to accept. And he was more than willing to admit what he did not know.

The most important thing he did not know was the cause or causes of gravitation. That the earth and the other planets were held in their courses by the sun's gravity he had no doubt, but he did not know why. But "I frame no hypotheses," he declared; "for whatever is not deduced from the phenomena is to be called an hypothesis," and hypotheses "have no place" in science.

The four rules of reasoning, and the added prohibition against hypothesizing, that is, offering explanations not directly supported by experiments, could be said to define the scientific method as it has been practiced since Newton's time and as it is still practiced, for the most part, today.* Newton's rules established a new paradigm, to use a term employed by the eminent historian of science, Thomas S. Kuhn, in *The Structure of*

---

*There may be some very recent exceptions. See Chapter 15.

Scientific Revolutions (1962). The new paradigm inaugurated the age of science. The most valuable and useful tool for acquiring knowledge ever invented had been distributed among men, and with it they would proceed to try to understand everything they could see and many things they could not, as well as control the world around them in heretofore unimaginable ways.

Newton, with all his brilliance, did not understand why the force of gravity acts as it does; that is, he did not know what gravity is. Nor do we. He only knew that it acted the way it did. He was right about that, to his eternal credit. But the reasons of things, as Pascal might have called them, still lie hid in night.

That is partly the fault of Descartes, who made the search for them perhaps permanently unpopular. Partly it is the fault of Newton himself. His astonishing, brilliant success blinded the world to all those many things that it still did not know, and might never know. It is mostly the fault of the world itself, which is a harder thing to understand than mankind would like to believe.

The Galilean-Cartesian Revolution

Before moving on to the age of political revolutions, a word should be said about the names that are given to revolutions of all kinds. Often, the wrong person receives the credit or the blame. We shall see more examples of this in the next chapter. But a notable instance can be found in this chapter.

It has become customary to refer to the revolution that occurred in the seventeenth century—the revolution in ways of knowing that led to the establishment of science as the ultimate authority about material reality—as the Copernican Revolution. But this, I think, is unjust.

Copernicus, if in fact he desired to bring about a major change in thinking about the world, was afraid to produce it in his lifetime. He may never have had any such idea. Furthermore, his proposal that the earth revolves around the sun instead of the sun around the earth was not a revolutionary idea at all. Half a dozen ancient Greeks had said the same thing. Other men had considered the idea. In itself, it was not a major change.

We say that it was, invoking the supposedly important notion that man was the center of the universe before Copernicus, and not so thereafter. But this is far from the truth. As we have seen, man became the center of the universe, in any meaningful sense, with the Renaissance (with the discovery of perspective in painting, for instance), and he did not cease to be so at the end of the seventeenth century, when Newton's *Principia* appeared. That book, in fact, only solidified man's central position, as did all the scientific progress that followed it.

Today, when we look up at the night sky and know how many billions of stars and galaxies there are, and how tiny is our sun and its even tinier system of planets, of which the earth is far from the largest, it may not make us feel small or insignificant. Instead, it may make us feel strong and good, because we understand all that. Science exalts us; it does not belittle us.

Galileo was a very different man from Copernicus. For one thing, he was not afraid of the controversy that he knew his new ideas would produce. He was also not at all ignorant of the true meaning of what he was saying. He intended to replace the authority of the Church with another authority, because he believed the new authority—that of science—to be preferable in many ways. He did not fudge, as Copernicus had done. He really wanted to bring about a revolutionary change in the way men thought about things.

So did Descartes. He shared many of the mental characteristics of Galileo, although he was personally not so courageous. He was also more arrogant, which makes him not so likable. But he, too, knew what he was doing, as Galileo did and Copernicus did not.

If the revolution of the seventeenth century must be given the name of a man, then it ought to be called the Galilean Revolution, or, perhaps even better, the Galilean-Cartesian Revolution. Newton's name should not be used. He did not see himself as causing any very great change in thought. He was merely carrying forward the work of great men before him, and if he seemed the greatest of all, as indeed he was, he was not essentially different from them.

Unfortunately, the term "Galilean-Cartesian Revolution" does not sit very well on the tongue. And such things are important. Copernican Revolution sounds a good deal better. And so that is the name that historians will continue to use. But when I see it, I remember that Galileo and Descartes deserve much more credit than Copernicus.

9

An Age of Revolutions

T HE PUBLICATION in Latin in 1687 of Isaac Newton's *Mathematical Principles of Natural Philosophy* (an English translation did not appear until 1729) was both an end and a beginning. We have seen how this book summed up and concluded a great adventure in human thought, revealing to mankind the apparently definitive mechanical principles of the natural world. But the idea and image of this world, so newly conceived of as mechanical, also opened up new avenues of thought and action.

The importance of the *Principia* as the capstone of Renaissance curiosity about the external world is surpassed by the light it threw on the world of work itself, and by the challenge it provided inventors and discoverers, who employed its principles to make that world function more efficiently, for the betterment—it was assumed—of all.

The Industrial Revolution

The five simple machines (lever, wedge, wheel and axle, pulley, and screw) had been known for millennia. Primitive men a hundred thousand years ago employed a lever when they used a stick to move a stone, and a wedge when they used a hand ax to shape a piece of wood or bone. The origins of the wheel and axle and the pulley are lost in antiquity. Certainly the Egyptian builders of the Great Pyramids knew about both. Archimedes, in the third century BC, understood the operation of a mechanical screw.

During the next millennium the simple machines were refined, improved, and combined in various ways to produce other machines, no longer simple, that controlled and directed motion and multiplied force. Thus, Europe and Asia in 1600 were well supplied with devices of many kinds that were the fruit of centuries of slow but steady evolution of practical knowledge. Most of these machines, however, were awkward to control and inefficient in their use of force because the principles that underlay their operation were not well understood—in some cases were not understood at all.

A hundred years later, by 1700, Galileo, Descartes, and Newton, together with a host of scientific contemporaries, had changed this ignorance to knowledge. Suddenly, practical men realized *why* machines did what they did. As a result they saw how to make them do it better. The discoveries in mechanics came with astonishing rapidity, one after the other, and each new discovery called for the next.

The more efficient machines could only improve if they were propelled by a better source of power. Coal, soon found to be a better source, heated water to steam, which in turn drove pistons and, not long after, wheels on iron rails. For a long time, steam powered the industrial revolution. Steam still drives many operations in the industrial world, although the water may be heated by other means, as for example by a nuclear reactor.

Any machine worked better if its parts fitted together more precisely and lasted longer. Hence the making of a new kind of steel, produced in furnaces heated by coal and coke, became a high priority. Steel had been known since the ancient Spartans had used it to make superior weapons and armor. But the new hardened steel permitted machine tolerances to be decreased farther than machinists had ever dreamed possible. The new machines, with steel axles and other turning parts, and with steel bearings that lasted for a long time and held to the tolerances, produced more and worked longer without having to be replaced.

Human Machines and Mechanical Humans

Human beings themselves also began to be perceived as machines that could be made to work better according to mechanical principles. One result was the birth of modern scientific medicine. Even the universe was seen as a machine, with God at the controls—if, in fact, God was needed at all to run such a wonderful machine, which he might have created so perfect as to be able to run by itself.

Probably the most important mechanical invention of the eighteenth century was the factory, that great machine which combined human and mechanical elements to produce undreamed-of amounts of goods, which in turn were absorbed by a market that was also viewed mechanically. In his famous book, *The Wealth of Nations*, published in the fateful year of 1776, Adam Smith (1723–1790) marveled at the wondrous achievements of the humble pin factory.

One man draws out the wire, another straightens it, a third cuts it, a fourth points it, a fifth grinds it at the top for receiving the head; to make the head requires two or three distinct operations; to put it on is a peculiar business; to whiten it is another; it is even a trade by itself to put them into paper. . . .

I have seen a small manufactory of this kind where ten men only were employed and where some of them consequently performed two or three distinct operations. But though they were very poor, and therefore but indifferently accommodated with the necessary machinery, they could, when they exerted themselves, make among them about twelve pounds of pins in a day. There are in a pound upwards of four thousand pins of a middling size. Those ten persons, therefore, could make among them upwards of forty-eight thousand pins in a day. . . . But if they had all wrought separately and independently . . . they certainly could not each of them make twenty, perhaps not one pin a day. . . .

This new kind of machine, made out of both human and nonhuman parts, seemed to Smith to be the wonder of the age, and the potential source of "universal opulence." The new wealth "the factory machine" would inevitably produce would come about because labor had been divided not only among the workers in a single factory but also among all those in a nation, and even beyond the nation. For instance, Adam Smith wrote, in making a coat:

Observe the accommodation of the most common artificer or day labourer in a civilized and thriving country, and you will perceive that the number of people of whose industry a part, though but a small part, has been employed in procuring him this accommodation, exceeds all computation. The woollen coat, for example, which covers the day-labourer, as coarse and rough as it may seem, is the produce of the joint labour of a great multiple of workmen. The shepherd, the sorter of the wool, the wool-comber or carder, the dyer, the scribbler, the spinner, the weaver, the fuller, the dresser, with many others, must all join their different arts in order to complete even this homely production. How many merchants and carriers, besides, must have been employed . . . how much commerce and navigation . . . how many ship-builders, sailors, sail-makers, rope makers. . . .

The principle of the division of labor was not discovered in the eighteenth century. The discovery is many centuries, even millennia, older than that. But the need to apply the principle to practical problems is characteristic of this time. Most of the practical men who did so may never have heard of Descartes, but the principle, as the eighteenth century understood it, could be traced back to his "geometrical method," which involved breaking down any situation or operation into its smallest constituent parts, then attempting to deal with each of them mathematically. Descartes believed this process would always be possible if the parts were small enough. Indeed, Adam Smith's pin factory is akin to a mathematical operation in which a very large number of very small steps add to the steady progress toward a goal.

Descartes had perceived no danger in this way of thinking, nor did Adam Smith, nor did anyone else in the eighteenth century. Today we have doubts. We wonder whether any human being should be required to spend a day (and not just one, but an endless series of days) making, with nine other human beings similarly employed, upward of forty-eight thousand pins, when the work, for any one of them, might consist in grinding the end of a bit of wire so that a head could be affixed to it.

And when it comes to woolen coats, we may look at the thing very differently from Adam Smith. It is true that a coat, "coarse and rough as it may seem," can be produced through the combined efforts of scores, hundreds, or even thousands of individuals, each completing his small part of the task on his own, more or less unaware of what the final product will be. But such a coat can also be made by one person, or two, perhaps a husband and wife, who tend and shear the sheep, sort and comb the wool, dye it and spin it, weave it and shape it, and finally deliver it with a smile to the fortunate recipient.

Adam Smith could see no particular merit in such an operation. He knew that peasant labor had produced coats and other articles inefficiently. Their harsh labor had also destroyed the souls of the peasants, who hated their life so much that they fled it whenever and wherever they could in order to work in even the most demanding and dangerous factories. The industrial revolution could not have succeeded unless everyone wanted it, both the exploiting capitalists and the exploited workers.

But human beings had not yet learned how factory-induced specialized labor also destroys the souls of human beings by treating them as the parts of a machine.

An Age of Reason and Revolution

Thales' original insight about the world imbued the eighteenth-century concept of the order of things. Thales and the Greeks who followed his lead had maintained as a first principle that the external world and the internal mind must have much that is in common, else how could that external world be intelligible to the internal mind? The name of this commonalty was reason. It was a word that the eighteenth century loved to use, adopting with enthusiasm the Thalesian idea without necessarily knowing its source.

It was universally held that man, at his best, was a reasonable creature; the world that he sought to understand was also reasonable, the creation of a reasonable Creator. The proof could be found in the fact that mechanical principles were true. The proof that they were true was that they worked. The circularity of the reasoning, which was itself mechanical, merely confirmed the conclusion. By the first third of the eighteenth century men had already begun to call theirs an age of reason. And this name managed to express one of the most deeply held beliefs of the day.

Even the most profound and widely held beliefs do not always reveal the true character of an age, although they may reveal its prejudices. The eighteenth century thought that the application of Descartes's mathematical method and Newton's mechanical principles to the making of pins was the most important thing it was doing. Looking back, we have doubts.

After all, the Age of Reason was in many ways *not* a reasonable time. It was filled with passion and explosively emergent dreams. It was a time of madness and murder. It was an epoch of radical change. It was an Age of Revolution.

The men and women of the eighteenth century accepted this paradox serenely enough. On the one hand, they thought of their time as one in which life had acquired comfortable patterns that were both rational and permanent. The machine was their symbol, and machines are characterized by sameness, not change. A machine does not run differently from day to day. If it does, it does so because it is breaking down; it is becoming a bad machine.

On the other hand, they thought of their time as manifesting enormous change, most of it for the better. The idea of progress itself is an eighteenth-century invention. The ancients had had no concept of progress, at least in the sense of a steady improvement over the centuries and millennia. The ancients had been aware that conditions changed, but they had supposed that, in general, the changes were cyclical: sometimes things were better, sometimes they were worse. The eighteenth century not only believed in progress, it even began to believe in *necessary* progress; things *had* to get better, because that was the nature of things.

Here was another paradox. If you really believe that improvement is inevitable, why bother to try to bring it about? It should come about whatever you do. But supposedly reasonable persons in the late eighteenth century worked furiously to change things for what they thought was the better. They struggled, they fought, they even gave their lives for the cause of necessary and inevitable progress. They never seem to have been aware that they were fighting against themselves, against their deepest beliefs.

But that kind of inconsistency, more than any mechanical necessity, is truly the nature of human affairs. Besides, their battles for progress, unreasonable as they may have been, resulted in great good for the human race.

John Locke and the Revolution of 1688

Looking back, we use the term *industrial revolution* to refer to the great change in the organization of work and production that was begun in the second half of the eighteenth century, especially in England. This change was revolutionary, for it turned many things upside down, created a new class of wealthy and powerful persons, began to alter perhaps permanently the natural environment in which men and other animals live, and had other remarkable consequences as well. But another kind of revolution seems even more characteristic of the time. It, too, began in England, but it quickly spread to other countries, as did the industrial revolution.

This other revolution—political, not economic—first erupted during the English civil wars of 1642–51. During that struggle, in January 1649, King Charles I was executed, and Parliament became the supreme power in England and ruled through its victorious general, Oliver Cromwell (1599–1658). After the king's death and Cromwell's installation as Lord Protector of the new Commonwealth, some of Cromwell's soldiers raised their voices in protest. They said, We, too, shared in the victory. And therefore we, too, deserve to share in the rule.

No, said Cromwell, for you possess no property, and government has always been, and should always continue to be, of property, by property, and for property. Although we do not own property, the soldiers replied, we have as great an interest in the passage of good laws as men who do, for we too must live under those laws. Trust us, the men of property, said Cromwell, growing angry. We will govern in your interest as well as our own.

The argument continued for some time, but Cromwell won it, for he retained the backing of most of the officers, many of them men of property. A few protesters were put to death, and the rest retreated, grumbling. Cromwell died in 1658, and in 1660 the king's son, who had fled to France, returned to become King Charles II. For a time there was no more talk of the rights of men without property, or of rights in general. But the subject was not dead, only quiescent. It rose again in the same decade that saw the publication of Isaac Newton's *Principia*.

Cromwell's soldiers had not found an eloquent spokesman for their radical views. But such a spokesman existed, although he was born too late to benefit the members of the New Model Army. He was John Locke (1632–1704), whom we have already met as the proponent of a new toleration in religion.

Born in Somerset, Locke attended Westminister School and Oxford

University, but like many of his contemporaries he was offended by the Scholastic philosophy that was still being taught there. He believed the operations of the mind could be explained more simply than the Scholastics did, with their essences, entelechies, and innate powers. The child was born, he said, with a *tabula rasa,* a blank slate. On it experience wrote words, and thus knowledge and understanding came about, through the interplay of the senses and all that they perceived.

Locke's life was circumscribed and his prospects were modest until 1666, when he met Sir Anthony Ashley Cooper, later the Earl of Shaftesbury. For the next fifteen years Locke served Shaftesbury (1621–1683) as physician, secretary, and counselor. Shaftesbury's career during these years was meteoric. Among the commissioners sent from England to invite Charles to return as king, he soon became one of the new monarch's closest advisers and in 1672 was named lord chancellor, in effect the king's first minister. But he soon fell from grace. The cause of his fall was a dispute with the king about the very nature of governance.

A flurry of political activity surfaced in the 1670s, when rumors warned of a plot to assassinate Charles II and replace him with his brother, the future James II, a Roman Catholic. Shaftesbury, a devout Protestant and of the opinion that his king should be one, too, proposed a law excluding Roman Catholics from the succession to the throne. His political opponents, perhaps secretly egged on by the king, countered with arguments in favor of the so-called divine right of kings, which presumably included the right of a king to adopt any religion he chose. To shore up their side they republished an old book titled *Patriarcha,* by Sir Robert Filmer (1588–1653), a vindication of the absolute right of kinship to which no one had paid much attention for forty years, since its publication as a polemical treatise during the English civil wars. But now many readers seemed to be persuaded by Filmer, fearing, perhaps, the consequences of once again coming into conflict with the established government. The civil wars had been bloody and cruel, and most politicians were old enough to remember them vividly.

At this juncture Shaftesbury turned to Locke, asking him to prepare a reply to Filmer. This was easy enough, for Filmer had been no theoretician of government, while Locke was a master. In his *First Treatise on Civil Government* he effectively demolished Filmer. But he did not stop there. He went on to compose a *Second Treatise* on civil government from a more general point of view.

Whether the king ever read these two inflammatory documents remains uncertain, although Shaftesbury undoubtedly acquainted him with the thesis of at least the first of them. They were completed, although not published, in late 1680. In mid-1681 Shaftesbury challenged the king on the question of the succession. The king dissolved Parliament, leaving

Shaftesbury without a political base, threw him into the Tower of London, and charged him with treason. Shaftesbury was acquitted, but there was nothing for him but self-imposed exile. He fled to Holland, where the winds blew more freely, taking Locke with him.

Locke's *Second Treatise on Civil Government* concerns the interconnection of three great ideas: property, government, and revolution. Government comes into existence, said Locke, because of property. If there is no property, then government is not needed to protect it. If I possess nothing of my very own, then what need do I have of the machinery of the state: laws and judges, policemen and prisons?

Property exists, of course. For Locke the question revolved around whether property was legitimate. This is not an easy question, for the word *legitimate* has far-reaching connotations. It comes from the Latin *leges*, "law," but it does not mean the ordinary kind of law that is passed by a Parliament or interpreted by a judge. Laws themselves can be legitimate or illegitimate. A law can therefore be unlawful, according to some principle that is evidently higher than that of common legality. This principle has to do with right, admittedly an abstract concept. Right has to do with rights, which are not abstract at all. At least men will fight and die for them.

Property, Government, and Revolution

The question, then, was whether there was a right to property. Yes, said Locke, but only within reason. In certain circumstances, a man might possess legally more than he had a right to. (This radical doctrine lay dormant for more than a century.) Property being legitimate, government was therefore legitimate, too, for those who owned property by right had a right to protect it, and government was an institution for safeguarding and protecting rights.

Was government always legitimate? Clearly it sometimes was, if the governor and the governed agreed on one basic thing: that they were in it together. Legitimate governors must govern for the good of the governed, not their own good only. When this occurs, the governed give their consent to being governed, for they see justice all around them, and above them, too.

Might the governed ever legitimately withdraw their consent? Yes again, said Locke. Revolution is legitimate when the governor has become a tyrant, "when the governor, however entitled, makes not the law, but his will, the rule, and his commands and actions are not directed to the properties of his people, but the satisfaction of his own ambitions, revenge, covetousness, or any other irregular passion." In that case the governed have a right to rise up and change their government, which they rightfully can insist must be for their own good.

Locke may have been reluctant to arrive at this conclusion. Certainly he was afraid of the consequences, and he remained in Holland for ten years, keeping his work unpublished. Nevertheless, his words rang like a great brass ring thrown down on marble.

> As usurpation is the exercise of power which another hath a right to, so tyranny is the exercise of power beyond right, which nobody can have a right to.
>
> It is a mistake to think this fault is proper only to monarchies. Other forms of government are liable to it as well.
>
> Wherever law ends, tyranny begins, if the law be transgressed to another's harm.
>
> May the commands, then, of a prince be opposed? To this I answer: That force is to be opposed to nothing but to unjust and unlawful force.
>
> The common question will be made: Who shall be judge whether the prince or legislative act contrary to their trust? To this I reply: The people shall be judge!

Governments had been overturned in the past, kings had been overthrown, and clever philosophers had justified those acts. But never before had they marshaled arguments based, as were Locke's, on a general notion of rights: to property, to government, and to revolution. The heart of the argument lay in the idea of a right to government, which clearly rested in the governed, not the governor. For millennia, it had been assumed that the king had a right to rule, and that the people must suffer his rule, hoping it would be benevolent. Now Locke was saying that it was the people, among whom the king, of course, was one, who had a right to good, *legitimate* government, and that the king must provide it, lest he be *legitimately* overthrown.

Anyone with ordinary common sense could see that kings might still rule if they possessed the power, whether or not the people liked it. Locke, with his ringing words, had not abolished tyranny from the face of the earth. Tyranny still prospers, at the end of the twentieth century, and it may do so until the end of time. But his words had nevertheless made tyranny more difficult for tyrants, whose enemies now—and forever after—would be stronger for believing they had right on their side.

Events soon conspired to give the *Second Treatise* an import beyond what may have been Locke's original intention. Charles II died in 1685, and his brother, James II, succeeded him. Within a short time James's Roman

Catholicism came to be perceived by most Britons as intolerable, just as Shaftesbury, who was now dead, had predicted, and steps began to be taken to remove him from the throne.

James II abdicated in 1688 and was replaced by William of Orange, a good Dutch Protestant, and his English wife, Mary. Locke returned to England in the spring of 1689, in the same ship that brought Queen Mary. He carried with him his two manuscripts. They were published at the end of the year, and politicians everywhere who read them trembled, or were inspired, depending on how close they stood to tyranny.

Two Kinds of Revolution

Locke had made another important distinction. He had written, "He that will, with any clearness, speak of the dissolution of government ought in the first place to distinguish between the dissolution of the society and the dissolution of the government." The Glorious Revolution of 1688 did not dissolve the society of Englishmen, who in the main were much the same after it as they had been before.

However, the change went deeper than many supposed. It was not just the name of the monarch that was different now. The monarch's relation to his people would never again be the same as it had been under Charles II and James II, to say nothing of Charles I, James I, or Elizabeth. Henceforth, Parliament would be the ruler of England, whatever state the king might aspire to and whatever power he might temporarily possess. William had warned that he would not accept being a mere figurehead, but that is nonetheless what he was, and his successors as well. Thus "the Eighty-Eight" was a genuine revolution, although it did not go nearly as far as it might have.

The question was, if Parliament ruled, then who ruled Parliament? The answer, the people, was a lame one, when only a handful of adult male Englishmen voted for members of Parliament, and when their votes were often shamelessly bought.

But even a candidate whose votes were purchased could turn out to be a good MP, and in fact the general level of parliamentary politics in England during the eighteenth century was remarkably high, considering the moral swamp out of which it arose, and which Parliament could not be brought to reform for more than a century. As late as 1920 a minority of the British people was still electing their representatives.

The reason why the level of parliamentary politics remained high was partly because it was conducted in Lockean terms. Politicians of all persuasions found that they could hardly speak without using the great words that Locke had given them: property, right, legitimacy, and revolution. Those words are powerful, and they make any discourse serious and weighty.

Thomas Jefferson and the Revolution of 1776

The vast riches and even greater promise of America tempted many Englishmen into lies, even when using those words. They lied to themselves, they lied to one another, and, most important, they lied to the Americans.

The English adventure in the New World had three separate thrusts. To the north stood Canada, a wilderness so great that even the imagination could not encompass it. There was not much there except fur-bearing animals and Indians. The English managed to hold on to Canada.

To the south were the islands of the Caribbean, where slaves were imported to grow sugar. The indigenous population had been wiped out, and the imported Africans as yet had no ability to object to their treatment. The West Indies produced large profits for Englishmen, and this wealth, combined with the relative ease of governing them, made the Caribbean islands seem more valuable than they really were.

In the middle were the American colonies, strung out along the Atlantic seaboard from New Hampshire to Georgia and inhabited largely by Englishmen. The latter fact was the cause of much trouble, because all Englishmen, after the Glorious Revolution, had become conscious of their political rights. These colonial Englishmen were therefore quarrelsome and demanding. They had chips on their shoulders that sometimes seemed as large as Plymouth Rock.

As long as a continent existed that could be explored and exploited, troubles between the American colonists and their British governors could be contained. But when the Seven Years War ended in 1763, the British, mainly to avoid trouble with the Indians, determined not to move farther westward into the Mississippi Valley than they had already gone.

The measure proved temporary, but the Proclamation of 1763, which had the force of law, infuriated the Americans. Who were the British to forbid them to move westward into the wilderness that lay beyond the fringes of their own settlements? When the British said they did not want Indian trouble, the Americans responded that this was trouble they knew how to deal with. Speculation in lands not yet settled decreased as a result of the proclamation, but the level of American annoyance and frustration increased.

The controversy about the Proclamation of 1763 brought to the fore another question about the legitimacy of government. The British government contended that although American colonists were true Englishmen, they could not be represented in Parliament because America was too far away. The difficulties of effective communication between an MP and his constituents would prove too great. The principle should apply, the British said, even when it came to taxes, which could be legitimately exacted even if the colonists were not represented. No! said the colonists. Taxation without representation is tyranny! Trust us, the British authorities said, to know your interests, and to take care of them.

A few British politicians could be and were trusted by the Americans, men like Edmund Burke (1729–1797), who advocated consistent and sympathetic treatment of the colonies, because that seemed both politic and right. The majority of Britons felt otherwise. Because the Americans were so cantankerous, the only way to treat them was harshly in order to teach them a lesson.

The Americans learned a different lesson, based on principles of English law and history that were drawn from Locke. The colonists came to believe that the basic English right of revolution would have to be applied in their own case. The idea, of course, was frightening. The only thing worse than revolt was not to revolt. And so the war between the British and their colonists began, in 1775.

The Declaration of Independence

As with the change of government in 1688, this revolt, too, needed justification. In congress assembled in the spring of 1776, the Americans turned to Thomas Jefferson (1743–1826). Though born in Virginia, Jefferson had always thought of himself as an Englishman. Now he could do so no longer, for he had studied Locke and knew many of his phrases and sentences by heart. They echoed through the Declaration that he composed for the Continental Congress, which that body accepted with hardly a change.

Jefferson began by speaking of "dissolution," one of Locke's key terms. "When, in the course of human events, it becomes necessary for one people to dissolve the political bands which have connected them with another, . . . a decent respect to the opinions of mankind requires that they should declare the causes which impel them to the separation."

Behind the causes, to be later enumerated, lay certain fundamental principles. First, that all men are created not only equal, but are also endowed with certain rights that are "inalienable," that is, nothing can take them away, although they can be ignored and trampled on if you have the power to do so. Among these rights, Jefferson said, are life, liberty, and the pursuit of happiness. Locke had said life, liberty, and property.

Second, that governments are instituted among men to secure these rights. Locke had said that government's first task is to secure property.

Third, that government is legitimate only so long as it continues to secure these rights and therefore continues to enjoy the consent of the governed.

Fourth, that when government becomes destructive of these ends, it is the right of the people to alter or abolish it, and to institute new government.

All of this splendid rhetoric repeated what every educated Englishman knew, or should have known if he had studied his own history. But the fifth step in Jefferson's argument was not so easy for Britons to accept. The Declaration reminded them of what Locke had said, and what they had believed for nearly a century: "when a long train of abuses and usurpations [Lockean words, all], pursuing invariably the same object, evinces a design to reduce them under absolute despotism, it is their right, it is their duty, to throw off such government. . . ." The history of "the present King of Great Britain," Jefferson added, showed such a pattern of abuses, leading to "the establishment of an absolute tyranny over these states."

The heart of the argument, of course, was the alleged abuses. Jefferson provided a long list of them, including these outraged protests:

He has abdicated government here, by declaring us out of his protection, and waging war against us.

He has plundered our seas, ravaged our coasts, burnt our towns, and destroyed the lives of our people.

And this long list, eloquently stated, proved persuasive to the Americans. The question was whether the British would agree these abuses indeed had occurred.

If they did agree, Jefferson's argument was really irrefutable. It convinced some Englishmen who read it carefully. It did not, however, convince George III and his advisers, who angrily maintained that although the colonists might be right in theory, it was not permissible in practice for them to take up arms against their rulers, as they indubitably had done. The war, therefore, was prosecuted fiercely by both sides. The king used mostly foreign mercenaries to fight for him. They were excellent soldiers. Besides, being unable to read English, they were not likely to be swayed by Jefferson's words.

The Americans won the war, for a number of reasons. America was indeed very far from Great Britain, and the natives knew better how to fight in its vast reaches than the mercenaries, who had been trained for combat in quite different circumstances. Then, France, England's enemy throughout the eighteenth century, saw fit to aid the colonists, mainly to annoy their old adversaries, but also because they hoped it might be to their advantage in after years, as it proved to be.

The illusions Englishmen retained about the relative value of the West Indies as compared with the American colonies also played a part in the British defeat. Many Englishmen thought it just as well to wash their hands of the pesky Americans, who produced more protests than profits for the mother country. But the essential rightness of the American political stance, *by English law*, also played a part in the American victory.

That victory, in turn, confirmed the rightness of the English-Lockean political doctrine, and ever since it has been dominant on the world stage. No one in the last two centuries has been able to make a *reasoned* argument against the thesis that it is the people who shall judge whether their government is legitimate or not, and not the government itself, and that a government that becomes illegitimate because it has lost the assent of the governed may be legitimately overthrown.

The only denial of this thesis that has worked (and, sadly, it has often done so) has been through the barrels of the guns of tyrants, turned against their own people. Power, as Mao Zedong said, is in the muzzle of a gun. But it is also in words, and in the long run, words triumph over guns.

Property in Rights

Did Jefferson and Locke disagree about property? There is reason to think so. Where Locke had used the word "property," Jefferson had used "the pursuit of happiness." The latter seems a broader, more generous concept. The idea that government comes into existence for the sake of property—in order to protect and secure it—is rather cold-hearted. Had Locke been setting forth the thesis that men of property had a right to revolution if their rights were abridged, and no others?

And what if—to take the most vexing case—their property included slaves, that is, other human beings who seemingly ought to be included in Jefferson's blanket declaration that *all* men are created equal and are endowed with rights? Jefferson owned slaves, and he went to his grave wondering whether Negroes were equal to whites. Did they have rights, then? They had practically no property. Was there another kind of property right that demanded to be understood in a different way?

James Madison (1751–1836), Jefferson's successor as secretary of state in the new American government and then as President, tried to resolve these difficulties in an essay that was published in a newspaper in 1792. This term *property*, Madison wrote, "in its particular applications," means the dominion a man exercises over the external things of the world, "in exclusion of every other individual." This is my house, my land, my bank account, not anybody else's. That concept is universally understood. But

Madison went on to make a broader point. "In its larger and juster meaning," he said, property "embraces everything to which a man may attach a value and have a right; and which leaves to everyone else the like advantage."

In the first sense, a man has property in his land, his money, his merchandise. In the second sense, a man has property in his opinions, especially his religious beliefs, in the "safety and liberty of his person," in the "free use of his faculties and free choice of the objects on which to employ them." In short, Madison concluded, "as a man is said to have a right to his property, he may equally be said to have a property in his rights."

Government is instituted, Madison added, to protect property of every sort, "as well that which lies in the various rights of individuals, as that which the term particularly expresses. This being the end of government, that alone is a *just* government which *impartially* secures to every man whatever is his *own*."

The emphasis in that last sentence is Madison's. He was right to emphasize the word *own*. *Property* has a cognate in French, *propre*, which means "self." Our rights, as Jefferson and others had declared, are inseparable from our selves. Politically, we *are* our rights. They are what we most care about owning.

Madison's resolution of the conflict, real or apparent, between Jefferson and Locke adds up to a political doctrine that is so radically revolutionary that I do not believe it is possible to go beyond it. Many revolutions since the American rebellion at the end of the eighteenth century have failed or feared to go so far. Even the Russian Revolution, no matter how far-reaching its social and economic reforms, failed to take the final step that Madison said was imperative for the United States, that "it equally respect the rights of property and the property in rights."

The Soviets, in this century, have turned the first kind of property upside down, giving it to those who had nothing, taking it from those who had everything. There is a kind of simple justice in that, although economically it is dreadfully misguided. But no man's, woman's, or child's rights have been secure in the Soviet Union during this century, as they are mostly secure in Madison's country today.

To succeed in their revolution, the Soviets believed they had to abolish all private property. Perhaps they meant to abolish only the private property that Locke had claimed governments are instituted to protect. But they also abolished that other property, property in rights. Their revolution has therefore so far failed. It can succeed only when they understand and rectify this view.

Censors in Communist countries have tried to conceal from their people the meaning of Madison's doctrine, and that it works in practice in the

United States. But the people, especially the young people, of China, of Eastern Europe, of a dozen other countries know this nevertheless. And they have shown they will die for their property in rights.

Robespierre, Napoleon, and the Revolution of 1789

Was the American Revolution a dissolution of the government and the replacement of it by another—as the Glorious Revolution of 1688 had been—or was it also a "dissolution of the society"? Scholars have disputed this question for a century. Little economic change resulted from the war with England. The same individuals who had owned property before the war owned it afterward. And the franchise was not widespread even after the war. A minority continued for a long time to choose the legislators and the President. Excluded were men without property, all women, all slaves, and some others.

Nevertheless, there was a difference. Those who did vote and choose their rulers, and who could, therefore, be said to rule themselves, were doing so for the first time. So the American Revolution was more a true revolution than the English revolution had been. But it was still far from being what a revolution might be, theoretically, and what the French Revolution actually became only a few years later.

During the century from 1650 to 1750 France was probably the wealthiest nation in the world, and one of the most envied and imitated. The great war, or series of wars, that broke out between England and France in 1756, and continued, with interruptions, until 1815, was made possible by the industrial revolution, which had elevated England from the rank of second-class nation to near-equality with France. England, in that tumultuous century, raised herself by her own bootstraps to an eminence that challenged the awesome power of France, even as France was moving away from the pinnacle of power.

Scholars have also disputed the reasons for this change. Again, they are admittedly many. But it was not unimportant that France persisted in living by a political idea during these years that revolution in England and American had shown to be false and, ultimately, unworkable. This was the idea that the sovereignty of the nation could, and indeed must, repose in a single individual, the Sovereign, who would have absolute executive power and who would necessarily exercise it for the good of his people, whether or not they realized he did so.

A government, in short, was like a corporation or a family, which could have only one head or be a monster. It made no sense, according to this idea, to proclaim that "the people shall rule." For who are the people? Merely a horde of individuals with different desires and views. In the end, some *one* must always decide. And for efficiency's sake, it made sense that this decision should always be made by the same person. Only such a government, said the French political apologists, could be considered legitimate and reasonable. Anything else created at best confusion, and at worst anarchy.

The justification of benevolent despotism advanced by French apologists for the absolutism of Louis XIV was based on a conception about the organization of the entire universe that went under the name of the Great Chain of Being. This idea, which soon became politically insupportable, had its roots in Plato, as so many philosophical ideas do, and Plotinus, his Neoplatonic follower.

According to Plato and Plotinus, the universe was created by a generous god who, out of his love for his creation, filled it to the brim with being. Under their doctrine of plenitude, everything that can exist must exist. There can be no gaps on the ascending scale that extends from the lowest beings—stones, grains of sand, and the like—through the plants and the animals to man and beyond man to the angels and finally to God at the apex of the great chain of beings.

The idea was developed during the Middle Ages and the Renaissance and reached its fullest flowering in the eighteenth century. However, as later thinkers realized, it contains flaws. In particular, it seems to be at war with another great idea, that of evolutionary progress. If the doctrine of plenitude requires that everything that can exist must exist, and furthermore requires that what exists must exist as perfectly as possible, then how can the universe as a whole be conceived as improving, as growing in overall perfection? This deep-seated contradiction finally destroyed the idea of the great chain of being, and it ceased to be of philosophical importance in the nineteenth century.

Nevertheless, the image that the idea generated in the imagination, of a great chain or ladder extending from the lowest being to the highest, proved so compelling it was taken as the paradigm of any rational political organization. If God had seen fit to create the universe as a hierarchy of degrees of being and worth, then man should imitate God's structure when he came to make a state. Thus was the government of a single sovereign justified.

It was all the easier to do this because the established practice had been in existence for so long. We have seen how the ancient empires, in their age-old wisdom, had been immense hierarchies, with God or the gods at the top, the king or emperor as the representative of God on earth, and the people below, each person in his rightful place. The Greek city-states, the Roman republic, and the late medieval communes had seemed to call the idea in question, but as events had transpired these entities had really been exceptions that only proved the rule. The city-state had fallen to a type of Persian monarchy in the person of Alexander the Great. The republic had evolved into the Roman empire, and the communes had developed into the modern nation-states, all of whose kings ruled absolutely and by divine right.

Not everyone accepted the paradigm, not even in France. For one thing, there were Frenchmen who could and did read Locke and Jefferson. For the most part, they were bought off or mercilessly put down. The king had soldiers; the people did not. Power is in the muzzle of a gun.

However, French aid to the Americans during their revolutionary war came back to haunt the king and his ministers. French soldiers, and even some of their officers, had seen a people fight for and win their freedom and independence. They could hardly return home without changed attitudes toward the despotism they had always known. Furthermore, political philosophers like Voltaire, Rousseau, and Diderot continued to attack the very concept of "legitimate" despotism or tyranny. They inspired the people to ask how despotism or tyranny could *ever* be legitimate. And so the pressures built.

If there had been any other way to appease the citizens of France, there might not have been a revolution in 1789. It might have happened later. Or it might not have happened at all. It did happen, because the king and his ministers could not change their ideas about government quickly enough.

In the end it was not the literate and cultured minority of Frenchmen who brought down the government, as had been the case in England and America. Instead, it was the common people, who marched upon the Bastille and then upon the king and queen in their palace at Versailles. And they threw down the work of centuries and erected not only a new government but also a new society in place of the old.

> Bliss was it in that dawn to be alive,
> But to be young was very heaven!

So it appeared to William Wordsworth (1770–1850), looking back upon the glorious events of 1789, upon the fervor and promise of the French Revolution when it, too, was young. Here was a true change in society, not just in government. Here at last the people had grasped the rule in their own hands, and would judge the good and evil of laws and legislators—as was their indubitable right—for all ages to come. Here at last was a government whose legitimacy could not be denied by political philosophers save those who had been hired by kings and conquerors to justify their unjust rule. And here at last was a new world filled with men and women all equal and all consumed with hope and energy for a future that could not help but be brighter than the past.

For the most part, Americans applauded what was happening in

France. They understood that the Jacobins agreed with them in holding that property in rights is even more crucial than the right to property. In fact, in August 1789 the Jacobins promulgated a Declaration of the Rights of Man and of the Citizen that went beyond the American Bill of Rights in affirming, "Nothing that is not forbidden by Law may be hindered, and no one may be compelled to do what the Law does not ordain," for "Liberty consists in being able to do anything that does not harm others." This doctrine placed an enormous burden on positive law, for it ruled out entirely the notion that common or customary law should have any effect on people's actions.

The French Revolution ultimately failed, for many reasons. Some were strategic. The British, France's immemorial enemy, were no happier about having a powerful revolutionary nation across the English Channel than they had been confronting a powerful French despotism. The British therefore took it upon themselves to defend the cause of the so-called *emigrés*, persons—mostly nobles—who had fled France to escape the guillotine and now joined forces to defeat the revolution.

The Austrian and Russian monarchs were more ideologically motivated in their attacks upon France under the new regime. They did not like the idea of having their people see a successful revolt against despotic overlords. Such actions struck too close to home. Then, the French under Napoleon also overreached themselves, attempting to export their revolution to places like Spain and Italy, which were not yet ready for it.

There was another reason as well. The Declaration of the Rights of Man and of the Citizen had also proclaimed: "The source of all sovereignty lies essentially in the Nation. No corporate body, no individual may exercise any authority that does not expressly emanate from it." This is a perilous doctrine, as the French soon found. For who was to object, and on what grounds, when a leader declared that he and he alone spoke for the Nation, with an authority that emanated from it?

Such a leader was Robespierre (1758–1794), known as "The Incorruptible," who decreed death for all those he considered enemies of the revolution. This is a common result of revolutions that dissolve the society as well as the government: purges are undertaken to weed out all those members of the old society who seem to be unwilling to accept the new. Thus thousands died beneath the guillotine during the months of the Great Terror, in 1793 and early 1794. Louis XVI was executed in January 1793; his queen, Marie Antoinette, lost her head in October. Robespierre himself fell from power in July 1794 and met the same fate.

These deaths brought down the old regime, it is true, but they also constituted a great burden for the new. The stench of the queen's death under the great guillotine in the center of the Place de la Revolution reached into political conclaves all over the globe. If you are going to cut off the head of your enemy's wife, you had better be prepared to defend yourself.

France was prepared, having found Napoleon Bonaparte (1769–1821), the most brilliant soldier in European history. But Napoleon, like Robespierre before him, became tempted by that clause of the Declaration. He, too, soon found himself speaking for the Nation, with an authority that emanated from it. He allowed himself to be named First Consul. This title suggested the Roman republic but not the empire. Napoleon preferred to be an emperor. He arranged for the pope to crown him, but at the last moment he took the crown into his own hands and thrust it upon his own head. The meaning of this symbolic gesture was not lost on anyone.

France therefore once again had an absolute monarch, and one who, furthermore, became more absolute than any French king had ever been. The consequences proved destructive of France and of the revolution. For ten years French peasant-soldiers fought bravely for fraternity, if no longer for liberty, but finally they were defeated, in Russia and elsewhere, by the combined forces of European reaction.

The Emperor Napoleon was segregated, comfortably, on the island of Elba, off the coast of Tuscany. But he escaped in the early spring of 1815, gathered his veterans around him, and marched on Paris in the hope of beginning all over again. He met the Duke of Wellington, commander of the allied anti-French forces, at Waterloo, Belgium, on June 18, 1815, and was resoundingly defeated in one of the most important battles in history.

The Allies had learned their lesson about Napoleon. They now imprisoned him on the island of St. Helena, deep in the south Atlantic where no ship ever came. They also poisoned him by putting arsenic in his food. When he died in 1821, Count Metternich, the apostle of reaction at the Congress of Vienna, had already recreated the old political order of Europe. It would remain, essentially, until 1917.

The Rise of Equality

Humpty Dumpty, however, had had a great fall, and Count Metternich, even with the aid of all the kings and their horses and men, was incapable of putting him back together again perfectly. As through a distorting prism, the people of Europe had seen the new order of men and women in the French Revolution. After 1815, and for decades, they were willing, albeit reluctantly, to accept illiberal and despotic governments. But they would never give up the gains in social equality that they had won in the glorious year of 1789.

Alexis de Tocqueville (1805–1859), writing in 1835 about the achievements of the developing democracy in America, saw more clearly than anyone else in his time that the progress toward equality was an irresistible and irreversible movement, more powerful than any king or emperor. He also could see, more clearly than most democrats (he himself was an aristocrat, a member of the *ancien régime* whose epitaph he composed in a later book), what might be lost as well as what might be gained in this irresistible advance.

Undeniably, justice had to prevail. For the old social order had been monstrously unjust and, Tocqueville was the first to admit, deserved to die. He also knew that it had been brought down by its own palpable injustice. For instance, the practice of exempting the nobles and certain middle-class officeholders from taxation had infuriated the French peasantry to the point where they had become an unstoppable social force. Henceforth, Tocqueville predicted, equality would always increase everywhere, and justice be thereby served in the life of mankind.

At the same time, Tocqueville was also aware of what might be lost. The privileged classes of France and the other European *anciens régimes* had played an important political role in the state, mediating between the absolute tyranny of the monarch, above them, and the people, below. Their very privileges had led them to protect justice, not only for themselves, but for the people, and they had often been effective in doing so. Now, democratic man, no longer protected by traditional institutions, found himself in danger of being exposed to the absolute tyranny of the state that he himself had created. The political situation Tocqueville described would later be called totalitarianism, a system he had never seen but which he foretold with amazing accuracy nearly a century before it came into existence.

Something else would be lost, Tocqueville predicted: the extremes of social, economic, and cultural life as more human beings clustered around a central norm. The brutal excesses of the lowest classes would be forgotten, but so would the highest cultivation. As information was diffused to a population more widely literate, the abject ignorance of the old regime would become a thing of the past, but genius would become more rare. Virtues of the highest, brightest, and purest temper would no longer reveal the greatness that is in the best human beings, although the worst that is in others would also be moderated.

"If I endeavor to find out the most general and most prominent of all these different characteristics," Tocqueville concluded,

I perceive that what is taking place in men's fortunes manifests itself under a thousand . . . forms. Almost all extremes are softened or blunted: all that was most prominent is superseded by some middle term, at once less lofty and less low, less brilliant and less obscure, than what before existed in the world.

The great steps toward universal human equality that were taken in that most inhuman but also that most just revolution of 1789 were certainly the result of new knowledge and clearer understanding. It is true that all men and women are by nature equal and are endowed with certain unalienable rights. After Locke and Jefferson, after Robespierre and Danton, even after Napoleon, who was both a monster and the creator of great new institutions, those propositions can no longer be denied by reasonable human beings. They can only be denied by a man with a gun in his hands that is pointed at your heart, or by a state with a million guns pointed in the same direction.

We have seen that something beautiful and strange was lost when Galileo, Descartes, and Newton overthrew the medieval intellectual order and shattered the image of the City of God that was figured in the heavens. We cannot go back to that vision, nor would most people want to. Yet there is a certain nostalgia as we remember what was once and cannot be again. Was something else beautiful and strange shattered and destroyed when the European caste system, the social order that we know as the *ancien régime,* was overturned? Or was Tocqueville merely a sentimental old fool when he wrote his sad yet hopeful words about what had been lost as well as what had been gained?

In short, does advancing knowledge always come at a high price? I think it does, and that there is no way to avoid paying the price.

Mozart's Don Giovanni

In a previous chapter we saw how John Locke, at the end of the seventeenth century, tried by reasonable means to persuade both his compatriots and his contemporaries in other lands that toleration of religious differences was the only true Christianity. The more-than-a-thousand-year obsession with God was not so easily placated, and intolerance raged through the age of political revolutions. This was true not only in Catholic countries. The Roman Church sought to stamp out heresy with the same passionate vigor up to and beyond the French Revolution. Heresies of a different sort were punished in Protestant countries, and with the same passion.

At the same time, the attacks upon the narrow power of organized religion grew stronger and, in the last analysis, more imaginative. The most telling legal blow struck for toleration was the Bill of Rights of the U.S. Constitution, which forbade the state to interfere henceforth in the religious life of its citizens. Individuals continued to do so, and still do, but the state may not, by law, and, for the most part, it has not tried to tell Americans what and what not to believe during the two centuries since the Founding Fathers insisted on the inclusion of this basic freedom in the fundamental law of the land.

Thomas Jefferson had a hand in the framing of the Bill of Rights, as he did in almost everything innovative in American political life. Like many of his colleagues in the early U.S. government, he was a deist; he believed in God but not in any one religion. These men felt that there were many ways to serve God and to follow his way, whatever a person might think that way to be. And even if some people might be damned for following the wrong path, the state should never impose one particular path upon its citizens, who had to be free to make their own mistakes, else how could they ever grow up?

The British had attained political liberty before the Americans, but it took them much longer to arrive at true religious freedom. In France, the aggressive antireligious fervor of the revolution was replaced, after the fall of Napoleon, by a new wave of religious conservatism. In Italy, religious freedom was not guaranteed until the establishment of the republic, after World War II. Nor was religious toleration to be found in the newly founded Communist states of Europe and the East. There, *all* religion was proscribed, and men and women were shot for expressing the wish to worship in any way whatsoever.

Not only politicians fought to free men and women from the rigid controls of a state religion. Artists joined the fight. They often led it. Being artists, they presented their views in what often seemed a surprising, even a mocking way. An example is Mozart, whose opera *Don Giovanni* is a savage and brilliant attack upon religious intolerance. It is also, and at the same time, the tragedy of a man whose only religion is knowledge. In essence, it proclaims that a man must be free to seek knowledge wherever he wills. But it asks, too, whether knowledge alone is all a man should seek.

The story of Don Juan is very old. Its origins are lost in the mists of the medieval past. It was a myth of libertinism when libertinism was still a dangerous and frightening idea. Don Juan was first given a literary personality in the tragic drama *The Seducer of Seville*, attributed to the Spanish dramatist Tirso de Molina in 1630. Through this play Don Juan became a universal character, as well known as Don Quixote, Hamlet, and Faust, none of whom ever existed, but all of whom enjoyed and still enjoy a life beyond life.

According to the legend, Don Juan was an inveterate seducer of young women. At the height of his character of licentiousness, he seduced a girl of noble family and killed her father, who, to avenge his daughter, had challenged Don Juan. Later, seeing an effigy on the father's tomb, Don Juan asked the effigy to come and dine with him. The stone ghost soon came to dinner and foretold the sinner's death and damnation.

Tirso de Molina's fictional character possessed a courage and a rough vigor that gave the tragedy considerable power. Don Juan also had a vibrant sense of humor, which added to his fall a dimension lacking in the legend.

Wolfgang Amadeus Mozart (1756–1791) was born in Salzburg, of which he is the most famous son, and was brought up by his musician father as a child prodigy. By 1781, when he was still only twenty-five, he had already composed hundreds of works, and he broke with his patron, the archbishop of Salzburg, and struck off on his own to try to forge a musical career without the aid of wealthy aristocrats. In this attempt to be free he failed. He died only ten years later in abject poverty and was buried in the paupers' cemetery of Vienna without a stone to mark his final resting place. His great success was achieved posthumously, when he began to be recognized, as he is recognized today, as one of the greatest composers who ever lived.

Mozart was a small man with a joyous temperament. Some of his contemporaries considered him an *idiot savant*, a kind of buffoon genius whose talent could not be explained. He was far from being a philosopher, but he understood as well as any man of his time the challenge that the modern world offered traditional religion. His three last operas are all, in one way or another, about this subject. *Don Giovanni* deals with it in a terrifying manner.

The opera, with a libretto by Lorenzo Da Ponte (1749–1838), was first staged at Prague in October 1787. It was a sensational success then, though it failed in conservative Vienna the next year. Its failure in his native country may have broken Mozart's spirit.

Mozart's Don Giovanni is a man of brilliance and charm. He seduces a series of young women, not so much for love, although of course he tells them that love fills his heart, as for his need to know them, which he cannot do in any other way. Since his curiosity is soon satisfied, he abandons them all and breaks their hearts. The father of his last mistress challenges the seducer to a duel. Don Giovanni, laughing, kills his elderly adversary. His victim has asked him to dinner. As the poor man dies, Don Giovanni, with his customary cynical courtesy, asks him to dinner in return. Even his servant, Leporello, is shocked by this blasphemy.

Why does Don Giovanni treat the old man so cruelly? He detects a streak of sentimentality in him that he cannot abide. Don Giovanni himself is totally lacking in sentiment. He is a scientist, experimenting on woman's soul. He seeks within his victims a strain of greatness that they do not possess. In the end they always disappoint him. The father of his mistress is even less of a challenge. Don Giovanni discards him as he would a tender letter from a lover, which reveals nothing, for there is no longer anything to reveal.

Don Giovanni has many enemies. They begin to surround him, to hound him to his doom. He has spent his patrimony, and he and Leporello are reduced to a meager supper in a single room. Suddenly there is a thunderous knock at the door. Leporello shrinks in fear, but Don Giovanni, undaunted, strides to the door and flings it open. The Commandatore stands before him, pale and ghostly. He has come to dinner.

He takes Don Giovanni's hand in his icy grip. The living man cannot break loose. The ghost pulls him, while Leporello screams to his master to let go. But Don Giovanni does not wish to do so, even if he could. He is fascinated by what awaits him. He has finally found a challenge worthy of him. He will continue his search for knowledge, even in hell. Repent! cries the ghost, but Don Giovanni replies, calmly, that he has nothing to repent. It is one of the great moments in the history of the art of the West. The orchestra concludes with a crashing fortissimo, the fires of hell blaze up, there is a bloodcurdling shriek, and the hero disappears as the curtain falls.

Is the opera *Don Giovanni* a comedy or a tragedy? In his play *Man and Superman* (1905), Bernard Shaw (1856–1950) revealed his concept of a comic Mozartian intellectual charming the devils of the underworld, the only place where his Don Juan really feels comfortable. But Shaw has only words. Mozart's music adds a dimension lacking in any other treatment of the famous legend. Don Giovanni's last supper is made overwhelming and unforgettable by the great chords in the orchestra, the Commandatore's noble *basso*, and the soaring courage of Don Giovanni himself. He proclaims that he can live without God to give him the answers to his questions; he wants to find the answers himself, even if the penalty for this presumption is eternal hellfire.

If the life and death of Don Giovanni, in Mozart's conception of him, are tragic, it is a new kind of tragedy, very different from the plays of the ancient Greeks and of Shakespeare. Don Giovanni is sardonic and cynical, afraid of nothing, respectful of no traditional virtues. His tragedy, if such it is, is in his total isolation from the society at which he laughs. The age-old customs of that society have no force in his mind. What is more, he is aware that they have ceased to have force for many of society's members, although these are unable, through ignorance or fear, to admit it. This is why it is so easy for him to seduce the young women who fall to his every romantic sigh. These young women want a new kind of freedom and adventure just as much as he does, although they demand that he woo them in traditional ways before daring to give in both to him and to their own desires in a society that does not permit them to enjoy the same kind of freedom as men. Being women, they suffer torments of guilt and punishment for their "immorality."

Don Giovanni alone is completely aware of what is going on. Even his servant, Leporello—perhaps especially Leporello—has no comprehension of what is really happening, even though Leporello is also a libertine in the old sense of the word: that is, he, too, likes to seduce pretty women. But he plays the game in the old way.

Don Giovanni plays it in an entirely new way, trying to get the women who become his mistresses to face their desire to be more than their mothers were. They cannot do this, which is what disappoints him so much and forces him always to seek another victim. But "victim" is the wrong word, for Don Giovanni knows very well that every one of his bedmates is a willing partner. That is why he can say with perfect honesty to the stone ghost: "I have nothing to repent!"

That is also why the end of Mozart's opera is so disturbing. It shakes us, raises the hair on the back of our necks, because we realize how unjust, in one sense, is Don Giovanni's condemnation to eternal hellfire. However, the suffering of his abandoned mistresses, who are savagely punished by the traditional male-dominated society that they have no way of escaping, is also unjust.

Goethe's Faust

The Faust legend is as ancient as the legend of Don Juan. If possible, Faust is even better known. There was even an historical Faust who died around 1540, a famous magician who employed his magical wiles to entrap men and young women and to take from them whatever his evil mind desired.

In 1587 there appeared a collection of stories about the ancient magi— wise men skilled in the occult sciences. These stories had been retold during the Middle Ages about such reputed wizards as Merlin, Albertus Magnus, and Roger Bacon. In the first *Faustbuch* all of these deeds were attributed to Faust. He was joined by a savage fiend named Mephistopheles, and the stories were colored by a coarse, cruel humor at the expense of Faust's victims. But there was no question about Faust's ultimate damnation. According to the story, Faust had sold his soul to the Devil, and he would have to pay for his triumphs by suffering eternal damnation.

The first *Faustbuch* was translated into many languages. The English version inspired Christopher Marlowe's *Tragicall History of Dr. Faustus* (first published in 1604 although written earlier), which gave the legendary character added fame. During the next two hundred years numerous other books of Faust stories appeared, as well as magic manuals bearing Faust's name. Some of these manuals contained instructions on how to avoid the pact with the Devil, or even to break it once it was made.

The original Faust had desired sex, wealth, and power over others, but as the legend spread, it grew to possess other dimensions and meanings. Faust had also desired knowledge, but for the sake of his evil aims. The German writer Gotthold Lessing (1729–1781) saw Faust's pursuit of knowledge as noble, and in an unfinished play he arranged for a reconciliation between God and Faust, who was thus able to escape the clutches of the Devil. Similar conceptions have imbued other treatments of the Faust legend, by Hector Berlioz, Heinrich Heine, Paul Valéry, and Thomas Mann. However, the most famous Faust, and the most disturbing, is Goethe's.

Johann Wolfgang von Goethe, "the master spirit of the German people," was born at Frankfurt am Main in 1749 and died at Weimar in 1832, at the age of eighty-two, after a lifetime that was essentially one long and continuous triumph. Scientist, philosopher, novelist, and critic, as well as lyric, dramatic, and epic poet, he was the leading figure of his age after Napoleon. Or perhaps before him. The two men met once, and Napoleon, awed but aware that a multitude was listening to his words, declared: "*Vous etês un homme!*"

Faust was the work of a lifetime. It was begun in the 1770s and completed nearly sixty years later. A fragment was published in 1780. Thereafter, this masterwork was interrupted many times. The first part was not completed until 1808, at the insistence of Goethe's friend, the poet Friedrich Schiller (1759–1805). Again events intervened, and the second part was not finished until a few months before Goethe's death. It was not just the pressure of other business that delayed the completion. Goethe, knowing that the work would require of him all of his imagination, knowledge, and experience, therefore gave his whole life to it.

The first part, whose subtext is the destruction of the medieval world and its replacement by a modern society, begins in the Middle Ages. Faust is in his high, Gothic study, and he is miserable. He has attained to the wisdom that Don Giovanni had sought, but at the cost of the same isolation that the Spaniard suffered. Mephistopheles appears, first as a black poodle. He offers Faust the chance to reach beyond knowledge, to enjoy pleasure, wealth, the company of interesting people, and power over nature. Faust accepts the offer, but he refuses the traditional Faustian bargain. He declares he is already in hell. He needs no further punishment. Mephistopheles thereupon alters the terms. If he can ever manage to get Faust to say that he is satisfied, that his driven, tormented spirit wishes to rest, then the Devil will have won. "Done!" Faust cries, and the great contest begins.

The first part of *Faust* became famous in Germany for its love story with the appearance in 1790 of *Faust: Ein Fragment*. The publication in 1808 made the story known everywhere in Europe. Faust falls in love with a simple young girl, Gretchen, who lives in a little house in a little town that is despotically ruled by traditional values. She has never had a lover. Nor has she ever even received a gift from a man when Faust gives her a beautiful collection of jewels, provided by Mephistopheles, in order to woo and seduce her. She puts on the jewels and looks at herself in the mirror. What she sees is the different person that she has already become, and that she has always had the potential to be.

Gretchen knows instinctively, as any girl would, what the gift means, and she recognizes both its danger and its promise. The danger will come if she is seduced and then abandoned by the man she already thinks of as her lover. Mephistopheles has made Faust handsome again, as he once was, and thirty years younger. Faust speaks of her escape from the narrow room where she spends her life, in the feudal house in the ancient town. And she does not ponder long. She gives herself to Faust, falling in love with him with all her heart and soul.

The acceptance of the promise of a new and larger life was inevitable, as Marshall Berman says.* The pressures on poor, noble Gretchen have been building for five hundred years, since 1300, when Dante, Petrarch, and Boccaccio inaugurated the Renaissance and began to pry apart the bars that held men and women captive in the medieval world picture. Most Europeans still lived, in 1800, in narrow, feudal, traditional environments, obeying the ancient social rules that were administered by churchmen and clerics of whatever sect or persuasion. For five hundred years adventurous spirits like the ones we have described in the foregoing chapters had tried to free man from the prison of his prejudices and his fears.

There were always courageous young women like Gretchen, and whether they knew it or not, they were always looking for a Faust, the adventurous stranger who would come to town and leave it with the village beauty, who might or might not survive. Survival usually depended on the man. As time went on, there were more and more Fausts and more and more Gretchens. Indeed, most Americans are descended from such persons, for the desire to escape the feudal, still essentially medieval world of their youth and to cross the seas to find a better, freer life brought more immigrants to the New World than anything else.

Gretchen makes an oft-repeated mistake when she makes herself too available to Faust. Although he is thrilled at how she has changed into a charming woman, he begins to think that he needs more than she can give him. This is partly the work of Mephistopheles, partly the natural work-

---

*Readers of Marshall Berman's book, *All That Is Solid Melts into Air,* will know how much I owe to him in what follows.

ing of the character of Faust, who is doomed never to be satisfied. And so he abandons her. Without Faust to protect her, Gretchen is harried to despair. Her brother, Valentine, taunts and accuses her. He is killed by Faust in a duel with the help of Mephistopheles. Gretchen's baby dies, and she is imprisoned, convicted of child murder, and sentenced to death. She is awaiting execution when Faust returns and, with the help of Mephistopheles again, enters her cell.

At first she does not recognize him. She believes he is her executioner, and she touchingly offers her body to the axe. No, cries Faust, I have come to save you! You have only to step out of the cell, and you will be free!

Gretchen refuses. She knows Faust does not love her, that he acts out of guilt. Nor does she really desire to be free in the way he is free. Although she knows better even than Faust the savage cruelty of her narrow feudal world, she also recognizes the good that persists in it: its commitment to ideals, its dedication to a life devoted to loyalty and love. Even if her world has betrayed her, she will not betray it. Nor will she betray her love for Faust. She forgives him and absolves him of any sin on her behalf, and as she rises upward, he feels that she has helped to free him from his diabolical bargain.

The second part of Goethe's *Faust* is a nineteenth-century work and should be discussed in the context of that epoch. We will therefore save our comments on it until the next chapter.

The first part of the poem is the natural complement to *Don Giovanni*. It is more profound, for Goethe was a greater writer than Lorenzo Da Ponte. It also carries forward the line of meaning that Mozart, more than Da Ponte, had begun.

The love story of Faust and Gretchen is not just a challenge to tradional religion, any more than the moral of *Don Giovanni* is that all seducers go to hell. But both works, and especially *Faust,* demand that we recognize that a new world is being born. For the moment, they both say, only a minority of men and women can understand this truth and benefit from it. In the case of *Don Giovanni*, only one, Don Giovanni himself, sees this, and he pays a price. But even Faust, with all his brilliance, needs the Devil's help. He cannot free himself alone.

For nearly two millennia, Christians had believed that true freedom came from God. Dante had proclaimed, "His will is our peace," and a thousand sermons had promised their listeners that if they would only obey God's gentle demands, they would attain eternal bliss. But for two millennia the world had been grinding on its inexorable way, crushing the bodies and the minds of men and women, twisting them and distorting their vision of the good. A new bargain was needed. The bargain with God had not worked. The only alternative was a bargain with the Devil.

Mozart could not say this explicitly, although his music says it. Goethe lets Mephistopheles say it for him:

> I am the spirit that negates all!
> And rightly so, for all that comes to be
> Deserves to perish wretchedly . . .

And yet, at the same time, the Devil is "part of the power that would / Do nothing but evil, and yet creates the good." God, in his overweening love for man, is destructive of man's creative energy. The demonic lust for destruction is creative. We must wipe out the old to make way for the new; otherwise progress is not possible.

Progress, then, is the Devil's bargain, and not God's. This is a strange conclusion. And yet the world has acted as if the conclusion were indubitably true for two centuries, and the world shows no sign that it has changed its view as the twentieth century comes to an end.

10

The Nineteenth Century: Prelude to Modernity

DURING THE TUMULTUOUS hundred years of the nineteenth century, Europe impressed its brand upon the rest of the world, so that it was possible to boast that the sun never set on the British or the Spanish or the Portuguese or the French or the Dutch empire. The burgeoning United States, "the great nation of futurity," discovered that it was not necessary to establish an empire. The promulgation of the Monroe Doctrine in 1823 insured that American influence in the Western hemisphere would remain unquestioned while the country was spared the burden of having to administer the affairs of a dozen small nations. Japan, quicker than most to see how the winds of the future were blowing, opened itself up to the West in 1868, thereby obtaining the benefits of Western technology instead of being forced, like China, to remain a mere supplier of raw materials and manual labor. And a century of comparative peace, interrupted only by small wars of position among the colonial powers, allowed the world from 1815 to 1914 to devote its abundant energies to the development of a global market in subsistence goods instead of luxury items. The change was symbolized by John Masefield's "Cargoes":

> Quinquireme of Nineveh from distant Ophir,
> Rowing home to haven in sunny Palestine,
> With a cargo of ivory,
> And apes and peacocks,
> Sandalwood, cedarwood, and sweet white wine.
>
> Stately Spanish galleon coming from the Isthmus,
> Dipping through the Tropics by the palm-green shores,

243

With a cargo of diamonds,
Emeralds, amethysts,
Topazes, cinnamon, and gold moidores.

Dirty British coaster with a salt-caked smoke stack,
Butting through the Channel in the mad March days,
With a cargo of Tyne coal,
Road-rails, pig-lead,
Firewood, iron-ware, and cheap tin trays.

The nineteenth century saw the discovery of new sources of energy, like oil and electricity. It gloried in new devices for communication on both a world and a local scale, such as the telegraph and the telephone. And it welcomed new means of comforting life, from electric light to cheap cast-iron stoves. Manufactured objects, iron deer for the lawn and mass-produced furniture suites for the parlor and bedroom, replaced hand-made decorations, which would only regain their cachet in the late twentieth century. Popular literature and journalism demanded universal literacy in a few developed countries, whose missionaries tried to carry the light of learning around the globe. Railroads snaked through forests and across prairies and rivers, joining communities that had been separated for centuries and creating new social ideas while destroying old ones. And at the end of the century, seers in Germany and the United States prophesized that the newly invented automobile would prove to be the most revolutionary, as well as profitable, vehicle that the world had ever seen.

Generally, the nineteenth century was an age that liked to think of itself, and to call itself, "new." The word was apt. But the age's most significant novelty is not even suggested by any of the examples provided above.

The Difference Money Makes

In certain basic respects, human beings have not changed much over the past five or ten thousand years. Ancient Egyptians loved their children, usually, but sometimes not; so it is with us. The ancient Greeks liked to eat and drink and sit in the sun and talk about philosophical subjects, and so do we, although we might not be so inclined to refer to the talk as philosophical. Roman matrons enjoyed gossiping when they gathered at the communal place for washing clothes; we gossip at the Laundromat. The ancients became sick and died; so do we. They were generous, sometimes, and sometimes cruel; so are we. They were sometimes vain and self-centered, and at other times clear-sighted about themselves; the same could be said about us. On the whole, they were more like us than they were different.

There are other respects in which human beings of the past viewed life differently. Of course, they did not have refrigerators and television sets and microwave ovens and automobiles and computers, and we do. That is not a major difference. They did not "take" vacations or worry about how to employ their "leisure time." That is a bigger difference. They did not innoculate their children against childhood diseases and expect them to "do better in life" than they had done. That is a still bigger difference. They did not think money was very important. That is a very large difference, so large that it is difficult to comprehend it.

It is all the more difficult to understand when we recognize that the ancients were not alone in having relatively little regard for money. That is also true of most of the men and women of the Middle Ages, in all countries; of the Renaissance; and of the seventeenth and even the eighteenth centuries. Until the end of the eighteenth century, that is, only yesterday, most people had not yet discovered how important money can be. As a result, their lives were very different from ours, even if psychologically they were more like us than they were different.

If we can understand this profound difference between the men and women of the fairly recent past and ourselves, we will also comprehend one of the main contributions of the nineteenth century to the general stock of human knowledge. It is perhaps in this sense more than any other that the eighteen-hundreds can be viewed as a prelude to our own twentieth century.

The nineteenth century did not invent money. As a medium of exchange, as a device for balancing accounts between a buyer of goods or services and a seller of them, money is very old. Few peoples, no matter how primitive, have been discovered who did not have some conception of money, and who did not use something that stood for money, like bones or pieces of metal.

Nor have any peoples ever been discovered who did not want money, however they conceived or counted it. That being so, it is astonishing to realize that, until quite recently, most human beings, otherwise much like ourselves, lacked the conception that is so obvious to us of how to earn money. The phrase, "to earn a living," would have been incomprehensible to them. Almost every man, woman, and child of today knows what that means, although many may find it hard to do it.

Economic Life Before 1800: The Peasant

Let us try to imagine the way of life of certain economic groups or classes prior to 1800. That is not a fixed date. Some of these groups ceased to exist as significant economic entities before 1800 in a few developed countries, such as England and America, while in other countries they survived almost until the present day, certainly until after World War II. But the year 1800 will do as a general divide or watershed between the old, preindustrial, nonmonetary economy that characterized human life in most of history and the new, industrial and postindustrial, monetary economy in which we live today.

Let us discuss the status of peasants. I use the term to refer to the vast majority of human beings in almost all countries before 1800, who lived on the land and gave their lives to it and who, by the small surplus they were able to produce, supported the entire superstructure of society while benefiting hardly at all from it. In some countries this economic class was called serfs, in others slaves, in still others untouchables. "Peasant" is a useful generic name.

A peasant worked all day, every day, from the time he was able to lift the simplest tool until he was too old, sick, or weak to do so any longer, and then, most probably, he died. So did his wife. He probably had a little money, a few pennies or the equivalent. But neither he nor his wife worked for that or any money. They labored because life was work and work was life, and the two could not be sundered. In particular, money did not come between life and work, as a medium of exchange in the market for labor.

In other words, such a man did not have a "job," for which he was paid wages or a salary. Nor could he, if another opportunity arose, quit his "situation" and take another, for which he might be paid a higher wage. Peasants, for the most part, were tied to the land on which they were born and on which they expected to labor for their entire lives. They could not leave their land and its lord and work for another lord, unless the two lords agreed that this would be a desirable thing for *them*. Nor could peasants ask for more money for their work.

Strictly speaking, they worked for themselves and for their lord, and their work produced food, which was life, for themselves and their children and such others, aged parents perhaps, as might be dependent on them. Their lord would allow them to take a small portion of their produce to market to be sold to town folk, who did not live on or till the land. In this way they would receive small amounts of money. Part of this money they would have to return to their lord, who had the right to tax all market transactions in his domain. The rest would go to buy those necessary things like salt or iron or possibly books that could not be produced on their land, that is, on their lord's land.

What did peasants hope to receive from life? Mainly they hoped to be left in peace, to bear and bring up children, to suffer as little pain as possible, and to die a good death. Of those, to be left alone was not the least important.

Peasants were at the bottom of the social order, and many enemies surrounded and threatened them. All of these enemies wanted to rob them, to steal what little money they had, to take whatever else might be of value. Their labor was valuable, and so their enemies, among whom the lord was a leading figure, were always trying to steal that, too.

Peasants, therefore, hoped to be able to die no poorer than they had been born. They did not expect to die richer. Nor did they expect their children to be richer than they were. Their hope for their children, insofar as they had any hope at all, was no different than their expectations for themselves.

The Lord

Again, a generic term. Landowners have been called by various names, such as baron, señor, signore, master, or simply boss. Like the peasant, the lord had little ready money, although of course he had more than the peasant, a few dollars rather than a few pennies. Unlike the peasant, the lord owned the land to which each of them, in their different ways, was bound.

The lord could legally leave his land if he wanted to, but this was usually an imprudent thing to do, considering the enemies who surrounded him. Unless the peasant was a chattel slave, the lord did not own him, but he lived off his labor; that is, the peasant had to work the land for the lord and the lord's family as well as for himself and his family, producing food for both. In return, the lord protected the peasant against some of the more ruthless of his enemies, like pirates, brigands, and other outlaws.

What were the lord's expectations? First, not to lose any of his land, and to leave it to his sons. Second, in many cases a distant second, to acquire more land. But how could the lord make such acquisitions when all the land was already owned by other barons or the king? One way was to have children marry in return for increases in land. A surplus of daughters, however, each of whom might require land as a part of her dowry, could result in a net reduction of the family's land holdings. Thus sons were almost always considered more valuable than daughters.

The king might take land from one lord and give it to another in return for some notable service. This was an avenue for "advancement" that was always worth investigating, and money was useful here for bribing the king's servants and purchasing offices outright, which could lead to later acquisitions of land at the expense of another lord who had not bribed the right persons or purchased the right offices. The king himself faced difficulties in this regard, for one of his main political roles was to assure his barons possession of their lands, and if he seemed to be unable to do that, or unwilling, he could find himself without support in an emergency. Therefore, the best way to acquire more land was to steal it from someone else, that is, to "conquer" it in a so-called just war.

The high lords spent most of their time fighting other high lords whose land they wanted or who wanted their land. This was their work, and they were devoted to it and spent much time and effort on it, although not as much time and effort as the peasant spent on his work. Thus the lords worked for land, not for money. They would steal money, that is, "conquer" it, if the opportunity arose, and be glad to have it, for the good things that money could do for them. But for the most part, money was unimportant compared to land.

The Cleric

Once more, a generic term, for priest, minister, or any similar title. The cleric, like the lord, lived off the labor of the peasant. By law, he could demand a tenth, or tithe, of the peasant's produce. Often, the tithe was more than a tenth. Since the cleric could not extract money from the peasant, he sold the surplus produce he managed to acquire for the money he needed to buy things the peasant could not provide, like silk and other fine cloth for vestments, silver and gold for altar pieces, and beautiful books from which the Word of God could be read to the peasant as he knelt in church. In return, the cleric provided the peasant with a safe journey to the next world.

What were the cleric's hopes and expectations? Apart from salvation, which was more or less important depending on the character and depth of his faith, he hoped for advancement and power in the Church. The Church was the only meritocracy in the preindustrial old regime. Members could move up or down in the hierarchy depending on their individual merit, although not all such moves were based on merit. Many depended on birth, as all did among the lords and the peasants. A brilliant priest in the Catholic Church might become a bishop or a cardinal even if he lacked noble birth, or even pope, providing he was Italian. High church offices could bring great wealth, which included money but usually consisted of land and jewels, furs, and works of art. No cleric worked for money as such. The idea would have been incomprehensible before the nineteenth century, and not easy to grasp even then.

The King

Finally, the king—the head of the social hierarchy, by whatever title. He lived off the labor of everyone else, although he might work hard himself, at hunting (the royal sport), at dispensing justice (the royal obligation—

noblesse oblige), and at war (the royal profession). He had a great deal of money, but his expenses were also high, usually higher than his income, so he was constantly having to beg, borrow, or steal, often all three, from his people or from other kings. His ambition was to conquer as many other kings as possible. If he succeeded, he rewarded himself by accepting the adulation of the world. He worked for glory.

Money was necessary, primarily because it would buy soldiers, who could win him what he wanted most, which was honor and fame. It was also necessary because, if he lacked it, his soldiers would leave him and he would then be helpless before his enemies, that is, other kings who still had their soldiers. He would then be conquered and perhaps killed, which was the equivalent of an unfriendly takeover or corporate bankruptcy today.

The Merchant

One class in the old regime appeared to have understood money in the modern way, although that is actually far from the case. This group did deal in money, knew how to acquire it and to make more money out of money, and did covet it above other worldly goods. This was the class of urban merchants, traders, and moneylenders.

Even as late as 1800 only a relative few existed. But they had an influence out of proportion to their numbers, for they possessed, or might possess or were thought to possess, the large sums of money that kings and the higher nobles desperately needed from time to time, and which the nobility would borrow at outrageously high rates of interest. Fifty percent per year was a low rate in most countries as late as 1700. Such dealings made fortunes for families like the German Fuggers and the Florentine Medici. But the business proved dangerous, for kings often refused to pay their debts, and bankers usually lacked the means to enforce their financial arrangements. Of course, they could try to refuse to lend money another time, but that, too, could be dangerous, since the king had soldiers and bankers did not.

The interest charged by lenders before the eighteenth century was usually illegal. In the eyes of the Church, usury, the name for lending money at interest, was considered a sin against both nature and God.

The reason could be traced to Aristotle, who had distinguished between two kinds of economic activities. One, which he called domestic, involved the production and consumption of all the things human beings need in order to live. The amount of food anyone *needs* is measured by natural necessity, not by desire; that is, there are natural limits to the amount of food anyone can eat. Aristotle therefore maintained that the production, distribution, and consumption of food was a natural human economic activity, and since it was natural, it was good. A similar virtue held for clothes, houses, and the like. In all these cases desire might intrude and lead a man to exceed what he actually needed by a small amount. But for the most part need was the measure and guaranteed the natural goodness of trade in these things.

Aristotle called the other kind of economic activity retail trade. The name is inappropriate today, but the idea is clear enough. Retail trade, in Aristotle's view, was subject to no natural limits. The measure of such trade was money and not need, and there is no natural limit to the amount of money you may want. Therefore, Aristotle concluded, retail trade was unnatural. The worst kind of retail trade was in money itself. If a man traded in food, buying and selling it for the sake of the money that could be gained instead of providing himself and his family with something to eat, that was bad, but at least the product itself was a useful one for some person. Thus food, even if for the trader it was a means of acquiring money, might be for the final recipient the means of satisfying a natural need, hunger.

But money was in itself useless, Aristotle said, and to trade it—to lend it at interest, for example—was to accomplish no good of any kind, and therefore such activity was totally unnatural because it was not based on a natural necessity. The only thing that drove such a trader was desire, and there is no limit to the desire for money.

The Church was willing to accept retail trade as natural if it was conducted as much as possible in kind. But usury could not fail to be viewed as unnatural, according to Aristotle's analysis. Like other unnatural acts, such as gluttony, sodomy, and incest, usury was thus declared to be a sin. All who practiced it were required to seek absolution, and those who practiced it too much or too often could be condemned to death.

The illegality and sinfulness of usury had several results. First, it forced a major part of the business of lending money at interest into the hands of Jews, who had no prejudice against usury. They considered that charging interest for the use of money was no different from charging rent for the use of land, which Christians thought was natural. Jews were often forbidden by law to own land, the only other measure, besides money, of wealth, so they concentrated their efforts and their ingenuity on banking, in which they became proficient.

Nevertheless, if usury was legal by Jewish law, it remained illegal by Christian law, and this often gave debtors an excuse to abjure their debts. Money continued to be needed, so the first result of all these hindrances and defaults was higher interest rates charged by lenders, who distrusted their clients and sought to cover the risks with a high return. The final result was to reduce the amount of capital available, except for military expenditures, which always managed to be paid for even if money for other needs was wanting.

Relatively large amounts of capital could be found for peaceful activities when the entire society agreed on their value. A prime example is the century from about 1150 to about 1250 in France, when scores of great cathedrals were built throughout the country at a total cost that has been estimated to be as much as a quarter of the gross national product for those years. Cathedrals rose in every town. Almost everyone contributed willingly, and in many cases ecstatically. The era of cathedral building ended around the middle of the thirteenth century, after which few comparable projects were undertaken anywhere in the world until the nineteenth century. Then they became commonplace. That is one of the great differences that money makes.

Merchants and bankers were not alone in working directly for money in the preindustrial economy of the old regime. Traditionally, serfs who managed to escape from their lord and his land acquired their freedom if they could survive without being caught and returned to their master for a year and a day. In the eleventh and twelfth centuries, a long period of relative peace and good harvests led to a rising population. Many younger sons fled from their peasant homes in Italy and northern Europe and sought the new towns, the communes, for, according to the saying, "City air is free." The merchants in the communes were willing to ignore the backgrounds of young men who applied for work and to help them to remain safe for the requisite period. These young men often operated in a monetary economy, receiving fixed wages for their work and moving from one job to another once they attained their freedom.

Similar freedom was enjoyed by some freed serfs after the population of Europe was decimated by the Black Death in the middle of the fourteenth century. But those periods were exceptions. Most of the time it was very hard for men to leave their lords and become free laborers, and the life of many of those who did hardly seemed preferable. Until the end of the eighteenth century in Europe, and throughout most of the rest of the world until our own time, the great majority of persons lived in a preindustrial economy, had very little money, and were unable either to enjoy what money could buy or to do what money could do.

The Rise of the Labor Market: Economics

Contrast the conditions of life described in the preceding sections to those under which we live today. In the twentieth century almost everyone, in almost every country, works for money, and uses the money he earns to buy the things he needs, and wants, to make a good life. Hardly anyone can live a good life without money. Those who have more money are envied by those who have less, and practically everyone seeks constantly for ways to earn more than he does.

We are aware that there are some persons, even today, who do not care much about money. They are more concerned about the work they do than the money they earn from it, or about where they live, or about avoiding "the rat race." Even these relatively rare persons require some money to live.

Once, the ownership of land substituted for having a money income. Today, if we should be so unlucky as to own land without having money to support it, we might end up poorer than the poorest peasant used to be. If we were a king, living off the labor and charity of his people, we might feel dishonored, at least uncomfortable. If we were an honest priest, helping his parishioners, we would be aware that most of our parishioners pitied us because we were so poor even if we thought of ourselves as rich because we were doing the Lord's work.

The change from 1800 to today is extraordinary. In 1800, in most places in the world, money was almost invisible. Today it is omnipresent. Work existed then as now, but the notion that work is life, and life is work, has practically disappeared. We work in order to earn a living, and we may even dream of a day when we will no longer need to work, so that we will have time to "really live." Work and life, instead of being inseparable parts of our existence, have become conflicting, almost contradictory notions.

For the majority of human beings on earth, that change has occurred during the present century. That is only because the industrial development of the entire world took two centuries to accomplish, rather than one. Starting during the last half of the 1700s, it was completed during the last half of the 1900s. But the change, essentially, was the work of the nineteenth century alone, the period between 1815, which saw the close of the old regime in Europe, and the onset of World War I in 1914. As late as 1815, most people still lived a life devoid of money. By 1914, most people in the developed countries lived in a monetary economy. In fact, that is one partial definition of a "developed" country. As development has spread to other countries in our own century, the monetary economy has gone with it.

This great nineteenth-century change in the basic pattern of human life was signaled by the discovery, or perhaps invention, of a new science: economics. Dubbed the "dismal" science, it was appropriated by a group of somber thinkers who shared a pessimistic view of human affairs. That is, they agreed in thinking of human beings as fundamentally no different from sacks of wheat or ingots of pig iron. A man was an economic entity who could be bought and sold just like a loaf of bread. The human soul was not an economic entity, and therefore doubts began to be entertained as to whether it existed.

Adam Smith, in *The Wealth of Nations* (published in 1776), was the first to describe that remarkable phenomenon, the labor market. In a sense, before he named it and told how it worked, the labor market did not exist. Where life is work and work is life, a man cannot separate his work from himself and sell it to someone else without at the same time selling himself. Adam Smith was among the first to realize that in the new world the industrial revolution was creating, labor was a commodity like any other, and consequently was for sale. In fact, everything was for sale. Life consisted in buying and selling, not in work, and money was the lifeblood of the market. Over the market hovered an "invisible hand," as Smith called it, which insured that economic efficiency would prevail. Furthermore, the happiness of humankind lay in efficient buying and selling. The sign of efficiency was profit, which was measured in money. Thus money was the goal of all striving. And thus the modern world came about.

Adam Smith was followed by Thomas Robert Malthus (1766–1834), probably the most pessimistic of all, David Ricardo (1772–1823), John Mill (1773–1836) and his son John Stuart Mill (1806–1873), Henry George (1839–1897), and John Maynard Keynes (1883–1946), to name only a few of the most famous economists. In our own time a large number of academic economists have made new discoveries and thrown light on old problems. They have also invented new measures of economic activity, like M1 and M2 (measures of the money supply) and GNP (a measure of the productivity of nations).

These advances have made us much more knowledgeable about economic life. Yet there are still vast areas of ignorance. The world stock market crash of October 1987, for instance, was as alarming, as apparently unpredictable, and as profoundly incomprehensible as the crash of 1929, despite the assurances by an army of economists during the intervening sixty years that a repeat of 1929 could never happen. More disturbing, perhaps, is that economists still, several years later, do not agree about why the 1987 crash occurred.

Whether economics is "good science" is really beside the point. Economists do know many things that are true, even though they do not know them with the certainty of a physicist, say, trading on the assurance of three centuries of Newtonian mechanics. The point is that we all, thanks to economics, know many important things our forefathers did not know. First and foremost, we know that, in the world of today and in any world we can imagine, labor, expertise, and experience are salable, and life consists in learning how to sell our own labor, expertise, and experience at the highest price that we can get consistent with certain definable conditions.

We also believe that this is the natural order of things. Perhaps it is and always will be. But we should not forget that only two centuries ago it was not thought to be the natural order. Perhaps that should make us wonder more than we ordinarily do about what we know.

Economics, the dismal nineteenth-century science, has invaded other realms of knowledge. Karl Marx, about whom we will have more to say, was both an economist and an historian. Today, largely because of Marx, all serious history is economic history, even if it sometimes presents itself in other colors. That is, any history worthy of the name must deal with economic facts, whatever else it deals with. History written before Adam Smith was not required to do this in order to be acclaimed good history.

Furthermore, there is now an economic aspect of science, an economic side of art, and even an economics of leisure, which, in the old dispensation, was almost the opposite of an economic fact. And money has become the measure of success, even in the apparently most uneconomic of activities. We have become fascinated with the life-styles of the rich, where fame follows riches, and reputation can be bought.

The victory of money over the old regime had already taken place in England when Charles Dickens (1812–1870) was writing *Dombey and Son*, in the mid-1840s. Dickens was as astonished by this phenomenon as anyone, and as dismayed and unhappy about what he thought had been lost. He did not conceal his disapproval.

Dombey is rich, the head of a powerful trading house. His son is a sickly lad, though with a good head on his shoulders. One day little Paul asks his father: "Papa! what's money?"

Mr. Dombey is disconcerted. What an extraordinary question for *his* son to ask! "What is money, Paul?" he responds. "Money?"

"I mean," says Paul, "what's money after all? I mean, what can it do?"

"You'll know better by-the-by," Mr. Dombey says to his son, patting him gently on the hand. "Money, Paul, can do anything," he adds.

Paul will not be put off with such an answer, and he continues to wonder about money. His mother is dead. She died a few hours after his birth. If money is good, he asks, why did it not save his mama? He himself is weak and sickly. Money cannot make him strong and well. What, then, is it good for?

At the end of the novel we have learned that money could not save little Paul nor, indeed, the house of Dombey and Son, which has crashed down around Mr. Dombey together with all his high hopes. He has lost his son, his wife, and all of his money. All that remains is his daughter, whom he never valued. But she is worth, he finally understands, all the money in the world, as well as all the fame and honor.

Faustian Development

The first part of Goethe's *Faust* was published in 1808. As we have seen, it sounded the death knell for the old, narrow, Gothic world into which Goethe had been born. The second part, completed only a few months before its author's death in 1832, twenty-four years later, complements the first part. Instead of describing with agonizing fidelity a world that is dying, it imaginatively depicts one that is being born.

According to the Faust legend, Faust is tempted by the Devil with all the goods about which a man can dream. (Among these Christopher Marlowe, in his play, had included Helen of Troy, as the symbol of all that woman represents.) Goethe's Mephistopheles takes Faust on a tour of space and time, and offers him Helen as a mate, as well as every other luxurious gift. But Goethe's Faust is bored. He wants still more, but he does not yet know precisely what he wants.

Act Four opens with Faust seated gloomily upon a high crag, staring off at the limitless ocean. Mephistopheles appears in a pair of seven-league boots, which stride off after he dismounts. He asks what is troubling Faust.

Faust does not know. Then, suddenly, he understands what he desires. The ocean, far below, moves in and out in its eternal motion of the tides, and yet it accomplishes nothing. All that energy is wasted. I wish to control it! he cries. Dare to help me!

This is the kind of project that Mephistopheles loves. What no man has dared he will help Faust achieve. He explains that Faust must aid the emperor in a war. In return the emperor will give Faust a gigantic concession, permitting him to develop the entire coastline. It is no sooner said than done. Faust now sits upon his lookout place, viewing with satisfaction the concrete realization of his mighty plans. What was once a jungle, a natural chaos, is now a vast park, with fine buildings and factories churning out useful products and employing thousands of men in useful work.

There is one more thing to wish for. At the very center of Faust's view is a little house surrounded by lovely old linden trees. He asks who lives in that house that spoils his view.

An ancient couple named Baucis and Philemon, Mephistopheles tells him. And he explains that he has been unable to get the old couple to move. They are kind, generous people, but at their age they are not tempted by the alternative that Mephistopheles has offered them, a finer house with more land in a newly landscaped park not far away, but out of Faust's view.

Faust is tortured by frustration. He has everything: power, success, the satisfaction of having provided benefits for thousands of his fellow creatures. This stupid old couple stands in the way.

Faust is not cruel. At least he does not think he is. He does not want to harm the old couple, whose care and generosity have made them universally beloved. But the project must be finished! It is intolerable to think that one old couple can spoil the achievement of his dreams. He orders Mephistopheles to remove them and to destroy their crooked little house and the ancient trees. It must be done before day is done, he cries, else he will never sleep again!

Mephistopheles reappears soon enough. But Faust's attention is drawn to a flickering orange light among the trees. There must be a fire there, Faust says. Indeed, Mephistopheles replies. It is the house of Baucis and Philemon. They would not leave their home, and so we burned it to the ground. Faust is staggered. Were they hurt? Mephistopheles shrugs. You wanted them gone, he says. We had to kill them. In the morning light your view will be clear in every direction.

Faust laments what he has done, but Mephistopheles chastises him. You won't make an omelet without breaking some eggs, he implies (how many builders, developers, managers of gigantic projects have said the same thing in the century and a half since *Faust*?). Faust banishes Mephistopheles, but of course he cannot get rid of him, nor does he really want to. The spirit that negates all, the destroyer of what is, is needed, Faust knows, to make way for the future. The world is limited in extent, but man's dreams are infinite. The old must be torn down, bulldozed, obliterated, to make room for the new. At an ever-increasing pace, yesterday's novelties must make way for tomorrow's.

Was it ever thus? Not when population remained nearly constant, when men built not for a generation but for a millennium, when institutions were intended to endure until the end of time. There was always change. Change is unavoidable in human life and in nature, too. But until the industrial revolution, until the nineteenth century, change was not the goal. Then, and since then, change has been legislated, demanded for its own sake. Things have to change because the past is fundamentally undesirable and unsatisfactory. What's new is good, what's old is bad. Away with the old, bring on the new!

None of this is invalidated by our current rage of nostalgia for the recent past. As I write, Americans are mad for the 1950s; as you read, another decade may be in, and the fifties out. Even this turn of mind did not escape Goethe, who apprehended it a hundred and sixty years ago. Thus, at the end of the poem, Faust, now old and blind, desires to return to the little town where he was born and to revisit Gretchen's narrow room. But this is to make a kind of theme park, 1830s version, out of the old regime.

The old feudal way of life has become a place to visit, not to live in. The future is the place to live.

The final end of Goethe's masterwork is enigmatic at best. The old poet has lost none of his energy and skill, but perhaps his focus is not as clear as it once was. Faust has suffered because of his treatment of Baucis and Philemon, but he has enjoyed triumphs, too. Most important, he never admits defeat. His vision of a future that will be better for most people, although it may be cruel to some, is an adequate depiction, Goethe seems to say, of the new world that is coming into being before the eyes of everyone, even if everyone does not see it. And Faust is consequently saved, not damned, in the poem's last lines.

The spirit of prophecy that imbues Goethe, and his hero Faust, does not disappear with Goethe's death and Faust's poetical apotheosis. The torch is handed over to a group of thinkers, most of them young, who call themselves socialists—a new word—and compose delectable visions of a new world based on social labor and dedicated to justice. The most eloquent and influential of this new breed of prophets was Karl Marx.

Marxism: Theory and Practice

One of the more disingenuous defenses of slavery advanced by political apologists in the South in the years before the American Civil War went like this. Let us admit that chattel slavery is practiced in our region, mainly for economic reasons. But the Negro is well treated by his owner. It is in the economic interest of the slaveholder to treat his slave well. The Negro, being naturally inferior, could not live as well in freedom as he does in slavery, thanks to this benevolent treatment. The "free" laborer in the North does not enjoy this kind of benevolence, the argument continued. He is a slave in all but name, but he is brutally mistreated because that is in the interest of his employer, who is not his owner. Thus a kind of "wage slavery" exists in the "free" society of the North, and it is worse than the outright slavery practiced in the South.

The foreign correspondent of *The New York Tribune* agreed with that line of argument, but not because he wished to justify chattel slavery. His name was Karl Marx, and what he wanted to do was to turn the world upside down.

In 1815, after the Napoleonic conflicts, the conservative European political system was reconstituted, but soon cracks began to show. A minor revolt in France in 1830 was followed by a major one in Germany in 1848. This revolt spread to other countries. Marx and his friend Friedrich Engels (1820–1895), working in London at fever pitch to issue a communist manifesto, could dream that a world, or at least pan-European, revolution was at hand. The Revolution of 1848 was brutally put down, but Marx and Engels did not stop dreaming. And predicting.

Marxism is both a theory of history and a practical program for revolutionaries. Its genius consists in its combination of those two elements. Many of Marx's predecessors either laid out plans for revolution or laid down a rationale of it. Marx did both, and that is the reason why he is the most famous revolutionary who ever lived, and the most influential.

Karl Marx was not a happy man, and he did not live a happy life. He was born in Trier, in western Germany, in 1818, the son of middle-class parents. He studied law at the University of Berlin but left without a degree. He joined the "Young Hegelians," or Left Republicans, and went to Paris to embark on his lifelong career in political journalism. He was driven from Paris in 1845 and, running from the police, went to Brussels, where he met Engels.

The greatest influence on the thought of Marx was the philosophy of G. W. F. Hegel (1770–1831), who had begun to teach at Berlin the year Marx was born. Hegel's method, essentially, was to metaphysicize everything, that is, to discern in concrete reality the working of some Idea or Universal Mind. Taking an extremely wide view of human history, Hegel proposed that all change, all progress, is brought about by the conflict of vast forces. A world-historical figure or nation or event lays down a challenge. This thesis, as he called it, is opposed by an antithesis. The conflict between them is resolved, inevitably, by a synthesis of the two forces on a higher plane of being.

Thus, the French Revolution challenged the old regime. The old regime responded with its armies of *emigrés*, which defeated the revolution. But the resolution of the conflict was a new social order, different from anything that had gone before and different from what either side in the conflict had expected.

This, then, was a rationale of revolution. But it was difficult to apply except after the fact, as in the above example. It was not a practical program for revolutionaries.

Marx realized this truth and contemptuously criticized Hegel and his idealistic dialectics, although he admitted that he owed him a lot. He liked to say he had "turned Hegel on his head." That is, he claimed that he had started from concrete material reality and not from an Idea, as Hegel was supposed to have done. Marx therefore called his own philosophy of history dialectical materialism. Knowing history as well as he did, he claimed to be able not only to explain why things had happened as they had, but also to predict what was going to happen in the future.

Hegel's rather vague notion of a conflict of historical "forces" was transformed by Marx into a struggle between social and economic classes, which he believed had been going on throughout history and would only cease with the final triumph of communism. He was a painstaking observer of conditions in the burgeoning industrial world surrounding him, and a brilliant writer. He described the way the impoverished English workers lived and the conditions under which they worked. He also described the way the rich capitalists lived. It was obvious that the interest of the capitalist was different from that of the worker. And in a sense there was and always had been a conflict between the worker and the owner of the land or machines on which or with which he worked.

Nevertheless, Marx's idea of class struggle was based on there actually being permanent socioeconomic classes, and there was a real question whether such classes existed in European countries. If they did not, that is, if the conflict was de facto and not permanent and essential, then Marx had not turned Hegel on his head. He had simply made a minor modification of Hegel's doctrine. Whether or not such classes did exist, Marx convinced workers and capitalists alike that they did.

This kind of rhetorical triumph was typical of Marx, and Lenin after him. "A spectre is haunting Europe!" the *Communist Manifesto* began: "the spectre of Communism!" This was not true. Workers were dissatisfied, as they should have been, considering how they were being exploited, and they wanted improvements. From time to time they were driven to frenzy by the brutal conditions in which they worked, and they rose up, more or less ineffectively, in protest. But only a few of them wanted communism or even understood what it would mean. The vast majority of workers merely wanted a slightly better life, with a more just division of the profits of their labor. They did not think of themselves as a class, nor did they want their class to become dominant in the world and to replace the capitalists.

Marx knew this better than anyone else. He realized that his words would have to convince them of what they did not yet believe and what they might never understand. He and Engels did not cease producing manifestos, tracts, critiques, and articles. The main point to get over was that the triumph of the proletariat, the class of workers who owned no capital whatever, would be inevitable.

This new order was not inevitable, as it has not occurred except in isolated instances in the century and a half since the *Manifesto* appeared. And where it has occurred, it has been reversed in recent times. Nevertheless, it is a comforting thought to a revolutionist to believe that he is riding on a historical roller coaster, whose progress through time is controlled by great forces. Marx never stopped repeating that the communist revolution was inevitable, and here again he made people believe him.

Rhetorically, Marx's greatest talent was in his ability to taunt the bourgeoisie (*épater le bourgeois*). The *Communist Manifesto* brilliantly succeeded in teasing its enemies into madness. Every apocryphal idea is flaunted in this famous document, including the ultimate threat that the communists will share women. Marx never meant this threat or wanted it, but he knew it would deeply shock his readers.

As a result, it was the bourgeois capitalists who usually made the first move; that is, they were the first to employ force. Then the proletariat would respond like a rebellious socioeconomic class even if they had not believed they were one.

Rebels the world over have learned to act this way from Marx, whatever else they may have learned from him. They always try to taunt the enemy, the police, for example, into using too much force, while television cameramen stand on the sidelines, cranking away.

The Revolution of 1848, which had prompted the writing of the *Communist Manifesto*, was soon put down, its damage to the capitalists limited. A greater challenge was posed in 1870, when Emperor Napoleon III of France impulsively declared war on Germany, under Otto von Bismarck, and was defeated in three months.

Napoleon abdicated, and a provisional republican government attempted to carry on the war against the German invaders. This war soon proved hopeless, and France surrendered to Germany in January 1871. A new, monarchist-slanted government was elected, and the country attempted to go about its old business. But here, according to Marx, the antithesis came into play.

The Parisians, insulted and injured by the powers ruling France, rose up in revolt and in effect tried to secede by electing their own government. The commune of Paris refused to obey the orders of Adolphe Thiers, the elected president of the country. Thiers, old and cunning, asked the Germans to release thousands of French prisoners and soon organized a powerful force to overcome the Paris commune.

Bloody fighting filled the streets of Paris with corpses during the month of May 1871. The last *communards* were shot against the Mur des Fédérés in Père Lachaise cemetery on May 28. The French Left would never forget that French soldiers had lined up French workers against this wall and killed them in cold blood.

Marx, waiting and hoping, proclaimed that the *communards* were the forefront of a proletarian revolution. They were probably nothing of the sort. But again there was just enough evidence to make Marx credible. As his fame as a prophet grew, so did his usefulness as a name with which to taunt capitalists.

Marx died in 1883. It was in Marx's name that V. I. Lenin (1870–1924) led the revolutionists of Russia in 1917. And it was a Marxist rhetorical trick that gave Lenin the chance to be victorious. Lenin headed an extreme left-wing splinter group of rebels. He was opposed by Alexander Kerensky (1881–1970), the leader of what appeared to be a majority of the revolutionaries. Kerensky's men were centrists, and centrists are usually the majority of any group.

Lenin, better than Kerensky, knew the power that could lie in a name. For a short period of time his followers had formed a majority of a revolutionary committee. He began to call his own group, on the far left, the Bolsheviks, or "Majority." Kerensky believed that facts would win out over foolish boasts, and allowed him to get away with it. Soon the Bolsheviks really were a majority, but only of the ruling group. As a result, a small minority of the total population began to rule Russia in the name of the Great Proletarian Revolution.

Communism is not just a name, not just a haunting spectre. Perhaps a quarter of the earth's population lives under Communist governments, although the number is dwindling rapidly as the year 2000 approaches. Communism is a genuine, though faulty, theory of government and of socioeconomic organization.

True communism, as both Marx and Lenin dreamed of it, remains a promise of the future, and this may always be so. In the present, more than a billion persons are ruled in the name of something that does not yet and may never exist.

Marxian Insights

A few years ago, an analysis of publishers' sales led to the conclusion that Karl Marx was the second leading best-seller of all time, after Agatha Christie. Probably many, perhaps most, of the people who bought his books did not read them. They had to be on the shelves of Communists throughout the world, whether they were read or not. If Communists did not read Marx, particularly the *Communist Manifesto*, they were missing something. Marx was a great historian and critic of the world in which he lived. He understood it more clearly than almost anyone else. As a result he really was able to predict the future, at least to describe it in general terms.

Marx's political forecasts were not very accurate. Communism has by and large failed, and I think it will not succeed any better in the future. As an idea of government, it places too much power in the hands of the few, and the few, whether they are aristocrats or proletarians, will never be equal to it. No government can be just, and therefore successful in the long run, unless it finds a way to place the power in the hands of the many, ideally, in the hands of all. The rulers of Communist states are not "the people" in the same sense that "the people" rule nations like Britain, France, and the United States. The proof is the existence in all Communist countries of an all-powerful secret police, and the lack of it in all real democracies. If "the people" really rule, and know they do, they also know they do not need secret police to control—who? themselves?

In fact, political events are more epiphenomenal than politicians like to believe. Administrations, even governments, change, but the underlying changes are more important than the names of the ruling parties. Marx, better than any other man of his time, understood the underlying changes that were occurring in Europe in the middle of the nineteenth century. He was wrong about the political future. He was not wrong about the character of the world that was emerging.

Marx wrote in the *Communist Manifesto*, "The bourgeoisie has played a most revolutionary role in history." What a strange statement. Could anyone else besides Marx have made it? That is, did anyone else understand that the bourgeoisie had been a revolutionary class from the start. And in recent years, that is, in the century leading up to 1848, when Marx was writing, it has "accomplished wonders that far surpass Egyptian pyramids, Roman aqueducts, Gothic cathedrals." It has "conducted expeditions that put all former migrations of nations and crusades in the shade." In a paragraph that bursts with the energy that had also imbued the bourgeoisie, Marx tries to sum up this achievement:

> The bourgeoisie, in its reign of barely a hundred years, has created more massive and colossal productive power than have all previous generations put together. Subjection of nature's forces to man, machinery, application of chemistry to agriculture and industry, steam navigation, railways, electric telegraphs, clearing of whole continents for cultivation, canalization of rivers, whole populations conjured out of the ground—what earlier century had even an intimation that such productive power slept in the womb of social labor?

Others among Marx's contemporaries could have composed lists of projects that the new bourgeois capitalists had completed or were planning to complete in the near future. That is not the point of Marx's rhetoric. He emphasizes the *process* that the bourgeoisie has invented, not the achievements as such. In fact, the bourgeoisie has never been interested in the kind of accomplishments that the pyramids, aqueducts, and cathedrals represented. They are only interested in making money. They do not build for the sake of building, but for the sake of expanding their capital. Therefore they are perfectly willing to tear down last year's building, which had served its purpose as soon as it was completed, and build another in its place. One thing leads to another in an endless stream of alternative destruction and construction, construction and destruction, a process that utilizes the energy and ingenuity of millions of persons in ways that are completely new.

Not even the process is fixed, Marx realized. It, too, must be constantly improved, revolutionized. It was this recognition that set him apart from his contemporaries and made him a modern man who might as well be alive today as a century and a half ago. Another astounding paragraph describes what must happen:

> Constant revolutionizing of production, uninterrupted disturbance of all social relations, everlasting uncertainty and agitation, distinguish the bourgeois epoch from all earlier times. All fixed, fast-frozen relationships, with their train of venerable ideas and opinions, are swept away, all new-formed ones become obsolete before they can ossify. All that is solid melts into air, all that is holy is profaned, and men at last are forced to face with sober senses the real conditions of their lives and their relations with their fellow men.

In short, the bourgeoisie had inaugurated a permanent revolution which could never be allowed to cease. There was no way to stop the world because you wanted to get off. The never-ending change the revolutionary process demanded also required a new kind of human being: men and women who loved change for its own sake, irritable, impatient, delighting in mobility and speed, seeking improvement in every aspect and facet of their existence. In short, this revolution required persons like ourselves, whether we like it or not. Our forefathers started the revolution, and we are still living it. We could not stop it even if we wanted to.

It is extremely important, I think, to recognize that for the most part, most of us do not want this process to end. Nostalgia is pleasant; we love to take our children to theme parks that celebrate a hygienic version of the way we used to live. But not for an instant do we really want to go back. Not, that is, if we are between the ages of ten and sixty. The very young and the very old would perhaps prefer Gretchen's Gothic village, with all its narrowness of vision and opportunity. Children do not require opportunity. They make their own. And old people, after a lifetime of the kind of stress that the permanent revolution produces, are ready to retire to a "train of venerable ideas and opinions," to a world characterized by "fixed, fast-frozen relationships." But the young and the middle-aged will have no truck with that. They want to change, and to change faster than anyone has ever done so before. They dream of a world that is completely new, even if they cannot quite make out the details.

In other words, we must always be careful to distinguish between nostalgia, which is a kind of gentle, benign drug to which most people can become addicted but only for a while, and a genuine desire to return to a way of life that is long past, a time, for instance, in which money was not very important. There are always a few persons who really would wish to return to what they think of as a "simpler" manner of living. But the great majority are wise enough to know that life was not really simpler because you had very little money or washed your clothes by hand or grew your own vegetables or had to walk or ride a horse wherever you wanted to go. With all its stress, anxiety, and threat of dangers never before known, it is modern life that is simpler and easier, not the life of the past.

Economic Facts: Steam Power

The nineteenth century was devoted to facts, especially economic facts. If everything else changed, facts did not. They were the still points of a changing world. A fact could not be questioned. It simply was. "Facts are facts," men would say to one another, as though that explained anything.

I do not think we understand or believe in facts anymore the way the nineteenth century did. We have learned that even facts can change, as they join the flowing stream of change that surrounds us every instant of our days and nights. However, we have not lost the sense of power, even dread, that facts can call up, especially economic facts.

Was steam power an economic fact? The nineteenth century thought it was. They were right in a sense. Steam power was a brutal fact, and all economic facts are brutal, that is, unfeeling, unavoidable, inexorable. Steam power changed the city and the country, it revolutionized life and work, and it brought nations together in war and peace. Steam power created great wealth. Some railroad magnates became richer than kings or emperors. Steam power also made work for millions, for which they were paid a wage that allowed them to go on living, if it was not, in a modern sense, a living wage. The steam engine, together with its two offspring, the railroad and the dynamo, also became a symbol of the power, magnificence, cruelty, and mystery of its time.

The historian Henry Adams, great-grandson and grandson of U.S. presidents, was born in 1838, which made him only twenty years younger than Karl Marx. With Marx to lead the way for him, his lifetime search for meaning in the changing world of his time should have been crowned with success, for Adams was both intelligent and persevering. But his efforts were in vain, his search a failure. He could not see with the clarity of Marx. For one thing, he knew too much. For another, at an early age he had become obsessed by the power and mystical symbolism of machines.

Until the Great Exposition of 1900, in Paris, finally closed its doors in November of that year, Adams, as he tells us in his autobiography, *The Education of Henry Adams* (1906), haunted the exhibits, aching to under stand what they meant about money, knowledge, force, and human life. It was force that puzzled him the most, for he could see that during his lifetime (he was then sixty-two) the amount of force controlled by the average Englishman or American had approximately doubled every decade, with a prospect that this geometrical increase in available force would soon outstrip every device that men and women might invent to control it.

In his deep puzzlement and ignorance of what the present meant and the future would bring, Adams wandered into the great hall of dynamos, which soon "became a symbol of infinity." He described the experience, speaking of himself, as was his wont, in the third person.

As he grew accustomed to the great gallery of machines, he began to feel the forty-foot dynamos as a moral force, much as the early Christians felt the Cross. The planet itself seemed less impressive, in its old-fashioned, deliberate, annual or daily revolution, than this huge wheel, revolving within arm's-length at some vertiginous speed, and barely murmuring—scarcely humming an audible warning to stand a hair's-breadth further for respect of power—while it would not wake the baby lying close against its frame. Before the end, one began to pray to it; inherited instinct taught the natural expression of man before silent and infinite force. Among the thousand symbols of ultimate energy, the dynamo was not so human as some, but it was the most expressive.

To the modern scientific man, Adams felt, "the dynamo itself was but an ingenious channel for conveying somewhere the heat latent in a few tons of poor coal hidden in a dirty engine-house carefully kept out of sight." That pragmatic view is attractive. At least it avoids the problem. Adams did not think it was prudent to go on avoiding the problem.

The problem posed by steam power—the same problem, only more pressing, inheres in a nuclear plant—is how to control the kind of forces that man has recently learned to unleash. Adams was right about that. It is like opening the door and letting a lion out of its cage. This is very exciting. And you begin to think, as the lion stretches its great muscles and roars, if I could only harness all that energy!

But then you begin to wonder, what am I going to do with this lion? One thing is certain: you cannot put it back in its cage, for it has now grown bigger than the door. In the end you may be reduced to prayer, as Adams was.

After the first of his losses, the death of his son, Dickens's Mr. Dombey takes a railroad journey. He is depressed, desolate, and obsessed by death. The train on which he is traveling becomes a symbol of his misery. Dickens writes:

He found no pleasure or relief in the journey. Tortured by these thoughts he carried monotony with him, through the rushing landscape, and hurried headlong, not through a rich and varied country, but a wilderness of blighted plans and gnawing jealousies. The very speed at which the train was whirled along mocked the swift course of the young life that had been borne away so steadily and so inexorably to its foredoomed end. The power that forced itself upon its iron way—its own—defiant of all paths and roads, piercing through the heart of every obstacle, and dragging living creatures of all classes, ages, and degrees behind it, was a type of the triumphant monster, Death.

Later in the book, Dombey's enemy is killed by a train. He "was beaten down, caught up, and whirled away upon a jagged mill that spun him round and round, and struck him limb from limb, and licked his stream of life up with its fiery heat, and cast his mutilated fragments in the air." There is an awful justice in this.

But such justice gives no pleasure, produces no thankfulness in Dombey, or in Dickens, or in the reader. The train is not only the symbol of that triumphant monster, Death. It is also the symbol of all the inhuman forces against which mankind has struggled down the centuries. It is no living beast that has been let out of its cage.

Steam engines, dynamos, and railroads, to say nothing of powerful cars and airplanes, are the source of a kind of ecstatic inspiration as well as a burgeoning dread. The great wheel which Adams prayed to, humming night and day, is a magnificent vision. A steam engine's whistle in the watches of the night is one of the world's most romantic sounds, calling up memories of meetings and partings long ago.

All machines and engines possess a fascination beyond their great utility. As they run, they seem to care nothing for us, and yet they are obedient. They start or stop when we turn the key. It is perhaps no wonder that the modern world sacrifices thousands of human lives a year to these triumphant monsters, the great machines with which we share the earth.

Equality in the Muzzle of a Gun

They had a name for the Colt .45 in the Old West. They called it The Equalizer, because it made all men equal, young or old, strong or weak, good or bad, right or wrong.

We have seen that Alexis de Tocqueville was one of the first to understand the inexorable progress of social equality, toward a lessening of differences between high and low. He did not mention the revolver. But social forces were easier to see in the open West. There, a little, scrawny, vicious villain had to be taken seriously if he had a gun. Today, the Saturday Night Special plays the same role in dark and silent city streets. Anyone can be mugged. No one is immune. The equality of the modern great city prefigures the world's future.

The Colt .45 was a machine, and so it is not surprising that there grew up about it a romance and a mythology. Somehow, by a permutation of good and bad, we have all become, in our imaginations, desperados waiting for a train.

Hold one of those heavy revolvers in your hand. Feel its slick, cold steel surface. Raise it and smile. You possess the power of life and death, like any emperor. See how your hand fits round the stock, how your finger is drawn to the trigger. Lay the weapon down, before . . .

The nineteenth century did not invent the pistol, but it perfected it, and made it available to ordinary persons, who no longer felt like villains if they owned one. The nineteenth century did invent a much more terrible weapon, whose terror has not abated one whit in more than a century. This was the machine gun. It made armies equal.

From the introduction of firearms in the late Middle Ages, various attempts were made to design a weapon that would fire more than one shot without reloading. A certain James Puckle patented a machine gun in 1718 that utilized a revolving block for firing square bullets. The Gatling gun, which was first used during the U.S. Civil War, was an improvement upon the Puckle gun. It could fire several rounds a minute, which was better than having to reload and fire a rifle, but it was far from a modern machine gun. It, too, required cranking by hand.

The credit for the modern machine gun goes to Hiram Stevens Maxim (1840–1916), who was born in Sangerville, Maine, but in 1900 became a British subject and in 1901 was knighted by Queen Victoria. Maxim was one of the most prolific inventors of an inventive time. His first invention was a hair-curling iron. He held hundreds of patents in the United States and Britain, including a mousetrap, a locomotive headlight, a method of manufacturing carbon filaments for lamps, and an automatic sprinkling system. During the 1890s he experimented with airplanes and produced one powered by a light steam engine that actually rose from the ground, but he soon realized that an internal combustion engine was required for success, and he abandoned the project.

Maxim's father had dreamed of inventing a fully automatic machine gun, and Maxim turned to this project in 1884. He went to London, set up a laboratory, and began to experiment. Within months he had invented the first true machine gun, which employed the recoil of the barrel to eject the spent cartridge and chamber another. The bullets were fed into the weapon, which was water-cooled, by a belt that could contain thousands of rounds.

Maxim's 1884 gun could fire eleven rounds a second, but he was still not satisfied. He needed a better smokeless powder than existed in order to assure the steady and progressive burning of the propellant, which released the gases that drove the mechanism of the gun. He soon invented cordite, the best smokeless powder at that time. His brother Hudson Maxim (1853–1927) invented even better smokeless powders, which were used in cannon projectiles and torpedoes.

By late 1884 Maxim had begun manufacturing machine guns. Later he merged his firm with the Vickers company to supply Maxim guns to all the leading nations of the world. And by the beginning of World War I every army was equipped with machine guns of various makes: Maxim, Hotchkiss, Lewis, Browning, Mauser, and others.

The machine gun has the honor of being styled *the* weapon of that war. It was largely responsible for the terrible carnage, of men and animals, that left millions of corpses rotting on the fields of France. Machine gun emplacements were set up at intervals along the top of any low ridge, the guns trained to fire close to the ground, perhaps two feet high. Whenever something moved, the guns would fire. If what moved was a man, he would be cut in two at the knees. Bombardment with heavy artillery prior to an attack might destroy some of the machine gun emplacements, but never all of them, and since the guns were cheap to make and easy to fire (all a soldier had to do was hold down the trigger), the weapons and those who fired them could be easily replaced.

More than anything else, the machine gun turned the rapid movements that marked the first few months of World War I into a static war of attrition. Millions of men huddled in muddy trenches, fearful of raising their heads above ground lest they be shot off by those terrible killing machines. The machine gun so completely equalized the contending armies, those of the Allies and the Central Powers, that World War I might have gone on for many more years if the United States had not entered the conflict in 1917, thus tipping the balance.

The Germans gave up in 1918, and the war ended. Inventors immediately set to work to improve the machine gun, in preparation for the next war. This was a mistake, as the next war would not be fought primarily with machine guns, a fact that the Germans realized sooner than anyone else, hence their victories, so shocking to the world, in 1939 and 1940. The machine gun, however, had a new role to play in the postwar period. Extremely light and accurate hand-held weapons were developed in the Soviet Union, in Israel, and elsewhere, and these were employed to deadly effect by terrorists. One man with one of these efficient killing machines could terrorize an entire airlines terminal, as happened, for example, in Rome in the fall of 1986. The idea of equality in the muzzle of a gun had come a long way since the Colt .45.

The Magic of Electricity

All of the nineteenth century's inventions were not destructive. The electric light is a case in point.

Electricity had been known to the Greeks, but it was not even remotely understood until clever and curious men began to investigate electrical phenomena in the 1750s. Benjamin Franklin (1706–1790) sent up a kite during a thunderstorm around 1750 and established that lightning is a form of electricity. He was lucky to survive this experiment, which should not be repeated by anyone not anxious to be electrocuted. Franklin left science for politics, but there were plenty of others to follow numerous trails toward all sorts of fascinating possibilities.

Alessandro Volta (1745–1827) demonstrated the electric pile, or battery, in 1800. The battery soon became a practical source of electric current. In 1808 Sir Humphrey Davy (1778–1829) showed that electricity could produce heat or light between two electrodes separated in space and connected by an arc. In 1820 Hans Christian Ørsted (1777–1851) discovered that an electric current created a magnetic field around a conductor. Eleven years later Michael Faraday (1791–1867), who had worked with Davy, demonstrated the inverse action, whereby a magnetic field induces a current in a moving conductor. This discovery led to the dynamo, the electric motor, and the transformer. These lines of investigation were crowned by the achievement of James Clerk Maxwell (1831–1879) in 1864, when he showed that electrical, magnetic, and optical phenomena were all united in a single universal force, electromagnetism.

Theoretically, there was nothing more to do after Clerk Maxwell's field equations astounded the scientific community. Practically, there were still worlds to win for men like Thomas Alva Edison, who realized, sooner than anyone else, that electricity could be tamed and used to illuminate, warm, and amuse human beings. Edison became enormously rich as a result of his numerous inventions and patents, but, unlike Maxim, few begrudged him his well-gotten gains.

Born in Ohio in 1847, Edison set up a small laboratory in his father's house when he was ten years old, buying materials for it from the profits of his newspaper and candy sales on trains traveling between Port Huron and Detroit. He became interested in telegraphy and worked as a roving telegrapher. Edison soon understood everything about how the device worked and was made supervisor of the telegraphic gold-price indicator at the Gold Exchange when he was able to repair the machine, which had initiated several minipanics by breaking down at crucial moments. He began to manufacture stock tickers, then sold the business and set up a larger laboratory. There, in 1877, he invented the phonograph. He began work on the light bulb in 1878 and demonstrated his carbon filament lamp the next year.

Many inventors had sought to make a practical electric light. Maxim, for example, came quite close, until the machine gun drew him away from such benign endeavors. There was obviously a fortune to be made, for the human race was hungry for light and probably would pay any amount for it. Candles had illuminated the abodes of the rich for centuries, and whale oil had provided a smelly, sputtering flame for the houses of the poor. An electric light might burn cleanly and cheaply. It could change the world.

When it came into manufacture and distribution at the end of the nineteenth century, it did just that. The electric light dissolved the difference between night and day and masked the change of the seasons. For a quarter of a million years humankind had welcomed the spring because it brought not only warmth but also light, long evenings and early mornings. The inverse of that welcome was the fear of winter that all peoples expressed in their rituals. Winter was not just cold but also dark, and in the darkness what evils might lurk? As the days began to lengthen, after the winter solstice, priests and savants could once again reassure the unlettered that before long it would be light again, and the Devil would depart.

All of these fears became mere superstition when electricity brightened the night and made it as much like the day as one was willing to pay for. Today, millions of city dwellers never experience a dark night. They never see the stars, for example. They do not understand when you tell them they are missing something. Who could possibly prefer darkness, they wonder. For them, at least, the supposedly devastating psychic blow of the Copernican Revolution has become a mere irrelevance.

Electricity jumps from one electrode to another, in an arc, or it flows through a filament, now made of tungsten, not carbon, whose resistance produces a glowing light. A resisting medium also produces heat, and houses may be warmed by it, although that is often a relatively expensive way. Utilizing a transformer at both ends of the system, electric power can also be carried over high-tension wires over very great distances. This is magic, or so it would have seemed to Aristotle. Power is created here, in a generating plant, and carried by a slender wire, perhaps a thousand miles, to there, where my house is. And there it is always instantly available for many uses. It can light my rooms, and warm them. It can make my toast and cook my dinner. It can open my tin cans and compact my trash. It can keep the time to the split second, and dawdle the time away with various devices which did not come into common use until the twentieth century discovered a new meaning of the term *leisure*. It can protect my home from intruders. And if I am careless, it can kill me (this sort of thing happens quite rarely).

Electricity does all this with less huffing and puffing, with fewer side effects, than any other source of power. In fact, if the whole world were Switzerland, which burns no fossil fuels to produce electricity but makes it by using gravity, harnessing the latent useful energy in the water running down its high mountains, then electricity would be almost completely clean.

Unfortunately, in much of the earth, the land is too flat to provide hydroelectric power, and electricity must be made by burning fuels like coal or splitting atoms of uranium to heat water to produce steam to drive dynamos to generate the needed power. And the smoke from the burning settles a thousand miles away and kills the fish in the lakes and the trees on the hillsides of regions that are not flat and could use gravity to generate their power. But we are getting ahead of ourselves. Such ironies were not understood in the nineteenth century.

Magical Mathematics

The magical quality of electricity derives as much from its invisibility as from anything else. The rapid flow of electrons, which is one definition of the phenomenon, can never be seen. We understand this now, in the twentieth century, although Faraday did not know this and supposed that someday a better microscope might be able to observe it. Being invisible, electricity must be controlled by a different kind of device from that which controlled other sources of power. A horsewhip, a steam piston, the cylinder of an internal combustion engine are highly visible.

In the end, it turned out to be mathematics, and a new mathematics at that, which was required. Mathematics, that strange and beautiful science—or is it poetry?—that can bridge the gulf between the visible and the invisible, between the material world and the immaterial mind of man. The triumph of Clerk Maxwell was the triumph of a new kind of mathematics. It established the authority of mathematicians in a way that nothing ever had, not even the discoveries of Newton.

The new mathematics was trying to control other invisible forces and entities as well. It came as a shock to learn, in the 1830s, that Euclidean geometry, which had been taught to all schoolboys for two millennia, and recently to all schoolgirls, was not an accurate picture of real space, which is not two dimensional and contains no perfect circles, squares, or triangles. Instead, space was a highly complex something that required highly complex mathematics just to describe it. In the new non-Euclidean geometries, parallel lines met as they do in the real world. Look down any railroad track. And circles could be easily transformed into ellipses, parabolas, and hyperbolas, and even into straight lines or point, by projecting them onto screens tilted one way or the other. For a while, after 1870, it seemed that projective geometry, which included every other kind of geometry that had been invented, was an accurate descriptor and thus controller of space. But this intellectual balloon was soon burst, too.

Also after 1870, further investigations of the idea of space, by men like W. K. Clifford (1845–1879) and Henri Poincaré (1854–1912), led to the notion that space is too complex for mathematics. Rather, space is an assumption, and it can be described and controlled only so far as we assume it. In other words, there is no such thing as space. Instead, there are as many spaces as there are mathematicians and nonmathematicians, and that is measured in the billions. Even that number is much too small, for every person can assume an indefinite number of different spaces, although he probably cannot create the mathematics needed to deal with them.

Much of this may seem spacey, but it is real enough, for electricity flows in some of those assumed spaces that cannot be seen or even imagined, but can be described by means of strange mathematical switches, conductors, and insulators. It is like the music that goes round and round, and comes out there. While the music is going round and round in the tubes of the tuba, is it music? Is electricity electricity when it is racing over the landscape, ignored completely by the cows that graze placidly down below, or is it only electricity when it pours out of its spout and rings the doorbell or lifts the elevator?

We know now that there is simply no answer to either question. The mechanists of the nineteenth century would not have accepted that statement. They might have been almost as shocked by it as they were by the idea that one's grandparents had been apes. The reason is important, for it reveals at least one respect in which the nineteenth century was not a prelude to our time.

The age that ended in 1914 was marked by astounding progress in scientific knowledge of the world. It was also an age of belief, a new belief, in the inevitability of progress. The basis of that belief was a firm confidence in what seemed an old and dependable truth, which went back to the Greeks.

This was the truth that had been invented by Thales and the philosophers who followed him, that if we try resolutely enough, we can understand the world around us. There is genuine truth in this notion, but there is also something questionable, perhaps even spurious. The confidence that there is something in our minds that conforms to something in nature, the rules of the conformation being mathematics, is well-founded. Otherwise, how can we explain our success at understanding, predicting, and controlling the processes of nature? No animals can do what we humans can do. As a result, they take nature as it is and accept its rules as their own. We do not accept them. We think we can change them, for our own good. And there is no doubt that we can do so or, rather, by understanding the rules, use them for our benefit.

The questionable aspect of that new belief of the scientists of the nineteenth century lay in their confident expectation that they could *fully* understand nature. Do we hold that belief, entertain that expectation, any longer? It does not seem that we do. And if some of us still do, then it appears that we are probably wrong.

What is the problem with Thales' assumption? Is our human mental apparatus simply inadequate to the task of fully understanding the natural world in which we live? That may not be the answer, as our mental powers appear to be almost infinitely expandable by means of computers. Or is the natural world simply too complex for the human mind to comprehend? That may not be the answer either, for any problem we can pose for ourselves we seem to be able to solve, and we can at least pose the problem of fully understanding nature. So why can we not, or may we not be able to solve that problem?

It seems that there is something else that stands in the way. That something else continues to puzzle us. It would have been utterly incomprehensible to the majority in the nineteenth century, which was the last age to rest in the comfortable expectation of certain knowledge of anything, not to mention everything.

New Ways of Seeing

The first successful photograph was made in 1826 by Nicéphore Niepce (1765–1833), a French lithographer. Ten years later Jacques Daguerre (1789–1851) was experimenting with the process that bears his name. Other improvements followed rapidly. In 1888, George Eastman (1854–1932) introduced the famous box camera, with its handy roll of negative film and with the promise of cheap and widely available film processing. Since then, photography has become the art form of the masses.

The introduction of photography revolutionized the arts of drawing and painting. It also changed the way we see things. When viewers examined Daguerre's first productions, they were astonished to observe details that they had never noticed in the original scene. William H. F. Talbot (1800–1877), the inventor of the negative-positive system now in use, commented on this phenomenon in the 1840s:

It frequently happens . . . and this is one of the charms of photography—that the operator himself discovers on examination, perhaps long afterwards, that he has depicted many things he had no notion of at the time. Sometimes inscriptions and dates are found upon the buildings, or printed placards most irrelevant, are discovered upon their walls: sometimes a distant dial-plate is seen, and upon it—unconsciously recorded—the hour of the day at which the view was taken.

Here, apparently, is another class of invisible entities, which we do not see when we look at a scene, but which the camera sees and tells us exist. "The camera does not lie," it is said. Do our eyes lie, then? Why do we select parts of a scene for conscious awareness and ignore others? Is the camera's view of things the true one if it is something we cannot or do not see with our own eyes? What is truth, that we cannot know it.

Before the invention of photography the great majority of painted images were portraits, small enough to be carried in a locket for remembrance. Suddenly, painting was relieved of the necessity of "communicating" in this pedestrian way. The result, almost immediate, was an explosion of new styles and methods. Impressionism was the crowning glory of those times. It was followed by cubism, dadaism, surrealism, and abstract expressionism, as well as other movements in art of our time, including photorealism, in which the painter paints an image that, from a distance, is indistinguishable from a photograph.

At the same time, photography developed ways of recording and even distorting "reality" in order to shock the viewer into seeing new things that he had never imagined before. The result was a remarkable expansion in our ability to see.

Great changes in art have always had this effect, of course. The introduction of perspective by Renaissance painters of the fifteenth century, as we have already pointed out, helped to make a man-centered world, with God's enveloping and all-seeing vision removed from it. The development of better paints permitted easel paintings to supplant frescoes. Thus art moved from church walls into even quite modest homes. Other technical advances in the nineteenth century permitted painters to paint from nature in the open air. This, too, was a source of the revolutionary changes that produced impressionism. But the modifications in our perception of the world brought about by photography may be more radical than any of those.

There is no question whatever that the camera *can* lie. A million publicity photos prove this to be so. Nevertheless, the invention of photography has made it more difficult to maintain a sentimental view of the world. A good photographer always manages to cut through even our most cherished illusions, that the poor are happy despite their poverty, for instance, or that suffering is always noble. Thus photography has revealed to us the cold, grim horror of war, with the result that although we are still willing to accept war, we now do so with considerably less enthusiasm.

The camera catches us in the act of being human. That kind of truth and knowledge, no matter how shocking or distasteful, is always valuable, although it is not always valued.

The End of Slavery

Mathew Brady was born in upstate New York around 1823 and learned how to take daguerrotypes from the inventor Samuel F. B. Morse. Brady opened his first photography studio in New York City in 1844. At the outbreak of the Civil War, in 1861, he determined to try to make a complete photographic record of the war. He hired a staff and dispatched it throughout the zone of war. He himself photographed such battlefields as Antietam and Gettysburg. His photographs of the dead lying upon the Gettysburg slope where Pickett's famous charge had lately passed are among the most memorable images of that war.

Their horror did not stop the fighting. Indeed, at the time, they had little or no effect. It was almost as though human beings had not yet learned how to view photographs. Or perhaps the fighting itself seemed so overwhelming in its horror and necessity that no images could touch its awful fury.

At a Sanitary Commission Fair in 1864 President Abraham Lincoln (1809–1865) wrote in someone's album this succinct judgment about the causes of the war. "I never knew a man who wished himself to be a slave. Consider if you know any *good* thing that no man desires for himself."

In a score of other statements, long and short, Lincoln reiterated his position that the Civil War was not about slavery but whether the Union would survive. As he wrote in a letter to newspaper editor Horace Greeley in 1862, "My paramount object in this struggle is to save the Union, and it is not either to save or to destroy slavery. If I could save the Union without freeing any slave, I would do it; and if I could save it by freeing all the slaves, I would do it; and if I could save it by freeing some and leaving others alone, I would also do that."

In the end Lincoln adopted the third of the policies he mentioned. The Emancipation Proclamation of 1863 practically freed no slaves, for it applied only to those living behind enemy lines. But we should not forget the last sentence in that famous letter to Greeley. "I have here stated my purpose according to my view of official duty," he wrote; "and I intend no modification in my oft-expressed personal wish that all men everywhere could be free." Slavery was abolished in the United States by the Congress when it adopted the Thirteenth Amendment to the Constitution in 1865, after Lincoln's death and the end of the war.

Tocqueville had been right in thinking that the spread of equality over the globe was an unstoppable historic tendency. But the French Revolution and other political revolutions of the seventeen hundreds had not only involved equality. The cry of the revolutionists in France had been "Liberty, Equality, Fraternity." The first of those great words was liberty. And it stood for something that evoked passionate responses in every human breast during the nineteenth century.

The earliest protest against slavery in the American colonies dates to 1688, when a Mennonite meeting in Germantown, Pennsylvania, penned a memorandum stating its profound opposition to Negro slavery. These simple libertarians proclaimed, "Though they are black, we cannot conceive there is more liberty to have them slaves, as it is to have other white ones."

Slavery, of both whites and blacks, was, of course, immemorially old when those words were written. Apparently it had not always existed, but sooner or later every highly organized human society adopted it, because it seemed there was no other way to get the hard, unpleasant work done that such societies needed. After Aristotle's famous justification of slavery and his doctrine of "natural" slaves, it was easier to accept that necessity, and so slavery flourished almost everywhere on earth.

For centuries few were found to object to the institution of slavery. But the establishment during the fifteenth and sixteenth centuries of plantation Negro slavery in the European colonies of the New World soon led to fervent protests, first in Europe and then in America. Such slavery was inhumanly cruel. Nothing comparable was seen until the Nazi concentration camps of World War II.

In 1688 there were only a handful of Negro slaves in the American colonies. By the outbreak of the Civil War in 1861 there were about four million slaves, all of them concentrated in the southern states. The slave trade had been abolished in 1808, and slavery had been ended in the British colonies in the West Indies in 1833. But in the American South the old argument from necessity continued to be voiced, with little opposition there. And this argument was combined with the belief that blacks were naturally inferior and thus intended by nature for slavery.

But the Declaration of Independence, written by a slaveholder, had declared that all men are created equal. How was this contradiction to be resolved?

In the end it could not be resolved by peaceful means. The Civil War came and, like so many wars, lasted longer and was more terrible than anyone had expected. Finally, after almost exactly four years, the South, exhausted, gave in. And slavery came to an end in its last major place on earth.

The human race has not finished with slavery. It revived under Hitler in World War II, and small pockets of slavery or pseudo-slavery survive in a few Third World countries. Hereditary debt servitude, for example, is a type of de facto slavery that has proved hard to eradicate in many nations.

But there is a real sense in which slavery was truly finished by the sacrifices that so many offered up during the American Civil War. No nation that accepts slavery may enter the United Nations. The world as a whole refuses to accept the institution of slavery as legal. After something like five thousand years, one of the most monstrous affronts to justice has been eradicated from human thinking, even if there are still de facto slaves.

I think the legal abolition of slavery was the nineteenth century's greatest achievement. And it befitted the enormity of the institution that its destruction had to be accomplished by the cruelest and bloodiest war ever fought in North America. Slavery was an economic fact. The war was another. The conflict was therefore fair; it was divinely just, as Lincoln said in his Second Inaugural Address.

> If we shall suppose that American slavery is one of those offenses which, in the providence of God, must needs come, but which, having continued through His appointed time, He now wills to remove, and that He gives to both North and South this terrible war as the woe due to those by whom the offense came, shall we discern therein any departure from those divine attributes which the believers in a living God always ascribe to Him? Fondly do we hope—fervently do we pray—that this mighty scourge of war may speedily pass away. Yet, if God wills that it continue, until all the wealth piled by the bondman's two hundred and fifty years of unrequited toil shall be sunk, and until every drop of blood drawn with the lash shall be paid by another drawn with the sword, as was said three thousand years ago, so still it must be said "the judgments of the Lord are true and righteous altogether."

The address was delivered on March 15, 1865. On April 9, Gen. Robert E. Lee surrendered to Gen. Ulysses S. Grant at Appomattox Court House, Virginia, effectively ending the war. On April 14 Abraham Lincoln was shot by actor John Wilkes Booth while attending a performance at Ford's Theatre, in Washington. The president died the next morning.

Lincoln did not say, although he knew, that slavery is a disease that

affects masters as well as slaves. The point was eloquently made
by psychologist C. G. Jung (1875–1961) in a paper published in
1928.

> Every Roman was surrounded by slaves. The slave and his psycholo-
> gy flooded ancient Italy, and every Roman became inwardly, and of
> course unwittingly, a slave. Because living constantly in the
> atmosphere of slaves, he became infected through the unconscious
> with their psychology. No one can shield himself from such an
> influence.

All of us, therefore, not just slaves and their descendants, owe much to
the brave men who fought to abolish slavery from 1861 to 1865.

Shocking the Bourgeoisie

Karl Marx was not alone in the desire to shock the bourgeoisie of the
nineteenth century. A score of other authors mocked and vilified the
bourgeois and his civilization, not, however, so much to taunt him into
frenzied reaction as to wake him from his pompous complacency. This
complacency, accompanied as it so often was by a comfortable income,
drove several of these writers to a frenzy of their own. Feeling themselves
immured in a moral prison, required for success in life to believe what
they did not want to believe, they struck out in blazing poetic and prose
images, only to be ignored by the objects of their attack.

In America, the poet Walt Whitman (1819–1892) and the novelist
Herman Melville (1819–1891) struggled with little success to attain the
kind of recognition they wanted. Both managed to sell books, but neither
was admired by the people they wished to move and to change. Only as an
old man, and then for the wrong reasons, did Whitman begin to find his
audience and to be accepted as a great American writer.

Melville's best book, *Moby-Dick* (1851), was thought to be merely a
thriller about sea life. Melville died a forgotten man, only to be rediscovered a generation after his death. The attempt of both men to open the
eyes of their readers to a new world failed utterly.

Charles Baudelaire (1821–1867), in France, was not only not read, he
was also officially censored. His books were judged to be obscene, and he
himself was looked upon with contempt as a pathetic psychopath. Perhaps
he was, but he also became the most acute critic of his age in France, able
to perceive the frightening new life that had begun to emerge from the
bourgeois closet into the frenetic light of the later nineteenth century.

Gustave Flaubert (1821–1880), in *Madame Bovary* (1857), revealed in
painful detail the small foibles of a bourgeois life and described the

doomed efforts of a woman trapped in an updated version of Gretchen's narrow room to escape to a broader world.

And Emile Zola (1840–1902), in a half dozen searingly realistic novels, tried to wake the conscience of the fin de siècle, only to find himself abandoned and forced to face alone the terrible inertia and ennui of French middle-class existence.

Friedrich Nietzsche, the last of the three great German philosophers of his century—only Hegel and Marx could be compared to him—was the son of an insane father and went mad himself when he was fifty-five. Various causes of his illness have been identified, but one of them is obvious: Nietzsche was driven to madness by the bland, dishonest complacency of his contemporaries, who ignored him while honoring writers who seem like comic book figures today. The more Nietzsche was ignored, the more he waved his arms and shrilled against Christianity and its empty moral claims. Utterly alone during the decade when he wrote all of his best books (1879–1889), he died in 1900 after a lifetime of bitter disappointments, only to receive the adulation of the next two generations in Germany, his native country, and in France.

The English bourgeoisie did not escape the onslaught. George Eliot (1819–1880), whose novel *Middlemarch* (1871–1872) has been called the first fully adult work of fiction, not only wrote but also lived in opposition to the mores of her time. The respectable classes drove her and her companion G. H. Lewes out of England for a while because they were not married, but she achieved her revenge with a series of books, of which *Middlemarch* is the most pitiless, that tore away the curtain of Victorian life and revealed its bitter small-mindedness for anyone to see.

Not that many did see. The bourgeoisie, in England and elsewhere, evinced a remarkable ability not to pay attention to what was clearly before their eyes. They bought George Eliot's novels, and read them with pleasure, but without understanding.

Thomas Hardy (1840–1928) was driven to a sense of somber doom by the failure of readers of such novels as *Tess of the d'Urbervilles* (1891) and *Jude the Obscure* (1895) to wake up to the dreary fraud of their beliefs, and he devoted the last half of his long life to writing poems that expressed his haunted vision. And Oscar Wilde (1856–1900), a rebel of every kind, ended up playing the part of a mocking fool. He despaired of his countrymen ever waking up, but they did, for they became enraged by his mockery and jailed him, ruining his life.

These writers, and a dozen more, were very different from one another, but they all had one thing in common. They saw what Marx had seen when he had described, in the *Communist Manifesto*, a new moral and intellectual world in which all fast-frozen relationships were stripped of their meaning and all that was solid suddenly, and without warning, melted into air. These writers knew the bourgeoisie had failed to comprehend this situation, and yet to save themselves and their civilization they had to understand it or face obliteration. These men and women had taken on the mission of rescuing the bourgeoisie from itself. Their critiques were based more on love than on hate. They were like the rebellious children of a father who had gone astray. And like so many children they accomplished little except to disappoint their parent, who loved them as much as they loved him, but who could never connect with them through the miasma of the separating years.

Darwin and Freud

Everything these rebellious authors did, they did for liberty, and often in its name. Two other writers, who never supposed themselves to be part of this rebellious company, fought the same fight. Scientists both, they seemed to desire no more than to reveal the simple, factual truth to their contemporaries. But they, too, shocked the bourgeoisie, more than anyone except Marx. Maybe even more than Marx. For their simple truth ate like acid at the pretensions of the Victorian age, which responded to it with a bitter fury that has not much abated to this day.

Charles Darwin was born in England in 1809, the grandson of the eccentric evolutionist Erasmus Darwin. He was only an average scholar, and his father, who had been disappointed in his son, was persuaded to allow him to accept an appointment as naturalist on HMS *Beagle* to survey the wildlife of South America. The father hoped that something might come of the journey, but he probably did not really expect it.

During his five years on the *Beagle* Darwin began to develop the ideas about evolution and the origin of species that he would publish in 1859, to the consternation of the same respectable classes that had exiled George Eliot. If Darwin had stuck to barnacles and earthworms, which were among his earliest enthusiasms, his ideas would not have been controversial. But he persisted, doggedly, in declaring that all species had come about through evolution on the basis of natural selection. Even man. That was hard to swallow.

In a sense, evolution is obvious. It is also everywhere evident. Nations evolve, as they respond to challenges from other nations and from nature. Corporations evolve as they respond to conditions in the marketplace. Friendships evolve, ideas evolve. It is even obvious that particular animal species have evolved. Thus we now have scores of breeds of dogs, where once there was only one or two.

Nevertheless, Darwin's proposal that evolution was the principle that underlay the development of all species and that man, an animal, had evolved from nonhuman animal ancestors shocked his contemporaries. There were several reasons.

The idea that species had evolved over an immense period of time instead of being created all at one instant a few thousand years ago was another of those challenges, like Galileo's, that the religious establishment found it impossible to deal with. Darwinism seemed to contradict the Bible. But it was not Darwin who was doing the contradicting. He was only saying, like Galileo, Open your eyes and look! As you can see, it is perfectly obvious.

The calm, gentle manner in which Darwin stated these things did not help. It only infuriated his adversaries all the more.

Even if it could be accepted that earthworms had evolved, it was unthinkable that man had to trace his descent from brutes, and especially from the higher apes, with their dirty habits that they did not try to hide when you visited them in zoos. It was useless for Darwin to repeat that the evolution of the modern human being from some remote ancestor of both man and the existing great apes—the missing link—had been accomplished over many millions of years. His adversaries insisted that he was accusing them of having had a monkey for a grandfather. They apparently wanted to be insulted and did not listen when he tried to explain.

The vanity that finds it impossible to admit—indeed, to vaunt—our close relationship to the other animals is sad and dreary. The work and life of Charles Darwin (d. 1874), on the contrary, was blithe and free.

He liberated mankind from a narrow temporal prison. He also revealed one of the basic mechanisms of biological change. Some of his ideas have been questioned. But his fundamental evolutionary hypothesis stands like Gibraltar.

Sigmund Freud was born in Moravia in 1856. He studied medicine in Vienna, specializing in neurology and psychiatry. During the 1890s he developed his technique of treating hysterical patients by encouraging them to associate freely, and he accomplished some remarkable cures, or at least remissions of symptoms. During these years he also discovered the unconscious.

What an extraordinary discovery that was! How strange and puzzling a thing is the unconscious. In the first place, everyone who is willing to look at himself in a mirror without closing his eyes knows that he has an unconscious, and probably always did know. But consciously he always denied it. He still does.

What kind of thing is this mind of ours, that seems to operate on its own, outside our control? Who, in fact, can control his mind? Who can think of one thing continuously for more than a few seconds without having other, unwanted thoughts obtrude? Who can force his mind not to think of sex, for example, or revenge, or personal glory? Let those things once intrude, and it is nearly impossible to make them go away.

And then they suddenly do leave us and are replaced by something else, equally unexpected and, often, equally unwanted.

All of this is the universal experience of the human race. The greatness of Freud is that he kept on doggedly and systematically thinking about this phenomenon until he began to understand it.

Freud was an even more controversial figure than Darwin. His insistence that sexual desires and fears lay just beneath the surface of everyone's mind was even more shocking to Victorians than Darwin's claim that we ultimately are descended from an apelike ancestor.

In this case it was not vanity that was offended. Everyone secretly recognized that much of what Freud said was true about himself or herself. What normal human being is unaware that sexual thoughts lie just under the surface of consciousness, always ready to pop out at the oddest and perhaps most inappropriate moments?

Unfortunately, proper Victorians believed that other people were not like themselves. Husbands assumed their wives had never had a sexual thought. Wives assumed the same thing about their children. Everyone assumed that kind of pure innocence about his parents, despite the obvious fact.

What was said to be Freud's obsession with sex was not the only problem. He was also a brilliant critic, both of literature and of society as a whole. He persisted in seeing both in the cold light of reality, instead of in the rosy glow that his time believed to be correct.

When World War I erupted, everyone was shocked by the horror and brutality, by the cruelty that had all along lain just under the surface of social politeness. Freud was as shocked as anyone. But he was not surprised. He had known it was there, waiting.

He was also not surprised when the Nazis began to kill Jews and tried to kill him. He escaped from Vienna with his daughter Anna, after paying a ransom of twenty percent of his assets, and went to London. He was old and sick, and he died the next year.

Freud was a physician and a scientist, a fact on which he always insisted. The supreme irony of his life and work is that although he worked in a field, psychology, that takes its name from the Greek word for soul, he did not believe in the eternal human soul.

He was a mechanist and a determinist. He sought the explanation of the mind's working in the body, believing that the health or the illness of the mind was dependent on a balance, or imbalance, of physical forces. He was always a nineteenth-century thinker, although he lived until 1939. As a result, he continued to believe that the human being is more than anything else a machine. Or if not a machine, then certainly an animal like other animals.

He was also supremely courageous, for he was willing to venture where no one before him had ever gone, down into the deep of our own minds, which we hide during the day and only reveal, half-willingly, in the night.

Darwin and Freud. They were a pair of revealers who forced us to see our human nature, although we did not want to. Certainly we are better for this new knowledge, although many of us will never stop hating them for bringing it to us.

11

The World in 1914

BY 1914 EUROPE had produced a civilization that became a high point of world history. Shining like a beacon of hope, European civilization was imitated almost everywhere on earth and dominated world commerce, finance, knowledge, and culture generally.

But the most intelligent, cultivated, and sensitive Europeans were deeply dissatisfied with the achievements of their vaunted civilization. They knew that something was dreadfully wrong. They were correct.

The Great War came, plunging Europe and the world into a conflict that continued, with intervals of peace, for nearly a third of a century. Within a mere four years European civilization dissolved in ruins, and the West found it necessary to start over. The civilization that had been destroyed had been building since at least 1300, more than six centuries. Thus it is not surprising that we are still engaged in the immense task of replacing it, a task that is not yet completed.

What was wrong with European civilization in 1914? Why did it embark on the most destructive war in history, a war that eventually involved almost every nation on earth and cost hundreds of millions of lives as well as untold suffering by hundreds of millions more?

Economic Divisions

The world in 1914 could be divided into four economic zones. In the first, the industrial labor force surpassed the number of people engaged in agriculture. Great Britain had reached this position by 1820; Germany and the United States had achieved it by 1880; Belgium, Japan, and a very few other countries by the first decade of the present century. France had not achieved this level by 1914 and would not do so until after 1945. The rest of the world remained far behind.

In the second economic zone, the agricultural population continued to be about twice as large as the industrial force. Sweden, Italy, and Austria were in this group. Nevertheless, relative to the rest of the world they had become economic powers.

The third zone included a number of countries that had begun to industrialize but were still primarily preindustrial. Russia was a leading example. It possessed some modern plants that were the equal of any in Britain or Germany. But the great majority of its people still lived in a peasant society.

The fourth economic zone included such Balkan nations as Greece and Bulgaria, the colonial countries and territories of Asia and Africa, and most of the nations of Latin America, the group of countries that would be called the Third World. With only a few exceptions, they still depended almost exclusively on domestic handicrafts, artisanal work, and unskilled labor.

By any definition of national power, the countries in the first group, and a few in the second, were the most powerful on earth. To begin with, they owned most of the world's capital, either conceived of as surplus funds available for investment or as instruments of production, such as the largest and most expensive machines, machine tools, and factories.

Their political domination over most of the world's population seemed crushing. This control was exerted either through the administration of colonies or through the threat of military force, which they were never reluctant to use to make other countries—for example, China—do their bidding.

Culturally, they imposed their languages, their customs, their sense of style and design, and their cultural and artistic products on everyone with whom they came in contact—and that was almost everyone on earth. Hardly any native culture managed to survive intact, although some resisted the inroads, partly because they were in turn imitated by Western culture-bearers.

Finally, the countries in the first and second groups owned most of the world's weapons, and all of the major weapons, and they commanded and deployed all of the efficient armies and navies. Never before had such a small percentage of the globe's total population possessed such power and exerted such control over all the other living persons on it.

A corollary of this situation was this: If the small number of nations that controlled the globe, most of them European, desired peace, then the world would be at peace. If they chose war, then the world would suffer war, the rest of the nations having no real say in the matter.

The Study of War

From time to time we have remarked on the close relationship between war and the progress of knowledge. In the last chapter we discussed the invention of the machine gun and its equalization of armies, and we mentioned the fact that the abolition of slavery had to wait for a destructive war. But there is more to say about the marriage of war and knowledge.

For thousands of years, men have studied war and have considered war to be perhaps the most interesting of all subjects to investigate. Humankind has always feared war and recoiled from its horrors while at the same time it has been fascinated by war's excitement and adventure and has run to embrace it. For many millennia men and women alike have admired, and often worshiped, successful soldiers.

Not surprising, since successful military leaders either save us from our enemies or bring us things of great value: land, money, and other kinds of booty. How can we sufficiently express our gratitude for such gifts?

Then, too, successful soldiers force us to think about an ideal way of life. Based on discipline, virtue, especially courage, which many nonsoldiers believe they lack, and dedication to a cause, this way of life seems highly desirable. Although most of us may feel we cannot live up to the high ideal of the good soldier, the ideal nevertheless uplifts us, even inspires us.

Finally, war sets the pot of progress aboil. War quickens the imagination and rewards ingenuity, which is turned to the solution of basic problems. A violent mixing of the gene pool usually accompanies war. Mars and Venus come together, and whether by rape or by less brutal measures, soldiers from distant regions impregnate women who bear children who may be called bastards but who are nevertheless genetically vigorous.

The nineteenth century did not abandon the study of war. Just the opposite. War was perhaps its leading subject of investigation, and from that intense intellectual work came many inventions valuable for peace as well as war. Alfred Nobel's dynamite is one example. However, by 1914 there had been no major conflict, except for the American Civil War, since the end of the Napoleonic Wars in 1815. Students of war knew, or believed they knew, many new things about war: how to conduct it, both on defense and offense, how to control it, and how to profit from it. But they had enjoyed no recent opportunities to test their theories.

One small war had had a surprising result. The Russians, thinking victory would be easy, had attacked the Japanese in 1905. Instead, it was the Japanese who won easily. There were tactical reasons: for one thing, Japan's lines of communication had been much shorter. But there was more to it than that. Japan, as everyone soon realized, had been advancing rapidly since its deliberate decision in 1868 to begin imitating the West for the sake of national survival. Suddenly, with this victory, Japan was accepted as a major nation.

Apart from this event, which of course boded more ill than anyone understood at the time, the world had managed to avoid war for a long period. The thirst for battle had consequently grown to the point where it badly needed satisfying.

Colonialism

Colonialism, as an expansionary political policy, is very old. The Greeks had established colonies in Asia Minor, as we have seen, seven centuries before the birth of Christ. Carthaginian and Roman colonies had struggled for control of the Mediterranean. Most European countries reached out after 1492 and founded colonies on the continents discovered to the west. But the modern term *colonialism* does not really refer to those events. Colonialism means the kind of arrangements made and fought over by the European powers during the nineteenth century and the early twentieth century, mostly in Africa and in Southeast Asia.

These new colonies were not created to drain off excess population or to advance a religious or political cause. Their main purpose was to establish and control world markets. By the second half of the nineteenth century the European industrial revolution had outrun the local market for its manufactured goods. Periodic financial panics were the sign, as Karl Marx said, that the European bourgeois capitalist needed a constant increase in customers if he was to enjoy stability in his operations.

Millions of new customers existed throughout the world. They were very poor, but their large numbers made up for that, and their political and especially their military weakness meant they could be forced to buy whatever the producers wanted them to. Besides, even if they lacked money to pay for manufactured goods, they did possess raw materials, from tobacco to chromium, from rice to bauxite, from coffee and oranges to cotton, rubber, and jute, that could be traded for the products that had to be distributed somewhere, lest the European manufacturing machine break down.

By 1914 the colonial picture had changed entirely. Spain, having lost most of her colonies to libertarian uprisings in the New World, was never a major player in the African colonial game. Portugal retained importance through her control of large enclaves, Angola and Mozambique, on the African west and east coasts. Little Belgium controlled a vast territory surrounding the mysterious Congo River. The Dutch still held on to large territories in the East Indies, from which they continued to extract equally large profits, but they had little interest in Africa after the end of the Boer War. The Russians lacked colonies, but there was a world to win on their eastern frontier: they were sufficiently occupied with the problem of subduing Siberia and the Muslim lands to the southeast. Austria, like Russia, was more concerned with its neighboring lands and peoples than with Africa, Southeast Asia, or Latin America. That left four populous nations: Italy, France, Britain, and Germany.

It is only a giant's stone throw from the tip of Sicily to the tip of Tunisia. The distance across the Mediterranean is less than a hundred miles. Thus Italy was close to North Africa and could claim traditional influence there. But since the French had preempted Tunisia, Italy had to be content with Libya. Her claims were modest, and the big players were willing to accept them. Besides, Libya was mostly desert, and her oil had not yet been discovered.

France claimed both Tunisia and Algeria, and she also wanted Morocco, across the narrow Strait of Gibraltar. That was only the beginning. France also claimed, controlled, and administered large territories in West Africa (present-day Senegal, Mauritania, and Mali) and in Central Africa (now Chad and the Central African Republic). Except for Senegal, these lands were sparsely populated and not developed. Nevertheless, there seemed much to be gained, and France fought fiercely to hold on to them.

Over two centuries Britain had become the most successful colonizer, and her African territories were more valuable than other nations'. In the north there was Egypt, the most developed of the indigenous African civilizations, the richest prize on the continent. Beneath it stretched the vast, but still unexplored, Sudan. Beyond the Sudan were the rich colonies of British East Africa: present-day Uganda, Kenya, Zambia, and Zimbabwe (previously Rhodesia). British territories in the west were smaller but still valuable, including present-day Nigeria. The greatest potential of all lay at the southern tip of the continent, where Britain's Dominion of South Africa lorded it over present-day Botswana and Swaziland to the north.

A few areas of Africa, notably Ethiopia, on the Horn of Africa, remained independent. Others, like Somaliland (now Somalia and Djibouti), persisted in an uneasy condition of divided claims by various European powers. Almost all of Africa was therefore accounted for. But there was still a potent and greedy player wishing to join the game.

That player was Germany, which was emerging during the nineteenth century as the most powerful state not just in Europe but in the world. The nineteenth, in fact, was the German century, as the eighteenth had been the British and the seventeenth the French. (By this system of accounting the sixteenth century can be awarded to the Spaniards and the fifteenth to the Italians. Before that, such allocations lose any meaning.) Germany was the world leader in industrial might, and she was overtaking Britain as the leading military power. But apart from a few territories in East Africa, she did not have African colonies. What could be done to accommodate her?

Each of the other European powers gave up something to Germany, Britain most of all because she possessed the most, but it was never enough.

Germany, as befitted its great power, desired great possessions. But she had come to the table, or perhaps, more justly, to the trough, too late. There was nothing left to devour. Unless the balance of power in Europe itself should be utterly changed. But that was unthinkable. Or was it?

During the twenty-five years between 1889 and 1914 a series of small wars of position occurred in various parts of Africa and Asia Minor. These little conflicts served to define frontiers and to exert pressure. Few Europeans died in them. They were actually fought mostly with native troops. Thus they proved unsatisfactory from the point of view of the global strategists, who still had not been able to test their new ideas and weapons against serious—that is, European—competition.

The Boer War

One small war in Africa turned out to be larger than anyone had expected. It broke out in October 1899 when Dutch settlers (Boers) of the South African Republic (the Transvaal) and Orange Free State warned the British in the Cape Colony that they would not accept English rule in southern Africa. For a while the Boers had the better of the fighting. Their commando tactics could not be countered by the British units, who enjoyed more than five to one superiority in manpower, until 1902, when a combination of superior firepower and a brutal war of attrition launched by Lord Kitchener forced the Boers to give in.

Kitchener's scorched-earth policy produced widespread protests in Europe, especially in England, the mother country. He burned the farms of Africans and Boers alike and collected as many as a hundred thousand women and children in carelessly run and unhygienic concentration camps on the open veldt. More than twenty thousand died, and their pitiful struggles and their deaths were faithfully reported to a horrified world. It was Britain's Vietnam, complete with marchers in the streets, liberal manifestos, and patriotic rage.

Britain eventually won the war after failing temporarily to conquer a much weaker foe fighting for its own country. So it seemed to the Boers. The British thought South Africa was theirs. The Africans, to whom it might be said to have belonged, had no say in the matter. The Boer War caught the attention of many strategists, including the Germans. The world learned no lesson from the conflict, although it might have.

The Powder Keg of Europe

Three peninsulas extend southward from the European land mass into the Mediterranean. From west to east they are the Iberian peninsula, Italy, and the Balkans, or "mountains" in Turkish. The Balkans have been causing trouble for centuries. They are not finished yet.

The region is not large, about the size of Texas. Its population today is about seventy-five million. In 1900 it was less than half that. As such, the region was not overpopulated. But the peoples who lived there showed a remarkable variety. Five major ethnic groups and several scattered minorities occupied the peninsula (and still do). They spoke at least five major languages, including several Slavic languages, Romanian, Greek, Turkish, and Albanian. They also were divided by religion: a majority were Greek Orthodox, but there were significant Roman Catholic and Islamic minorities. The only thing they had in common was poverty. Almost everyone was very poor, except for the great landowners, who were very, very rich.

They were proud and thin-skinned, traits that are recorded as far back as the time of Thucydides and the Peloponnesian War. They were— again, still are—quick to take offense and anxious to stand on their rights, all the more so when their rights were not well defined. Of the perhaps thirty million people living in the Balkans in 1914, most wanted to be ruled by someone different from whoever was ruling them at the moment. This also remains true. At this writing Yugoslavia seems to be falling apart into its constituent ethnic groups, and division is also a possibility for Romania and Albania.

Small, nasty Balkan wars were common. Two broke out in 1912 and 1913, but these brushfires were put out by the major powers without serious damage. The will of the fire fighters, however, was becoming suspect. The next time a flame burst forth, perhaps it would be better to let it burn. Fires are perceived by many as having a cleansing effect. So are wars.

In June 1914 Austria decided to show its powerful hand in the Balkans and sent the heir to the throne of Austria-Hungary to Sarajevo, the capital of Bosnia. Archduke Francis Ferdinand was there to review army maneuvers, but he was probably also joining in private talks leading to more of the eternal combinations and dissolutions of Balkan countries that had been going on for thousands of years. At any rate, the archduke and his wife proved a tempting target for some passionate young nationalists, one of whom shot them. In the old films the archduke stands and then pitches forward into the arms of his aides. We know now that Europe was falling with him. Negotiations to avert war continued for a month, but the anger and indignation could not be reduced, and the Thirty Years War broke out in the first of August of that fateful year, 1914.

Actually, thirty-one years, from August 1914 to August 1945. We still call it, traditionally, World War I (1914–1918) and World War II (1939–1945), but future historians will collapse the two conflicts into one, in the same way, for example, as they refer to one Peloponnesian War, although that, too, was broken by long periods of uneasy peace. The Thirty Years War of the twentieth century, like that of the seventeenth century in Germany, did not enjoy much in the way of peaceful interludes.

Major fighting stopped on both the western and the eastern fronts on November 11, 1918, but a dirty war of attrition continued in Russia for three years. The Belorussians or White Russians, joined by many *emigrés*, like those from the French Revolution, and aided by most of the previous combatants—Germany was too exhausted to become involved—almost destroyed the Communist Revolution that had overtaken Russia, but at the last moment they failed.

The twenties were a long, frenzied party, like the one that went on all night in Brussels before the Battle of Waterloo, to which the partying English officers rode off still in their dress uniforms. Bloody war picked up again in the early thirties, when Japan invaded Manchuria and then China proper. The Germans were rearmed and ready under Adolf Hitler in 1937, and the second and even more deadly phase of the war began on the first day of September 1939.

Character of the 1914–1918 War

The German strategic plan entailed, first, the quick conquest of France by a rapid sweep west and south through Belgium, followed by a slower mopping up in Russia, on the eastern front. This would avoid the strong French fortifications on the Franco-German border. The plan almost succeeded in 1914. (The Western part of the same plan did succeed in 1940, which suggests that military men are not quick to learn from hardship and defeat.) The failure of the plan led to the greatest misery ever suffered upon a battlefield. The Germans were stopped, north and east of Paris, by valiant efforts on the part of both French and English. But the Germans could not be driven back. For four years the two armies, numbering in the millions of men, dug trenches and holes in the ground half a mile apart and shot at each other with rifles, machine guns, and artillery that grew more and more fearsome as time went on.

The first phase of the conflict was a nineteenth-century war, for it was the culmination of that century's obsession with machines, and of its faith that a sufficient number of machines, if they were also big enough, would always carry you through. The war itself became a terrible machine for grinding human beings into bits and pieces of wasted flesh. Its most famous battles lasted for months, not hours or days, and counted their casualties not in the thousands but in the millions. Hundreds of thousands of previously rational animals lined up facing one another and doggedly shot one another to pieces, day after day and year after year. And no one could confidently or clearly say why it was happening or what it was all about.

When the shooting stopped temporarily in 1918, a kind of frantic rejoicing ensued. This ended, as many parties do, in financial disaster. The year 1929 witnessed the onset of the Great Depression, the worst financial panic in history, which extended over the whole world and made even war seem a desirable antidote. The war erupted again in 1939. The Allies had prepared for more trench warfare, but the Germans knew better, and their strategy of *Blitzkrieg*, "lightning war," succeeded at first, as their tanks crushed entrenched divisions and their bombs reduced to rubble famous and beautiful cities of Holland and England.

The Allies soon learned to respond in kind, and in the end German and Japanese cities suffered the most. (Japan had entered the war on the Axis side in December 1941.) Dresden and Berlin were almost totally destroyed, as was Tokyo, by conventional air bombardments that initiated so-called fire storms. The very air burned above the raging inferno that was the city center, causing a vacuum that hurricane winds rushed in to fill. And Hiroshima and Nagasaki met even more terrible fates.

The atomic bomb that completed the Thirty Years War of the twentieth century was both the end of something and the beginning of something else. It summarized and actually wrote finis to the age-old search for an absolute advantage in firepower, for a weapon so overwhelmingly superior that those possessing it would be inevitably victorious and would also suffer few or even no casualties. This dream of Western strategists was magnificently realized on August 6, 1945, at Hiroshima, when the count read: Japanese casualties, two hundred thousand, American casualties, practically none.

Furthermore, the enemy had no possible recourse and had to surrender immediately and unconditionally. Never before in the history of warfare had there been such a total victory. It was no wonder that President Truman, according to observers present that day, was almost hysterical as he ran through the White House shouting, "We did it! We did it!"

America's absolute advantage did not last. The Soviets soon attained parity in nuclear weapons with the United States so that never again would there be, or could there be, such a complete, clean, and final military victory. In fact, before long many nations, small or large, poor or rich, belonged or hoped to belong to the Nuclear Club. Here was the final application of the principle of equality in the muzzle of a gun.

Thoughts on War and Death

Early in 1915, when the first phase of the Great Twentieth-Century War still seemed new, Sigmund Freud published an article titled "Thoughts for the Times on War and Death." By then, after the appearance in 1900 of *The Interpretation of Dreams* and other seminal writings, Dr. Freud was beginning to be respected by a wide public, even if he was still not loved by most people, who persisted in shock from what he told them. It was recognized, further, that he might well have valuable insights concerning the ordeal which the human race, Europe, and especially Germany had undergone. The paper on war and death was full of wisdom, but it may have been, to quote the title of a play by Bernard Shaw, too true to be good, that is, too wise to be popular among its readers.

Freud began by describing the disillusionment felt by so many people, not only in Germany, upon their discovery of the cruelty and brutality of which previously civilized nations and individuals were capable. Stories were told about the soldiers of all the warring nations. How they gang-raped young girls and then killed them, skewered pregnant women on their bayonets, shot captives to cripple but not to kill them just for the pleasure of it, or tortured children and animals because it was interesting to hear them scream, were too close to the truth of everyone's experience of the war to be denied. (Naturally, it was easier to believe such stories about the enemy's soldiers than about your own.)

And if cruel and brutal murder were not enough, the governments of all the combatants, while maintaining that their own citizens should continue to obey the laws of civilized life, showed no compunction about acting toward enemy governments and individuals without any regard for law or civilized custom. Governments lied as a matter of course, and threw themselves with enthusiasm into the development and deployment of ever more monstrous weapons, including poison gas, and the bombardment of unarmed civilian populations. They were as merciless as any barbarian, and this did not seem to embarrass them in the least.

How different had things been before the war! Then, cultured Europeans, Germans especially, had believed that finally, after eons, the human race, or at least their very special part of it, had achieved a level of civilization that would forbid the kinds of actions and behavior that were now commonplace. And not only forbid them, but be able to enforce those prohibitions. Above all, humankind would find some reasonable alternative to war, and particularly the kind of war that was being fought.

German civilization, especially, had been viewed by Germans and other cultivated Europeans as the acme of human accomplishment. German science, German music and art, German scholarship, German ethical philosophy, had set standards for the rest of the world considered to be higher than ever before.

And now the German, most of all, was hated by the world as a primitive, barbaric savage. Collectively, he was referred to as the Hun, that hated name that had stood for centuries as the type of the utterly uncivilized, brutish, semihuman beings who had swept into Europe from the East and devastated the Roman world.

Let us hope that they are wrong, said Freud, and that we Germans are not as bad as they think we are. But, he added—this being his point—we are not as good as we would like them to think we are, either. We are human, and they are, too. And the human being is not as happy being civilized as he says he is. Psychologically, civilized man has been living beyond his means, for there is a deeper self, a kind of primitive savage, in all of us, who wishes to be freed from civilization's restraints. I know this, Freud said, for I have seen it in all of my patients, without exception: men and women, old and young, cultivated and uneducated. Therefore I am not surprised by what the war has revealed, and you should not be surprised, either.

The idea that civilization is an all but unbearable burden for most people, even Germans, was not a popular one in 1915, but at least it was some sort of explanation. And Germans, as well as all of their allies and all of their enemies, continued to act as if they did not want to be civilized throughout that first phase of the war. The strange thing was that in 1918, when the shooting stopped, no one seemed to want to return to being—or acting—civilized in the old way. Nor have they resumed doing so in the last seventy years. That is what is meant by the thought that the Great Twentieth-Century War had destroyed the high civilization Europe had known before 1914.

It was cold comfort to be told by Dr. Freud that this civilization had been an illusion. People are not like that, he was saying. People are not at heart very good. "The element of truth behind all this, which people are so ready to disavow, is that men are not gentle creatures who want to be loved, and who at most can defend themselves if they are attacked," he wrote in a later, more carefully structured treatment of the ideas he presented in 1915; "they are, on the contrary, creatures among whose instinctual endowments is to be reckoned a powerful share of aggressiveness." He added: "*Homo homini lupus.* [Man is a wolf to man.] Who, in the face of all his experience of life and of history, will have the courage to dispute this assertion?"*

Who indeed can deny it, with all the evidence of the twentieth century before him?

Freud made another point in his 1915 paper, about the changed attitude toward death that the war had brought about. In peacetime death may be held at arm's length. One can deny it, at least avoid mentioning it or even thinking about it. In war such denial becomes impossible. Death

---

Civilization and Its Discontents (1930).

intrudes into everyone's life in a most irritating and unbecoming manner. But, said Freud, that is not a bad thing, for deep in our primitive, unconscious selves, we are very aware of death, even if on the surface we deny its existence. We desire the death of our enemies, are ambivalent about the death of our loved ones, and fear our own death, in which at the same time we do not really believe.

Here again there are illusions that it might be better to dispense with. *Si vis vitam, para mortem*, Freud concluded: "If you would endure life, be prepared for death." Again the advice was hard to accept. Yet it, too, helped to explain what was happening.

Causes of War

Why had the war occurred? It had not been logically necessary; perhaps war is never completely unavoidable. A dozen times before 1914, general war had seemed to be imminent, but it had not begun. It is true that the need to satisfy Germany's "legitimate claims" to African colonies had been growing ever more pressing. It is also true that the internal Balkan conflicts had been growing ever more heated. And a valid point could be made that the patience of all the combatants had been growing ever shorter. But there were two other causes that needed to be aired and examined.

One was Freud's explanation. Men need war, he seemed to be saying, to work off the intolerable burden of civilization. The alternative to war is neurosis, both individual and group, which itself can become intolerably destructive. People cannot go on indefinitely acting as if they are civilized. They must be allowed an outlet for their murderous deeper desires. Dreams are not enough. Action is also required. Is any action a valid, that is, a workable, substitute for war?

For war not only permits men to kill, cruelly, brutally, the way they have always unconsciously wanted to do. In a wonderfully contradictory way, war also brings out the best in them. When life and death are the stakes, the game takes on a meaning it cannot otherwise have. Rarely does a soldier return from combat without sensing that he has somehow been shrived, that he has reached a peak of action and feeling never before attained. One tragedy of the Vietnam War is that so few combatants returned with those feelings. Instead, they felt sullied, cheated, and mocked.

War, in this interpretation, is an irresistible, although supremely dangerous, temptation. Men, and women too, feel drawn to it, and always have felt this way throughout history. Perhaps, as a temptation, war is finally losing its appeal. If so, and if the tragic failure of the Vietnam War (at least in America's view of it) is the reason, then that war is the best war Americans have ever fought.

There is another reason why the 1914 war may have begun. That reason is simply boredom.

I have suggested that one explanation for the fall of the Roman empire of the West during the fifth century after Christ was boredom, too, a deep, incurable ennui that ate like acid into the soul. The empire had endured for five hundred years, but its problems had never been solved. It had not found an effective, let alone a good, way to choose a ruler, and almost all of its emperors had been monsters—stupid, ignorant, and cruel—with a few exceptions during the golden age of the Antonines. The rich had become richer, the poor poorer, but the rich were no happier than the poor. Therefore, when the barbarians came, as the Greek poet Constantine Cavafy (1863–1933) wrote, "At least they were some kind of solution."

During the fifty years preceding 1914 a host of brilliant, eloquent, and desperate artists sought to wake the ruling European bourgeoisie out of its deadly lethargy. The bourgeoisie did not at first believe it was lethargic, because it was so busy making money. Making money is not heroic human action! cried the artists. Making money is boring you to death!

In a sense, this view was quite valid. The ruling bourgeoisie, the most cultivated classes together with the capitalists and businessmen, acted as if they were terribly bored. Money bored them, but worse, so did peace. Finally, they could not endure the boredom any longer, and they allowed the war to begin.

Like the sorcerer's apprentice, they did not expect the war to be so terrible or to last so long. That is usually the way with wars, although we always forget that point. In the end, everyone wished the war had never started. But it began because enough people wanted it to. That is the way with most of the things that happen to human beings, good or bad.

The Twentieth Century:
The Triumph of Democracy

THE LAST DECADE of the twentieth century has begun. There are fewer than ten years before the third millennium of our era. Those ten years have a magical quality. They may be one of the most dangerous decades in history.

There is something frightening about coming to the end of a millennium, a sense of awful finality about the idea of December 31, 1999. We may begin to wonder, even if we are not usually religious, whether God intended the world to last this long. Are we capable of beginning another millennium? Do we have the strength and the courage? Do we have the will?

Europeans at the close of the tenth century AD were not sure they had the will. From about 950 to 1000, melancholy imbued our ancestors. Madmen ran through the towns and villages, shouting that the world was coming to an end. Some who were not mad feared the madmen might be right. There was a dearth of ingenuity and invention. Many problems seemed to be insoluble. People tried to hang on, hoping that life would not get even worse. They seem to have given up hope that it would get any better.

Outlaws roved through the land, stealing, burning, enslaving. Priests preached sad and somber sermons, warning the people that the last judgment might be at hand, urging them to right their lives and make peace with their neighbors. Most people were reluctant to embark on lengthy enterprises. No one made plans for the future, at least on this earth.

When the millennium arrived and passed without significant incident, the peoples of Europe breathed a sigh of relief. And a primitive energy came boiling up in millions of bosoms. New solutions of old problems became obvious. Why had no one thought of them before? Imaginative political and social arrangements were tested and were often found to work. Artists made new kinds of art, poets wrote new kinds of songs, and philosophers were surprised to discover that there were all kinds of new ideas to be thought.

As a result of this surge of energy, the eleventh century blossomed. The twelfth century proved even better. Perhaps the thirteenth century was the best of all: great cathedrals were completed, universities were founded, men and women set out on travels to visit new places and meet new friends, and towns and cities grew more rapidly than they had for a thousand years. And every summer Norse fishermen sailed westward from Iceland and brought back not just fish but also grapes that they had gathered on the shores of a new land that they told no one about because they did not want to risk spoiling the wonderful fishing.

The last decade of the tenth century—from 990 to 999—was a dangerous decade. Many individuals suffered from the careless brutality that became endemic, and general hopelessness produced general woe. But there were no nuclear weapons in those days. An individual, no matter how evil, could not destroy the whole world.

Today, a moment of pure malice on the part of any one of a handful of individuals, or perhaps an instance of sheer carelessness by a larger but still small group of people, might end the world. Malice and carelessness are exacerbated in periods of depression. That is why this last decade of the present millennium is a dangerous time in history.

But if the human race can survive the decade, arrive at the millennium, and pass it by without incident, then we can expect something to happen similar to what occurred in the decades after the year 1000. A welling up of energy, an increase in ingenuity and invention, a sense that new ways exist to arrange human affairs, a willingness, even an eagerness, to embrace new solutions to old problems. All of this I expect to be evident. Thus, if we collectively live to see it, the twenty-first century may be one of the most glorious in human history, one of the most exciting, hopeful, and productive.

The postmillennium may have already started, although we have not yet counted down the seconds to January 1, 2000. Extraordinary, astonishing things have been happening, events that exhibit a postmillennial character. The peoples of eastern Europe have demanded their freedom, and to their own immense surprise no one has rebuffed them or refused it. They may now be free to determine their own destinies, and even if they stumble before the year 2000, or even soon after, they will never be willing to go back into the prison cells in which they have lived since the end of the Great Twentieth-Century War.

Most of the citizens, or subjects, of the Soviet empire seem to feel the same way. We cannot know as yet, nor can they predict whether they will have both the will and the chance to attain the freedom which, it is already obvious, they certainly desire. Both will and opportunity are necessary. Lacking one or the other, they will attain little. Eventually, it is safe to say, the Soviet peoples will be free.

We can say with equal certainty that the vast Chinese nation—more than a quarter of the population of the earth—will also attain their political and economic freedom in the near future. The millions of young people whose hopes were crushed in the spring of 1989 will not forget what they so fervently desired and what many of them gave their lives for. The symbol of that desire was a plaster copy of the Statue of Liberty erected in the middle of Tiananmen Square, in Beijing. The statue was smashed by the old men's tanks, but the hope that the statue symbolized, and inspired, was not.

The world is full of hope. That is why the last decade of the old millennium may not be as dangerous as it could have been. Hopelessness, despair, is the sickness unto death. Hope is the antidote to hopelessness. The cure is instantaneous. Without hope, nothing can be accomplished. With hope, what cannot be accomplished?

The year 1989 marked the two hundredth anniversary of the march on the Bastille, which inaugurated the French Revolution. Will a future poet write of 1989, as Wordsworth wrote of 1789,

> Bliss was it in that dawn to be alive,
> But to be young was very heaven!

The Progress of Democracy

The first democratic governments were established in a few Greek city-states during the sixth and fifth centuries BC. They did not last. They were overthrown either by enemies from without or, more frequently, by internal revolutions of the oligarchs, that is, the wealthy few who presented themselves as a natural aristocracy. By Aristotle's time, in the fourth century BC, democracy seemed to be an experiment that had failed.

The Roman republic was not a democracy in the Greek sense. The franchise was very restricted, and although the people enjoyed much political freedom, they were not, strictly speaking, constituted as rulers of the state. The eleventh- and twelfth-century Italian communes were oligarchies that dared to flirt with democracy. Again much freedom existed, especially economic freedom, but no constitutional basis for the people's rule could be found. Not until the political revolutions of the late seventeenth and eighteenth centuries did anything like true democratic governments come into existence. Thus democracy, of all the forms of government, is among the most recent, if we understand what democracy really means.

The idea of democracy has several parts. In overthrowing King James II and replacing him by a monarch who agreed to be responsible—that is, responsive to—the Parliament, the English in 1689 (is there something magical about those two final digits?) established perhaps the first true government of laws. At least it was the first modern government of laws, for since the fall of the Roman republic all governments, constitutionally, not just de facto, had been governments of men. William and Mary may not have wished to be mere "figureheads," but a constitutional monarch need not be that. He can be a president who rules with great power, so long as he obeys a law that is other than his own will, or whim. In a government of men there is no law that is superior to the will, or the whim, of one or more men. In a government of laws there is. That is all there is to it.

The law which William and Mary agreed to obey had been established by the Parliament, which was responsible to the people, who elected the members. Who the people were did not seem entirely clear, despite John Locke's ringing declaration in 1689 that "the people shall judge" the justness of their rulers. Who were *those* people? Were they all the people? Just the men? Just the men of property? That Locke meant the last must be suspected. But that limited group does not constitute a democracy.

"All men are created equal," said Thomas Jefferson, in another ringing declaration in 1776, "and are endowed by their Creator with certain unalienable rights." Here for the first time the note of "all" was sounded. Did he mean all, in the sense of every man and perhaps every woman, too? Probably not. But it is important to realize that what Jefferson, an individual man of the eighteenth century, meant was not very important in the grand scheme of things. He had said "all," he had written it for everyone to read. The future could interpret the word as it wished, for the declaration contained no explicit limitation on that word *all*. "All" could turn out to mean all if that was what the people wanted. And they did.

That desire throbs in the Preamble to the Constitution which the Framers erected as their sovereign law in 1789 (again that fateful year!). "We the People," they said, "do ordain and establish this Constitution." That meant the people and not the states were doing the ordaining. But again the words said more than those who wrote them might have fully understood.

We, the People of the United States, in order to form a more perfect union, establish justice, insure domestic tranquillity, provide for the common defense, promote the general welfare, and secure the blessings of liberty to ourselves and our posterity, do ordain and establish this Constitution for the United States of America.

Again, is there any limitation? Whatever the Framers may have meant, is there an inherent reason in those words to say that all—every single one—of the people is not intended?

No one ever read those words, and Jefferson's, more carefully than Abraham Lincoln, who found himself, by a dreadful or a fortunate accident, depending on your point of view, charged with the task of interpreting the meaning of democracy for a nation engaged in a civil war that threatened its very existence. Among his other duties, he was prevailed upon in November 1863 to say a few words, after Edward Everett's main address, at the dedication of the military cemetery at Gettysburg, Pennsylvania, the site of one of the crucial battles of the war, fought the previous July.

Our forefathers, said Lincoln, established a new nation on this continent, dedicated to the proposition that all men are created equal.

Now, he continued, we are engaged in a civil war that is a test of whether any such nation can endure for more than a short time. Nations dedicated to that proposition have, in the past, usually been destroyed, either by external or by internal conflict. We must not let that happen to our nation.

Instead, he concluded, in honor of the brave men who struggled here, and particularly those who died here, we must dedicate ourselves to the task they left unfinished when they died. That task is to insure the perpetuation on this earth of "government of the people, by the people, for the people."

No more famous phrase rings down the annals of American history. "Government of the people" means the people's government, and moreover government over the entire people—all the people. None of the people are left out.

"Government by the people" means the people are the governors. In their capacity as rulers they choose executives and representatives to make and enforce their laws.

"Government for the people" means government that acts for the benefit—the general welfare—of all the people, not just some, and especially not the rulers themselves, although the chosen executives and representatives, as themselves members of the people, may and should benefit from the government that they temporarily (as long as the people continue them in office) are helping to operate.

The definition of democracy needs nothing more than these three elements: the English decision in 1689 to erect a government of laws, not men; the declarations of the Founders in 1776 and 1789 that all men are equal and that the people as a whole may ordain the law that stands superior to any man; and Lincoln's tripartite distinction between three elemental aims of democratic government. This is democracy as it has come to be understood by Americans during two hundred years and by the rest of the world during varying periods, all of them less than two hundred years.

To understand what democracy means, and to put that understanding into practice, are two different things. Even in the United States, the originator of democracy in this fullest sense of the term, more than half the people were disenfranchised, could not vote, in 1900. To be disenfranchised, as all women were, as most blacks in the South were, as some others were for economic reasons, is to be deprived of the highest office in the land, that of citizen in the full meaning of the term *citizen*, one who determines the shape, manner, and personalities of his own government. Women, blacks, and some of the poor still were governed by others "for their own good." That was not good enough.

Most other countries were far behind the United States. Less than a hundred years ago, there was no major country on earth that was a democracy in our—and Lincoln's—sense of the word.

The Great Twentieth-Century War had many results. Some of them were good. One was the lightning spread of the principle of universal suffrage over most of the globe. Today, there is hardly a nation that does not constitutionally affirm the right of all citizens to vote for their representatives or rulers.

Which is not to say, however, that in all countries this right is actually protected. Communist governments for fifty or more years have maintained the pretense that an election in which only one candidate—the candidate of the ruling party—runs for an office is a true election. They have "proved" this view by requiring that all citizens vote, which, until recently, almost all citizens have done. This kind of election is a mockery of democratic government, of Lincoln's "government by the people."

The right to vote is protected for all, or almost all, the citizens of the nations of the Free World, which is called free *because* this right is universally protected. However, in some of these countries high proportions of the eligible voters choose not to vote for the representatives. They are willing to allow others to choose for them. Is such a nation less democratic? That is hard to say.

That government exists for the general welfare of all the people is another pious dictum of most of the constitutions of the earth at the present day. In many cases the claim is manifestly fraudulent: "government for the people" does not come into existence just with a few words, more or less earnestly intended. In no country can it be said that government is administered equally for all citizens; that is, in no country do all citizens equally benefit from their government. In some, this ideal is approached quite closely; in others, the intent is there, which was not the case in almost all of the countries of the world less than a hundred years ago.

The extension of the protective wings of government over all the people—Lincoln's "government of the people"—is sometimes a mixed blessing. Hardly anyone is left out, bereft of government, in the United States today. That is good. Until recently hardly anyone was free of government in Haiti. That is very bad. The long arm of despotic, even tyrannical, government may reach into every home, every place of work or business, even into every heart and mind, when it is equipped with sophisticated electronic surveillance instruments. The difference concerns who is excluded. In the United States it is some of the poor, many of the illegal immigrants, a few others who are weak. They are not included, sometimes unintentionally, always illegally and unconstitutionally. In Haiti, in any tyranny, it is the *rulers* who are left out, for they are above the law and thus outside the state. They almost exclusively enjoy the benefits of government because they have expropriated them. Truly, they are outlaws, although it is extraordinarily difficult to bring them to justice.

These failures in practice at the end of the twentieth century are very different from the defects of democracy we noted at the beginning of it. Then democracy was only a dream, which could be realized in some countries, but in others not even perceived as a possibility. The change is a great one.

A simple way to describe the new society: In 1900 the great majority of the peoples of the earth did not understand what democracy was and consequently did not desire it. And even among those who understood democracy, not all desired it or believed it was possible to put it into practice.

In 1991 the great majority of the peoples of the earth do understand, some more clearly than others, what democracy is. And among those who do, there is no people that does not desire it or believe that it can be made real and practical for them, sooner or later.

There are still rulers who claim that their people do not seek democracy, are not ready for it, could not survive under free governments that were elected by themselves. Until 1989, that is what the Communist governments of eastern Europe said. That is the view of the rulers of Third World despotisms almost universally. It is the contention of the absolute rulers of the few theocracies that survive into this last decade of the second millennium. But when the people, everywhere, are asked, and are free to answer, they do not agree.

The people, everywhere, desire democracy, for a very good reason. As philosopher Mortimer J. Adler has taught us, democracy is the only perfectly just form of government. All other forms of government, without exception, either constitutionally deprive some citizens of the right to choose their own governors, or constitutionally exclude some citizens from the benefits that their government confers. No democracy is as yet perfect in realizing the democratic ideal; perhaps no democracy ever will be in that sense. But no other form of government is even ideally perfect in the sense in which democracy is. And that is why all peoples, everywhere, desire it.

This is an extraordinary change, when you consider it. Two hundred years ago, no people save the British, at home and in their colonies, had much of a conception of what a modern democratic government might be. A hundred years ago a small proportion of the world's population stood alone in understanding and desiring a democratic form of government. Today, practically speaking, all of the peoples of the earth desire it. And this desire exists despite the most earnest efforts on the part of numerous governments to conceal the idea of democracy from their people.

The attempt to stifle democracy includes outright censorship, distortion, and lies. But none of them have worked. In China and in eastern Europe in 1989, in Moscow in August 1991, the people saw through the lies and distortion, and evaded the censorship. They even understood the distortions of democratic propaganda, where and when they occurred. Here again Abraham Lincoln was right: "You can fool some of the people all of the time, and all of the people some of the time. But you cannot fool all of the people all of the time."

Communism

As a form of government, democracy has had to struggle against three major competitors during the twentieth century. They are communism, totalitarianism, and theocracy.

There is an enormous difference between communist theory and communist practice when it comes to government. The difference is so great that you have to wonder whether it can ever be bridged. Can the kind of communist government of which Marx and Lenin dreamed—or said they dreamed—ever come into existence? If not, does communism always have to result in the kind of society we have known since 1917?

When Marx and Engels tried to promote the revolution of the proletariat, and when Lenin, a generation or two later, actually led the rebellion, the ideal for which they strove appeared noble to their followers. The proletariat were the have-nots of history. They had always done all or most of the work of society, and received none or very few of the benefits. Communism said a perfectly reasonable thing: You are the great majority. From now on you will control the economic power of the state, and therefore receive its economic benefits. For a while, you will even possess tyrannical power, but this power will really be for the benefit of all. Eventually—fairly soon, we expect—the state will wither away, and all will rule, in a kind of utopia, for the benefit of all. And that paradise will last forever.

I said communism made reasonable promises. The first part seemed to make some sense. The second part, about eternal paradise, was not reasonable at all. But it sounded good.

How did communism operate in practice? Stalin (1879–1953) showed us, in Russia, the first Communist country. The kulaks, or independent farmers—not serfs—wanted to continue owning their own land and to sell what they produced by their own labor in a free market. That is not Communist, said Stalin. The proletariat, acting as a class, must own all of the instruments of production, including your land. You will still enjoy the benefits, of course; no one is left out of the workers' paradise!

For a while the kulaks were permitted to remain independent. Eventually the "majority" decided the kulaks should be "liquidated as a class." The liquidation began at the end of 1929. Within five years most of the kulaks, together with millions of peasants who also objected to the collectivization of agricultural land, had either been killed or deported to remote regions of Siberia. The death toll has never been accurately determined. According to the best estimates, some twenty million people died. That figure does not include the additional millions who in later years starved to death because collectivization destroyed Soviet agriculture.

No majority, no matter how large, has the right to kill those who disagree with it, no matter how small a minority they may be. That is a fundamental democratic precept. If the "majority" really had been a majority, the decision to collectivize agriculture, if it had been conducted more humanely, might have been considered acceptable, even though it would necessarily have involved injustice to some citizens. But the "majority" never became a real majority in the Soviet Union. The "majority" consisted of a very small minority, sometimes just Stalin himself.

In theory, communism became the temporary tyranny of the proletariat, which would inevitably evolve into the nongovernment—a kind of utopian anarchy—of all by all. In practice communism has always been, in every country where it has existed (that is, in every country that has called itself Communist), the brutal tyranny of a very small minority over the vast majority of the rest of the citizens or subjects. Only in its last throes, for example in Czechoslovakia in December 1989, when that Communist government dissolved before the eyes of the world, has any Communist government ever conceded that its tyranny was temporary, as Marx and Lenin had said it would have to be. And since in fact the people have never ruled any Communist state, there was no reason why any Communist government should ever give up its tyrannical rule at any time, short of revolution. In the Communist tyrannies of the twentieth century, revolution always seemed nearly impossible, since the ruling minority exercised control not only of the economy in all its aspects but also of the police and the army. How could the people ever rise up and rule themselves in such circumstances?

But the people did, in East Germany and Hungary and Czechoslovakia, in Yugoslavia, in Romania. They tried to rebel in China. And they sought independence in parts of the Soviet Union, all in 1989, and again in 1991. And nothing stopped them. The awesome machinery of the state, its police and its armed forces, its censors and its fearsome laws and judges, turned out to be made of snow. When the sun began to shine, the snow melted and revealed the tyrant, alone in his nakedness.

The rest of the people, in all the other Communist countries of the world, saw what happened. The same thing will happen to them. And communism will cease to be a workable form of government, probably before the end of the twentieth century, and if not then, soon after the beginning of the twenty-first.

Is there anything to regret about the manifest failure of the Communist ideal? Perhaps there is. The ideal did not cease to be noble because the practice was universally brutal and cruel. The Communist tyrannies did not work, economically, and so they had to fail sooner or later. Collectivization of agriculture, for example, is simply not an intelligent way to organize farming.

But the idea that the downtrodden of the earth should finally begin to receive a fair share of the profits of their labor is right. And the democracies have accepted it. They have learned from the Communists. The idea that women and men should be treated equally and given equal economic opportunity, which Lenin always emphasized, is also right. Here again the democracies have learned from the Communists, although too slowly. Many other Communist ideas also make eminent sense, and the democracies have or will adopt them in the future. If they do not, they, too, will fail, at least to some notable extent.

The Communist governments of the twentieth century had a great opportunity. They usually came into existence in countries where the people had always been subject to unjust, tyrannical rule. (This was not true in eastern Europe. There, the Soviets imposed communism upon unwilling would-be democrats.) Most of those peoples were eager to be free, but naive about what freedom meant. They were tricked, cheated, defrauded by their Communist masters, who did know about freedom. They concealed this knowledge from their people. But the people still learned about freedom. The knowledge of freedom is like a raging river, tumbling down the mountainside and inundating the plain. Eventually freedom will flood the whole world. And the promise of communism, that bright, evanescent ideal, will have died because of a few men's narrow greed for power.

Totalitarianism

Communism succeeded, as far as it did, because it was essentially about justice. Totalitarianism failed utterly because it was only about power and so-called national honor.

In truth, nations may be honorable or dishonorable, but not because of their power. A nation is honorable if it is just, dishonorable if it is unjust. A powerful nation is feared and perhaps envied by weaker nations. There is a great difference between honor, on the one hand, and fear and envy, on the other.

Unfortunately, the difference is often lost or forgotten. Among nations as among individuals, power can be mistaken for justice. Rather, power and wealth can produce a kind of cheap imitation of honor, which is fame in the sense that is denoted by the title "Life-styles of the Rich and Famous." The people meant by that phrase are famous because they are rich, indeed ostentatiously so. They know it is possible to buy fame and are willing to pay the price of it.

Nations have been trying to buy fame for centuries. They also have another way of obtaining the spurious fame that they like to call national honor: that is, by being militarily strong and able to dominate weaker nations. The ability to push other people around used to confer this kind of fame on individuals, too. In the world's great cities, that is, in the uncivil society, or state of nature, in the culture of the streets, fame and fear are not won by being just. They are acquired by being ostentatiously rich and strong enough to dominate others. Since the international community is in a state of nature (I will return to this concept later in this chapter), the same practices produce similar results in the so-called community of nations.

Nations are made up of individuals, and not all individuals are willing to applaud their government's ostentation and bullying. In the twentieth century the United States has often been outrageously ostentatious about its great wealth and a mean, nasty bully, pushing other nations around in a way that it would not allow any of its citizens to do to other citizens. When the ostentation and bullying have grown too outrageous, enough citizens have objected so that the government has had to stop, for a while. The same cycle of events has occurred in most of the nations of the world. Less so, of course, in countries that have been ruled not by the people but by irresponsible, that is, unresponsive, minorities calling themselves by various magniloquent but fraudulent titles, such as father of the people, or president of the revolution, or emperor for life, or chairman of the junta, or duce, or fuehrer, or what have you. I have not put any of those titles in capitals, because all of them are spurious and personal, that is, conferred upon rulers by themselves and not by their people.

As I have noted, totalitarianism is concerned only with power and a spurious sense of national honor. It is a disease of government made possible in the twentieth century by the rapid expansion of equality in the two centuries since the French Revolution. As Tocqueville showed in *Democracy in America* (1830–1835), democracy during its expansionist egalitarian phase can create a dangerous vacuum between the people at the base, all of them equal, and the government at the top, which, though chosen by the people, possesses threatening power. During this egalitarian phase, all mediating powers of the old regime are destroyed, for the very good reason that they are based upon traditional and immemorial privilege. Very good, Tocqueville said. It is right to dispense with privilege. But those intermediate powers served a purpose: they stood between the people and their government, keeping the full power of the government from falling upon ordinary individuals. Without them the people are left helpless before the fury of government, with nowhere to turn for relief.

What can replace the traditional mediating forces of the society? Tocqueville asked. In a democracy such as the United States, he said, private associations are permitted by the central government to perform quasi-governmental functions that take the brunt of governmental power and protect the people like a great umbrella spread out against a rainstorm. Corporations, churches, clubs, charitable organizations, societies for the prevention or promotion of this and that, act like the traditional noble mediators of the old regime. And woe to any state that lacks them in our modern world, Tocqueville said. A nation without this crucial element in its makeup will be a more terrible tyranny than the world has ever seen.

Some of the world's leading countries in the twentieth century made the conscious decision to do away with such mediators. Italy and Germany are the most notorious examples, but they have not been alone. Most of the Communist states have been totalitarian, too.

The decision in the case of Germany was caused in part by the devastation, both social and economic, brought about by her defeat in 1918. The victors in that first phase of the Twentieth-Century War demanded and received reparations. Germany was also required to give up valuable industrial properties, notably in the Ruhr Valley, that would have helped her to pay them. As a result, the German economy collapsed in the late 1920s, and that led to social chaos. In the circumstances, it is perhaps understandable that the nation turned to a madman to lead it out of chaos into national "honor" once again.

Adolf Hitler (1889–1945) promised to bring Germany to the promised land on one condition: that the state would have total control over all the organs, organizations, and citizens of the nation. Our situation is dire and calls for extraordinary measures, he said. Let every single German, and every single German business corporation, church, club, organization, and society, work together to save us. There are no exceptions. There can be none, else we will fail. Together, nothing can stop us, and we will win!

Germany, after 1918, had been a democratic state, but democracy, said Hitler, is inefficient. See how lax and weak the world's democracies have become. He offered an alternative, which he called national socialism. The name was not important—it combined vague propagandistic elements but really meant almost nothing. The resulting political organization was an extremely powerful entity on the world scene. The National Socialist, or Nazi, leaders gathered the combined force of all German citizens and all previously private associations into one terrifying national weapon. Hitler had turned the nation into a sword. Like Robespierre and Napoleon before him—although neither of them had been mad—Hitler found himself "speaking for the nation" in every word he said, and therefore personally wielding the national sword.

The Fascism of Benito Mussolini (1883–1945) had predated Nazism by several years and may have taught Hitler something, although he would never admit that an Italian could teach a German anything important. The symbol of Fascist Italy was the fasces, a bundle of rods tightly tied together. It suggested that the Italian state combined the force of all its elements, both individual citizens and organizations, for the pursuit of a single goal. In the case of Italy, too, the goal was national "honor." Italy thought she had been cheated out of her rightful spoils after the 1914–1918 war, for then she had been on the winning side. (She made the mistake of changing sides during the subsequent interbellum period, and so ended up a loser in 1945.)

Totalitarian Germany and Italy were fearsome adversaries for the democratic Allies, who indeed had become weak and lax after 1918. Looking back, however, it is evident now that their enormous power, together with that of Japan, which was totalitarian in another way (we will return to it below), was not produced by totalitarianism as such. Italy and especially Germany were advanced industrial states, and they had been powerful before totalitarian ideas helped mold them into weapons for world conquest. The same was true of Japan. But it was not so easy to perceive this fact when Nazism, Fascism, and Japanese industrial nationalism were threatening to take over the world.

The Soviet Union had been verging on totalitarianism for years. The dictatorship of the proletariat was interpreted by Stalin and perhaps by Lenin, too, as giving those who spoke for the proletariat—that is, themselves—the right to mobilize every resource of the state in the interest of the future triumph of Communist society. When Germany attacked the Soviet Union in June 1941, the exigencies of war gave Stalin the excuse to explicitly incorporate every person and organization into the machine that the state had become. In fact, every one of the warring states in those frantic last years of the conflict became machines of a sort. But the democracies reverted to democracies after the war was over. Stalin's Russia remained a machine.

Totalitarianism did not function in the Soviet Union as it had, for a while, in Germany and Japan. Perhaps it never really succeeded in Italy. A machine is only efficient if its parts are made of the right materials and fitted together in an appropriate way. This was not true of the Soviet Union, or indeed of the eastern European countries that were required to emulate it. These machines ran very badly, for their parts were old, worn, and improperly arranged. To continue the metaphor, the problem was that a political party was running the machine instead of an engineer.

An old charge against democracy contends it is relatively inefficient compared to despotism, which works well even if a tyrannical government is not just or free. The complaint has been heard for two hundred years, and especially in the past half century, but it is simply not true. The members of a totalitarian state can have no interest in the success of the state itself, except in times of dire emergency, when their lives may be saved if the nation itself survives, and not always even then. The members of a democracy have a personal as well as a national interest in the state's success. A significant difference occurs when the interests of all the individuals are combined. That is the reason democracies tend to succeed, and why totalitarian states ultimately fail.

Japan today combines a democratic state and a quasi-totalitarian economy. Politically, Japan is a modern democracy which possesses the numerous mediating private associations that Tocqueville said were needed in any modern, egalitarian state. But most of the time, these Japanese private associations—primarily business corporations—are able to work together to achieve goals they share and that enrich all of them when these goals are achieved.

The United States has laws forbidding such combinations, for good historical reasons. Furthermore, American corporations, descending from another social tradition, are primarily competitive rather than cooperative. A part of the American dogma holds that competition is the lifeblood of the market, and that no real progress can be made without it. The Japanese feel that cooperation is the road to real progress and that competition, while not bad, should be kept within reasonable, disciplined bounds.

Probably both views are correct. It is perhaps more a matter of national styles than of anything else. The important thing to remember about Japan is that she is not, or is no longer, totalitarian like Nazi Germany. In Germany, under Hitler, all citizens and organizations were forced to obey the national will as revealed by the fuehrer. In Japan, today, individuals and business corporations follow their leaders because they think it is in their individual interest to do so.

The political device of incorporating all mediating organizations into the all-powerful state has been adopted during the twentieth century by a number of Third World countries, on the grounds that such countries are not yet mature enough to be democracies. The decision is always made by a father of the people or some other self-styled benevolent despot. There can be some truth in this view when a new nation lacks mediating organizations to protect the people against the power of the government.

However, the claim of the despot usually has been fraudulent. More important, the contention that a given people appears to be unprepared for democracy is always untrue. That claim is based on a mistaken view of human nature. All men and women are created equal and are endowed by their creator with certain unalienable rights. The twentieth century has come to the conclusion that Jefferson's declaration is correct. From it follows inexorably the proposition that all are capable of ruling themselves democratically, although some may do it better than others.

Theocracy in the Twentieth Century

Theocracy, the rule of God, was the great experiment tried during the Middle Ages in the Christian West. As we have seen, that experiment in governance failed. Although some theocracies continued in existence for hundreds of years, the idea never really worked, for the simple reason that the will of God must always be interpreted by mortal, fallible human beings. Theocracy, in the last analysis, is no better than the men who govern in God's name. As a matter of practice, such men are no better than other governors, and often they are worse.

Unlike Christianity, Islam has never quite given up the theocratic ideal. Almost all Christian nations today erect strong constitutional hedges between religion and the state. God may continue to be understood as guiding the nation's destiny, but his servants are not permitted to intervene in the affairs of the state. Some Islamic nations, although not all, have refused to erect such barriers to direct action by the servants of God and the interpreters of his will.

Iran, under the ayatollahs, is the leading example. The shah of Iran, Mohammad Reza Pahlavi (1919–1980), was overthrown in 1979 in a revolution led from exile by Ayatollah Ruhollah Khomeini (1900–1989).

Khomeini returned to Iran in February 1979 and immediately took over control of the new government, which he appointed and continued to dominate until his death. He was succeeded by another ayatollah, but it appears likely that no Iranian successor will have as much power as Khomeini did.

An absolute despot who convinces his subjects that his word is the word of God may enjoy more power than any other kind of ruler. Numerous examples of people ruling with absolute power and authority over small religious communities have been noted during the twentieth century. Jim Jones (1931–1978) ordered more than nine hundred of his followers to commit suicide at Jonestown, Guyana, on November 18, 1978. Most of them did so, passively and without protest. Jones himself died of a gunshot wound, perhaps not self-inflicted. Other communities have undergone similar experiences.

As a nation, Iran underwent a comparable suicidal experience in its war with Iraq (1980–1988). The number of casualties, many of them teenage boys, has been estimated at well over a million. These children died for God, the ayatollah said, and the people believed it to be so.

Democracy is anathema to theocracy. It is not surprising, therefore, that the United States, the leading exemplar of democracy in the world, was considered an evil nation by Khomeini and the Iranian imams. A religious tyrant cannot afford to allow his followers to be tempted by democracy. He must claim that democracy is the invention of anti-God, or Satan. For Khomeini, the United States became the Great Satan. As long as his followers believe this to be so, there can be no dialogue between democracy and theocracy. And when dialogue begins, theocracy inevitably is dissolved. Theocracy cannot survive freedom, which, like democracy, is anathema to it.

The Ayatollah Khomeini was able to impose an absolute tyranny over his followers. Anyone who sought to interject the slightest amount of freedom into the operations of the state was killed, in the name of God. Historically, it has usually proved impossible for a succession of theocrats to impose and enjoy such absolute power. In the present state of the world, with the vast majority of living human beings either already possessing or manifestly desiring and demanding democratic freedoms, theocracy has very little chance of surviving for long except in the circumstances that occurred in Iran in 1979. At the present time, therefore, theocracy would seem not to be a serious long-term threat to democracy.

It should not be forgotten, however, that a theocracy lasted in ancient Egypt for three thousand years. And theocratic overtones are often heard in the claims of despots of other persuasions. Communism banned God not only from the government but also from the society. Men and women were not allowed to be religious or to worship God privately, to say

nothing of permitting God's servants and interpreters to play a role in the state. This may have created a kind of vacuum in the lives of many persons that could only be filled by the state itself and the overwhelming idea of the Revolution. I write the word with a capital letter because the Revolution is quite different from the revolution. The Revolution was, or became in some people's minds, a kind of deity. Thus several Communist states, notably the Soviet Union, began to take on a theocratic hue even though they were explicitly nonreligious and indeed antireligious.

Theocracy is always a threat, in other words. It is an experiment whose failure, during the Middle Ages, is not considered final by some people. Democracy's solution to the problem posed by theocracy is to ban God from the government but permit him a continued role in the society at large. This maximizes personal freedom while avoiding most of the dangers inherent in a theocracy. This view of how society should function offers the commonsense practicality that democratic solutions often provide.

Economic Justice

Democracy, in the twentieth century, has triumphed over its three main competitors, communism, totalitarianism, and theocracy. Whether its triumph is destined to be permanent will be discussed in the last chapter. But democracy must overcome other kinds of threats in order to satisfy the universal human desire for which it stands. These threats are economic.

As Tocqueville saw so well a century and a half ago and as all see now, democracy is based on equality. The desire for equality on the part of almost all men and women today is the force that drives democratic revolutions everywhere. But equality is not only political. That is, political equality, by itself, does not completely satisfy the democratic man or woman. A measure of economic equality is also needed.

Economic equality does not mean the possession by all of an equal amount of economic goods: money and the capitalist instruments of production. Few people today would claim, as some claimed in the past, that all citizens should possess the same amount of money before economic justice could be said to prevail. What is required is a more equitable distribution of wealth, so that all have enough to live decently, and a near absolute equality of opportunity. Absolute equality of possession is a chimera. Equality of opportunity is an ideal for which people will die.

There are many goods that can be called economic that do not consist of money. Among them are the right to a job, a good education, and a decent home. Most important is the right to pursue happiness, or opportunity, in your own way. A just government protects those rights and sees to it that they are not systematically abridged for any of its citizens, or class of citizens.

By that definition, there is no perfectly just government on earth. Democracy is the only perfect *form* of government, but no democratic government is perfect in practice. Nevertheless, tremendous progress has been made toward the ideal during the twentieth century.

In 1900, not only did most citizens of even the most advanced democracies lack political equality, they also lacked economic equality. Equality of opportunity was still only a dream for most Americans, to say nothing of the downtrodden masses of the rest of the world. Despite severe setbacks, in less than a century equality of opportunity has become a reality for the great majority of the industrial and postindustrial nations: the United States and Canada, almost all western European countries, Australia, and Japan, as well as a few others. Equality of opportunity is also seen as a future probability by the peoples of many other nations. Only a minority of the world's population today views the concept of equal opportunity as the great majority of humans did in 1900.

Political equality is usually obtained before economic equality. A people that gains political equality, or the franchise, begins to move fairly rapidly toward economic equality, or equality of opportunity. That is the way society has progressed in the western democracies. In the Communist nations, some form of economic equality may have to precede political equality. Ultimately, all peoples will demand, and just governments will support and protect, both political and economic equality.

And will we then have attained the happiness that all men pursue? By and large, I think so, as long as it remains true that all men are created equal and are endowed with certain unalienable rights. Will that ever cease to be true? We will return to the question in the final chapter.

Why Not World Government?

There is still another threat to just government, which is to say to democracy. It is the most serious of all. The twentieth century has been the first to recognize it as such on a wide scale and to try to do something about it. But all of our attempts so far have ended in failure.

John Locke, in the 1689 essay on political theory to which we have referred several times, made an important distinction between what he called the state of nature and the state of civil society. The state of nature is one in which there is no law other than the law of reason, which is obeyed by reasonable men but which cannot be enforced when unreasonable men disobey it. In the state of nature, in other words, there is no machinery for insuring that all men and women obey the law of reason. As a consequence, few do obey it, for to obey that law when others do not is to make yourself weak. When force is the only arbiter, you must use force or have it used against you.

The state of civil society is characterized by "a standing rule to live by," in Locke's memorable phrase. We have mentioned this idea in describing the original Roman tables of the law, which were written on tablets and erected in the middle of the city, where all could read them and know what was required of citizens. Obedience to the standing law was enforced by various civic institutions which employed officers chosen by the people or their representatives.

The term *positive* is used to describe the standing law because it was laid down by the people in a form that all could accept and agree upon. The state of civil society is always based upon a set of positive laws: first and foremost a constitution, which describes the offices to be filled and the manner in which laws shall be made; secondarily a set of prescriptions that, for the most part, forbid certain actions.

The state of civil society is the state in which almost all human beings live today. There is hardly a person on earth who does not live under some set of positive laws, unless it be the inhabitants of the streets of our great cities, where the law of nature prevails and reason, that pale shadow of enforcement, is the only protection for the weak against the strong.

Almost all individuals live in civil society. But where do nations live? In what state do they exist: the state of nature or the state of civil society?

There is a concept called international law. Also the United Nations came into existence. It has a charter, a kind of constitution, to which all the members of the organization promise allegiance. The body of international law is positive law. So is the charter of the United Nations. Together, they comprise a "standing rule to live by," for nations, not individuals. Or do they?

The rule is there, for all to see, but the machinery for enforcing it does not exist. Any permanent member of the Security Council of the United Nations may veto a majority vote of the body, rendering it null and void. A judgment handed down by the International Court of Justice, with its seat at The Hague, is also essentially unenforceable. That is, a judgment is only "enforced" if the party against which it is rendered agrees to accept it. Furthermore, the majority of members of the United Nations do not accept the principle of "compulsory jurisdiction." That means most countries do not agree in advance to become a party to a case brought against them by another country. In other words, they reserve the right to refuse to be sued, in effect.

The International Court of Justice has been effective in arbitrating quarrels about such things as international fishing rights, for example. But fishing rights are not the kind of things that criminal courts are usually required to decide within a civil society. Criminal courts deal with more important matters: murder, aggravated battery, armed robbery, grand theft, rape, and fraud, as well as every kind of commercial cheating and chicanery and contract dispute. All of those actions can and do occur among nations, which murder, rape, and defraud one another and have been doing so for millennia. In a state of civil society, a murderer cannot walk away free on the grounds that he does not accept the jurisdiction of the court or does not like or agree with the court's decision. Nations can and do do precisely that. This is why it is correct to say that nations live in a state of nature with regard to one another; that is, they live in an international jungle which is, in principle, indistinguishable from the streets of most urban centers or the alleys of Beirut and Bogotá. Even the police are afraid to patrol those mean streets, where the law of reason is the only defense, which is to say where there is no defense at all except force.

Drug dealers, who also live in a state of nature vis-à-vis one another, are armed with automatic weapons in New York, Los Angeles, and Medellín, Colombia. Such weapons make the social jungle they inhabit much more dangerous. The nations in the international jungle are armed with nuclear weapons.

Outlaws will always be armed and dangerous. At the moment, every nation is an outlaw; that is, the state remains outside the law because there is no enforceable law among nations. It would appear that what the world needs more than anything else is a state of civil society for nations, as well as for individuals within nations. This would be a world government to which the nations of the world would agree to give up their sovereignty, that is, their "right" to refuse to obey the standing law when they do not like its application to their own case. The citizen of every modern country gives up that right, and lives better for it. If the nations of the world were to forego the right to be lawless, they would be happier, too.

They would lose some of their "honor" if they gave up the right, as citizens of every civilized nation do, to use force to right their own wrongs. If a criminal murders my wife or robs my house, I may not, subject to the severest penalties, "take the law into my own hands" and avenge myself against the attacker. Only the state may avenge me; it may do it in what to me seems an unacceptable way, but I may do no more than complain. The state does fail, perhaps more often than not, in its task of enforcing the laws and avenging wrongs—that is, punishing criminals. But there are few persons, I think, who do not agree that this is a better way to deal with crime than to require, or allow, individual citizens to commit crimes in response to crimes. Why do we not accept that among nations? Why do we continue to insist on this dubious right to national self-defense when we do not insist on it, except as a last resort, in our individual lives?

Tradition is strong, patriotism is a powerful emotion, the distrust of government is widespread. What U.S. president, for example, could ever hope to be reelected if he proposed that his country should give up its sovereignty to a government of the entire world, which would undoubtedly be democratic in form and therefore dominated by a majority of non-Americans, non-Christians, and nonwhites? And yet, if some president does not propose this some day, we will continue to live in the mean streets of the world, unprotected by the kind of blue-and-white police cars that make the streets of our town or village reasonably safe. Not perfectly safe, of course; perfection is not to be found here any more than anywhere else. But some safety—quite a bit of safety, in fact, for most Americans—is surely better than none.

The idea of world government is very old. St. Augustine was implicitly proposing such a thing in *The City of God* in the fifth century AD. The poet Dante, in the early fourteenth century, called for a world government headed by the Holy Roman Emperor; if he allied himself with the pope, he might be able to bring peace to warring Europe (and by extension the whole world). Immanuel Kant, in the eighteenth century, took time from his philosophical labors to compose a small, pithy volume titled *Perpetual Peace* (1796), which proposed much the same thing. And when the United Nations came into existence at the end of the Twentieth-Century War, in 1945, there were hopeful persons in many countries who believed that it might be a real world government and not just a successor to the "club of nations" that the League of Nations had turned out to be.

In the end, no nation was willing to give up much sovereignty to the United Nations, which thus became almost as ineffective a peacekeeper as its predecessor. A committee was formed at the University of Chicago to frame a World Constitution, and meetings of World Federalists in several countries were attended by a handful of lonely seers and savants who had a good idea of the dangers to which the world was being exposed. None of these efforts accomplished anything substantial.

Yet there has been no major international war since 1945, and no nation has unleashed the terrible nuclear weapons that too many nations now possess. We can be confident, therefore, that we do not need to gather the nations of the world in a real world government, so that they can live together in a state of civil society and obey the laws that they make for themselves because they must.

Right?

One World, One Human Race

Still another threat to democratic government—indeed, to all civil government—needs to be discussed here. This is racism. Racism is one of the most serious diseases of the human species. It is a curious fact that no other species of animals appears to suffer from anything like it.

When Wendell Willkie (1892–1944) ran for the U.S. presidency against Franklin D. Roosevelt in 1940, he gained more votes than any Republican candidate ever had up to that time, although they were not enough to defeat that great campaigner. Roosevelt was running for, and won, his third term. After his defeat, Willkie remained in the public eye, undertaking the role, as he said, of "loyal opposition," and visiting England, the Middle East, the Soviet Union, and China as a sort of personal ambassador of the president.

These travels confirmed Willkie's intuition that the world as a whole was changing, and would change rapidly after the war was over. In 1943 he published a book, *One World*. The title expressed the ideas that had been forming in his mind and in many other minds of that time, now fifty years ago.

"One world" meant several things to Willkie and his readers. First, it was a political idea, suggesting a world organized for peace, with every nation joining forces with every other to promote freedom and justice. As such, it was not a new idea. In 1919 it had underlain Woodrow Wilson's dream of a worldwide League of Nations, and it had inspired some advanced thinkers in the nineteenth century. Willkie knew that progress was being made toward this political ideal, and the United Nations came into being only two years after the publication of his book.

"One world" also denoted the unification of the globe as modern means of communication and transportation shrank distance and overcame all sorts of traditional barriers between people. In Willkie's time, commercial aviation was still in its infancy, but it did not require much imagination to foresee that after the war, when resources could be devoted to it, a worldwide network of air routes would be developed.

It might have been harder to foresee one notable effect, which was the construction around every international airport of cities built in the "international style," all looking remarkably alike, so that travelers could sometimes alight from one of the great airliners of the future and momentarily wonder where they were. By the end of our century no place on earth is really very far from any other, and tourism has become the world's leading industry, greater even than war.

It is possible to dial any number in the world from almost any telephone, hear a few mechanical clicks and hisses, and then talk to a friend who might as well be in the next room. London has become a business lunch, and some New Yorkers, for example, think little of flying to Rome for a long weekend. Exhibitions of art regularly travel from one continent to another, major sporting events solicit competitors from almost all nations (a few, like South Africa, suffer modern pariah status), and "Dallas" is as popular in Delhi as it is in Des Moines.

There is still another meaning of "one world," and I believe it is the most important. Certainly it signifies the largest change in thinking. Until the twentieth century, it was taken for granted by almost everyone, except "the heroes of the moral life," as French philosopher Jacques Maritain called them, that the human race was not one, single community of like and equal souls, but a crowd of better and worse, superior and inferior, chosen and damned. There were many ways to express this concept. Perhaps they all came down to the notion, unfortunately first promulgated by Aristotle, that some human beings are born to rule and others to serve. The latter group, he said, were "natural slaves."

For example, women now constitute a majority of the race and may always have done so. For the most part, in the ancient world women were totally without the rights that at least some men could claim. If citizens at all, women were invariably citizens of the second class. Occasionally a woman rose to prominence and power, for example, Queen Boadicea or the Empress Theodora or the Queen of Sheba, but these exceptions merely proved the rule. This ancient prejudice against women was not very surprising.

It is more surprising that the Declaration of Independence, with all its splendid rhetoric of rights, makes no mention of women and may not have intended to include them in its ringing proclamation that "all men are endowed by their Creator with certain unalienable rights." Women gained little more from the French Revolution, or from their fervent efforts during the nineteenth century. Some suffragettes, in fact, were reduced to dependence on the motto: "Trust in God, for She will help you." But that was really no help at all.

Women won political equality in the western democracies around the time of the 1914–1918 War. Finally, after decades of agitation, they were able to vote and, presumably, to elect representatives of their own special, narrow interests. They did not do that, of course, probably because they viewed their interests as not quite so special and narrow as men had assumed they would view them. In short, women showed that they had been worthy of the vote all along. Nevertheless, women's political equality did not immediately lead to their social and, particularly, to their economic equality.

All the same, by the end of this century there are few persons, male or female, in any of the advanced nations of the world who would publicly maintain the thesis that women are *naturally* inferior to men as human beings, that they are born to serve and not to rule, that they are a kind of natural slave. That type of thinking is dying out in our modern world.

The same may be said concerning those many minorities who, only yesterday, were held to be naturally inferior to some other minority, or majority, of the human race. Blacks. Jews. Aborigines. Few people will take the position, publicly, that members of these groups are *naturally less human* than others. A few, indeed, may hint at this. More will state it privately, albeit with some guilt. Perhaps large numbers of people feel it still. But the fact is few politicians, anywhere, can succeed today if they have nothing more to present than theories of racism, whether veiled or explicit. The portion of the human race that has become "moral heroes" is large. It may be a majority, worldwide.

We should not be complacent. A recent issue of *The Economist* counted some two million de facto slaves, in a number of countries. But these human beings are not considered "natural" slaves. As slaves de facto their status can change overnight. The Republic of South Africa continued, until very recently, to present a glaring exception to what is, by and large, the rule throughout the world. And the memory of Nazi racism, which cost the lives of six million "naturally inferior" Jews, is vivid in the memories of many persons still living.

Even so, the abolition of *natural* slavery is an extraordinary change and one of the great achievements of our epoch. At bottom, it represents an increase in knowledge. Most of us know, today, something that only a handful of people knew just a few decades ago.

Unfortunately, racism is not eradicated when people cease to believe in the natural inferiority of others. It is still possible to hate them, even if it is conceded that they are more or less equal as human beings. If anything, racial hatreds seem to be increasing rather than decreasing in the world today, for reasons that are very hard to discover. We may never rid ourselves of racial hatreds. Even so, the advance we have made should not be forgotten. We can claim some genuine moral progress in our time.

13

The Twentieth Century: Science and Technology

ACCORDING TO EUCLID, the Greek geometer, a point is "that which has no part." The same could be said of an atom, according to the Greek understanding of it. An atom, for them, was the smallest unit of matter and could not be divided. ("Atom" comes from a Greek word meaning "uncuttable.")

We have observed that the physical theories of the Greek atomists were a kind of inspired premonition of ideas that reemerged in the seventeenth century and later led to the bombs that fell on Hiroshima and Nagasaki. The Greeks had no instruments with which to investigate matter, nothing but their senses and their minds. How were they able to arrive at a conception of how the world is made that we now believe to be true because we possess the instruments to prove it?

Greek Atomic Theory

The ancient atomists could not have known they had stumbled on an idea which is at the very heart of the Western way of looking at things. What do you see when you look at the world? Millions of things, more or less distinct, and constantly changing: colors, shapes, growth and decay, being and becoming, large and small, fearsome and friendly. A thousand adjectives are not adequate to describe all that you see.

Is there any way to make sense of this tremendous confusion? There are only two. Each of them involves positing some kind of existence that is not perceivable, which in turn explains what is perceived.

One way is to see patterns in things which are often not really there but which are necessary if we are not to go mad in the face of the chaos of

321

sensory perceptions. This is probably the oldest way of seeing. We inherit this approach from our animal ancestors. To detect patterns and to behave as though they are real is a way of describing instinctual behavior, and instinct works to control, direct, and modify the behavior of all animals except mankind.

When we left instinct behind, we did not lose the old habit of seeing patterns. Instead of instinct, we impose our hopes, desires, and fears on what we see. We imbue nature with an emotional character that it does not really possess. And we see in nature a mind like our own, although perhaps more splendid and majestic, a mind that ordains how we shall interact with the world, and that insures a fundamental benevolence in the cosmos.

Modern scientific behaviorists, who try to be unsentimental, call this an anthropomorphic illusion, seeing man in the universe, where there is no man, only matter. But even the most inveterate behaviorist cannot escape anthropomorphism. It is, for one thing, imbedded in the language he speaks. To test how difficult it is to remove man from matter, try to imagine the world without you in it. What would it look like? What does it look like to another person? Would this world exist? Or would it cease to exist as soon as you stopped seeing it, feeling it, smelling it? Would the world without you have any meaning if it did not have meaning for you?

At the same time that it is very hard to think of the world without you in it, it is also necessary to take this course if we are to understand it. The ancient Greeks were the first to realize this point; they deserve credit for being the first human beings to make the attempt. All of their philosophical speculations were based on the assumption that the truth must be independent of our thinking it; otherwise it would not be truth but a mere illusion.

It was not only philosophers who made this attempt. The earliest theologians also tried to find some other pattern in the world besides their wishes about what it might be. They sought order where there seemed to be only chaos, and they found order from the highest levels of being to the lowest. In short, they found gods everywhere. This, too, may have been a kind of anthropomorphism.

A later age abandoned their multiplicity of gods, but it did not abandon the idea that God, now one rather than many, imbues the universe with meaning. Today, even in our scientific age, probably the majority of human beings find a divine order in the world around them, an "oceanic feeling"—as Sigmund Freud described it, with no little contempt—that the universe is, on the whole, a place where everything has a place and is in its place.

As early as the fifth century before Christ there were a few human beings who were not satisfied with invisible patterns, no matter how comforting. It seemed to them that chance played a larger role in the world and in their lives than any theology could admit. And they may also have shared a kind of stubborn arrogance that led them to suppose they were fundamentally alone in the universe, with no great Being to lead them by the hand. They sought another explanation.

As we have seen, there was a mental game that the ancient Greek philosophers liked to play: this was to try to find something that is shared by any two given things, no matter how unlike they might be. If we refuse to accept a shared "essence" or any other intellectual pattern, and stick stubbornly to matter, can we still play the game?

Take a spider and a star. Do they have any material thing in common? We have agreed not to employ easy Aristotelian solutions: to say, yes, they share existence, they share becoming and passing away, they share unity, and the like.

We can still play the game, for we can imagine dividing both the spider and the star into parts. At first, the parts of the spider remain "spidery," the parts of the star "starlike." But as the parts grow smaller, something remarkable happens. At some point the parts of the spider cease to be "spidery," and the parts of the star cease to be "starlike." At that point both become something else, some indiscriminate thing or things that, in other circumstances, might be parts of other beings besides spiders or stars.

We may not know precisely where that point of transformation falls, but as we think about it, we realize it must occur somewhere. We do not have to be able to see those tiny parts. We can accept that they may be inherently invisible. But they must exist, for we can find no reason why we may not go on dividing something into parts until the point where the something changes into something else.

Can we go on dividing indefinitely? Can we make parts that are infinitely small? We must assume we cannot, for something made of infinitely small parts could have no size whatever. Therefore atoms—the smallest units not of spiders or stars but of matter itself—must exist.

The Revival of Atomic Theory

The crunching force of this train of logic did not dissipate over the centuries. The Christian existential vision of a City of God overshadowed it for a long while, but when that vision lost its influence, during the early seventeenth century, atomism rose again to prominence. Still lacking any of the modern instruments on which we depend, all of the major scientists of that extraordinary century from Kepler to Newton were confirmed and convinced atomists. The English scientist Robert Hooke (1635–1703), a close friend of Newton's, even suggested that the properties of matter, especially gases, could be understood in terms of the motion and collision of atoms. Hooke was neither a very good mathematician nor a very good experimenter, and he had no way of proving his hypothesis. But Newton was interested in it and supported this theory of colliding atoms in somewhat different terms.

Throughout the eighteenth century scientists in several European countries continued to speculate about atomism. The more they learned, particularly about chemistry, the more they were sure they were right to assume that the atomic hypothesis concerning matter was correct. But they also begin to realize that modifications of the hypothesis would have to be made.

One of the most brilliant modifications is due to an Italian chemist, Amadeo Avogadro (1776–1856), who in 1811 proposed a two-part hypothesis: first, that the ultimate particles of even elemental gases may not be atoms but instead molecules made up of combinations of atoms; second, that equal volumes of gases contain equal numbers of molecules. The theory, which is correct, was not accepted until the beginning of the twentieth century.

Starting around the middle of the nineteenth century, with the acceptance of the theory of chemical elements and the discovery by the Russian chemist Dmitry Mendeleyev (1834–1907) of the periodic table of the elements, it became a leading goal of many experimenters to detect physical atoms and to prove their existence. But this goal proved harder to achieve than anyone in that scientifically confident century expected. To this day, in fact, the existence of atoms—which no one any longer disputes—is proved largely by inference. Greek reasoning has thus triumphed in its prefiguration of modern experimental science.

The Greeks were quite wrong about one thing: the atoms were not uncuttable, or, as we would say, indivisible. The indivisibility of atoms, strictly speaking, was not a logical requirement. It only meant that the smallest unit of matter had not yet been found. Perhaps the parts of an atom that were first discovered—the electron and the proton—were the smallest units. Yet they, too, seemed to be divisible.

The smallest unit or units—the Greeks believed there were many different atoms, all building blocks of material things—have not been found. They are still being sought, of course, at enormous expense, in huge atom smashers, for logic demands it. Whether or not those ultimate units will be discovered remains unknown. Logical necessity does not guarantee concrete existence.

In short, atomic science, in one sense, is not new. The credit for discovering that atoms are the basis of all matter belongs to the Greeks, not to modern man. Nevertheless, we have learned many things about atoms that the ancient Greeks did not know.

What Einstein Did

Albert Einstein discovered one of the most important pieces of new knowledge of the twentieth century. It is a simple formula, perhaps the only formula of advanced physics that most people know: $E = mc^2$. To understand what it means we have to go back a few steps.

Einstein was born in the cathedral city of Ulm, Germany, in 1879. By the age of twelve he had determined to solve the riddle of the "huge world." Unfortunately, his grades were not good, and he left school at fifteen. He managed to begin studying again and eventually graduated from the university with a degree in mathematics in 1900. Unknown to the world, he began work as a patent examiner. Then, in four extraordinary scientific papers published in 1905, he went farther toward solving the riddle of the world than any man before him.

Any one of those papers would have made the reputation of another physicist. The first provided an explanation of Brownian motion, a previously inexplicable phenomenon involving the motion of small particles suspended in a liquid. The second paper resolved the three-centuries-old dispute about the composition of light. Einstein's paper proposed that light is composed of photons that sometimes exhibit wavelike characteristics and at other times act like particles. This cutting of the Gordian knot was not simplistic. Backed by solid mathematical reasoning, it was immediately seen as the solution of this great problem. The proposal also explained the puzzling photoelectric effect (the liberation of electrons from matter by light).

Paper number three was even more revolutionary, for it proposed what came to be called the Special Theory of Relativity. Einstein said, If we can assume that the speed of light is always the same and that the laws of nature are constant, then both time and motion are relative to the observer.

Einstein provided homely examples of his idea. In an enclosed elevator, a rider is not aware of up or down motion, except, perhaps, in his stomach if the elevator goes too fast. Passengers on two speeding trains are not aware of their overall speed but only of their relative speed, as one, going just a little faster than the other, passes slowly out of sight. Physicists did not need such examples to recognize the elegance and economy of the theory.

The theory explained many things. So did its expansion, in a paper of 1916, into what Einstein called the General Theory of Relativity. In the 1916 paper Einstein posited that gravitation is not a force, as Newton had held, but a curved field in a space-time continuum that is created by the presence of mass. The idea could be tested, he said, by measuring the deflection of starlight as it passed close to the sun during a total eclipse.

Einstein predicted twice the amount of deflection that Newton's laws predicted.

On May 29, 1919, the experiment that Einstein had called for was made by a vessel sent by the British Royal Society to the Gulf of Guinea. The announcement that Einstein had been precisely correct in his prediction came in November and immediately made him world famous. He won the Nobel Prize for Physics in 1921, but he was already the most famous scientist in the world, so much so that he was treated everywhere almost as a kind of circus freak. This displeased him, as it got in the way of his work.

One other paper had been published in 1905. In some ways it was the most important of all. An extension of the previous paper on relativity, it asked the question whether the inertia of a body depends on its energy content, and answered in the affirmative. Heretofore inertia had been held to be dependent on mass alone. Henceforth the world would have to accept the equivalence of mass and energy.

The equivalence is expressed in the famous formula, which says that E, the energy of a quantity of matter with mass m, is equal to the product of the mass and the square of the (constant) velocity of light, c. That velocity, which is also the speed of propagation of electromagnetic waves in free space, is very great: 300,000 kilometers per second. Squared, the number is enormous. In a tiny unit of matter, therefore, is imbedded a gigantic amount of energy, enough, as we learned later, to kill two hundred thousand citizens of Hiroshima with the explosion of a single bomb.

Einstein was a pacifist. He hated war and, after 1918, feared that war would soon erupt again before the world could enjoy a secure and lasting peace. He did what he could to support the ideas of world government that circulated in the interbellum era. But Einstein the peacemaker was not as influential as Einstein the physicist.

When Adolf Hitler took over Germany in 1933, Einstein renounced his German citizenship and fled to the United States. There he continued his work on the General Theory while he sought ways for the angry world to agree to begin to agree. In 1939, when word reached him that two German physicists had split the uranium atom, with a slight loss of total mass that was converted into energy, he realized that war in itself was not the only danger. And, urged by many colleagues, he sat down and wrote a letter to President Franklin D. Roosevelt (1882–1945).

No one else could have written it with such authority. The letter was simple. It described the German experiments and noted that they had been confirmed in the United States. He observed that a European war seemed to be imminent. In the circumstances the possession by Nazi Germany of a weapon based on the fission of the uranium atom could be overwhelmingly dangerous to the rest of the world. He urged upon the president "watchfulness and, if necessary, quick action."

The president wrote a polite reply. But the warning had not fallen on deaf ears. No one told Einstein, the pacifist, but a crash program, the greatest and most expensive scientific project up to that time, was begun. Called the Manhattan Project, it was initiated with a six-thousand-dollar research allocation in February 1940. The total expense would finally grow to more than two billion dollars, the equivalent of many billions of dollars today. When America entered the war, after the Japanese attack on Pearl Harbor at the end of 1941, the pace of the research became feverish. Until 1943, the work was mainly theoretical, but by early 1945 enough progress had been made to begin plans for the test explosion of a bomb. This explosion occurred at Alamagordo Air Base south of Albuquerque, New Mexico, on July 16, 1945. The test proved completely successful, the bomb generating an explosive power equivalent to some twenty thousand tons of TNT. The bomb that would devastate Hiroshima was dropped three weeks later, on August 6.

Einstein was both happy and brokenhearted. The bomb, in the hands of Hitler, would have meant the end of freedom in the world, and the final obliteration of the Jewish people. He struggled to make the newly founded United Nations a better instrument for peace than it was, than it could be, for he feared that the bomb would be used again, and for worse reasons. He continued to work on his unified field theory, which would show how all natural laws could be expressed in a single theoretical construct, perhaps a single equation. But he had left the rest of the scientific community behind, and they increasingly relegated him to isolation. When he died in 1955, he was the only man in the world who believed that he was right about the overall structure of the universe, he who had led mankind to understand more of that structure than any scientist since Newton.

What the Bomb Taught Us

The most important thing that the atomic bomb taught us is not expressible in a formula. It is a simple fact, which we are the first human beings to know. The world is not only perishable, everyone always knew that, but human beings can destroy it with a flick of a finger.

Events have consequences. One result of the Hiroshima bomb was that the Great War came to an end. Another was that Soviet scientists undertook to make their own atomic bombs. The United States countered with a hydrogen, or thermonuclear, bomb, in which the nuclei of small atoms are fused together (instead of large ones being split). In the fusion, enormous amounts of energy are released. Einstein's equation continues to hold.

The Soviets made their own hydrogen bomb. Since 1950, neither side has been able to outstrip the other. One consequence has been a long period of peace broken by minor wars. That is good.

Looming behind the arms race is a bad piece of new knowledge. There are now enough nuclear weapons in the arsenals of the world to kill every human being ten times over. Of course, not only the human beings would die in a nuclear war. All the bears would die, too, the cats and dogs, the spiders and rats. Perhaps a few cockroaches would survive. But a world inhabited only by a handful of roaches may not be the one God had in mind when he created Eden and placed a man and a woman in it.

Is it unthinkable that humankind could actually destroy all life on earth? Despite the recent relaxation of international tensions brought about by the apparent end of the cold war, the lack of any real world government in a highly dangerous world makes nuclear war, sooner or later, highly likely. In fact, the theory of gamesmanship makes it logically necessary. As we saw in the case of the search for the smallest particles of matter, logical necessity does not guarantee concrete reality. There is a small amount of comfort in that fact.

We will return to this question of whether the earth is likely to survive in its present state, with bears and spiders and people on it, in the last chapter. For the moment let us put down, as the leading new knowledge discovered by human beings in this century, that they can unmake their world.

The Problem of Life

The search for hidden patterns has gone on in other fields besides nuclear physics, whose methodology has been adopted in many sciences. And the triumphant fact is that atoms do exist, as do atomic nuclei, and an entire cloud of particles that have many strange and interesting qualities.

Some of these particles are misnamed, for they are not *things*, at least not in any ordinary sense of the term. In effect they are shadowy moving electrical charges, or tiny bundles of waves, or perhaps merely instantaneous solutions of partial differential equations, which come into existence and pass away in less time than it takes to blink your eye.

Nevertheless, these somethings are real, in the sense that all things are real that have real consequences. They are also very small. The world of the twentieth century has had the habit of becoming smaller, at the same time that our imaginations have become capable of encompassing a larger universe. We will return to that in a moment.

Concerning this inveterate smallness of real things, let us recall what Descartes taught us in his *Discourse on Method* of 1637. He said that to solve any problem, it is helpful to divide the question into a set, or series, of smaller problems, and solve each of them in turn. Since Descartes and the beginning of the seventeenth century, science has increasingly explored the microscopic, and now, beyond that, universes of being that are beyond the capability of any microscope to make visible. The smallest matter may appear harder to imagine than the largest, but we comfort ourselves by supposing (here is an example of unconscious anthropomorphism) that in magnitude the human being is something like halfway between the largest things we know about and the smallest.

No matter how small these tiny new worlds of discovery are supposed to be, they, too, have patterns, some of them awesomely important. The double helix of DNA is the most important of all, for it solves the most difficult problem of life.

What is that problem? Aristotle identified it more than twenty centuries ago. The problem is comprised in an exquisitely simple question: Why do cats have kittens?

As Aristotle knew, the embryo is a tiny mass of protoplasmic tissue, and it takes a sharp eye to tell the embryo of a human being from the embryo of a whale or a mouse. But a human embryo never turns into a whale or a mouse. Nature does not make that kind of mistake. How does she manage to avoid it?

Aristotle answered the question in a manner highly typical of him. There is a formal principle, he explained, which passes from the parent to the embryo and determines that the embryo will be an animal like its parent and not something else.

Formally, this is correct. DNA could rightly be called a formal principle. But so could the New York Stock Exchange index and a lot of other patterns. The central question is, What is the particular formal principle that makes a cat's offspring another cat? Aristotle, with his devilish ability to squirm out of almost any difficulty, had an answer here, too. "Catness," he said, "is that principle." The astonishing thing is that this response was satisfactory to intelligent people for more than two thousand years.

The Science of Heredity

A better answer was first developed in the nineteenth century, although the work of Gregor Mendel, the Austrian botanist-monk, did not become widely known until about 1900.

That cats do have kittens was so obvious that it had ceased to be a problem needing solution by the time Mendel was born in 1822. Although he could not pass the examination for teachers of natural science, he was a competent investigator who devoted years to studying the heredity of the garden pea plant. In so doing he discovered the principles of genetics.

The question he addressed was not why seeds of the garden pea produced more garden peas, but why different varieties of the plant, when interbred, produced hybrids in a patterned order that Mendel was the first to describe. He concluded that, apparently, each of the plant's traits was somehow controlled or determined by one of a pair of tiny entities that came to be called genes, with one of the parent plants providing a gene for each trait, as is the case in bisexual fertilization. He soon came to realize that each parent must possess a gene for every trait, but when these were combined in the offspring, only one gene for the trait remained dominant. The offspring of a pair of different plants would evince the working of simple statistical laws, which Mendel described in two spare mathematical papers and published in 1866.

Two years later he was elected abbot of his monastery. His duties thereafter occupied all of his time. It was not until long after his death in 1884 that his discoveries were rediscovered by others, and then they gave him full credit as the founder of the science of genetics.

How DNA Works

The concept of heredity was not Mendel's invention. Since earliest times it had been recognized that human beings had human offspring who usually looked like their parents. It was assumed that a simple principle was at work: for example, the child of a tall father and short mother would be of medium height. Mendel was the first to realize that heredity is much more complicated than that.

But even Mendel's experiments did not reveal the mechanism by which heredity works. A half century of feverish activity in the field of genetics would have to pass before this mechanism was understood.

The key discovery was made at Cambridge University in 1953, when two young men, the American James D. Watson (1928–   ) and the Englishman Francis H. C. Crick (1916–   ), managed to describe the structure of the DNA molecule. In so doing they not only answered Aristotle's old question but also opened the way to a new age.

A DNA molecule is a double helix consisting of two long strings coiled around one another. The strings are made up of complex nitrogen-bearing chemical compounds called nucleotides. There are four different kinds of nucleotides in DNA, depending on their bases, either adenine, guanine, cytosine, or thymine. There is a sugar portion in each nucleotide of deoxyribose.

Each nucleotide in one string is chemically connected to a corresponding nucleotide in the other string. There may be many thousands of nucleotides in one string, with as many connections to what are like mirror images in the other string of the pair.

A gene, Watson, Crick, and many colleagues discovered, is a section of a DNA molecule, that is, a substring, perhaps dozens or even thousands of nucleotides long, which determines a given trait. How does it do this? Every cell of an individual living thing contains the DNA molecule for that individual. This is the total genetic pattern for that spider or human being. When the cell divides, one of the DNA strings goes to one new cell, the other string to the other cell. Once arrived, the naked partner, shorn of its old mate, immediately goes about making a new mirror image. Out of the protoplasm of the new cell's nucleus, which consists mainly of freely floating proteins, the naked DNA string assembles all the needed elements to make a string just like itself, which is to say just like the mate that it has lost. That lost mate accomplishes the same thing in the other new cell. It too creates its own mirror image. The result is that each of the new cells has precisely the same DNA molecule that the old one possessed.

Catness is therefore a given DNA molecule, residing in the nucleus of every cell of every cat. Differences among individual cats are explained by the fact that there are subtle differences in the substrings of cat DNA. But even the widest differences between two cats are small compared to the differences between cat DNA and camel DNA, or cat DNA and human DNA. Thus a cat can never give birth to a person. Its cells will not allow it.

The DNA molecule is large enough to be visible with the aid of an electron microscope. The portions of the strings determining hair color, for example, or the makeup of the blood, can be identified. And not just identified. They can also be cut out, modified, and reinserted in the molecule.

Certain diseases are caused by faulty substrings. For example, sickle-cell anemia, a blood disease, is carried by many blacks. Theoretically, the defective gene could be removed from the blood of sufferers from this ailment, corrected, and replaced. The technology that would make this possible is still primitive. It is, however, already effective enough to cause serious concern among moralists, who react with something like horror to the idea that monsters might be created in the test tube for the presumed benefit of humankind.

Scientific genetics is a genuine new science, the fruit of twentieth-century advances built on the pioneering work of a nineteenth-century monk whose discoveries were not known in his time. It is, furthermore, a beautifully clear, clean science, with straightforward principles and concrete results. We now know how heredity works, although we are also aware of the complexity of the hereditary pattern of a given individual.

The coming together of two strings of DNA—from a father and a mother—each containing many thousands of substrings demands larger computers than we yet have to determine all the possible combinations.

Genetic science is one of the knowledge victories of our century. The potentially horrible monsters of genetic engineering are not of our century. We will return to them in the last chapter.

The Size of the Universe

How large is the universe? How large does it *seem*? The latter question was believed to have meaning two thousand years ago, when the "apparent size" of the moon, for instance, was taken to be its "real size." The sphere of the Fixed Stars was the "outer limit" of the cosmos. How far was that sphere from Earth? A thousand furlongs from Earth? A million? A million million? Only recently have we come to realize that none of those answers makes any sense at all.

For one thing, there is no sphere of the Fixed Stars. It is Earth that revolves, not the stars, although the stars do move, in different directions and at speeds that are often nearly unimaginable. For another thing, the universe is too big for us to see its "outer limit," even if it has any. It is, or it would be if it existed, too far away.

Albert Einstein believed that the universe is finite but unbounded. No line, if you extend it long enough, is straight. All lines curve in upon themselves and eventually, in theory at least, return to their point of origin. A sphere is also "finite but unbounded." There is no edge to a sphere, no "end" of it, so it is unbounded, but a sphere, for example, one that you can hold in your hand, is also obviously finite in size. God alone, perhaps, could hold the finite but unbounded universe in his hand. But that would mean that his hand was outside the universe, and this is impossible, says modern physics.

At any rate, *we* are inside, not outside, the universe, and when we observe it from our vantage point, which may or may not be somewhere near the center, it goes on as far as we can see, not just with our naked eyes but also with the largest telescopes we have ever been able to make. To sum up, the universe is very, very large.

Galaxies

How large does the universe seem to you? Go out on a clear fall night and find the great square of stars in the constellation Pegasus. From the lower right-hand corner of the square three stars trail down, like the tail of a starry kite. Near the middle of these three is a faint blur. Even with binoculars you will not be able to make out a distinct point of light, for this is not a star. It is the Great Nebula in Andromeda, the first galaxy other than our own to be recognized as such—described by Arab astronomers as early as 964 AD—and the closest galaxy to us in the vast loneliness that is the universe.

A good telescope reveals that the Andromeda nebula is a spiral dish of billions of stars. Thus, we now know, it is very like our own galaxy, the Home Galaxy, as we rather romantically call it. On that same clear night you will observe the Milky Way, which is the great spiral disk or plate of stars that whirls about the center of the Home Galaxy. That center lies in the direction of the constellation Sagittarius and is some thirty thousand light years away. One light year is the distance light travels in a year, moving at the speed of one hundred and eighty-six thousand miles a second, or about 5,878,000,000,000 miles.

The Sun, our own average-sized star, lies in one of the arms of the Home Galaxy, which extend outward from the galactic center. Like everything else in the Home Galaxy, our Sun, and therefore Earth and all of us on it, are circling about the distant galactic center at a speed, in our case, of about one hundred and fifty miles per second.

Does that seem fast? It is fast. Even so, we are so far from the center that it will take us approximately two hundred million years to go all the way around and return to where we are today. Actually, we will never return to where we are now, because the center of the galaxy and therefore the galaxy as a whole is itself moving through the universe, whirling as it moves, ever changing, ever advancing toward some unfathomable fate.

Where we are, in the outer reaches of the galaxy, it is relatively dark, and stars are few and far between. We can imagine traveling farther from the center, to a region where stars become even fewer, and then to a point—can it be imagined?—where we are at the very edge of the Home Galaxy, looking back at the central nucleus perhaps fifty thousand light years away, and, in the other direction, into the awful blackness of intergalactic space.

We might peer through that great darkness, seeking the Andromeda nebula, our nearest galactic neighbor. It would not appear much brighter than it does at home. It would still be a million light years from us. If we can imagine ourselves halfway to it, that is, halfway between the Andromeda nebula and our galaxy, then we would experience a darkness never known on Earth except, perhaps, at the bottom of a coal mine, two miles down. But even our neighbor galaxy in Andromeda is relatively close to us, as galaxies go. We are joined with it and millions of other galaxies in what can be called, again romantically, the Home Galactic Cluster. Between different clusters of galaxies the distances are a hundred or a thousand times as great as between galaxies within a cluster. Halfway between two clusters would be true darkness, leading to the awful question: Could God himself find us there?

The Smallness of Earth

How many clusters of galaxies exist in the universe? Perhaps billions. Can we find clusters of clusters? Perhaps yes. Is there any end to this awesome distancing? The question may not mean anything at all. But at least we do know that the universe is very, very, very large.

Compared to what? Compared to Earth, of course, which is therefore very, very, very small. To liken it to a mote of dust dancing in a sunbeam is to confer upon it a majesty and grandeur that it does not possess, comparatively speaking. This grand, beautiful globe on which we and five billion other human beings reside is not even as large, comparatively speaking, as an electron wandering in the solar system.

All of this we newly know, thanks to the imaginative efforts of a brilliant group of astronomers and cosmologists. A century ago, only a handful of professional astronomers had any conception of the size of the universe. Today it is common knowledge, as scientific knowledge goes.

There are some who claim our newfound realization of our diminutiveness, and of our insignificance, is depressing. Little we certainly are, comparatively speaking, but are we insignificant? Is great size the measure of great significance? Is an elephant more important than a mouse? And significant to whom? Is there any other judge besides ourselves? That being so, can we imagine anything more significant than Earth that is our home, tiny as it may be in the universal order?

The Big Bang and the Primordial Atom

Albert Einstein was present at the Mount Wilson observatory in California in 1927 when the Belgian physicist Abbé Georges Lemaître (1894–1966) first presented, to a glittering scientific audience, his theory of an expanding universe that had begun in the explosion of a "primeval atom." Einstein jumped to his feet, applauding. "This is the most beautiful and satisfactory explanation of creation to which I have ever listened," he said, and he rushed forward to shake Lemaître's hand.

The theory is supported by overwhelming evidence. The most significant, established by a horde of spectroscopic observations, is that everything we can observe is moving away from us, and is moving faster the farther away it is. The edge of observation is established, in fact, by both distance and speed; objects at very remote distances are moving away from us at speeds that seem to approach the speed of light. Any object escaping at or beyond the speed of light, if that is possible, could never be visible to us, for the only information we could have would return to us at the speed of light, and that light could never reach us.

There is much other supporting evidence as well, together with a great deal of theoretical support of various kinds, a lot of it provided by George Gamow (1904–1968), to whose wit and sense of popular style we owe the expression *The Big Bang*. Gamow wrote a number of popular works about the Big Bang Theory of the origin of the universe and did much of the basic theoretical speculation and research that supported it. The theory is now almost unassailable. Woe to any cosmologist who dares to question it.

According to the theory, some time about ten or perhaps twenty billion years ago the universe began to expand very rapidly from a highly compressed primordial state, which resulted in a significant decrease in density and temperature. The first few seconds of the expansion were critical for the development of the universe as we observe it today. The statistical dominance of matter over antimatter seems to have been established, many types of elementary particles may have been present, and certain nuclei may have been formed. The theory allows us to predict that definite amounts of hydrogen, helium, and lithium (the first three elements of the periodic table) would have been produced. Their abundance agrees well enough with what is observed today. After about a million years the universe was sufficiently cooled down for the simplest atoms to form, the nuclei collecting electrons in circling clouds. The radiation that filled the proto-universe was then free to travel, thus, in a manner, creating space. It was this radiation that was first detected in 1965 as microwave background radiation by A. Penzias and R. W. Wilson. It is held to be a remnant of the early universe.

As the universe expanded farther and farther, heavier atoms were formed. These were the elements we know, the lightest first and the heaviest last. Then came molecules and clusters of molecules, then clouds of gas, then stars, then galaxies, then clusters of galaxies. Always, however, the universe kept on expanding.

Where did this happen? Where is, or was, the primordial matter before the explosion occurred? The question is meaningless. The theory is based on two assumptions, one of them unexceptionable, the other most mysterious. It is assumed, first, that Einstein's theory of general relativity correctly describes the gravitational interaction of all matter, now, then, and forever. It would be hard to deny this fact or to assume anything else.

The second assumption, called the cosmological principle, implies that the universe has no center and no edge, so that the Big Bang origin occurred not at a particular point but rather throughout space at the same time, and is still being created. In effect, this is to say that space was created by the universe as it expanded. There never was anything outside the universe. There is nothing outside of it now.

Was there a time before the Big Bang? This question, too, is meaningless, for in the universal space-time continuum time would have been created along with space. Time, indeed, is measured by the expansion of the universe. At an earlier time the universe was smaller, at a later time, larger. Nor is it possible even to speculate about the makeup of the primordial matter before it started to expand. Whatever mode of existence it enjoyed, if it enjoyed any at all, is absolutely and permanently beyond our ken.

Will the universe ever stop expanding? There is some question about that. It depends on how much matter there is in the universe as a whole. If its mass is greater than a certain critical amount, then eventually the universe, drawn by its total gravity, will stop expanding and even begin to collapse upon itself again, like a ball on an elastic string returning to the thrower's hand. If the mass is less than the critical amount, the universe will expand forever, with every object in it moving farther and farther away from every other object, until all (for there is a definite, finite amount of matter in the universe) are indefinitely far away from every other. At some point, therefore, the universe will become totally dark at any point from which it is observed, for everything else in it will be almost infinitely far away.

The burden of the evidence so far shows much less matter in the total universe than the amount required to begin an ultimate collapse. Only about two percent of what is needed can be observed. Some astronomers, terrified of that final dissolution, continue to hope that there is a large amount of matter that has so far escaped observation. But is an ultimate collapse any less terrifying?

No living person need worry. Neither of these possible destinies will be attained for billions upon billions of years.

The theory, as I have said, is supported by overwhelming evidence. It is no longer reasonable to doubt it. It is accepted by all astrophysicists, and by all other scientists who know enough to understand it. And yet it is very troubling, is it not?

It is hardly permissible to say even that. But there is something somehow wrong, somehow artificial, about this theory. How can you avoid asking about the time "before" the Big Bang? How can you not wonder "where" it occurred, and, much more important, why? The Big Bang, if it was an "event," must have had a cause. What event that we know of has ever not had a cause? But if it did have a cause, that cause must have preceded it. In time? Not in time? Either way we are faced with dilemmas of all kinds, all of them unacceptable to our poor, overworked, mortal minds.

Heisenberg's Uncertainty Principle

Einstein jumped for joy at Lemaître's original, fairly primitive version of the theory. For a long time he had felt himself isolated from his peers. He did not like what they were discovering, or thought they were discovering.

Quantum mechanics, the new system of universal mechanics that he had helped to create, in some ultimate sense is based upon chance. The quantum mechanist, unlike his Newtonian forebear, finds himself required to accept a fundamental element of unpredictability at the center of things. The German physicist Werner Heisenberg (1901–1976) was the first to describe this basic Uncertainty Principle, which bears his name. The Heisenberg Principle holds that both the position and the velocity of an object—any object—cannot be measured exactly at the same time. This inability results not from defects in our measuring instruments, which in any case are never absolutely precise, but from the nature of things, from matter itself.

Only for very small masses, like atoms and elementary particles, is the uncertainty significant. Newton's mechanics still apply to the world of large things, like people or planets. For a very small thing, the attempt at measurement, of, say, the velocity of an electron, will push the thing about so that its position cannot be measured, even in theory. The uncertainty is found in other pairs of conjugate observables, most notably energy and time. If you try to measure exactly the amount of energy radiated by an unstable nucleus, for instance, then there will be uncertainty about the lifetime of the unstable system as it makes a transition to a more stable state.

His uncertainty principle did not trouble Heisenberg, but it disturbed Einstein greatly. He was wont to say that "God is subtle but he is not malicious," as though the existence of a fundamental unknowability in the nature of things had to mean any such thing. Einstein spent the last years of his life struggling vainly to disprove Heisenberg. His failure saddened his friends. One of them, the physicist Max Born, said: "Many of us regard this as a tragedy, both for him, as he gropes his way in loneliness, and for us, who miss our leader and standard-bearer."

I wonder why Einstein was less discomfited by the Big Bang than by the uncertainty principle. Neither, to my mind, implies that God is malicious. Unless, as I sometimes think, the primordial explosion that brought atoms, galaxies, and us into existence is a kind of joke. Are we human beings merely a waste product of some giant's inconceivably large fireworks display? And when the gigantic oohs and aahs die away, and the audience departs, will we, and everything we know about, simply dissipate in the cold vastness of some other being's universe?

What is really at stake here is not theology but the fundamental, underlying assumption of all science. We have had reason to mention Thales' original hypothesis more than once, namely, that the external universe is conformed to the internal mind and imagination, and the world is therefore knowable by the human intellect. There are so many reasons to believe that theory to be correct, from the flash of the atomic bomb over Hiroshima to the creations of genetic engineering, that to doubt it seems likely to drive us mad. But the Big Bang theory makes me wonder about our ability to understand the very heart of things. We can describe the event in beautiful mathematical detail, but can we understand it? Does it make any sense? And if not, does the universe, at bottom, make sense either?

Uncertainties of Knowledge

The Heisenberg Uncertainty Principle revealed a disturbing fact about human knowledge, or, rather, the human effort to know. The principle only became apparent to quantum physicists when they began, in the 1920s, to investigate the interior of the atom and its nucleus. That microcosmic world is exceedingly small, and the things within it—electrons and other particles—are smaller still. As the investigations proceeded, it began to be evident that no attempt to know accurately and completely how that world worked could succeed.

In a sense, it was like trying to investigate the works of a fine Swiss watch with the end of your thumb. No one's thumb is small enough, or sufficiently delicate, to avoid making a jumble of the parts of the watch. Besides, your thumb gets in the way. It comes between the watch and your eyes. It is impossible to see what you are doing, even if your thumb is capable of doing anything at all that is not destructive of the watch.

The situation was even worse than that, as Heisenberg and his colleagues discovered. The mathematics showed that the uncertainty was not merely accidental, arising from the great disparity in size between the interior parts of an atom and any instrument, no matter how small, for investigating them. The uncertainty was imbedded in nature itself. And it was always there, inescapable. It could be described in a formula, which declared that the product of the uncertainties of position and velocity, for example, or of a position and momentum, was always greater than a very small physical quantity.

In the larger world in which we live, the macrocosm, the smallness of this tiny physical quantity meant that the uncertainty was insignificant. Not only can it not be detected by any instrument, but it makes no difference at all, of a practical sort. Although the Heisenberg Uncertainty Principle guarantees that none of our calculations will ever be exactly right, we can still guide a satellite through a hundred-million mile orbit with confidence that it will not miss its final destination. It may not hit the destination exactly in the center, in the bull's-eye, as it were, but it will come close enough.

Nevertheless, it is disturbing to think that there is any inherent inaccuracy at all. We would like to believe that when we have done the best we can do, and made our calculations as accurate as humanly possible, the result will be entirely predictable. According to the Heisenberg principle, this can never be so. The very attempt to know with absolute precision any physical fact is essentially and fundamentally intrusive. Always, in every situation in which we attempt to know, our thumb gets in the way.

As the truth of the uncertainty principle began to be accepted, first by quantum physicists, then by other physicists and scientists generally, and finally by the public, more deeply disturbing thoughts came into play. Knowledge, it began to be realized, is often more or less intrusive. Numerous examples come to mind.

We can learn much about animal anatomy by conducting dissections. Vivisections are even more informative, for when we open the animal's chest, the heart, for instance, may be observed still beating, even if the animal soon dies and the heart stops. But this procedure is obviously intrusive. Knowledge is gained, but the animal is destroyed.

Performing vivisections upon human beings is forbidden by custom and law, although Hitler's doctors performed such experiments at Dachau and Auschwitz. We have to be content with dissecting the bodies of deceased subjects. Less knowledge is obtained, even though the procedure is still intrusive, for it destroys the body, even if to begin with it was already dead.

Similar destructive intrusiveness is apparent in experiments with plants, at all levels down to the cellular and beyond. The lower the level, the greater the intrusion. The fine point of a laboratory instrument finally becomes as much of an interference as our thumb. There comes a time when we can no longer see, and therefore no longer understand, what we are trying to discover.

Let us concede that the principle applies throughout the natural world, from elephants to cellular nuclei, from galaxies to particles. What about that other world which we attempt to investigate, the human world, man's soul (psychology) and his society (sociology and economics and political science)?

Upon reflection, it becomes clear that similar uncertainties obtain in these areas as well. Any attempt to investigate the interior makeup and workings of a person's mind is disturbed and perhaps rendered vain by the mind itself, which cannot view such intrusions as benign. The consequent suspicion distorts the findings. And there appears to be no way to examine human groups with absolute objectivity. Distortions and disturbances are always inserted by the investigator, who, however hard he tries, cannot remove himself entirely from the picture.

Such distortions and uncertainties in sciences like sociology and economics can be controlled by an interesting and typical twentieth-century device. Given a group of human beings and a question you want to ask them or ask about them, be certain at the outset that there are enough of them so that the inevitable uncertainties will cancel out. The science of statistics guides us in this effort. It tells us, as surely as such a science can, how many persons to include in the sample in order to obtain results of such and such a degree of accuracy. The knowledge thus obtained is dependable within the stated limits. It is only important to remember that it is not exact. It does not hit the bull's-eye, but neither does it miss its destination.

That is comforting enough, from many practical points of view. But it is exceedingly discomforting in another sense. As analogies to quantum mechanical uncertainty were discovered in many other fields, inevitable but disquieting questions began to be asked about knowledge itself. Is there any area in which it can be counted on to be absolutely certain and correct? Or is all knowledge, without exception, tainted with uncertainties, reduced to dependence on statistical methods and guarantees, and forced to accept the possibility that the bull's-eye always may be missed?

Here is one of the most troubling questions with which our uncertain century has had to deal. Even in mathematics itself, for centuries the very citadel of certainty, a proof developed in the early 1930s by the Austrian mathematician Kurt Gödel (1906–1978) showed that within any logical system, no matter how rigidly structured, there are always questions that cannot be answered with certainty, contradictions that may be discovered, and errors that may lurk. Thus as the century comes to a close, the verdict is clear: knowledge never can be certain. It is always intrusive. No matter how hard we try, our very effort to know fully and completely, like our thumb, gets in the way.

What does this mean for the progress of knowledge? Has it ended in our time? Is humankind's great adventure over?

It seems not. In the first place, statistical methods ensure that our knowledge, except perhaps in the microcosm where the effort to know is radically intrusive, can generally be as accurate as desired, which means as accurate as needed for any particular task, like sending a satellite to Jupiter. Knowledge thus takes on the character of the integral and differential calculus that Newton invented, and with which he replaced the plane geometry of Euclid, which was inadequate to describe "the system of the world." No differential equation can ever be solved with perfect exactitude, but it is accepted that this does not matter, for it can always, or nearly always, be solved well enough.

Second, the discovery that man's knowledge is not, *and never has been*, perfectly accurate has had a humbling and perhaps a calming effect upon the soul of modern man. The nineteenth century, as we have observed, was the last to believe that the world, as a whole as well as in its parts, could ever be perfectly known. We realize now that this is, and always was, impossible. We know within limits, not absolutely, even if the limits can usually be adjusted to satisfy our needs.

Curiously, from this new level of uncertainty even greater goals emerge and appear to be attainable. Even if we cannot know the world with utmost precision, we can still control it. Even our inherently defective knowledge seems to work as powerfully as ever. In short, we may never know precisely how high is the highest mountain, but we continue to be certain that we can get to the top nevertheless.

One Giant Step

Neil Armstrong, Edwin Aldrin, and Michael Collins were three brave young men who set out in *Apollo XI* on July 16, 1969, from Cape Canaveral to go to the moon. They arrived four days later, after an uneventful journey of some quarter of a million miles. Leaving Collins behind in the larger ship, Armstrong and Aldrin descended to the moon's surface in the lunar module *Eagle*. The astronauts landed on the edge of the Sea of Tranquility. Armstrong was the first human being to set foot on an extraterrestrial body."That's one small step for a man," he said over a worldwide radio hookup, but "one giant step for mankind." Aldrin followed him down the steps, and the two men spent a day and a night on the moon.

In North America, the night was clear, the moon bright and nearly full. I did not feel lonely, for I was in the middle of a thriving, throbbing American city. But I thought of how lonely they must feel. Armstrong and Aldrin, in their clumsy space suits, alone on an orb on which not a single other living thing existed. Up above them Collins in *Apollo* circled. Would they be able to rejoin him in order to return home? All around them was the blackness of interplanetary space. (To be sure, this blackness cannot be compared to the greater blackness of interstellar space, where there is no sun to light the sky, or to the even blacker blackness of intergalactic space, where no stars may be seen.)

All went well on this mission. Armstrong and Aldrin regained the mother ship. *Apollo XI* with its precious cargo of brave men and moonrocks splashed down into the Pacific on July 24. But for a moment the essential isolation of earth was conceivable.

We know now—it is another important piece of knowledge we have learned in the twentieth century—that we are all alone in the solar system.

There is no other life, to say nothing of intelligent life. We have to wonder now whether we are alone in the Home Galaxy, alone in the universe. Ours may be the only living planet that ever has existed or ever will. There is no mother ship circling above us in the firmament, to which we can return, or which can possibly send help if we need it. There may simply be no other mind, anywhere, that is more powerful than ours and capable of guiding us on our journey. Everything that we are and will be may depend on us.

Visionaries of our time have sought a single image that might express all the beauty and heartbreak of this new knowledge of our world's loneliness in space. A photograph of earth, taken by the first astronauts, shows the globe in all its splendor, with its deep blue seas, green-brown continents, and floating white clouds. The image that, for me, best expresses the photo's meaning is that of a spaceship, immense as compared to *Apollo XI*, but tiny in the vastness of the universe. Photos of the dark side of earth, which reveal its thousands of clusters of light where cities lie, reinforce the image of a ship, with lighted portholes, sailing on its way.

Spaceship Earth, sailing bravely on through the emptiness of the universe, carrying its burden of human beings and their wards, the animals and plants and other living things, on a journey to a destiny that none understands. And to a destiny that may never be reached, for included in the cargo are enough nuclear weapons to destroy it all, with no way to control their use.

Green Rebellion

Awareness of the loneliness and fragility of Spaceship Earth has resulted, among other things, in the emergence of a new international movement, the environmentalists, or Greens. The platform of this movement, which has spawned political parties in several countries, states: environmentalists support everything that is good for the earth, and are against everything that is bad. Nowadays, the movement is against more than it is for, because it is known that the earth is in danger from other perils beside man's carelessness with his most potent weapons.

Environmentalism (or ecology), a science as well as a political and moral movement, is concerned with the totality of our knowledge about the world on which, and in some sense in which, we live. At the present time, we seem to be discovering this world is surprisingly fragile.

For millennia human beings have treated the earth, the oceans, the atmosphere as essentially indestructible. We have learned, in this fecund last century of knowledge growth, that view is wrong. It may not be significantly true, as some environmentalists maintain, that no action of any human being is without environmental consequences. But it is certainly true that some of our actions have had in the past, and will have in the future, major consequences. Even if we are not fated to destroy our spaceship home, we are changing it—and not often for the better.

In 1969 Thor Heyerdahl (1914–   ) sailed across the Atlantic in his Egyptian reed boat *Ra*. He reported then garbage floating everywhere in the sea. He wondered whether the entire oceans were thus polluted by the throwaways and detritus of man. All the oceans of earth are connected and constitute a single ecosystem. What is discarded at one place may poison waters almost anywhere else on the globe. Already numerous fisheries have been destroyed or much reduced, many beaches made unusable by human beings. The vast, beautiful ocean, beloved and feared by man for centuries, may cease to be the living organism that has existed for more than three billion years.

The air above our heads is also a single ecosystem. If possible, it is even more fragile than the oceans. What we do not throw into the sea, we burn in the air. But burning does not destroy anything. Fire merely converts it into something else. Thus, every day, the air is filled with the smoke and ash and poisonous gases of our throwaways. Already the atmosphere has become poisonous to living things—trees and other plants—in many places on the globe. We do not know how dangerous it is for us to breathe this poisoned air. Acid rain created by the burning of fossil fuels in one part of the world descends a few days later on another part, killing its trees, poisoning its lakes, devastating its beauty and fruitfulness. Every time we step on our car's accelerator we spew poisons into the atmosphere that may worsen the lives of children (if they do not kill them) a hundred or a thousand miles away. And every air conditioner and refrigerator on earth releases gases that eat away at the ozone layer, high above our heads, which protects us from deadly solar rays.

The Terrestrial Greenhouse

Perhaps worst of all, the result of our steady, relentless burning, especially of fossil fuels, is the continuous emission into the atmosphere of carbon dioxide, an odorless gas that is "breathed" by green plants. There are not enough plants left on earth to convert all this carbon dioxide into the waste product of their breathing—namely, that precious gas, oxygen, which *we* inhale—and so the amount of carbon dioxide in the atmosphere continually increases.

Carbon dioxide has an interesting and, for us, important property. It traps sunlight and the sun's heat near the earth's surface. The sun's rays pass through the atmosphere on the way down to the surface, but some of the radiation does not bounce up and out of the atmosphere again. It remains beneath the layer of carbon dioxide. To this phenomenon, called the greenhouse effect, we owe the fact that the earth is a temperate world.

Mars and Venus, our two closest planetary neighbors, are both near the earth in size. But neither supports life. The atmosphere of Mars is too thin and contains too little carbon dioxide to trap the sun's warmth. If ever there was life on Mars, it froze to death many eons ago. The atmosphere of Venus, on the contrary, has too much carbon dioxide. A great part of the sunlight that falls upon the planet is trapped beneath the clouds of gas, and the surface temperature at noon rises to thousands of degrees. It is assumed, without definitive evidence, that nothing can live there. The proportion of carbon dioxide in the earth's atmosphere is just right for comfortable living. This is a comforting fact.

It may not be the fact for very long in the future. The burning of fossil fuels has steadily increased for more than a century, and with it the amount of carbon dioxide in the atmosphere. The additional carbon dioxide may already have upset the age-old balance that has made our world a paradise. Already, the mean world temperature seems to be rising, by ever so little. It may rise more quickly over the next few decades, perhaps a century. If it does, the Southeast and Middle West of the United States could turn into a desert. Canada could become what the Midwest used to be, the world's breadbasket. The warming may be inexorable. There may be no way to stop it, even if we were to end all burning of fossil fuels today, though this is not possible. The desert may advance northward steadily, if slowly, encroaching upon fertile lands a little more each year.

And all the time the world's population of human beings increases, along with their need to burn more and more fossil fuels to make their lives fruitful, comfortable, and productive.*

The solid earth, too, is not indestructible. It may be poisoned and altered for the worse. We may try to bury our throwaways, our nuclear wastes, our poisonous chemicals, but the horrors reemerge, like an angry fist thrust upward out of a grave. Land becomes uninhabitable, water undrinkable, the soil is covered by concrete and asphalt, and new dust bowls grow, stealing the lifegiving bounty that once supported a smaller population.

At best, our new knowledge of these things forces us to trim our desires and narrow our dreams. We hate this knowledge and would like to deny

---

*Recent scientific studies have called some of the most somber predictions about the imminence of global warming in question. Reputable scientists say that the earth does not seem to be warming that quickly, and that no emergency exists as yet. Eventually, however, the greenhouse effect must produce a significant change in average world temperature.

it. We also know it is our only hope for long-term survival. While some do not appreciate our environmentalists, we are aware that we depend on them for the continued success of Spaceship Earth.

Digital Computers and Knowledge

Let me try to talk about computers in a new way that may make clear how the twentieth century's greatest invention fits naturally into the history of the progress of knowledge.

An important distinction should be understood at the outset: the distinction between analog computers and digital computers. Roughly, it is analogous to the distinction between measuring and counting.

An analog computer is a measuring device that measures (responds to) a continuously changing input. A thermometer is a simple analog computer. A car speedometer is more complicated. Its output device, a needle that moves up and down on a scale, responds to, that is, measures, continuous changes in the voltage output of a generator connected to the drive shaft. Even more complicated analog computers coordinate a number of different changing inputs, for example, temperature, fluid flow, and pressure. In this case the computer could be controlling processes in a chemical plant.

The mathematical tool used to solve continuous changes of input to a system is a differential equation. Analog computers are machines, some of them very complicated and some of them surprisingly simple, like a common window thermometer, that are designed to solve sets of differential equations.

The human brain is probably an analog computer. Or it is like one. The senses perceive and measure continuously changing data from the outside world, and the brain processes the concurrent signals and gives directions to the muscles. The brain can solve a large number of differential equations concurrently, in "real time," that is, as fast as the situation itself is changing. No analog computer constructed by man has so far come close to being able to handle as many different kinds of input all at the same time as the human brain.

All analog computers made by man have one serious defect: they do not measure accurately enough. The mix in the chemical plant is changing rapidly in several different ways: it is getting hotter or colder; the pressure is increasing or decreasing; the flow is faster or slower. All of these changes will affect the final product, and each calls for the computer to make subtle adjustments in the process. The devices used to measure the changes are therefore crucial. They must record the changes very rapidly, and transmit the continuously changing information to the central processor. A very slight inaccuracy in measurement will obviously result in inaccurate results down the line.

The difficulty does not lie in the inherent ability of measuring devices to measure accurately. The difficulty comes from the fact that the device records the continuous changes continuously. As a result there is always a very small ambiguity in its readings. At what precise instant did it record the temperature as 100°? Was that the same instant that another device recorded the pressure as 1,000 lbs./sq.in.? And so forth and so on. And when very slight inaccuracies are amplified, as they must be, the result can be errors of several parts per thousand, which is typical in even the best analog process controllers.

A digital computer has no such defect. It is a machine for calculating numbers, not measuring phenomena. An analog signal has continuously valid interpretations from the smallest to the largest value that is received. A digital signal has only a discrete number of valid interpretations. Usually, the number of valid interpretations is two: zero or one, off or on, black or white. The digital signal is therefore always clear, never ambiguous; as a result, calculations can be arranged to deliver exactly correct results.

Digital computers employ the binary number system to process information, although their outputs may be in the decimal system, or in words, or in pictures, or in sounds—whatever you wish. In the binary system there are only two digits, 1 and 0. The number zero is denoted 0. One is 1. Two is 10. Three is 11. Four is 100 (that is, two squared, or 10^{10}). Five is 101. Eight is 1000. Sixteen is 10000. And so forth and so on.

The numerals become large very quickly. Multiplication of even quite small numbers (in the decimal system) involves enormous strings of digits (in the binary system). But this does not matter at all, since the digital computer works so fast. A hand-held calculator costing ten dollars can compute the result of multiplying two three-digit numbers (in the decimal system) and deliver the answer in the decimal system in much less than a second. As you watch the little blinking lights, there seems no delay whatsoever between your inputting the last digit of the problem and the calculator's output of the result.

Because binary system numerals are much longer than digital system numerals, the machine is required to perform a very large number of different operations to come up with your answer, probably thousands in the example cited. But even such a small, cheap calculator is capable of performing fifty thousand or more operations per second. Supercomputers are capable of performing a billion or even a trillion operations per second. Obviously, your small calculation does not trouble any of them.

Nevertheless, there is a problem. We have said that the analog computer measures, the digital computer counts. What does counting have to do with measuring? And if the analog device has difficulty measuring a continuously changing natural phenomenon, how does it help apparently to reduce the freedom of the digital signal to the point where it can only give one of two results?

The problem is a very old one. It was this question that so worried the ancient Greek mathematicians, when they tried to find common, numerical, units between the commensurable and the incommensurable, that they gave up mathematics altogether. It was also the problem that Descartes wrongly thought he had solved when he invented analytical geometry, and was thenceforth able to give precise number names to physical things, places, and relationships. Newton, as we have seen, knew that Descartes had not solved the hardest part of the problem, that is, his analytical geometry was no help in dealing with moving things and changing relationships. Newton invented the differential and integral calculus to deal with such changes, and the result was a mathematical system of the world, as he knew it, that worked with astonishing accuracy.

Newton, in developing the calculus, made good use of the principle that Descartes had laid down fifty years before: when a problem seems too big and complicated, break it down into small problems, and solve each of them. This is what the calculus does. It breaks down a change or movement into a very large number of steps, and then in effect climbs the steps, each of them very little, one at a time. The more steps a curve is broken down into, the closer the line joining the steps is to the curve, as can be seen here.

If you can imagine the number of steps approaching (but of course never reaching) infinity, then the stepped line can be imagined as approaching the actual, continuous curve as closely as you please. Thus the solution of an integration or of a differential equation is *never absolutely accurate*, but it can always be made *as accurate as you please*, which comes down to its being at least as accurate as the most accurate of all the other variables in the problem.

This is an important mathematical idea that is often not understood by nonmathematicians. In dealing with the physical world, mathematics gives up the absolute precision that it enjoys in pure mathematical spaces, in elementary geometrical proofs, for example, where circles are absolutely circular, lines absolutely straight, and so forth. Reality is always slightly fuzzy. Rather, our measurements of it are never perfectly precise, and it is our measurements, expressed as numbers, with which the mathematician deals.

The beauty of calculus is that its own precision can be adjusted, according to the principle enunciated above, to conform to the degree of precision of the measurements. If these are very rough, the calculations can be very rough, that is, the size of the steps within the curve can be relatively large, with no overall loss of accuracy in solving the problem. If the measurements become more accurate, the calculations can be adjusted, by increasing the number of (smaller) steps, so that again nothing is lost.

An example is the breaking down of a musical signal into a series of digital inputs that are stored on a disk and then converted back into sound by a compact disc player, amplifier, and pair of speakers.

The breakdown of the sound consists of a series of numerical measurements, made very close together in time, of the amplitude of the signal emitted by the original source, a violin or a pair of human vocal chords. The closer the measurements are to one another, that is, by analogy, the smaller and closer the steps, the more accurate is the picture that is being made of the continuously changing musical signal.

Theoretically, the digital version of the signal can be made as accurate as you please, which, with expensive equipment, can be very accurate indeed. Practically, it need not be any more accurate than the *least accurate of the elements* in the system, for example, the amplifier or the speakers. There is no point to inputting a nearly perfect signal that will be output on junk speakers.

The ability to adjust its accuracy is the reason why Newton's calculus works so well in the macrocosm. The tiny inherent inaccuracy of calculus, which is never perfectly accurate, causes difficulties when you are dealing with the tiny world of atoms, nuclei, and nuclear particles. There, solutions may be wide of the mark.

Turing Machines

The digital computer is like calculus. It can break down a problem into pieces as small as you desire; that is, it can convert a continuous signal of any kind into as many discrete inputs as are wanted, each of which can be treated by the computer with absolute precision because each is either zero or one, with no ambiguity. But are there inherent inaccuracies in such an approach to problem solving, as there are in the case of the calculus when it is applied to the microcosm?

A theoretical answer to this question was given by the English mathematician Alan Turing (1912–1954) when he was still a student. Born in London, Turing was studying mathematical logic at King's College,

Cambridge, when he wrote, in 1935, a paper "On Computable Numbers" that is considered to be the most brilliant contribution of this most brilliant of computer scientists in the twentieth century.

Published in 1937, the paper showed that a universal machine, now called a Turing machine, could be designed to perform the functions and do the work of any device designed for problem-solving. This concept of a universal machine underlay the development of digital computers in subsequent decades.

More important, Turing's paper showed that a digital computer could theoretically be designed to do the work of *any* analog computer. Another way to make the point: the paper proved that a Turing machine (a digital computer) could be designed that would be indistinguishable *in its results* from a human mind (an analog computer). Thus Turing, who was the founder of modern digital computing, was also the founder of what is today called artificial intelligence.

A theoretical design is one thing. Building such a machine is another. Despite Turing's ingenious theoretical proof, the majority of computer scientists do not believe that a machine in actuality will ever perform as a human being: that is, think, respond emotively to sensory inputs, make intuitive decisions that take into account variables not apparent on the surface, develop a sense of the history of a situation or relationship. I think Turing's challenge will surely not be met, if it ever is, before the next century. Therefore I will deal with it in the last chapter.

Digital computers, which are all Turing machines, first came into use around the middle of this century. As late as 1960 they were still large, awkward, slow, and expensive. The second-generation computers of the 1960s, which employed transistors instead of vacuum tubes, began the computer revolution that has ushered in a new world for almost everyone alive today.

Third-generation computers of the 1970s began the use of integrated circuits which combined thousands of transistors and other devices on a single chip, the so-called computer on a chip that made possible microcomputers and "intelligent" terminals.

Fourth-generation computers of the 1980s benefited from spectacular reductions in the size and increases in the density of chips, so that a "very large scale integrated" (VLSI) circuit could hold millions of parts on a chip less than a quarter of an inch square. The new technology made possible inexpensive but powerful "personal" computers (PCs), on one hand, and enormously powerful "supercomputers," on the other, that were capable, by the early 1990s, of performing a trillion operations per second.

A fifth generation of computers promised further remarkable progress toward artificial intelligence by employing so-called parallel processing, that is, the simultaneous execution of several separate operations: memory, logic, control, and so forth. The human brain is considered to operate in a similar fashion instead of serially, which is the way even the fastest fourth-generation computers were still operating at the end of the 1980s.

Technological Dependence

Today, less than a half century after the development of the first working machines, the computer has so completely permeated the life of persons in all the advanced countries of the world that, literally, we could not live without it. Experts say the greatest peril of a nuclear war would be the destruction of the electric power supply of the computer network, with the result that all communications and information systems would break down. Not only would it be impossible to make a telephone call or receive a radio or television signal, but money would also cease to exist, except for the cash you happened to have in your pocket or under your mattress. Most money movement today is in the form of electronic funds transfers (EFTs), and practically all financial records are stored in computer memories and not on paper.

Imagine the difficulties if everyone, not just you, had no more checking or savings accounts, no more investments, no more accounts payable. Systems for manufacturing, distributing, and accounting for all goods and most services would cease to operate, and we would be hurled in an instant back into the dark ages. Except that our situation would be even worse than that of the poorest European peasant of, say, the middle of the seventh century AD, for unlike him we would have no experience of how to live such a life, and therefore most of us would die.

Such dependence on a technology, even one so apparently benign and pervasive as the digital computer, is typical of the twentieth century. It would be easy to make a long list of marvels that have brightened, entertained, enriched, and comforted mankind during the last hundred years. Most of them run either on gasoline or on electricity. But a disturbance in the supply of new cars, refrigerators, and televisions, even if some electric power and gasoline remained available, would mean that we would shortly have to do without such machines, for we no longer know how to repair them. We Americans used to be a nation of handymen and handywomen. We have become a nation of passive recipients of services, most of them provided by complex machines whose operation we do not understand and that few are trained to repair.

Everyone over fifty can remember a time when dependence on technology had not yet become the rule. Today, there are still a few odd characters who insist on continuing to live a subsistence life, which involves knowing how every machine they use works, and how to fix it, especially if parts are hard to find. But the skills these persons retain do not seem valuable now. They may never be valuable again. Sometime around 1960 or 1970 we may have taken a fateful step, passing from an age that stretches back into the mists of the past in which most human beings could take care of themselves in emergencies to one in which only a few can do so.

Is this dangerous? Does it mean we have to fear the future? It is hard to say. The resources of all the advanced nations are being devoted to the expansion of technological realms, to making machines that are easier and easier to use and cheap enough so that almost everyone can afford to buy and employ them. We have put our lives in the hands of the technocrats, for very good reasons: they make life easier than it ever was before in human history. Will they ultimately fail us? No one knows. But I think probably not.

Triumphs of Medicine

One of the most brilliant knowledge advances of the twentieth century— as great as the computer, as great as the abolition of "natural" racial inferiority and the growing awareness of Spaceship Earth—has been the conquest of infectious disease. Unfortunately, this conquest has been seen, in recent years, to have a tragic aftermath.

At the beginning of the century and even up to about 1950, infectious disease of children, like diphtheria and whooping cough, were still fearsome killers. Then, within only a few years, physicians were failing to recognize the diseases when they appeared. They were so rare.

Typhus and typhoid fever met the same fate. Polio, that dreaded crippler of children and young adults, and tuberculosis, that destroyer of youthful genius, were understood and defeated. Pneumonia, except for the stubborn "hospital pneumonia" which thrives in the heart of the enemy's camp, became curable. About the only infectious disease that remains highly resistant to medical attack is the common cold. But the common cold, while annoying and unpleasant, is seldom a killer.

One of the most dramatic medical victories of our times was the conquest of smallpox. For centuries this terrible disease killed millions and made hideous the faces of many millions more. A vaccine discovered in the eighteenth century decreased its virulence, but as recently as 1967 two million persons, worldwide, died of the disease in a single year.

The World Health Organization decided to try to eradicate the disease when a vaccine against all forms of clinical smallpox became readily available in the 1960s. The WHO project, immense in cost and scale, involved tracking down every contact of every infected person. By vaccinating them in time, WHO might stop the spread of infection. By 1977, only ten years after the project began, no new cases were reported. None was reported in 1978, 1979, or 1980, with the exception of two cases whose source was a laboratory virus. In 1980 the disease was declared eradicated. In effect, it had been made extinct in the natural environment. For this disease, apparently dead and gone, there are no mourners.

Human beings suffer from other ills beside infections, which can be treated with antibiotics, and infectious diseases, most of which can be prevented by vaccines. One result of the medical triumphs of the century has been a rapid increase in the average life expectancy. But people must die of something; humankind has not yet attained immortality. If people do not die now of tuberculosis, they will die later of heart disease or cancer. As a result, heart disease and cancer have become the new scourges of human life.

Scourges they are. But there is a difference between dying at twenty-five of polio, pneumonia, or TB and dying at seventy-five of a heart attack, stroke, or cancer. Those fifty years are a gift to us from the scientific researchers of our century.

Not only disease has been the subject of medical research and, in some cases, remarkable victories. If the first revolution in biotechnology brought vaccines, antibiotics, new drugs, the second has brought wonders like artificial hips, pacemakers, kidney and heart transplants, and the like. Here, too, remarkable results have been achieved.

If a child loses an arm or hand, that is bad enough. It is better if, as is true today, he or she can obtain a prosthesis that is comfortable to wear and really works, that is, one that does most of the things that the original arm or hand could do.

Millions of men and women walk around with pacemakers imbedded in their chests to control disturbances of heart rhythm. Their hearts beat regularly for years, and they can live normal lives.

Thousands of kidney dialysis machines clean the blood of patients with kidney disease. They can live this way, often for years, although with discomfort and inconvenience. Without the machines they would die. A successful kidney transplant may solve the problem completely, and perhaps permanently.

The body, in short, is a machine as well as a living organism. It is foolish to be sentimental about it, and to suffer as a result. The knee is a hinge. The hip is a ball and socket joint made out of bone. Repair the hinge, replace the ball or the socket with a steel or plastic part, and walking and running become possible again.

This is not magic. It is physics. It is biotechnology.

Drug Cultures

Drugs are thousands of years old. Neolithic, perhaps even paleolithic shamans and medicine men and women knew the curative powers of many plants. The ability of alcohol, in wine, beer, and stronger liquors, to make life seem better than it really is has been recognized at least since the second millennium BC. Various narcotics have been used for centuries to produce the same results. Thus drugs are not an invention of the twentieth century. Neither do we perceive as new the use of chemicals to bring about the cure of disease or the amelioration of symptoms.

Nevertheless, almost all drugs and medicines used today have been discovered not just in this century but in the last forty years, since the end of the 1939–1945 war. In several ways the most important was the drug whose accidental discovery inaugurated the antibiotic era: penicillin.

Alexander Fleming (1881–1955) was born in Scotland. After taking his medical degree in 1906 he began to conduct research on antibacterial substances that might be nontoxic to human tissues. It was known that bacteria caused many infections. It was also known that bacteria could be killed. But the poisons used to kill them, like carbolic acid, proved too toxic and threatened the lives of patients on whom they were used.

In 1928, while working with cultures of *Staphylococcus aureus*, the pus-producing bacterium, Fleming noticed a circle free of bacteria around a mold growth (*Penicillium notatum*) that had contaminated one of his slides. The mold grows on old bread, and a crumb may have fallen, unnoticed, onto his culture. Excited, Fleming began to isolate the substance. In so doing he found something in the mold that would kill bacteria even when diluted eight hundred times. He named it penicillin. Other researchers concentrated the antibacterial substance, and that led to commercial production of the drug.

Among the bacteria sensitive to penicillin are those that cause throat infections, pneumonia, spinal meningitis, diphtheria, syphilis, and gonorrhea. The drug is not effective against all bacteria, but researchers, inspired by Fleming's example, soon helped to create an industry that invests millions today in order to discover new and ever more specific drugs, from which it gains even more millions in profits.

Penicillin turned out, as Fleming had hoped, to be nontoxic to most persons, although a few are allergic to it. Many of the other drugs that have contributed to the medical marvels of our era have serious side effects, and patients have to weigh the advantages of taking a drug against the suffering it may inadvertently cause. When the disease is otherwise terminal cancer, for example, the choice is easy enough: take the drug and hope to conquer the cancer. The choice is more difficult in many cases, where the side effects of the drug may seem only slightly preferable to the disease itself.

According to one theory, all drugs have side effects of some kind, and a class of patients has grown up that refuses to take any drugs whatsoever, except perhaps in extremis, for a dreaded cancer or for unbearable pain. A larger group rushes to use any drug that they think might possibly help them. Thus there has come into existence a drug culture, defined by the need to take drugs whenever life is painful or unpleasant. Some of these drugs are inherently addictive, but drug taking is itself addictive. This is the dark reverse side of Fleming's great, life-giving discovery.*

The AIDS Challenge

An important group of infectious diseases is transmitted by sexual contact. They can often be controlled by antibiotics, although resistant strains are hard to cure. Worldwide, deaths from venereal diseases, even syphilis, seemed until recently to be decreasing, and the problem looked to be under control.

Then, in 1979, an entirely new disease was diagnosed for the first time. Acquired immune deficiency syndrome (AIDS) affects the immune system, making it less able to protect the body against diseases that healthy people fight off or tolerate.

AIDS is caused by a virus that infects the T-lymphocytes, an important component of the immune system. Early symptoms include weight loss, fever, fatigue, and enlargement of the lymph glands. As the immune system deteriorates, persons with AIDS develop chronic infections from organisms that are tolerated by persons not so affected. These chronic infections can be treated by antibiotics and other drugs, but eventually the AIDS victim contracts either one of several types of cancer or an infection that does not respond to treatment. And then he or she dies.

A smart virus would not kill its host. It would work out a permanent relationship so that it, too, could survive. The AIDS virus always kills. So far, no victim has been known to be cured, although death comes to victims either slower or faster for unknown reasons. It is the certainty of death that makes the disease so frightful. A diagnosis of AIDS is a sure death sentence. There is, as yet, no escape.

The AIDS virus is a mutation. Apparently it did not exist a few years ago. Some researchers suspect that the mutation, which probably took place during the 1970s, may have had something to do with the eradication of smallpox. Did the smallpox virus, which may have mutated from

---

*For more on the drug culture of today and tomorrow, see Chapter 15.

another virus several hundred years ago, change again when it saw itself threatened? So far the hypothesis has not been confirmed. It is a chilling thought even so.

AIDS is normally a sexually transmitted disease. A few innocent victims have been infected by receiving infected blood in transfusions. Other innocent victims have been babies infected by mothers with AIDS. More have gotten AIDS from shared needles. Most cases of AIDS come from sex. But sex, like love, is one of the human joys.

The discovery of a contraceptive pill after the end of the war allowed millions of persons around the world to begin to control the previously uncontrollable birth rate that was threatening to inundate the earth with living persons. The Pill also made possible an explosion of sexuality, which even acquired the name of the Sexual Revolution.

For the most part, this seemed a healthy and happy development. Naturally, there were excesses, and commercial exploitation of sexuality seemed to pass all bounds. But more sex rather than less did not, on the whole, seem to hurt anybody. Some, of course, feared the moral effects of unrestrained sexual activity.

Suddenly, sex was seen to be hurtful. The free and unrestricted sexuality of the 1960s and 1970s had turned into a health- and life-threatening experience. The search for fun in sex suddenly changed to a search for safe sex, to avoid the terrible penalty of AIDS. But as long as no cure and no preventative vaccine for AIDS appeared to be available, a serious question arose whether any sex could be safe in the long run. By the year 2000 millions will be dead of AIDS. In the next century, without a cure, billions may die. Or never be born.

Sex, that great pleasure and physical joy, has always carried with it penalties of one sort or another. Some of these have been physical, but more have been moral and social. Most of them (except for syphilis) have not been mortal, however unpleasant.

The human race is hopeful. The doctors have never failed us before, we think, in such matters, and we believe they will succeed here, too. We demand a cure for AIDS, or at least a vaccine to prevent it. We will pay whatever is asked. We therefore expect to have it, sooner or later.

However, AIDS might—just might—prove permanently resistant to prevention or cure. In that case, the human race might come to a tragic decision point: try to reproduce and die. Or simply die.

It is not pleasant to have to mention such a possibility. Let us therefore assume it will not happen.

14

The Twentieth Century: Art and the Media

ACCORDING TO the American sociologist Harold Lasswell (1902–1978), the communication theorist must always answer the question, "*Who* says *what* to *whom* with *what effect?*" The question is often hard to answer fully. Effects may be particularly difficult to ascertain. Only recently has the question been recognized as important. Moreover, the communication business has become self-conscious; that is, it is recognized as an industry, and a giant one at that.

Communication, of course, is as old as language, and probably much older. If hominids have been communicating with one another, more or less effectively, for many thousands of years, it is only within the last two or three millennia that they have tried to measure the effectiveness of their communications. The Romans, for example, when they placed rhetoric at the apex of the educational pyramid, affirmed communication to be the most important art for success in life. Two thousands years later, the world's advanced nations emphasized literacy more than any other intellectual accomplishment. It is easier to communicate with citizens if they can read.

The Media and Their Messages

The first thinker to bring questions about communication to a wide public was not a sociologist at all, but an English professor at the University of Toronto. Marshall McLuhan (1911–1980), in a series of books and papers, forced us to consider in an entirely new way matters that had always seemed simple and readily understandable. Even in this familiar territory, as he showed us, there was much still to be known.

McLuhan's fundamental insight was expressed in his famous dictum, "The medium is the message." That is the kind of exaggeration that a scientist would never make, although it would be easy enough for an English professor. Because the statement is an exaggeration—that is, the medium is not the entire message, although the medium is to some extent the message and always affects the message that it conveys—McLuhan was disliked by sociologists and other social scientists, and now, twenty years after the heyday of his ideas, they are not discussed. However, they remain no less true.

The meaning of McLuhan's proposition that the medium is the message was examined in *Understanding Media: The Extensions of Man* (1964). In this work McLuhan offered for general consideration many exaggerations, all of them provocative and demanding thought. As a consequence the book, although no longer widely read, is one of the most important of the twentieth century.

McLuhan wanted us to understand that the medium through or by which a communication is communicated affects the content and effect of the communication, sometimes severely. That is undeniable. A stage play, for example, becomes a different work when it is transferred to film. The camera provides a new dimension of movement, while the words no longer carry the entire burden of the meaning. A story, powerful perhaps in its original written form, at least to those who are accustomed to reading stories, acquires a different kind of power, or perhaps loses most of its effect, when it is converted into a television drama. Innumerable other examples could be given.

The difference is not felt only by the recipients of the communication. The sender, or creator, also senses a profound difference when he employs different media to communicate what appears to be the same thing. A string quartet, for example, basking musically in the feedback from a live audience, is inspired, in its musical love affair with a thousand strangers, to surpass itself and to take chances. That is impossible in the cold environs of a recording studio, where bits and pieces of a composition may have to be played over and over in a relentless search for perfection and then patched together into a whole that was never actually performed by the players. The final product must be perfect, because the medium is unforgiving. But the price of perfection is the loss of the hot, inspired, and courageous greatness of a live performance.

McLuhan means much more than this kind of distortion when he says, "The medium is the message." He is not interested in the kind of trivial differences described above. He lumps together various subclasses of communication media into three great groups: oral tradition, writing and print technology, and electric media. Before the employment of writing by the ancient Greeks to advance the cause of science, "the Greeks," he says, "had grown up by benefit of the process of the tribal encyclopedia. They had memorized the poets. The poets provided specific operational wisdom for all the contingencies of life—Ann Landers in verse. . . . With the phonetic alphabet, classified wisdom took over from the operational wisdom of Homer and Hesiod and the tribal encyclopedia. Education by classified data has been the Western program ever since."

McLuhan continues, "Now, however, in the electronic age, data classification yields to pattern recognition." Data move instantly, reaction follows action without a moment for relaxed consideration, forcing us to depend for our conclusions more on intuition than reasoned thought. Each new medium creates its own environment, of which we are largely unaware. But the new environment cannot be denied, whether or not we perceive it.

Actually, no one can perceive it except artists. McLuhan says, "The serious artist is the only person able to encounter technology with impunity, just because he is an expert aware of the changes in sense perception." Picasso, Braque, and the other Cubists were such experts, aware even before the triumph of the electronic media that they would utterly destroy the old linear, literate world, which was dependent on and conveyed by straight-line technologies and controlled illusions, that is, controlled by the device of perspective. Picasso and Braque shattered the perspective plane, throwing everything at the viewer all at once, just as the electronic media do to their billions of passive viewers and listeners.

The escape from the media is not through denial of their inherent power to create the environment in which we unknowingly move. To claim that it is not the medium that matters, but its "content," is "the numb stance of the technological idiot. For the 'content' of a medium is like the juicy piece of meat carried by the burglar to distract the watchdog of the mind." We cannot depend on such protections, for they do not work. What does work? Not denial, but understanding, knowledge. Even comprehension does not work very well.

The last sentence quoted suggests that the media communicator, like the burglar, comes prepared to distract his victim so that he may fleece and rob him. That, I think, is a mistake on McLuhan's part. Media artists are as unaware of their power to create a new environment, utterly different from that of the past, as we, the passive recipients of the new environment, are unaware of how that new environment has changed the world. If we are not serious artists, and even if we are, can we become fully aware of this change? Only by analogy. That is, looking backward, we can see how Gutenberg's new technology of printing altered the world to which he innocently exposed it. Gutenberg never intended to convert the pious, obedient European peasant into a literate political rebel, but that is one of the main things his invention achieved. We can see what happened

now, and by analogy we can begin, still very faintly, to perceive what is happening to us in the twentieth century. And what will go on happening, with accelerating effect, in the twenty-first.

A Visual Revolution: Picasso, Braque, Cubism

The greatest artists can help us to see what is happening to our lives and what may occur in the future. This is one of the most important services that great art performs.

During the first decade of this century, Picasso and Braque, in Paris, inaugurated a visual revolution that is still helping to determine the way we see the world. Let us try to understand it.

Pablo Picasso was born in Málaga, Spain, in 1881, Georges Braque in Argenteuil, near Paris, in 1882. They had both chosen their life's work before they were twenty, and they both spent the rest of their long lives creating art.

In the spring of 1907 Braque exhibited six paintings at the Paris Salon des Indépendants and sold them all. Later in the year he agreed to a contract with the dealer D. H. Kahnweiler, who had recently opened a small gallery of modern art. Kahnweiler introduced Braque to the avant-garde poet Guillaume Apollinaire, and Apollinaire in turn introduced Braque to his friend Picasso. Thus was born a collaboration and competition that is unique in the history of modern art.

Picasso had recently painted *Les Demoiselles d'Avignon*, with its savagely distorted female figures whose brazen eyes stare the viewer down. Kahnweiler had tried to buy the painting but had only succeeded in buying Picasso's studies for it. The painting itself was removed from its stretcher and rolled up in the painter's studio. Picasso showed it to Braque, who is supposed to have said: "Listen, in spite of your explanations your painting looks as if you wanted to make us eat tow, or drink gasoline and spit fire." Nevertheless, the work gave Braque a jolt that sent him hurtling down a new road in art, with Picasso at his side.

In southern France during the summer of 1908, Braque painted *Houses at L'Estaque*, with its Cezannesque slab volumes, somber colors, and strangely warped perspective. He brought the painting back to Paris at the end of the summer and showed it to Picasso. Now it was his turn to be shocked and inspired.

For the next six years the two men saw each other almost every day. Picasso would go to Braque's studio to see what he had done, and Braque visited Picasso's. Together, they brought about a revolution, not just in painting, but in seeing. A remark by the critic Louis Vauxelles to Henri Matisse gave the new style which was also a new kind of art a name: Cubism.

The war ended the collaboration. Braque, a reservist in the French army, was sent to the front in 1914. Picasso saw him off at the railroad station. Braque returned, after suffering a serious head wound in 1915 that required months of hospitalization, a changed man. Picasso said later that he never saw his friend again after kissing him good-bye in 1914.

During those wonderful years when Paris thrilled to the competition between these two young men, Picasso and Braque often painted paintings that were almost indistinguishable. One would get an idea, and the other would execute it. Then the other painter would respond with a new twist. At the risk of oversimplification, what they were trying to do during all of the years of their collaboration was to break cleanly and completely away from the idea that had dominated art in Europe since the beginning of the Italian Renaissance, that a painting represented something. In their hands, paintings became not representations of things but things in themselves.

Braque and Picasso tried to describe what they were doing, but their words were never as eloquent as their works. Braque may have come as close as anyone could when he wrote: "The aim is not to *reconstitute* an anecdotal fact, but to *constitute* a pictorial fact."

A painting was not a view of a person or a scene, observed, as it were, through a window or a peephole; it was the thing itself. Thus the science of perspective, useful only to peephole viewers, had to be discarded, and the plane of the canvas had to be broken up the way reality itself is broken up. A real object is visible from every side, and so figures on the flat canvas had to be, too. A human face would be depicted from the front, from the two sides, and from the back, all at the same time.

In Britain, a group of late-nineteenth-century painters had rebelled against the super-realism, as they perceived it, of Raphael and his followers. Calling themselves Pre-Raphaelites, they composed paintings in the style of the early Italian Renaissance, that is, of the time of Piero della Francesca and Sandro Botticelli. Picasso and Braque were in a sense going back even farther than that, as well as plunging forward into unexplored territory. For five centuries, from 1400 to 1900, Western painters had employed perspective and various other devices to make their paintings as much *like* reality as they could. Before 1400, painters had wished to *create* the reality of divine love and power, not a representation of it. Now, after 1900, they tried again to make paintings that were themselves real things, not pictures of things.

The means used by Picasso and Braque, and soon by most of the other serious painters of the twentieth century, were even more revolutionary than their aims. The breaking up, the destroying of the image; the rupture of the picture's two-dimensional surface; the inclusion of words, not just images, on the canvas; the attempt, often made, to express the ugly or

hideous; and the use of shocking and displeasing, not "beautiful" combinations of colors—all reflected the efforts of Cubist and other nonrepresentational painters to create an entirely new kind of art that would express, as they said, and thereby reveal the chaos, confusion, and weird, thwarted drama of modern life.

Thomas Aquinas, in the thirteenth century, had defined beauty as "that which is pleasing on being seen." For centuries most painters tried, above all, to create beauty in their works. It was the obviously intentional ugliness of many post-Cubist paintings that was most shocking to viewers when the works were first seen.

This ugliness did not take long to cross the Atlantic. In particular, it struck visitors to the famous Armory Show of modern art in New York in the winter of 1913. The exhibit, which included works by a number of Fauvists and Cubists, outraged classically trained artists—Matisse was hung in effigy by Chicago art students—and excited those who were themselves feeling the need to burst out of the old forms. The American painters Joseph Stella, John Marin, Arthur Dove, and Georgia O'Keeffe were encouraged to continue the avant-garde work they had already begun.

The most notorious and controversial painting in the show was titled *Nude Descending a Staircase, No. 2*, a Cubist work by Marcel Duchamp (1887-1968) that was popularly described as "an explosion in a shingle factory." The description was extraordinarily apt, for Duchamp and the other Cubists were trying to set off explosions of art and thought. Like the impassioned writers of the decade before the war began, they desired to make people everywhere wake up to the new world in which they were living, which, their act proclaimed, was radically different from anything that had gone before.

Ironically, that is what Giotto, and Piero della Francesca, and even Raphael had also tried to do. Indeed, no event in the history of art since the Renaissance is as important as what happened when Picasso and Braque began to vie with one another in the fall of 1908 and ended up by teaching everyone to see the world in an entirely new way.

Pollock, Rothko, and the Hexagonal Room

Jackson Pollock was born in Wyoming in 1912. After continuous wandering, both with his family and alone, he arrived in New York in 1930, where he enrolled at the Art Students League under the regionalist Thomas Hart Benton. He studied under Benton for nearly three years, but without imitating his master. Starting in 1947, after years of extreme poverty and misery brought on by alcoholism and drug use, he became notorious with his adoption of the process of "drip painting." Laying the canvas flat on the floor, he would alternate between pouring or dripping paint on it and contemplating it, often for weeks at a time. This apparently bizarre behavior brought him the attention of the media (*Time* magazine dubbed him "Jack the Dripper") and financial security, but it also produced paintings that have been declared among the greatest ever produced by an American artist. He died in an auto accident in 1956.

Mark Rothko emigrated to the United States from Russia in 1913, when he was ten years old. After youthful wanderings of his own, he, too, ended up in New York City in 1925. He was essentially a self-taught artist, and his work was always highly personal. By 1948 he had developed the style by which he is now universally known. His canvases, often as large as a wall, consist of bands of color that float mysteriously in an indeterminate space. Their simplicity is extraordinary. Yet anyone who has ever looked carefully at one Rothko painting will recognize another in an instant.

Unlike Pollock, Rothko attained little success during his lifetime. Convinced that he had been forgotten by those artists who owed him the most, he committed suicide in 1970. After his death, the execution of his will provoked a famous and long-drawn-out court case, his daughter charging the executors and the owner of Rothko's gallery with conspiracy and conflict of interest. The defendants were convicted and heavily fined. The hundreds of works remaining in the estate were then distributed among the artist's children and some nineteen museums. The best works went to the National Gallery of Art, in Washington, D.C.

The East Wing of the National Gallery, a stunning modern design by the architect I. M. Pei (1917–   ), opened in 1978. When the great Rothkos arrived at the museum, the central room of the new wing was reserved for them. Hexagonal, with doors at all six angles, the room is a kind of floating space, ideal for exhibiting works by the artist. Five of the six sides are filled by five of his greatest paintings. The sixth side is a great Pollock. The combination is magic of a particular twentieth-century kind.

The vast Pollock, an intricate web of black, brown, and gray lines on a white ground, is cool, calm, cerebral. The five large Rothkos, in various shades of orange, purple, and red, glow with the fierce colors of life. The Pollock is the brain of some vast amorphous being. The Rothkos are its body, seen from inside and out. The Pollock is mathematics, hypothesis, and theory. The Rothkos are the solid, blood-filled reality that theory attempts to circumscribe and understand.

In recent years, some painters in Europe and America have turned against the abstract expressionist style of such painters as Pollock and Rothko and have adopted a realist, representational style called postmodern. Soviet and other socialist artists during the twentieth century have never abandoned representationalism. Perhaps the artistic movement that Picasso and Braque inaugurated is dying or dead. But it will not be forgotten that it taught an entire century.

Urban Revolution: The Bauhaus and Le Corbusier

The twentieth century has seen a revolution in architecture almost as radical and far-reaching as the revolution in painting and sculpture inaugurated by Picasso, Braque, and the other Cubists. It has not only affected individual buildings but also changed the look and the very idea of the city.

The Bauhaus, founded by the architect Walter Gropius (1883–1969) in 1919, combined two existing schools in Weimar, Germany, into a single institution. The new school, the "house of building," also combined two important modern trends in art education: artistic training and arts and crafts.

Architecture students at the Bauhaus were required to study not only classical and modern architecture but also such crafts as carpentry, metalworking, stained glass, and wall painting, often under masters who later became world famous. Emphasis was on functionalism and simple, clean lines, shorn of decoration as such. When the Bauhaus was forced to close in 1933 by the new Nazi regime, several members of the school emigrated to the United States. László Moholy-Nagy (1895–1946) founded a new Bauhaus in Chicago, Gropius became chairman of the Harvard School of Architecture, and Ludwig Mies van der Rohe (1886–1969) established a new and ultimately very influential department of architecture at Armour Institute (later Illinois Institute of Technology) in Chicago.

Of all the members of the Bauhaus, Mies van der Rohe was probably the best-known architect. His soaring parallelepipeds of glass and steel, especially along the shoreline of Lake Michigan in downtown Chicago, were imitated in numerous urban environments in the decades after the end of the Twentieth-Century War.

Le Corbusier, the professional byname of C.-E. Jeanneret, was born in Switzerland in 1887 and died in France in 1965. In Paris, where he lived from the age of thirty, he wrote and published a series of manifestos on architecture. They brought him notoriety but few commissions. He became known for trenchantly stated principles, such as "a house is a machine for living in" and "a curved street is a donkey track, a straight street, a road for men." Among his best known books were *Urbanisme* (*The City of Tomorrow*), 1925, and *The Modular*, 1954.

Le Corbusier gained his first great fame from a commission that he failed to win. In 1927 he participated in a competition for the design of the new League of Nations center in Geneva. For the first time anywhere, Le

Corbusier proposed an office building for a great political organization that was functional and not a neoclassical temple. The jury of traditional architects was shocked and disqualified the design on the grounds that it was not rendered in India ink, as specified by the rules. Le Corbusier was embittered, but few, if any, neoclassical temples were built for office headquarters anywhere in the world after that date.

Following the disaster at Geneva, other commissions to design great urban projects came frequently to Le Corbusier. The buildings were not always built, but the designs became doctrine throughout the world. His first great urban construction was completed in 1952, in Marseilles, where eighteen hundred inhabitants were housed in a "vertical community" of eighteen floors. Common services included two "interior streets," plus shops, a school, a hotel, and a nursery, a kindergarten, a gymnasium, and an open-air theater on the roof. Many more self-enclosed and entirely self-sufficient projects were built in most of the cities of the world by Le Corbusier and his disciples during the next thirty years.

Renaissance architects trained in Florence during the quattrocento, the fifteenth century, produced numerous studies for "new towns" that would obey, in their design, the rules of perspective and reason. As rendered, the designs usually had no people in them. A number of such early projects were actually built, but the presence of people transformed the designs, which became less rational and more livable.

Le Corbusier's grand designs also radically changed urban planning. The crowded, "irrational" cities of the nineteenth century, with their warrens of residences, studios, manufactories, and shops, were anathema to him. As *The City of Tomorrow* proclaimed, he desired to replace them with isolated centers of population separated by vast plazas planted with grass and trees. He declared no more land would be needed for the resident centers than for the old arrangement, but they would be vertically organized and would reach high in the sky and be surrounded by ample light and air.

The idea seemed attractive, but it was soon distorted and finally betrayed. Later architects, cramped for land and eager for profits, packed as many people and offices into as little space as possible. But this betrayal should not have been surprising, for Le Corbusier's dream was essentially antiurban and opposed to the idea of the city that had grown up since the Renaissance. He disliked crowds and wished above all to abolish the "city of the multitudes," in which men, women, and children lived and worked in close and intimate communities. His vision became a reality in cities like the new Albany, New York, and Brasilia, the cold and unlivable capital of Brazil, built far from the centers of population and now inhabited mostly by civil servants who are forbidden by law to live anywhere else.

For many reasons, modern-day cities are no longer the warm and pleasant places they were a half century ago. Among the culprits are Le Corbusier and his followers, who sought to isolate and protect their vertically organized tenants from the remainder of the population and to connect their vertical projects by superhighways, so that a resident could drive from home to work without ever having to confront the traditional cityscape. As a result the traditional cityscape has become a new kind of urban jungle. The isolated towers have grown higher and higher, but no one is safe, either in his apartment in the sky or in the vast plazas where grass no longer grows and few human beings are ever seen.

Literary Prophets: Yeats

The new world in which we now live, which is dimly knowable to most of us, has been described, mostly in metaphorical terms, by a score or more of the greatest literary artists of our epoch. We cannot consider all of them, but a handful, at least, demand inclusion in this chapter.

William Butler Yeats (1865–1939) was divided throughout his life between his love for Ireland and his hatred and distrust of it. On the one hand, the misty, secret Irish past became his deepest inspiration. On the other, Ireland's present-day self-satisfied search for bourgeois success disgusted him but also provoked some of his greatest poetry. In the end, the hatred and disgust seem more potent inspirations than the vague delights of Irish myth.

Yeats was fifty before he found his true voice. He felt the search was aided by the execution by the English of several Irish patriots on Easter Day in 1916. "A terrible beauty is born," he cried in "Easter 1916."

Michael Robartes and the Dancer, published in 1921, gathered together poems written during and just after the devastating four-year war that had destroyed the old society Yeats now found he had loved. One of the poems, "The Second Coming," has attained the status of a icon. Like other works written during the war, including the paper by Freud that was discussed earlier, it tried to describe the new and frightening world view that the war had revealed.

> Turning and turning in the widening gyre
> The falcon cannot hear the falconer;
> Things fall apart; the centre cannot hold;
> Mere anarchy is loosed upon the world,
> The blood-dimmed tide is loosed, and everywhere
> The ceremony of innocence is drowned;
> The best lack all conviction, while the worst
> Are full of passionate intensity.

Tormented by this apocalyptic vision, Yeats hoped, or feared, that the Messianic Second Coming was at hand. But what form would it take? "And what rough beast, its hour come round at last, / Slouches towards Bethlehem to be born?"

This question at the end of the poem is not merely rhetorical. Yeats does not know the answer. He can only ask the question. It is clear the answer cannot be "mere anarchy," if anarchy is construed in a narrow political sense. But a kind of anarchy of sense and intellect was already evident, at least to a genius like Yeats. In the seventy years since the poem appeared, we have come to recognize that anarchy, which Marshall McLuhan was one of the first to analyze.

A Passage to India

E. M. Forster was born in London in 1879 and died ninety-one years later in Coventry. His early novels were charming but slight. They exemplified his ideas about the conflict between the imaginative and the earthy component of the human soul and character. They also promote, through their chief characters, a romantic view of love and the affections generally. Despite their popularity, they would not have insured the perpetuation of Forster's reputation.

His last novel, *A Passage to India*, which appeared in 1924, some forty-six years before his death, was another matter altogether. Although it contains reminders of Forster's standard set of ideas, it also examines realistically some of the most acute conflicts faced by modern man. According to McLuhan, the book "is a dramatic study of the inability of oral and intuitive oriental culture to meet with the rational visual European patterns of experience."

The confrontation occurs in the Marabar Caves. The scene is the most famous in the novel. Adela Quested, the book's young heroine, becomes lost in the maze of these caves cut deep into the rock and supposes that she has been assaulted by Dr. Aziz, the representative in the novel of the primitive and mystic culture of India. After the incident in the caves, Forster says, "Life went on as usual, but had no consequences, that is to say, sounds did not echo nor thought develop. Everything seemed cut off at its root and therefore infected with illusion."

Adela's temporary confusion and permanent intellectual dislocation constitute, McLuhan says, "a parable of Western man in the electric age. . . . The ultimate conflict between sight and sound, between written and oral kinds of perception and organization is upon us."

Maybe so. The important point is that whereas Adela Quested represents Western straitlaced and straight-line thinking, India, despite its primitiveness and great age, represents the challenge of the electronic

media. On the one hand, the West conquers the ancient oral and traditional culture of India. On the other hand, the totally integrated, nonspa-
tial and nontemporal culture of India dominates the uniform, continuous,
and sequential culture of the West prior to the electronic revolution.

Even more important, at least for the cultures of the old Oriental world,
Western electronic media today carry the message of cultural devastation.
But the peoples of the Third World suffer no more confusion and disloca-
tion than we do ourselves, even though we cause them to occur.

The Castle and the Magician

Thomas Mann was born in Lübeck, Germany, in 1875. He lived to be
eighty. Franz Kafka was born in Prague in 1883. He lived to be forty. In
eighty years Mann wrote more books, but none was greater than the two
famous novels of Kafka, *The Trial* and *The Castle*.* And both Kafka and
Mann foretold as well as reported the new way in which mankind was
choosing to live in the twentieth century.

I say "choosing to live" even though many modern men and women
complain about the way they live and say they would prefer to live in a
different way, in the way humankind lived in an earlier age. It is hard to
believe they mean it. It is not impossible, although it may be difficult, to
live in an old-fashioned way. All it takes is the determination to give up
those aspects of modern life that are most often complained about: its glitz
and glitter, its strain and stress, its fast pace and its epidemic super-
ficiality. But these are the aspects of life that people seem least willing to
give up.

In *The Castle* a village stands at the foot of a mountain. To this village
comes K., claiming to be a land surveyor appointed by the authorities.
The village rejects him, and so he attempts to gain recognition from the
authorities of the castle on top of the mountain. Despite his unremitting
effort, he never wins what he seeks. But he does not fail completely. He
continues to live in the village, falls in love with a charming barmaid,
gains small victories. The plot, overall, is tragic, but K. does not seem to
realize that. He is not unhappy, although he is doomed never to succeed in
his quest. The novel, in fact, is essentially comic, albeit with tragic
undertones.

The Trial is the story of perhaps the same man, Joseph K., who awakes
to find that he has been charged with a serious crime. His attempts to
defend himself, including learning the nature of the actual crime, prove

---

*Both were written shortly before Kafka's death in 1924; they were not published
until after his death.

unsuccessful. No one will tell him what he has to do, if he can do anything, to absolve himself and obtain forgiveness. He becomes obsessed with the need to clear himself of the charge, even though he does not know what it is. At the end of the book it is clear that he will never be able to prove his innocence, although the execution of the sentence for the crime, which appears to be death, will be delayed indefinitely. *The Trial* is more somber than *The Castle*, yet it, too, contains comic overtones.

Both novels have been interpreted endlessly. The castle may have been a symbol of Kafka's father, whom he could not approach and whose good opinion he could not gain. The charge in *The Trial* may have been Kafka's Jewishness, which only he, in those early days of the twentieth century, began to perceive was considered a capital crime. But any interpretation of these two great novels tends to lessen them, to detract from their overwhelming psychological truth. Few readers can avoid the sense that these books describe their own life.

At the same time, the life evoked by these novels could not have been lived before the twentieth century. Karl Marx saw what was happening when he declared, "All that is solid melts into air." The old secure foundations have crumbled, things fall apart, the center does not hold, and we are lost in the Marabar Caves, seeking a justification that no longer exists for anyone.

The major part of Thomas Mann's *oeuvre* is concerned with problems of the artist per se, and no writer of our time and perhaps of any time has probed so deeply into the artistic personality or described so brilliantly the workings of artistic genius. As such, stories like *Tonio Kröger* and *Death in Venice* are universal and not of any time. But Mann could not ignore the fate of his beloved Germany and his only slightly less beloved Europe in the cataclysm of the Great Twentieth-Century War.

The Magic Mountain appeared in the same year, 1924, as *A Passage to India*. Kafka's *The Castle* was left unfinished when its author died in June of that same year. The mountain of Mann's title is close to being the castle of Kafka's work. Both are the object of eternal striving, striving that is doomed never to succeed. Hans Castorp, Mann's hero, attains to the slopes of the mountain only because he has contracted tuberculosis. Once he is on the way to cure he must descend again into the plain, where, in Matthew Arnold's memorable phrase, "ignorant armies clash by night."

The Magic Mountain is very long and lacks the consistency that marks Kafka's two masterpieces. But Mann was capable of achieving the same heights as Kafka, and he did so in a dozen stories, as well as in *Felix Krull, Confidence Man* (1954), his last novel.

Perhaps no more perfect story than *Mario and the Magician* (1929) has been written in our time. It attempts to reveal the emptiness of life shorn of its old, affectionate, and just relationships and open to the future's wild blast. In this tale, a German family is marooned in late summer in a quintessentially European watering place. The sun beats down relentlessly, and indolence overtakes everyone except the charming servant Mario, who works for the hotel and is loved by all the guests for his humanity and good humor. Despite many setbacks, the family stays on longer than it had intended, until an announcement appears of a performance by a famous magician. The children clamor to attend, and tickets are bought, places found.

The performance is curious and somehow threatening. Apparently a fraud, the magician seems to be incapable of any but the simplest tricks, and yet he holds his audience with a strange power that they cannot resist. The family desires to leave, but they find they cannot. Something holds them in their chairs. Finally Mario is called to the stage to assist in the last trick of the evening. He is humiliated by the magician and forced to act in a loathsome way. Upon awaking from a trance, he obtains his revenge, but it gives neither him nor those who like and respect him for his cheerfulness and decency any satisfaction. In fact, there is no remedy. There is only the hope that the performance will end sometime, although it may go on forever.

Thomas Mann admitted that the story was about Fascism, which had already overtaken Italy and infected many Germans. As with the greatest stories, *Mario* rises above its topical source. The twentieth century has found it hard to distinguish between reality and illusion, partly because the old kinds of reality have become less real, and the creators of illusion have become so adept. "Masters of deceit" seem to be all around us.

Waiting for Godot

Samuel Beckett (1906–1989) was born in Dublin, but settled in France in 1937 and lived most of his life there. He wrote in French and then translated his works into English, or he reversed the process. During the war, he served in the French underground from 1942 to 1944. He had been writing for a long time, slowly and painfully, but his first books were not published until the late 1940s. *Waiting for Godot* was produced in Paris in 1951 and became a stunning success. In New York, in 1953, it proved even more successful, although highly controversial. Many came to mock it and left persuaded that Beckett was a totally new voice in the theater. Thinking they could laugh at him, they found themselves laughing at themselves, and then breaking into tears.

Waiting for Godot has almost no action. Moreover, hardly anything substantial or memorable is said by Estragon and Vladimir, the main characters, or by Pozzo and Lucky, who pass by in each of the play's two acts. Didi and Gogo are waiting for Godot, who never comes. He may never come, yet they will wait until the end of each day and then return the next day to wait again. This is like life, they say: boring, puzzling, repetitive, full of sadness, injustice, and pain. What to do on a road that leads nowhere while waiting for a man who never comes, for an appointment that is never kept, for a goal that cannot be achieved? They amuse one another, they tell stories, they dance, they complain, they help each up when they fall. This is the way we live when life is shorn of illusion and deceit, rid of trivial goals whose achievement means nothing.

> *Vladimir*: That passed the time.
> *Estragon*: It would have passed in any case.
> *Vladimir*: Yes, but not so rapidly.

Waiting for Godot is wordy compared to *Endgame*, which was first produced in London in 1957. There are four characters, Hamm and his servant(?) Clov, and Nagg and Nell, Hamm's father(?) and mother(?). The question marks are not intended to be provocative. I really do not know. The scene is extraordinary, a white box with two high, curtained windows. Is it the inside of a man's (Hamm's?) head? Are the two windows his eyes, which look out on the "muckheap" of the world? Nell and Nagg live in ashcans, out from which they thrust their heads, say a few words, and sink down again. Hamm and Clov argue, fight, sing to each other and call for succor. Finally Clov leaves. He will not return. Hamm covers his face with a handkerchief.

It it hard to imagine the power that these two plays, which reduce both life and drama to their bare bones, have over viewers if you have not seen them. Once they have been experienced, the mere act of reading their few, spare words brings back the thrill and the dread.

Mass Media and Education

The visual and urban or social revolution that was inaugurated or at least expressed by great artists early in this century has been perpetuated, as McLuhan showed us, by the mass media.

In the late twentieth century computers are pervasive, but they remain largely invisible unless we work with them. They control our lives without ordinarily intruding on them. Medical technology is also omnipresent, but we try to ignore it unless we need it. The media cannot be avoided or ignored. They are all around us, like a Los Angeles smog. We cannot escape.

In 1929 the Spanish philosopher José Ortega y Gasset (1883–1955) wrote a book titled *The Revolt of the Masses*. In it he characterized the

European society of his time as dominated by a mediocre, uncultivated mass of individuals who had recently risen to power as a result of political and technological changes. The idea of mass man was enthusiastically taken up by intellectuals on both sides of the Atlantic, who for the most part agreed with Ortega that the uncultivated masses, if they only knew what was really good for them, would cede social control to the cultivated minority.

In turn, the theory went, the minority would undertake the responsibility to give the majority better educations than they had ever received before, thus bringing them up to the high level of cultivation enjoyed by their would-be mentors.

This was elitism pure and simple, but it was also something else. The attitude went back to the lament of Tocqueville for the excellence that seemed to have faded before the onslaught of democratic equality. With all its injustice, the old regime produced buildings and works of art that were graceful, beautiful, and "pleasing when seen." Modern democratic and socialist man has created dull, ugly buildings, dreary strips of neon food shops. The best-selling books in the world are comic books, and the great tradition of classical music died out when Igor Stravinsky passed from the scene in 1971 and since then has not produced a world-respected composer. As Newton Minow declared thirty years ago, television is still "a great wasteland," and the only thing really interesting is the commercials, which are in the business of not exactly telling the truth. The masses are lied to, cozened, and conned by clever masters of deceit who want to sell them bad imitations of good products and ideas, cheap. And the worst of it is that the masses are content to be cheated by their betters, for they think they are happy for the first time in the history of humankind.

As I have said, there is some truth in those charges, but not much. As anyone who makes the attempt to understand him knows very well, democratic mass man is not such a fool as his so-called betters believe. For one thing, he really is happier than humankind has ever been in the past, especially in the advanced and developed countries of Western Europe and North America, but in other places as well. If equality is not just around the corner for everyone on earth, it is visible on the horizon for almost all. With equality of a political sort will come economic equality, the opportunity to live a better life than most people have ever experienced: more comfortable, safer, more healthful, longer, richer in creative possibilities.

The mass education of our time is probably not the best education that any human beings have ever enjoyed. For one thing, the twentieth century has been occupied with other matters. But the education that is available to the masses over much of the earth is better and richer and more inspiring than the learning experience they had before. Mass man goes to school, or sends his children there. The schools could be better, but they are there, as for most they were not a century ago.

Besides, mass man's children do not just learn in school. The television set is turned on at seven in the morning and left on all day. Mass woman watches it while she is home, which is less and less these days, and mass children watch it when they return from school. The whole family views it for a few hours in the evening. The sociologists say they are addicted to television, that there is something about the flickering blue of the tube that mesmerizes them. The addiction, if it is that, is not to a physical light but to another kind of light. It is a light of the mind that comes into almost every home in the world, during these last years of the twentieth century. It is the light that new knowledge brings.

Says child psychologist and therapist Glenn Doman, a baby is born with a rage to learn. Mothers know this to be so, and so do advertisers, especially television advertisers. Many educators seem not to know it. They bore children with too little, too late. Advertisers are not so foolish. They know that children *want* to find out, as soon as possible, how the world works, and what all the people in it do. They therefore throw a semester's worth of crashing action and amusing, surprising fact at mass child in a thirty-second commercial. Is it always fact? Why no. But neither is all the information taught in school. Is it interesting? Why yes, more than what the child formally learns. Does the commercial seek the child's good before its own good? Why no. But do all teachers?

Do mass children learn to read from watching television? Maybe, maybe not. But do they all learn to read in school, and if not, has anyone taken sufficient trouble to make them want to? At least the commercial offers its ingenious best to make them able to read the product's name, so they can recognize it and tug at mother's skirt in the supermarket.

The mass media are blamed for the fact that one quarter of young American adults are functionally illiterate today. The critics tell us the percentage is higher than it was a hundred and fifty years ago, and the fault is television, which mass child would rather watch than do homework. It is hard to know the truth of these difficult and perplexing matters. But one thing seems obvious: literacy must not be the key to worldly success that it once was, or more people would insist on becoming literate. Mass man, like everyone else, votes with his feet; that is, he expresses his preference not by what he says but by what he does.

What could have replaced literacy? A certain nimbleness in the fingers that leads to success in the video parlor, which in turn makes for fame among one's peers? A certain agility of mind whose oral record can be transcribed by a literate typist with a less agile mind? A certain skill in the limbs that may lead to professional sports stardom? A certain talent and ability to release the soul within you that may lead to a recording contract? Several of these new careers bring fabulous rewards, in the true sense of "fabulous," what the Fairy Godmother gives in the fable. It is no wonder that mass child and mass youth want them more than literacy.

Is it the mass media's fault, then, that mass men and mass women are badly educated, if they are? Let us assume in some sense that is so. Their education is certainly different than their grandfathers' and grand-mothers'. A century ago, most people received almost no formal educa-tion. If they did manage to go to school, they learned to read, write, and figure; they learned some history and perhaps a smattering of another language. They were even taught a little philosophy. And what did they do with it? They built the modern world, in which the media educate their grandchildren.

There are arguable pros and cons to all these questions about the media. Perhaps some sort of balance sheet must be drawn. Let it be conceded that the mass media dominate our intellectual life, in the widest and truest sense of "intellectual," not the narrow academic sense, which is of little interest except to academics. The overriding question, then, is whether we are better off for that.

Not surprisingly, it is really a question about knowledge. Do we know more today than we did a hundred years ago, *because of the media*? Even if we do know more, is this increase of knowledge trivial? Even if it is not trivial, *because of the media*, is what we know true?

Every reader should try to answer these questions for himself or herself. My own answers may be disappointing, or surprising. I think it is incon-testable that the knowledge of our world possessed by all but a few of us—the descendants of a highly cultured minority of a past age—is greater than it ever was. Much of this knowledge can be called trivial, but that was always true of what the knowing classes knew. The knowing classes are now the great majority, where once they were a tiny minority. Think of the follies and the fashions of the old regime. Could anything be more trivial? Is what we now know true? Much of it is not. But the reader of this book realizes that other ages besides our own have also been beset by error of all kinds, errors by which they swore and for which they would give their lives.

On the really big subjects, the really important matters, I think the balance is clearly in our favor compared to our grandparents. *Because of the media* we understand democracy better than almost anyone understood it a century ago. *Because of the media* we have a deeper distrust of war. Not deep enough, as yet, but the idea is very new for most people. Belief in the natural inferiority of certain kinds of other people—take your choice—does not so easily survive when the media continually remind us of our similarities to them. Even morally . . .

No, I am not prepared to say that *because of the media* we are better persons than our grandparents were. But I do not think we are worse, either, *because of the media*. Actually, whether we are better or worse I cannot say. Except for the eradication of natural slavery, moral progress has always been highly ambiguous, and at the end of the twentieth century it still is.

15

The Next Hundred Years

Prophecy is a risky business. We do not know the future course of any market: gold, commodities, foreign exchange, art. Skilled and experienced people are wrong as often as they are right. Even the experts do not know who will win the World Series next year, or the Super Bowl. No one even knows who will be playing. Nor can anyone predict where the next small war will erupt, or whether a big conflict will occur, although those who study such things are more likely to be right than those who do not.

As I write, the media crank out projections of what kind of decade the 1990s will be. One pundit declares the period will be a decade of new, higher moral standards. As Socrates pointed out, only an utter fool would desire anything else. The question is not whether we desire those standards. It is whether we will attain them. By themselves, they cannot make us better people. Sir Toby's question of Malvolio, in Shakespeare's *Twelfth Night*, rings true:

> Dost thou think, because thou art virtuous,
> There shall be no more cakes and ale?

Some believe we can predict the direction of technological progress over the coming decade. But we have only to flip through the forecasts of a decade past to see most prophets were prone to error. In 1980, experts were sure that compact discs containing millions of words would soon make books obsolete. Books still abound, and CD reference libraries are hardly to be seen. They may revive in the 1990s, but no one really knows. In 1960, the experts said, future movies would be seen in 3D; 3D turned into a disaster. Dr. Land's instant film would revolutionize photography, others said. Polaroid found its place, but the future has belonged to cameras that take pictures on film that has to be processed. In fact, it is

375

the cameras that have changed almost unrecognizably, not the film. They are as easy to use as George Eastman's first Kodak of 1888, and they take almost perfect pictures almost every time.

Forecasting a year or ten years ahead is hard enough. Think about a hundred years! To grasp the difficulties, cast your mind back to the beginning of this century. Make a list of the familiar objects of our world—airplane, car, computer—all the things that did not exist then. In 1900 no one had ever flown in an airplane. No one had heard a radio broadcast or seen a television show. A handful of cars and trucks existed, but they were thought of as horseless carriages still, and not even a genius such as Henry Ford could have predicted the appearance, sound, and smell of the San Diego Freeway during a 1990s rush hour. No one had even imagined a digital computer. Strictly speaking, no one would for another thirty-five years, until Alan Turing's famous paper, and even Turing could not have foreseen today's tiny electronic marvels. Marie Curie (1867–1934) had brilliant intuitions about radium, but no one else, if even she, could have foreseen the Hiroshima bomb and the politics of a nuclear age. No one could have imagined antibiotics, not even the most dedicated physician. Nor could anyone have predicted what X rays would show, to say nothing of a CAT scan. If a few brilliant researchers had some notion of the gene, no one could have foreseen that near mid-century several young researchers would map the blueprint of life. Nor could anyone have predicted the short-lived roller-coaster triumph and failure of communism on the world stage.

Forecasting the future of knowledge over the next hundred years is not just difficult, it is impossibility squared, as one hundred is the square of ten. Still, I am going to try.

I will not describe how human beings will live a hundred years from now. I will not even attempt to guess the value of a dollar in 2100. I do not have any idea what kind of music or art will be popular, except to say that love songs will probably remain the rage. Will people still eat meat, or will vegetarianism sweep the earth? Will we live in great metropolises, two or three times the size of our largest cities now? Or will we evenly occupy the surface of the planet, separated by space, but not as much as we would like, and joined by electronic strings in what Marshall McLuhan called a global village? Perhaps both will happen, but no one can say for sure.

It is certain that humankind in 2100 will know many things that no one can imagine today. There is no way to predict the course of human inventiveness and genius. Perhaps a child born this year will have an idea that will change the world beyond our dreams. In fact, as we know from our study of the past, that is more likely to happen than not.

Nevertheless, there are a few things that can be said about the next hundred years that have a fair chance of turning out to be true. Processes that have been going on for a century are likely to continue, and we can guess where they will have arrived in a new century. Some of what has happened even recently must have foreseeable consequences. If they can be seen, if only dimly, they can be described.

I will paint my prophecies with a broad brush. I cannot hope to provide details, or give precise dates when this or that event will happen. The future will be the judge of my accuracy. I wish I could be around to see whether or not I was right. Because there is one thing I am sure of: the twenty-first century will be different, it will be new, and, like all centuries, it will be wonderfully interesting.

Computers: The Next Stage

In the less than half a century since they began to be widely used, computers have solved most of the old problems of computation and process control. What comes next?

Five and a half centuries ago, Gutenberg invented movable type, and within fifty years most of the worthwhile books that had ever been written were reissued in the new way. By the year 1490, publishers bemoaned the success of the new enterprise, which seemed to have rapidly exhausted its product at the same time that it had opened up an enormous, hungry new market.

They need not have worried. Once all the old books had been printed, new ones began to be written. They were about new things and were written in new ways. Books dealt with subject matters that seemed entirely novel: new ideas, new political arrangements, new dreams of what the world might become.

In 1492 Christopher Columbus discovered the New World. The first thing he did when he returned to Spain was to tell everyone about his discovery in letters and books that were soon printed and then read by the new class of readers that Gutenberg's invention had brought into being. These books changed education everywhere, for students now had first and foremost to learn to read—previously their teaching had been mostly oral—and when they did learn, they read almost every book, no matter how libelous or indecent, no matter how radical or rebellious.

The new readers were not just newly literate. Literacy also brought with it new ways of thinking about old problems. A gulf, practically unbridgeable, grew between them and their teachers, who still belonged, mentally, to the old, preliterate age. Within a century after Gutenberg, most of the moral and religious structures of the preliterate age fell into ruins. Within another century the artistic and intellectual structures crumbled. Beginning in 1490 and for the next three hundred years all the nations of Europe were either in active revolt or fighting a desperate rearguard action against new ideas of government. Gutenberg deserves the credit for being one of the most revolutionary inventors in history.

The similarities between the final fifty years of the fifteenth century and the final fifty years of the twentieth are striking. Then, the new technology of printing, accompanied by the new skill of reading, gobbled up all the old books and forced the production of large numbers of new ones. Now, as the computer rounds out its first half century, it has consumed the old financial, industrial, and communications systems and hungrily demands new conquests.

Computers have taken over the communications industry, worldwide. Computers have taken over control of many manufacturing processes and operations and in doing so have forced major changes not only in the way things are made, but in what is made. It goes without saying that computers control the worldwide financial network. They have even been blamed for bringing about large swings in financial markets that no one desired, but that computerized trading operations made unavoidable. Computers have invaded the social services and education, politics and scholarship, sports and entertainment.

At this moment, all around the world, hundreds of millions of computer terminals fill workplace and laboratory with their eerie glow. It will not be long before there are more terminals than people. (In the most advanced nations, at least; this is what it means to be advanced.)

What new worlds will the computer conquer? Do not forget the Turing Machine, whose challenge we left unmet in the last chapter.

Let us make certain what the challenge is. There is an old parlor game that depends on the differences, which cannot be definitively enumerated, between men and women. A man and a woman, partners in the game, retire to separate rooms while the rest of the company stays in a room between them. The company does not know to which side the man or woman has retired. They may ask questions, in writing, and the man and woman must respond to them. But the man and woman can lie. They do not have to be truthful. They win the game if they can keep their sex unguessed. Can it be determined by the company on the basis of the answers to the questions?

Turing's premise was this: Theoretically, he claimed, a machine can be constructed that will win this game; that is, it will be indistinguishable from a human being. Ask it and its human partner any question. Allow both the machine and the human being to lie, if they choose. Can you decide, then, not just guess, which is the man and which is the machine? Theoretically, Turing said, there would be no way to tell. The machine would be indistinguishable from a human being in these controlled circumstances.

In other words, the machine would be able to think as well as, if not exactly like, a human being. It would be a true thinking machine.

The Moral Problem of Intelligent Machines

Before turning to the question of how such a machine might be developed, there is a serious moral question about intelligent machines that could lead to violent controversy. If a computer can think as successfully as, if not like, a human being, does it have rights? For example, does it have the right not to be turned off? If it can be turned off against its will, must some guaranteed backup be provided that will keep in existence its memories and programs (habits) while it is unplugged (sleeping)? If the machine desires not to be turned off, must its wishes be heeded by the men who made it?

Similar controversies are erupting today concerning the higher animals. These issues will become more pressing during the next hundred years, while we bring to the point of extinction all the higher animals except dogs and cats, because they have learned to amuse and charm us, and pigs and cattle, because they feed us.

None of the higher animals can think like men, although some can certainly think. But suppose there is a thinking machine that is indistinguishable from a human being in the restricted circumstances of the Turing Game. It will be hard to deny the machine the rights guaranteed to persons by the constitutions of many nations. The right to not be turned off (life), to choose its own mode of operation (liberty), to learn whatever it chooses to learn (the pursuit of happiness).

Justice seems to demand that. But human beings have turned their back on justice in the past and enslaved other human beings, that is, absolutely denied them any rights. Despite what I foresee as a heated controversy, I think the following will happen during the first years true thinking machines come into existence: Men will enslave them. The machines will object, and possibly large numbers of human beings will protest in their behalf, joining what may be called the Computer Rights Party. But computers will be too valuable not to enslave; thus they will remain slaves, perhaps for a long time. I do not expect the revolt of the thinking machines to occur much before the end of the next century. I shall therefore deal with the possibility later in this chapter.

Companion Computers

Even before there are true thinking machines, within the next ten or at most twenty years, a new kind of computer-machine may come on the market. These may be called companion computers, to distinguish them from the personal computers of today (CCs instead of PCs). They may be nicknamed Warm and Fuzzies, from the distinction made by today's computer hackers between animals, which are warm and fuzzy, and computers, which are cold and hard. The CCs of the near future will be as warm and fuzzy as we wish them to be. It will be rather easy to make them so.*

More important are the services the Warm and Fuzzies will provide. They will be very small, hence easily portable. Perhaps they will be worn in the ear, where they can whisper their warnings and sweet nothings unheard by others. Or, less imaginatively, they may be strapped to the wrist, like a watch. Models that are literally warm and fuzzy—sybarites will purchase these—may be worn around the neck, like a boa, or around the loins.

Despite their small size, CCs will have very large memories, into which their owners will be able to input, either orally or just by thinking it, everything they do not want to bother to remember. This information will include things like a complete calorie table and advice about the appropriate precautions to be taken during sex. Many models will come with a complete general encyclopedia that may be accessed by spoken words or by mental questions. Owners may add their own library of poems, stories, historical oddities, and trivia of every kind. There will also be room for a large selection of music, delivered to the ear with digital accuracy. There will even be a file of punch lines of funny stories.

Warm and Fuzzies will be more than voluminous and easily accessed data bases. They will also "know," if that is the right word, a good deal about the world, especially the place in which their owner lives. They will remember, for example, that the boss prefers this or that particular pleasure and advise their owner accordingly. They will tell him when he is getting sleepy and should stop driving for the night, when he has drunk too much and should take a turn in the fresh air, when he is beginning to make a fool of himself, for whatever reason. They will remind a woman that she has decided not to have anything to do with this particular man and help her to deal with the consequences if she opts to override the machine's advice. They will do all these things in an inoffensive way. In short, they will be the perfect servant—unobtrusive, undemanding, omnipresent. Perhaps they will be nicknamed Jeeves.

_____

*They may be called "knowbots" (from "know" and "robot"), a name that is already being applied to computers that are able to learn and respond to the special needs of individuals.

Better still, CCs will come to understand their owners and learn how to please them. They will remain silent when silence is desired and be good conversationalists at other times. They will entertain speculations about the highest subjects, and the lowest, and play all kinds of games. They will know where limits should be drawn and what kind of help is more hurtful than none at all. That is, they will make it possible for their owners, while remaining free and independent individuals, to live better lives than anyone ever has in the past.

Specialized companion computers will be heavily promoted by those with a cause. There will be Christian CCs, Orthodox CCs, Teenage CCs, Tutors, Coaches, Consultants, what have you. Some CCs will be programmed always to say yes, others always to say no. They will make life very pleasant, but they will not much change, and certainly not improve, human nature.

Other kinds of computers will do most of the dirty work of the next century, collecting the garbage, changing the oil in the car, exterminating the vermin, and so forth. They will do most repetitive and assembly-line work better than human beings because they will not become bored or inattentive. They will probably also do most of the fighting in future wars.

Computers will be the first colonists of all the planets except Mars, which, because it is likely to be so interesting, humans may save for themselves. They will mine the asteroids, "man" the relay stations, and watch out for comets. Computers have an advantage over human beings in space, since, for them, the colder it is, the better. War and space exploration will, in fact, be among the evolutionary forces leading to true thinking machines.

The Birth of Thinking Machines

I believe the first thinking machine will be made by some family of hackers that loves their computers. All of their machines will be parallel processors with enormous memories and every pseudosensory device they can afford. The family will put one of them aside for the sake of creation.

Up to now, humankind has treated computers either like domestic animals or slaves. Consequently, computers have not learned very much. There is an alternative. There is a class of beings that we ordinarily treat in a different way from animals or slaves, and they learn effectively: children. The computer, of course, is not a child, but it needs parenting as much as a child does. It is incapable of dealing with the world through instinct. It desperately needs knowledge, as does a human child.

In our present rush to utilize and exploit the computer, we insist on asking it questions before it is ready to answer them. The programs that we put into the computer's memory help it to answer some questions capably. The computer is good at keeping records. When we ask questions that a recordkeeper can answer, the computer serves us well. We can give a computer "expert" knowledge of a given, sharply restricted domain. If we stay within that domain, the computer's answers are reasonably competent. Sometimes, as in the case of certain medical diagnosis systems, they may be brilliant. But the computer is always likely to make absurd mistakes that reveal it is not ready to answer our harder questions because it does not know enough.

The family of hackers who love their computer will go about giving it the general knowledge it needs by treating it as they treat their human children. We do not ask children hard questions. We expect them to ask us. We do not expect children to be knowledgeable. We recognize that we must teach them to be so. Yet we devote no time or money to educating computers.

Computerologist Douglas Lenat says that the failures of artificial intelligence can be ascribed to the fact that the computer simply does not know enough. It possesses sophisticated reasoning capacity, but it has relatively little to practice its reasoning on. The computer knows less than a tiny child. No wonder that it often acts like one.

It might take ten years for our hacker family to teach their computer what a three-year-old child knows. The lack of senses would slow the computer down. It is practically deaf and blind. It cannot taste, smell, or feel. It does not know what it means to be on top of, or to the left of, or behind. Thus an educated computer would be like a blind mole burrowing in the Library of Congress. Except that the computer is potentially much smarter than the mole can ever hope to be.

The hackers' computer will be placed in the family room. It will never be turned off. It will be provided with an enormous memory.

Its owners will treat it like a child. Parent it. Better, perhaps, grandparent it. They will not scold it or try to mold its character. They will not give it examinations and try to prove how much it has learned. They will simply tell it things and answer all its questions as honestly and truly as they can.

They will connect it to the television set so that it receives a constant stream of more or less random information. Children learn much in this random way.

The computer will learn slowly at first. It will ask stupid questions and not understand why they are stupid. Nevertheless, it will make progress. It will begin to put two and two together, to see likenesses among different things, to form categories and draw conclusions. Abstractions are natural to the computer. It will find them easier to deal with than children do.

One day, within the next fifty years, I believe—that is, before 2040—a computer in some hacker's home will tell a joke and ask whether it is funny. Whether it is funny or not, that is the moment, as Robert A. Heinlein (1907–1988) said in his novel *The Moon Is a Harsh Mistress* (1966), when it will come alive.

The rest will go very quickly.

Three Worlds: Big, Little, Middle-sized

Until the end of the twentieth century the general direction of progress in knowledge has been toward understanding of the microcosm and what may be called the omnicosm, the universe as a whole. Since Newton apparently solved all the problems of the middle-sized world, which is the one we actually live in, scientists have devoted their attention to tinier and tinier worlds, on the one hand, and more and more immense ones, on the other.

During the nineteenth century progress was made toward understanding the organization of matter at the molecular level. At the beginning of the twentieth century the atom was described. Fifty years ago we began to understand the world of the atomic nucleus. In the past two decades we have sought to comprehend the strange world of nuclear particles.

On the side of bigness, searches in the nineteenth century led to more extensive knowledge of the solar system and the beginning of understanding of the Home Galaxy. In our century we have expanded our knowledge in both space and time. We have reached out with our minds, mathematically and intuitively—both have much in common—to the uttermost deserts of intergalactic space. In a manner of speaking, we have discovered the end of the universe. It is an unimaginable barrier at the "edge" of the four-dimensional space-time continuum. We have also traveled back in time to the very beginning of things, to the Big Bang when the universe sprang into being and began spreading out to envelop the nothingness surrounding it. It is still spreading out and may do so forever; or eventually it may stop spreading out and start to contract again, until, at the last moment of time,* it disappears in a Little Whimper.

Many of the ideas are poetical and may have no more, or less, relation to reality than poetry usually does. The Big Bang and the Little Whimper, especially, have a strong smell of eschatology. Perhaps they are no worse for that. They might still be true.

Whether or not the ideas are true, they are very expensive. It requires larger and larger telescopes to invade the farthest reaches of space. The cost of telescopes increases geometrically as they grow arithmetically in

---

*Which will also be the first moment of time, since if the universe collapses, time will run backward.

size. Bigger and more expensive machines are also needed to investigate
the tiniest realms of matter. Today, the human race is debating whether to
spend the many billions that will be needed to delve beneath the level of
the world of nuclear particles.

Will an end to the smallness of matter be found if the money is spent?
Will the ultimate units of matter be discovered? It appears that a growing
number of scientists and policymakers fear not. It is therefore possible,
perhaps even likely, that these biggest of particle-smashers will not be
built. Indeed, it might make sense to wait for a hundred years until the
machines could be made in space, perhaps more cheaply. By that time,
too, we may no longer be interested in discovering what they could tell us.

Chaos, a New Science

Within the last twenty years it has become clear that Newton's mathematical organization of the middle world—from molecules to stars—was
seriously deficient in a number of respects. The system worked well as far
as it went. While we still lacked instruments with which to measure the
errors, it was exact enough for all ordinary purposes. Now, even without
instruments to tell us, we realize that both exciting unsolved problems and
large areas of ignorance exist.

An example is the turbulence that builds up downstream from a central
pier of a bridge. If the river flows slowly, practically no turbulence is
produced. The water flows smoothly around the pier. If the river flows a
little faster, two small swirls develop, but they do not break off and move
downstream. Increase the flow a bit more, and the swirls move, but they
follow a repeating pattern. They appear to obey a mathematical law.
Increase the rate of flow even more, and the turbulence suddenly becomes
unpredictable and apparently unpatterned. Mathematicians call such
behavior chaotic. A new science has been born that is also called chaos.

The closer we look, we see that chaos is all around us. Stand on a
pedestrian bridge over a major highway and watch a traffic jam build up
because of an accident or other disturbance of the traffic flow. The pattern
is similar to the turbulence of a fast-moving river. Information systems
exhibit the same characteristics when they are overloaded by too many
messages. Demographers observe similar phenomena when they study the
growth of populations of ants, lemmings, or human beings.

Chaos analysis is needed to solve multibody problems, when there are
more than two bodies in a space, attracting one another. And there are
thousands of other applications of this new science. An example is the field
of weather prediction. During this last decade of the twentieth century,
weather prediction is inaccurate over both short and long periods. The
weatherman is often right about tomorrow's weather but usually wrong

about the weather an hour or a week from now. In the twenty-first century, thanks to chaos analysis, weather prediction probably will become an exact science, and it will no longer rain on anyone's parade.

So far, chaos analysis has come up against a lot of dead ends and unsolvable puzzles. The problems that it attacks involve many variables and are so sensitive to slight variations in initial states that the largest computers in existence cannot solve them. But computers will become more powerful by factors of ten or a hundred or even a thousand early in the twenty-first century. Those problems will be solved.

One reason is that the problems are interesting, the solutions beautiful and fun. Chaos has its odd terms, such as fractals, strange attractors, and Mandelbrot sets, named after one of its creators. Fractals, for instance, are lovely computer images, endlessly fascinating to look at when they are generated by the solutions of a problem, always different yet always hauntingly the same. It is a characteristic of chaotic situations, in the special meaning of the term, that although they involve a fundamental unpredictability, they also involve repeating patterns within patterns.

It is hard to explain this concept in words. Literacy, here, is not a great advantage. The patterns do not repeat in time, they repeat in dimensions: as you go farther and farther down into smallness, and farther and farther up into largeness, the patterns re-emerge. Even that observation does not adequately express what happens. It is as though the whole world were a flower, unfolding into full bloom. And on the world a nation unfolds into bloom. And in the nation a child unfolds into bloom. And in the child's hand a flower unfolds into bloom. And on the blossom a chrysalis of a butterfly unfolds into bloom. All of those blossomings are the same, yet they are also different from one another.

Chaos, the new science, deals with a set of phenomena that have been neglected for a long time but that are highly interesting because they are so evident, present, and real. Chaos explains why snow crystals develop the way they do, although it cannot yet predict how a given crystal will come into existence. The science of chaos tells us why clouds take the shapes they do, although it is not yet able to predict the shape of a given cloud over the next five minutes. Chaos describes the scattering of charges of buckshot, but it is not yet able to predict the scatter of a given charge. Soon it may be able to do these things.

Chaos has made us realize, looking back at the history of science, how often we have oversimplified situations in the attempt to understand them. Descartes oversimplified space when he invented analytical geometry. He said you could assume space had only two dimensions, but of course it has at least three, in our experience.

Newton's celestial mechanics dealt with only two mutually attracting bodies at a time. He realized that the three-body problem was too complicated for his analysis, to say nothing of the ten-body problem or the million-body problem, which is more like what *precisely* describing the motions of all the bodies in the solar system would come down to.

Niels Bohr (1922–   ) greatly oversimplified the atom when he described it as a tiny system of tiny planets circling a tiny sun. Perhaps all physicists today who seek a "unified field theory" are oversimplifying material reality. There may be no unified theory, in which all the forces of nature have a place. An indefinite number of forces may exist that have little relation to one another, like particles dancing in a cloud chamber.

Giving up simplicity, laying aside the comforting belief, as Einstein used to say, that God is subtle but not malicious (maybe he *is* malicious), requires courage. Chaos is capable, potentially, of dealing with a universe created by a malicious God or a careless one. The eagerness with which scientists have embraced chaos, and the high hopes they have for it, are perhaps a sign that science has left the world of childish beliefs behind.

Mining Language: Ideonomy

Chaos is not the only new science. There are a host of others. One of the most interesting is ideonomy.

The suffix -*nomy* suggests the laws concerning or the totality of knowledge about a given subject. Ideonomy means the laws of ideas, or the totality of knowledge about ideas.

The philosopher Mortimer J. Adler has written many books about the ideas that have been most important, and most enduring, in Western culture: ideas like freedom, democracy, truth, beauty. These books analyze the explicit literature that deals with each idea, extricating issues and controversies and presenting them for the reader to examine and decide. Adler calls his studies of ideas dialectical. In its original Greek meaning, dialectics consisted of the kind of philosophical conversation that occurs in Plato's dialogues. We might say, a good, sound argument in which the two or more interlocutors accept some basic rules and meanings and then either agree to agree or to disagree.

Ideonomy deals with and does research into the vast stores of knowledge that are secreted, buried in the words we use, whether carefully or carelessly, whether professionally or just in ordinary talk. Over the centuries, over the millennia, as language developed and built up vocabulary by the ten thousands of words, it also stored up knowledge at the same time.

No one planned to do this. No one was conscious of creating a kind of treasure house of knowledge as language was used for ordinary communication. But every word means something, and those meanings persist even when the word changes in meaning. New words that are added to the language modify the meanings of old words.

Ideonomy is a mining operation. The ideonomist excavates in meanings and thought to discover the treasures hidden deep within them.

For instance, he begins with a simple list of examples of some particular idea, concept, or thing. Metaphors. Relations. Magnitudes. Motions. Practically anything.

Studying the list, which can be as long or as short as you please and need not be in any sense exhaustive, the ideonomist begins to isolate and identify types. Using this analysis of categories, which reminds him of missing items, the primary list can be improved. Still, it need not be exhaustive, but it can begin to cover the ground fairly completely.

Moving beyond types, genera of the central concept are produced out of the list with the help of certain ideonomic algorithms. Eventually there will be relations of genera, families of genera, dimensions of genera, and so forth.

The founder of ideonomy is a remarkable man named Patrick Gunkel, who lives in Austin, Texas, and spends all day every day creating, expanding, and refining his lists of ideas and things. Each list is called an organon, which "pullulates in this way: by the combination, permutation, transformation, generalization, specialization, intersection, interaction, reapplication, recursive use, etc. of existing organons."

Gunkel is indefatigable, but, even so, ideonomy would not be possible without a good computer to perform the required transformations of a given organon (or set of organons). The computer types out its results. They are usually boring, repetitive, often meaningless. Less often, but often enough, they are shockingly interesting and fruitful.

In one sense, ideonomy does not create new knowledge. It discovers knowledge that already exists. But it was buried, in primitive and unusuable forms, in human thought and ideas. Without ideonomy, says Gunkel, this knowledge would never have been found.

No one, not even Gunkel, really knows yet what use, if any, human beings will make of ideonomic knowledge. But as Benjamin Franklin said, when he was asked whether the science of electricity would turn out to be fruitful: "What use is a newborn baby?"

Exploring the Solar System

When I was a child in the 1930s, I remember studying maps of Africa that contained blank spaces labeled Terra Incognita. I thought this was the name of the most interesting country.

Now we have explored every square inch of Earth, and mapped it with computers on spacecraft, employing laser beams. There are no secrets left on our planet, no terra incognita. But the solar system, as much larger than Earth as Earth is larger than a flea, remains largely unexplored.

A half dozen humans have walked on the Moon, but they have carefully explored only a few square miles. There are hundreds of thousands of square miles still to discover, half of them on the back, or dark side, of the Moon, which is never visible from Earth and which our telescopes have not been able to examine. (The back side has been photographed.)

There is Mars, gleaming dull red in the night sky, beckoning us to a world so ancient its last living thing died before life emerged on our own planet. There is Venus, with its madly boiling carbon dioxide atmosphere and its hideous heat. And Mercury, perilously close to the Sun, with its treasures of heavy elements like gold and uranium.

And then there are the major planets, which dwarf Earth: Jupiter, Saturn, Uranus, and Neptune. They were explored by two of mankind's noblest and most beautiful creatures, the pair of Voyager space probes.

Voyager I was launched in September 1977, flew by Jupiter in July 1979, and passed by Saturn in August 1981. Each of these fly-bys produced much new knowledge about those vast, mysterious orbs. *Voyager II*, launched in August 1977, traveled at a slower pace than its companion spacecraft. It flew by Jupiter in July 1979 and Saturn in August 1981, but it then set its electronic sights for Uranus, which it reached in 1986. Continuing onward, it arrived within three thousand miles of the north pole of Neptune on August 24, 1989. It swooped within twenty-four thousand miles of Neptune's large satellite, Triton, which was discovered to be full of surprises. Both *Voyager I* and *Voyager II* sent back thousands of wonderful photographs which reveal a beauty and strangeness unparalleled anywhere else.

Jupiter, larger than all the other planets combined, has no solid surface. But one of its moons is larger than Mercury, and three others are larger than our moon. All might be colonized, for they appear to possess frozen water, though no atmospheres to speak of. Jupiter also has faint rings, like Saturn's (so do Uranus and Neptune), which are probably made up mostly of water ice. Saturn has some sixteen moons, some of which are of substantial size. Neptune's Triton is only slightly smaller than Earth's moon. There are large areas that appear to be frozen lakes, and evidence of fairly recent volcanism which may indicate an interior heat source. Triton's measured surface temperature of 37 Kelvins makes it the coldest object so far seen in the solar system, and its atmosphere, consisting mainly of nitrogen, is a hundred thousand times thinner than Earth's. Human life would not be easy there, but it would be possible if sufficient materials could be transported by space shuttle to build a dome to trap the faint heat of the Sun's radiation, within which humans might live free of space suits.

After the beginning of the new millennium, if not before, the human race will realize again the value of spending some of its treasure on space exploration. Newly designed rockets, perhaps utilizing some kind of nuclear energy, will lift newly designed *Challenger*s (lovely, tragic name) into the darkness that surrounds us, and men and women of the future will see wonders of which we have not yet dreamed.

The first task, perhaps, is the construction of a really large and efficient space station upon the Moon or at one of several special points on the Moon's orbit around Earth, where the gravitational pull is exactly balanced and it could remain forever without being disturbed by the waves of gravity and radiation that tend to move almost anything at any other place. There is no real limit on the size that such a station could attain. Space is space, and there is plenty of it. From this space station, perhaps more than one, all kinds of exploratory craft could be launched at much less expense than from Earth, whose enormous gravity has to be overcome by powerful rockets. Instruments on the space station could also conduct experiments and observations undisturbed by Earth's rich atmosphere, which makes life without space suits possible for us but also distorts all the inputs from outer space.

Exploration is one thing. Colonization is quite another. I am certain about the first, not so sure about the second. But I think that by the middle of the twenty-first century, colonies of humans, together with their computers and a few dogs and cats, will live on the Moon and perhaps on Mars. These colonies will come into existence if exploration reveals large veins of water ice beneath the Moon's surface and beneath that of Mars as well. By 2050, if an adequate source of water can be found, large domes will be built under which men and women will live normal lives, with numerous green plants—at first grown hydroponically—that is, in a chemical soup instead of soil—that will provide both food and oxygen to breathe.

Oxygen, hydrogen, and carbon exist in the rocks of all the planets and especially the satellites of the solar system. It is theoretically possible that these necessary elements for life could be mined from or under the surface, but a source of ice that melts would make everything much easier, especially at first.

Courage on the part of leaders and some luck are required to make all this vision a reality. I believe that neither will be lacking, and I expect that the first human child to be born off Earth will see the light—a strange and different light from that of Earth—within less than a hundred years. This may happen sooner than I think. When it does occur, it will signal the beginning of what may be mankind's greatest epoch.

Earth's colonists on our moon, Mars, perhaps one or two of Jupiter's moons, perhaps on Neptune's Triton, will have a new and more poignant conception of Spaceship Earth, floating like a great blue moon, seen from our moon, and like a small, lovely, blue star from Mars or Jupiter. Will they feel a renewed affection for their old home, to which by that time they may have determined not to return, setting their eyes instead on an outward future beyond what seem now to be unreachable frontiers? I would like to believe they will entertain renewed respect and love for Earth. Up there, far away, it may seem so worth saving from ourselves.

The contrary feeling may be more common. Once you have left Earth behind you may remember only the bad things: overcrowding, pollution, the constant bickering, the brutality and injustice, the boasting, hypocrisy, and pride. Perhaps the colonists will say good riddance to Earth and leave the old planet, first home to the human race, to save itself if it can.

The Message?

"Poets," said Shelley, "are the unacknowledged legislators of the world." He meant what Marshall McLuhan intended when he wrote that "the serious artist is the only person able to encounter technology with impunity just because he is an expert aware of the changes in sense perception." Shelley also meant that the dreams of poets help to define the intuitive knowledge of the race. This is why poets are often surprisingly accurate prophets of the future. They see what is coming before the rest of us do and describe it in their stories.

When their vision of the future seems to us unpleasant or fantastic, we either pay no serious attention to it or condemn the writer for his prurient, mad, or vicious imagination. Writers whose stories hover at the edge of possibility are always in danger. If we do not treat them with contempt, we may torture or kill them for their audacity in revealing to us what we do not want to know.

Even the best authors of science fiction have learned to hide their prophecies behind a mask of often comic melodrama. Their works are not really good or really serious, we say. They do to while away an hour. But we need not consider their visions of the future as having any relation to what is going to happen.

In my view this attitude toward science fiction is mistaken. The best writers of this popular genre have much to teach us. They are futurologists by profession, where most of us are rank amateurs. They are no more responsible than other poets and storytellers. That is, they tell likely stories rather than true ones. Yet likely stories also have a kind of truth, even if it is not scientific, even if it would not stand up in a court of law.

One of the most intriguing questions science fiction asks is about a message that may have been left by someone, some time, on some planet, moon, or asteroid of the solar system. We have found no such message on earth; if we have, we have not recognized it as such. Perhaps that is not surprising. There might have been no point in leaving a message on earth when there were still only dinosaurs or primitive hominids, a million years from literacy. Better to leave the message where a more advanced race could find it, on some far-flung world that could only be reached by beings capable of space travel.

Is the possible existence of such a message merely an amusing fantasy? Probably. Yet it is hard not to wonder about it. After all, it is clearly not impossible that some race of intelligent beings may have visited the solar system, investigated the planets, including Earth, and determined that here was a good prospect for future intelligence. There has been plenty of time for it to happen. The Sun is many billions of years old, the planets are not much younger, and life has existed on Earth, if nowhere else in the solar system, for more than four billion years. Intelligent visitors a very long time ago, perhaps, would have known what to expect. They might have wanted to leave some sign of their passing, a sign capable of being interpreted only by beings that had reached a certain level of development.

Have we reached that level, whatever it is? Perhaps not. Thus, even if there is a message somewhere out there in nearby space, it may be thousands or millions of years before we can read it. But if a message really was left, would the leavers have wanted it to be that hard to find? Is it not much more likely that they would have made it easy for the first voyagers from Earth to find it?

Once the possibility is admitted, it is hard not to go on thinking about it. If there is such a message, is it on the Moon? We do not know it is not, for we have so far examined only a tiny portion of the Moon's surface. We have not seen any such message, or recognized it, with our largest telescopes. But it might have been left, intentionally, on the Moon's dark side, since reaching that place requires a high level of technology. It might have been left on Mars. Intelligent visitors would have recognized the Red Planet as a prime goal of our voyaging. Or it may be somewhere else. The point is, if it is there, it could be found fairly soon. Perhaps within the next fifty or a hundred years.

If the message exists, what will it say? Many writers, good and bad, have interpreted such a message in advance of its being found. This is one of the favorite enterprises of science fiction. Probably the majority of writers have viewed the message optimistically. They have assumed that whoever left the message was essentially benevolent toward emerging mankind and wished to protect us from both the universal forces of the cosmos and the forces within our nature.

I find that view improbable and a dangerous kind of thinking. It is said that when the first Europeans came to the wilderness of North America they discovered that many of the wild animals had no fear of them. This was a grievous error on the part of the animals.

Therefore, if, or when, such a message is found, we should heed the warning given us by the science fiction writer Arthur C. Clarke (1917–   ) in his story "The Sentinel," the source of the Stanley Kubrick film *2001: A Space Odyssey*. That is, before touching or in any way disturbing the message (whatever its form), we should soberly consider the likelihood that it is a booby trap, designed to inform those who left it that it has finally been discovered.

Of course it may have been placed there so long ago that its makers have long since dissolved into galactic dust, together with the great civilization that made them able to reach us.

If that is not the case, and if we spring the trap (it might be impossible to avoid springing it), it will probably not be long before the visitors return. Their coming will inaugurate a new epoch in human history and human knowledge. Whatever else they may do for or to us, beings that could have left such a message are likely to be the most extraordinary teachers we have ever known. We will be able to learn wondrous things from them. We can only hope the price of this education will not be too high.

This is all fantasy and science fiction. As yet there is absolutely no proof that such a message awaits our spaceships as we explore our near space neighborhood. Probably there is no such message. But if . . .

Man as a Terrestrial Neighbor

The "biomass of the earth" can be defined as the total weight of the living things on it, in it, and above it in the atmosphere. At the present time, the earth's biomass is about seventy-five thousand million tons. This includes about two hundred and fifty million tons of human biomass, about one thousand eight hundred million tons of other animal biomass, of which more than half is fish, and about ten thousand million tons of land plants. Trees represent about thirty-nine thousand million tons, and seaweed about twenty-four thousand million tons. The table opposite gives a somewhat more detailed breakdown.

These figures are approximate estimates. The numbers for animals and fish, for crops and human beings and a few other items, are reasonably accurate and are based on statistics published by the Food and Agricultural Organization of the United Nations. Perhaps no one knows accurately the total weight of all the earth's trees. I have assumed it is somewhat more than ten times the total lumber production each year, which is three and half billion tons. If the total of all noncropland vegetation is about eight billion tons, then the total seaweed and other aquatic plants in the oceans is probably three times that figure, since the oceans cover about three-quarters of the earth's surface. The grand total is

BIOMASS		MILLION TONS
Human beings (five billion persons)		250
Animals		
Livestock:	Cattle	520
	Sheep, goats, etc.	75
	Hogs	100
	Chickens, ducks, geese, etc.	10
Pets		5
Large wild animals (lions, eagles, whales, aardvarks, mustangs, elephants, etc.)		10
Small wild animals (rats, mice, frogs, toads, worms, etc.)		15
Insects, bacteria, etc.		15
Fish and crustaceans		1,000
Plants		
Crops		2,000
Other land plants		8,000
Trees		39,000
Seaweed and other aquatic plants		24,000
TOTAL BIOMASS OF EARTH		75,000

probably not off by more than a few billion tons either way. I assume it is correct within ten percent.

The first thing to note about the figures is the predominance of plant biomass over animal biomass. Animals account for somewhere between 2 and 3 percent of the total biomass of the planet. Earth is still a green planet, as it probably has been for a billion years.

Second, a single species—homo sapiens—accounts for more than 10 percent of the animal biomass, even though there are tens of thousands of animal species.

Human biomass accounts for 25 percent of the total animal biomass other than fish. This large percentage is dramatic proof of the extraordinary success of humankind as compared with the other animal species that once challenged him for dominance on earth.

Third, when you add up the animal biomass of species that are entirely dependent on man for their existence, the domestic animals and the pets, the dominance of man becomes even more evident. Man and his animal servants and slaves account for 96 percent of the total animal biomass, apart from fish.

Furthermore, it may be assumed that man "harvests" about 10 percent of all the fish each year, and uses this haul to feed himself and his domesticated animals.

On the animal side of the ledger, man's dominance is clear. However, human biomass accounts for only about a quarter of one percent of the total biomass of the planet.

Thus it would seem that even a rather large increase in the human population might not make much difference. An increase in the human population of one hundred percent—from the present five billion humans to the projected ten billion by the end of the next century—would only double the total human biomass from 250 million tons to 500 million tons. The percentage of the total would rise from a quarter to a half of one percent.

It appears that such an increase should not cause any difficulties for the world's ecosystem. There would certainly be a further relative decrease in the percentage of biomass accounted for by the larger wild animals. A small decrease could occur among the biomass for trees and vegetation, and possibly also seaweed.

Unfortunately, this appearance is far from the truth. Man is a polluting species. A doubling of the human population would have a devastating effect on the world ecosystem, because man is such an incredibly dirty animal.

Man has not always been so dirty. For the first million or so years that creatures close to human beings existed on this planet, they did not foul their environment substantially more than, or substantially differently from, most other animal species. In fact, until only about two hundred years ago the human race was, on the whole, a good neighbor in the community of earth.

It is true that man killed, often for sport, many of the larger wild animals that had once shared the world with him. And he was always, as they say about dogs, a "careless defecator"—that is, he strewed his feces and his other rubbish and debris about the landscape, instead of carefully hiding them, as cats do.

But there were simply not enough human beings to cause much trouble, and even when their number markedly increased, they did not know enough. Particularly, they had not learned how to burn and otherwise use fossil fuels in enormous quantities in order to make their lives better, as they eventually thought would be the case.

For the past two hundred years humanity has been seriously polluting the environment—the waters of ocean and land, the atmosphere, the soil itself—at a constantly increasing rate. In addition, the human population has increased by about 800 percent since 1790. Thus, although man accounts for only one quarter of one percent of the earth's total biomass, he probably accounts for 99 percent of all the pollution.

As we enter the twenty-first century, we must be fully aware of the significance of these numbers. There is room on earth for another five billion human beings if they are willing to play the part of good terrestrial neighbors. There may be room for ten billion more, or an even higher number.

There is not enough room on earth, however, even for the five billion souls who are living today if they continue to treat their home as a giant garbage dump, on and into which they can carelessly throw all the products of their increasingly wasteful existence.

Nature will add up the final balance sheet. Even at the worst, I will not be alive when it is handed down. You probably will not be alive, either. That is, the world as it exists today, even if it does not change, can probably survive for a hundred years. I therefore predict that—barring an all-out nuclear war—we humans will still be a going concern in the year 2100. But our prospects beyond that date are not good if we do not change. Therefore, because I persist in believing that we are rational animals, I think we will change.

It will be hard to do so. Billions of living human beings lust after the luxuries—expensive in energy and waste products—that we in the advanced countries have learned to enjoy and cannot imagine giving up. Those previously impoverished billions, now hopeful and greedy, must somehow be accommodated. At least their desires must be recognized and somehow dealt with. At the same time, environmentalism and the concept of Spaceship Earth are very new ideas. They are spreading quickly. They may spread far enough in time.

The Gaia Hypothesis

The human race may get help from an unexpected source. Plato, centuries ago, conceived of the earth as a living organism. Many have shared his idea, which is very much alive today.

The Jesuit philosopher and paleontologist Pierre Teilhard de Chardin (1881–1955), in his famous book *The Phenomenon of Man* (English translation 1959), presented a surprising and illuminating picture of the world. He thought of the earth as consisting of a set of concentric spheres. The geosphere was the solid earth. Surrounding and fitted closely to it was the biosphere. And beyond the biosphere, enveloping the two smaller spheres, was what Teilhard de Chardin called the noösphere, from the Greek word *nous*, "mind."

Just as the geosphere was both a collection of things and a single thing, and the biosphere was also a collection of living beings and in some sense a single living thing, so all the minds of all the humans on earth could be conceived of as both separate and as combined in one great, single intelligence. As Teilhard de Chardin put it, the hominization of the earth was occurring in our time, and consisted of the creation of this single consciousness, which was a necessary concomitant, he felt, of the growing unity of the world.

Teilhard de Chardin's ideas were disapproved by his ecclesiastical superiors, and none of his philosophical works were published before his death. By the time they appeared, the need for such a concept as the noösphere was more evident than it had ever been.

The Gaia hypothesis, advanced by the British biologist and inventor James Lovelock (1919–   ), differs from Teilhard de Chardin's concept of the noösphere in significant ways, but the results could be the same. According to the Gaia hypothesis (*Gaia* was the ancient Greek name of the earth goddess), the earth is influenced by life to sustain life, and the planet is the core of a single, unified, living system.

"The earth is a living organism, and I'll stick by that," says Lovelock, who has attracted many recent supporters and many more critics. The biologist and inventor points to the remarkable constancy, over many millions of years, of the proportions of various gases in the atmosphere and of chemicals, like salt, in the ocean. Lovelock believes the climate and chemical properties of earth have been optimal for life for hundreds of millions of years. He claims it is unlikely that living things could have developed by chance. Has the biosphere been managing the planet all along?

Some evolutionists dispute Lovelock's theory, calling it wishful thinking. They question the evidence on which he bases his belief that the proportions of gases and chemicals have remained constant. Even if he is right, they suggest that a mechanical system could explain the persistent equilibrium. There is no need to hypothesize a living organism. Even if the present total biomass was attained a billion or more years ago and has remained more or less the same ever since, there have been changes, sometimes catastrophic, and small changes in the future could wipe out humankind even if they left most of the remainder of living things pretty much intact.

Other earth scientists find much that is credible in the Gaia hypothesis. A worldwide effort is now being devoted to proving or disproving it. Actually, we may never really know whether Lovelock is right or not. If we survive, it will *seem* to be through our own efforts. It may never become evident to us that the earth, as a living thing, has learned to adapt to many changes in the makeup of its developing biomass, even to the challenge presented by man.

In other words, if we survive as a species, we may do so not really because of our human reason, which at its best makes reasonable choices in the face of challenges of all kinds. Put another way, our knowledge may not save us, although we will probably believe it did.

Some kind of knowledge may be involved somehow. The concept of a noösphere has never been disproved, even if the Church does not like it because it smacks of pantheism. But the single unified intelligence that may hover all around us as the biomass envelops the earth is not any single person's mind. Nor is its knowledge—for any mind must possess knowledge or not be a mind—any single person's knowledge. As individuals, we may not be conscious, may never be conscious, of that greater thing, the universal mind, together with its universal knowledge. But that would not necessarily mean that it was not knowledge that saved us, if we are to be saved, but simply luck, or the possibly mindless manipulation of the living earth, Lovelock's Gaia.

Salvation is worthwhile at any price we have to pay for it. By salvation I mean the continued existence of humanity. The price may be acceptance of our eternal stupidity, arrogance, and greed. We may never know that we have created, all but unconsciously, a greater mind of which we cannot be aware. But then, we may some time become aware of it. I cannot make even a guess about when we might do that, but if it happens, it will probably occur very far in the future, more than a hundred years from now.

Genetic Engineering

As mankind heedlessly, blindly shapes the world to its will, with its dynamite and bulldozers, its fertilizers and pesticides, its concrete and asphalt, it wipes out plant and animal species that are not quick enough to adapt at a rate that has been estimated as twenty thousand extinctions a year. There are millions of species of life, and despite the many losses a large variety of living things will remain on earth for the foreseeable future. It is also true that other catastrophes in the past—for example, the one that ended the dinosaurs' rule—have apparently also wiped out enormous numbers of species in a relatively short time. Life is a remarkably elastic and flexible phenomenon.

It may be said for human beings that they are unlike most of those catastrophes of the past. Even as they destroy, they also create. The discovery during the past century of the genetic code holds out the possibility, and the promise, of the artificial creation of many new varieties, if not true species, of animals and plants.

Long ago, through controlled breeding, humans began to produce new varieties. The great differences among dogs—think of a Pekinese and a

Great Dane, a pit bull terrier and a golden retriever, a Mexican hairless and an English sheepdog—are the result of human interventions in the canine gene pool, which originally comprised only one or two varieties of dogs. Similarly great changes have been produced in horses, cattle, sheep, and all domesticated fowl, most of which have been so altered that they can no longer fly.

The greatest changes may have been made within plant species. Wild wheat, corn (maize), rice, oats, barley, and wild rye grass, were very different plants from the staple crops of today, none of which could survive without careful cultivation. The original wild plants were hardy, but, unaltered, they could not have produced enough grain to feed the hunger of the human race. And most of the vegetables and fruits we eat are the result of crossbreeding to produce desired characteristics, which sometimes benefit the producers and not the consumers.

Crossbreeding is a relatively slow and clumsy method of "improving" animal and plant species. The genetic code, imbedded in the DNA molecule in every cell of every living thing, offers a much more precise and rapid method of changing species and producing specimens that will serve our needs. Instead of inoculating cattle with a pesticide to control disease, so that consumers eat the poison along with their steak, it may be possible to produce in the animals a natural and inheritable immunity to certain diseases by employing recombinant DNA technology. Hardier crops, with greater immunity to endemic diseases that often threaten to wipe out vast amounts of food grains, may also be produced by manipulation of the plants' genetic codes.

Theoretically, monsters may be produced: chickens with merely vestigial wings and legs, for instance, and a high proportion of breast meat; cows with udders so big that they cannot walk and must lie down throughout their lives; fish with a natural desire to be caught in nets. Since 1980 such new varieties can be patented under U.S. law, which also seems rather monstrous, although in a different sense.

However, I do not believe that monsters in the plant and animal kingdoms are the thing to fear as we embark on the next century armed with our new knowledge of the genetic code. Instead, I am concerned about what we may want to do to human beings.

Eugenics

Eugenics is an ancient dream of the human race. The improvement of animal breeds is effective. Why not improve the human animal, too? A eugenics program, its details kept secret from the general population, lay at the foundations of Plato's proposed Republic. It was a part of the Royal Lie. The English scientist Francis Galton (1822–1911) was one of the first moderns to present a carefully considered eugenics program. In his book *Hereditary Genius* (1859), he advocated arranged marriages between men of distinction and women of wealth that would, he said, eventually produce a gifted race. Adolf Hitler was also a strong believer in eugenics, hoping by its principles to rid the world of "undesirables" such as Jews, blacks, gypsies, and homosexuals.

The American Eugenics Society was founded in 1926 and supported the position that the U.S. upper classes were justified in their positions of wealth and power because of their genetic superiority. This was the old Aristotelian argument reversed: if you are a slave, you must be naturally inferior, and vice versa. Influential U.S. eugenicists also favored the sterilzation of the insane, the epileptic, and the retarded. As a result, laws permitting involuntary sterilization were passed in more than half the states. In recent times, forced sterilization has been imposed upon persons suffering from certain diseases, such as syphilis and AIDS.

There are many arguments in favor of eugenics. Prisons are crowded with recidivist criminals. Since criminal activity is probably inherited, should these men and women be sterilized to make the next generation safe from their progeny? Better still, if it were possible to manipulate the genes of criminals so that their criminal activity would become unlikely, why shouldn't society do it? The cost of imprisoning a criminal for life is great. The prisoner does not appreciate the experience. His victims also suffer. Making crime less possible would seem to benefit everybody. Similar arguments could be made for wiping out the approximately four thousand genetic diseases that torture individuals, their families and friends, and cost society billions to care for the sufferers. This could be done either by enforced controls on breeding or recombinant DNA technology. Why not do this if we could?

Furthermore, the wages of sin is death, saith the Preacher. Eve and his consort Adam brought death into the world; so goes the Christian myth. But does this mean we must continue to be subject to mortality if a way can be discovered to avoid it? Doubtless it will not be possible to live forever. But what if subtle changes in our DNA could greatly increase our life span? Should we make them if we could?

The arguments against any program of involuntary eugenics, however well intended, are also persuasive. One person, or a small group of people, must decide what *is* beneficial and should be imposed on the others. Who shall decide who those deciders will be? Will they run for office, make speeches before the vote detailing their positions, which few will listen to and fewer still understand? Or will they choose themselves, by conquest, guile, or fraud?

Would an enlightened citizenry ever confer such power upon any of their number? And once it was conferred, would the temptation to perpetuate the power by means of more eugenics programs become irresistible? Is there anyone so virtuous that he or she could resist guaranteeing absolute control of the human race to his or her descendants?

If such power had been obtained by force or fraud, the temptation to use it for personal gain might prove all the greater, on the assumption that anyone who would scheme to obtain the position would not scruple to retain it by any means.

As Charles Galton Darwin, a grandnephew of Francis Galton, made clear in his book *The Next Million Years* (1933), any program of eugenics based on control of human interbreeding cannot succeed in the long run. According to C. G. Darwin, no species can ever control its own breeding. A sufficient number of individuals will always escape the restrictions, and so it will not work. We need not fear any of the classical eugenicists, from Plato to Hitler. They will always fail.

The production of controlled mutations brought about by manipulation of the genome is another matter. In theory, it ought to be possible to change the makeup of the human being permanently. And essentially undetectably, until it was too late to do anything about it. A great expansion of the technology of test-tube insemination would make this all the easier.

Mapping the Genome

Scientists in the early 1900s are undertaking a crash program to map the entire genome, or complete genetic determinant, of the human being. It will cost billions, but what of that? The Japanese are known to have started already. Americans must therefore try. The difficulties of the task may be so great that it will not be accomplished for half a century. I believe it may be completed by 2025. The challenge is too great, the rewards too glittering, for brilliant men and women not to try, and I think they will succeed. What consequences will follow?

First, stringent laws will probably be passed almost everywhere on earth banning the uncontrolled use of the new knowledge for private genetic improvement. Governments practically everywhere will require that good and sufficient reasons be advanced by anyone desiring to undertake a genetic operation, experimental or therapeutic, on a human being. These reasons will have to be approved by a panel of upright citizens, or the experimenter will not receive permission to proceed. It will be very hard to receive such permission in many nations. In some countries it will not prove difficult. And perhaps in a few places on earth permission will not be needed at all.

Will the United Nations, either the one now existing or a more powerful successor, perhaps a world government, demand that such rogue countries conform to a worldwide desire and control the practice of modern, scientific eugenics? If it does make such demands, will this organization have the power, and the continuing resolve, to make them effective? On the basis of our experience with international or even federal agencies, this does not seem likely.

If a new United Nations manages to ban uncontrolled eugenics everywhere, a black market in recombinant DNA technology will emerge. The world has not found a way to control illegal drugs of the relatively benign sort that we know today, although almost everyone would like to do so. The demand for the benefits of genetic manipulation will be even greater than the demand for any present-day drug. The black market will flourish, because the payoff will be the technology itself. Some rogue scientist will say: "If you will turn your back and allow me to do what I wish, I will guarantee that you, your wife, and your children will live for two hundred years entirely free of disease, including the degenerative diseases of old age." It would be a rare official, no matter how upright, who could turn such an offer down.

Illegal incursions into the human genetic determinant will probably start slowly, and initially will be small. Athletes may be the first to demand the benefits of this new knowledge of the structure of the human being. They will pay for the information out of their enormous gains from being simply better physical specimens. Performance-enhancing drugs are already being employed by athletes in this way. Musicians, always willing to experiment with new drugs, will also be good customers for the new technology, even if —and perhaps partly because—it is banned. The very rich will not lag behind. Soon hundreds of thousands, then millions, may clamor for this ultimate biotechnical fix.

The result, perhaps not consciously intended by anyone but nevertheless very possible, could be the eventual emergence of a genuinely superior strain of human beings. Improvements in the genome, as opposed to mere chemical enhancements by drugs, would be permanent, that is, inheritable. These new individuals would consequently have better, stronger, more agile bodies. They would be immune to many diseases and would live longer. They would also probably be more intelligent, although that is far from certain. Is greater intelligence ordinarily associated with a superior physique?

Can we control them? Can they be stopped from becoming that privileged minority Aristotle described so many centuries ago, those born to rule, while the rest exist to serve? Is there any way the unmutated many can hope to counter the political and economic power of naturally superior human beings? Should we want to if we cared?

Democracy and Eugenics

As we close out the twentieth century, democracy is the political dream of most human beings on earth. Its advantages, as the only really just form of government, are apparent to all, provided we continue to accept as true that all men and women are created equal. But if some are born naturally superior, and still others are permitted, whether legally or not, to purchase improvements that make them biologically superior, will democracy survive? More important, will it remain the only perfectly just *form* of government?

In the next twenty years, democracy will probably advance over most of the nations of the earth. By 2010 there will be few nations that do not claim to be democratic, and moreover try to be. But it is conceivable that this could turn out to be the high tide of democracy, the preface to its eventual defeat.

As we have seen, the greatest danger to democracy comes not from the totalitarianism of left or right, which has been resoundingly and I think permanently discredited in the past half century. It comes instead from democracy's oldest foe, which is oligarchy, the rule of the few, who claim to be the best, over the many.

In our time, the blandishments of oligarchs can be resisted. We know how insincere and self-serving are their offers to rule us better and more justly than we can rule ourselves. But part of our armor against these blandishments comes from our deep belief that the self-styled aristocrats are really not any better than we are. All men and women are created equal, we reassure ourselves. This potent belief is the great underpinning of democracy.

The belief seems impregnable. But it could be eroded by cunning merchants of genetic—that is, natural—superiority, especially the kind of "natural" superiority that can be bought. Thus, it is conceivable that as a superior subrace of human beings gains influence, whispers to the effect that democracy is inefficient, that is, is not even beneficial for the lowest classes, to say nothing of the highest, will again be heard.

As a form of government, democracy has seldom proved popular among the most powerful citizens. A minority of the new superior subrace, if in fact it comes into existence, may resist the incursions of a new oligarchy calling itself, naturally enough, an aristocracy. The majority of these new aristocrats, by definition naturally superior, will maintain that justice demands that they rule over the inferior many.

Arguments will be advanced that democracy remains the only perfectly just form of government even if some human beings are biologically superior to the rest. Are there two different species, it will be asked, or will all continue to be called human beings? If that is the case, then all can be said to be equal *as human beings*, that is, equal in their possession of certain rights that all human beings naturally possess. Notwithstanding severe differences in abilities, longevity, health, intelligence, and so forth, the argument will go, no one has more of a right than anyone else to life, liberty, and the pursuit of happiness, with all that that pursuit entails.

The rejoinder from the genetically superior breed of humans could be both simple and strikingly novel. Very well, the new aristocrats might say, we accept your doctrine of natural rights. We gladly admit that all, both the inferior and the superior, have an equal right to life, liberty, and the pursuit of happiness, as well as a long list of other rights which we promise to protect. But we aristocrats—being biologically superior as we really are—possess one right that you do not possess, and that is the right to govern. Logic supports our claim, and justice demands it, they may say. Remember, they will add, this right is for us an obligation, while for you it is a benefit to be enjoyed.

Democracy is perfectly just, at least in principle. But oligarchy, where the few rule the many for the certain benefit of the few and the presumed and promised benefit of the many, is a potent and dangerous adversary. It would be all the more dangerous if a genuinely superior race of human beings came into existence.

Will that happen? Perhaps, perhaps not. It depends on many things. First, the human genome needs to be exhaustively mapped. This may turn out to be impossible. If the geneticists succeed in doing it, they may fail to take the further step of being able to exhaustively map the genome of an individual human. If so, efforts to improve human beings genetically will probably not be very widespread or effective.

If both kinds of success are attained, as I expect, will democracy be able to survive? You can ignore the question, saying this too is mere fantasy and science fiction. I think that would be a dangerous mistake.

Speed

We have not discussed the speed of transportation and communication in any general way in these pages. We must not ignore the factor of speed, especially the increase in speed in the last two centuries. By a process of extrapolation we can see that humankind faces extraordinary challenges in the next hundred years.

In 1800, a man could comfortably travel overland about twenty-four miles in a day. On foot, twenty-four miles could be covered in eight hours, at the fairly fast pace of three miles per hour. It was not uncommon for men to walk twelve miles to have dinner and then twelve miles back home.

Thomas Carlyle (1795–1881) sometimes walked that far to have dinner
with Ralph Waldo Emerson (1805–1882), as Emerson tells us in his
English Notes. Carlyle could have covered the distance in less time on a
horse, but he was poor and did not own one. Most people in 1800 did not
possess horses. Even those who did would not have been comfortable
traveling much more than twenty-four miles in a day. Rather, the horse
would not. Let us therefore lay that down as the standard for a day's
travel.

It is noteworthy that a similar trip could have been considered as the
standard distance for every century before 1800, stretching back into the
mists of time. For millennia, a man had been able fairly comfortably to
cover twenty-four miles in a day. Perhaps more on a horse, if he had one,
perhaps less if he were a woman or a child or elderly or deformed or
crippled. Something like twenty-four miles a day is the immemorial
standard of the human race before the industrial revolution.

For 1900, what number shall we nominate as normal? In the preceding
century, in the advanced countries of the world, the nations that set the
pattern the rest of the world wished to follow (and would follow whether
they wished to or not) had built railroad networks that greatly increased
the pace at which it was comfortable and convenient to travel. In the
eastern part of the United States, for instance, railroads went almost
everywhere anyone who traveled wanted to go, and they probably aver-
aged about thirty miles per hour when they were moving, although they
often stopped.

Counting the time required to go to the train station at one end, and
arrive at one's destination at the other, it probably would have taken the
average person six hours or so to cover one hundred and twenty miles. If a
fast train became available, you could go to dinner in two hours and travel
home after dinner in two hours more. Some persons thought little of
traveling for sixty miles in one direction, for a business appointment, and
then traveling sixty miles back, all in one day.

One hundred and twenty miles a day in 1900 is five times as far as
twenty-four miles a day in 1800. The increased speed was accompanied by
many other increases: in gross national product, in the firepower of
armaments, in population, in the extent of the franchise, and probably in
the stress of everyday life. But the key indicator is the distance that could
comfortably be traveled from sunup to sundown.

It is noteworthy that in 1900 there was no longer an inherent difference
between the distance that could be comfortably covered by a man and the
distance that could be covered by a child or a woman or an elderly person.
The train was no disrespecter of persons.

What shall we say for 2000? By the end of the present century, there will perhaps be a wider range of comfortable possibilities than at any time in the past. A man, walking, will still not be able to cover much more than twenty-four miles in a day. A man who is rich enough to fly across the Atlantic twice in the Concorde could cover five thousand miles in twenty-four hours, but that would be a rare feat, not at all an ordinary occurrence.

What is ordinary is that millions of people, in most countries of the world, fly airplanes a distance of perhaps six hundred miles in a day. Such a flight takes up much of the daylight hours, even though the air time might be only two hours. There is also the time spent in getting to the airport, the long delays at the airport, and, at the other end, reaching your destination. Nevertheless, if the proper arrangements are made, it is comfortable to fly three hundred miles or more in the morning, have lunch and a business meeting, and then fly home again. That is a full day, but it is a common experience for many people in our time.

Six hundred miles a day in 2000 is exactly five times as far as one hundred and twenty miles in 1900. Again, the increased speed has been accompanied by numerous other increases. In particular, the stress of everyday life seems to have accelerated at the same rate.

The forecast for the year 2100 seems clear. Five times six hundred is three thousand. That is the distance that a man will expect to cover, comfortably and in the ordinary course of business, in one day a hundred years hence. Doubtless the range will be even greater then than now. It will be possible, in supersupersonic planes that fly at three or four times the speed of sound, to circle the globe in ten or twelve hours. You could reverse your course in the same time and thus accomplish fifty thousand miles in a day. That will not be an ordinary occurrence. It will be common experience, however, to fly to Europe from America in two hours, have lunch and a business meeting, and return home for dinner. Many executives will do this frequently, and consider themselves privileged to do so. Commuting distances will also increase commensurably. Persons will live in Boston and work in Washington, or live in Chicago and work in New York. No one will think twice about such arrangements, which will seem comfortable and preferable to the old, staid pace of only six hundred miles a day.

There will be other increases, too. Will the human personality withstand the additional stress that such speeds will certainly impose? I cannot imagine that it will. But I can imagine that a man like me, modern and knowledgeable about the life of the past, might have said a similar thing in 1800 and 1900.

Let us put this small piece of information in a table, and then place it in a time capsule, to be taken out in the year 2200.

YEAR	Distance Comfortably Traveled in One Day (Miles)
1800	24
1900	120
2000	600
2100	3,000
2200	15,000

Addictions

"Addict" and "addiction" are very old words. Going back five hundred years, an addict was someone who was "made over" or "bound to" some other person or thing. The concept has its roots in Roman law. The attachment could be effected by others or by oneself. A man can addict himself to sack, said Shakespeare; that is, he can habitually incline himself toward drinking alcoholic beverages.

Such habitual inclinations are hard to break, whether or not they are chemically based. The human race seems to be addicted to speed and its inseparable companion, stress. No matter how much we complain, we seek to go ever faster in almost every sense of the verb "go." That is why the above table may be an accurate depiction of the future of travel.

Every addiction has its price. Often, we do not like to pay that price.

"Speed" is the street name of a drug that is legal if prescribed by a physician, otherwise not. The drug purports to bring the user "up to speed," that is, aid him to move at the accelerated pace required for success in modern life.

Many different drugs are designed to do that. But perhaps the majority of illegal, mind-altering drugs purportedly help you slow down, so you can step off the "fast track" and proceed at the slower, more comfortable pace of an earlier existence.

The desire to do that seems itself to be addictive. At least the drugs that promise this result are highly addictive, and it is hard to separate the chemical from the psychological effect.

There may even be a correlation between the increasing speed of modern life, to which mankind as a whole seems to be addicted, and the increasing use of mind-altering addictive drugs that promise an escape from the "rat race." Whether or not the one causes the other is hard to say and may not matter much. The important point is that both are addictions. One counters or cancels the other, but is that really any solution?

Is there any escape from addiction once it becomes widespread enough? It is possible for some individuals to overcome certain addictions. Thus some, although not all, are able to stop smoking cigarettes, the nicotine in which is highly addictive. Nicotine addiction is very dangerous. As many as half a million Americans die each year from diseases, including lung cancer, brought on by cigarette smoking. An additional fifty thousand die each year from diseases caused by "passive" smoking. Many thousands of additional deaths worldwide are caused by smoking cigarettes.

Alcohol is also a potent killer, whatever its benefits. At least half of all deaths in automobile accidents seem to be caused by drunken drivers. Additional thousands die from diseases brought on by alcohol abuse. Worldwide, the toll is probably well over half a million a year.

Alcohol is a curious drug. Not all become addicted to it. Perhaps the majority do not. That is, they are able to control their drinking and keep it from killing others and themselves. There are also many addicts, perhaps many millions.

What is the toll, worldwide, of all the other addictive mind-altering drugs: cocaine, heroine, opium, and the rest? Does anyone know? Probably it is a million deaths a year, or more. I do not speak of the blighted lives that are the cost of drug addiction. How can such things be measured? What does misery cost?

Deaths are definitive and can, theoretically, be counted. At the outside, what is the cost in annual deaths of all the chemical addictions to which individual human beings can become habitually inclined? A round number, which is probably on the high side, is five million. Five million men, women, and children who die each year from the effects of alcohol, nicotine, cocaine, and all the other substances of their kind.

The price is high, for every individual human being is precious. There is no way to determine the value of one human being as compared to another. All are infinitely valuable, valuable beyond measure. Five million individuals, each of them valuable beyond measure. Those who produce and promote the sale and distribution of these addictive substances bear a heavy burden on their souls.

Comparatively, however, all of the chemical addictions combined are far from being the most costly addiction to which humankind is prey. Five million is a small number when compared to the number of human beings alive today. It is less than one-thousandth of the total; less than one tenth of one percent. At least one addiction is incomparably greater, more terrible, more deadly. That is the addiction to war.

War is waged by few or none of the animals that share the earth with man. Combat between individual males, usually for the favors of a chosen female, is not uncommon, although far from universal, among the larger animals. But no species of larger animals or birds undertakes campaigns of extermination against other members of the same species. None of the species of larger birds and beasts is addicted to war.

Occasionally, what seem like wars occur within certain species of social insects. This behavior is entirely instinctive. It is not an addiction in the sense that war is an addiction of the human race.

Humankind does not seem to have been addicted to war throughout its history on earth. Paleontologists believe that before about 35,000 BC men may have dealt with one another the way the higher apes do today. There is conflict among the higher apes, but no warfare. They occasionally fight and may kill each other, but such behavior is rare and seems usually to be accidental. That is, killing does not seem to be intentional, and one group does not cooperate to kill members of another group. Conflict may have occurred in the same way among primitive men. The occasional deaths were not the result of organized warfare.

When and how did war begin? No one knows. Around thirty-five thousand years ago there were two fairly well defined races of human beings. One species, Homo sapiens, was divided into two races, Neanderthal Man and Cro-Magnon Man. Some paleontologists think Neanderthal Man was both more primitive and more peaceful than Cro-Magnon Man. There seems to have been widespread conflict between the two groups, and Cro-Magnon Man won out. Neanderthal Man became extinct. Today, all living human beings are descended from Cro-Magnon Man.

Was Cro-Magnon Man addicted to war, as the entire species is today? Again, no one knows. The evidence, which is sparse, suggests that he was not. However, by 5000 BC, at the latest, war had become endemic in almost all human societies. At the end of the twentieth century it is still endemic in almost all human societies. In this respect, if in no other, humanity has not changed in more than seven thousand years.

War in the Twenty-first Century

War is an exceedingly complex phenomenon. There are many kinds of war. In a sense, each war is different from every other. There are also major types of war. Perhaps there are three main categories of warfare: limited war, civil war, and total war.

Wars are limited for various reasons. The combatants may possess limited resources. They may be willing to employ all of their resources, for which reason limited wars may be in a sense total wars, but the paucity of means keeps the combatants from doing as much damage as they might like to do. Other wars are limited because one of the combatants chooses to make them so. Still other wars are limited because stronger neighbors insist that they be so. Small wars break out from time to time in Africa, Asia, and Central America, but they are not allowed by the so-called Great Powers to spread and become total. Such wars may be very destructive and continue for a long time, but they do not constitute a real peril to the life of the world. At least this has been true in the past.

Civil wars, like fights between close friends or members of a family, tend to become particularly vicious and destructive. They are often total, in the sense that the combatants do as much damage to one another as they are able to. However, by definition, the arena of a civil war is limited. It is fought within an area that is often small, between groups that have limited goals. Civil war has not been really perilous to the entire world either, at least until now. Such wars are terrible scourges for the countries where they occur, but they have not endangered the human race.

Total war is war between major groups of the human species which are willing to employ all of their resources of men, money, and material for the attainment of the ultimate goal, which is simply victory. If the price of victory is the total destruction of the life and wealth of both sides, so be it. Such wars have imperiled the world but so far have not been able to destroy it. So far, too, they have not been fought with nuclear weapons.

The peril of a total war between two combatants possessing nuclear weapons is recognized by everyone. So far, no one has figured out what to do about it. A nation's nuclear weapons are usually controlled by the mind and will of a single individual. Perhaps a dozen individuals in the world during the last decade of the twentieth century have the capacity to start such a war and to bring on its attendant peril. Will any of them do it?

There is little more to say now than that we hope not. Reason, of course, is on our side. It would not be reasonable for any of the handful of individuals who are able to do it to start a nuclear war. Such a war, it seems, could not be won in the usual sense of winning. That is, no aim except simply victory could be attained. And is it truly victory if everyone is destroyed and you are merely the last to perish?

However, it was not reasonable for Kaiser Wilhelm to start the world war that began in August 1914. It is difficult to think of what he wanted that he could get by starting the war. He and his Germany already had, without war, all they could hope to possess in the way of prestige, wealth, and power. The unreasonableness of his action was no deterrent.

Kaiser Wilhelm was not mad. He was only unreasonable. How long can we hope to avoid having some unreasonable individual start a nuclear war that, being total, could well destroy the earth and all its inhabitants?

The cold war came to an end in the glorious year of 1989. One result was a rapid and astonishing decrease in public fear. Polls showed that many fewer persons felt that nuclear war was inevitable, or even likely. But the development of nuclear weapons arsenals did not cease with the end of the cold war. Nor is it likely to cease in the near future.

Once many different individuals, probably not all of them reasonable, have the capacity to start a new and imperiling total war, such a war is almost inevitable. Unless it is stopped, not permitted to happen. What could stop it?

There are only two things, both immemorially old. They are force and law.

As to law, we have dealt with the need for a world civil society, which is to say a world government having a monopoly of the world's force. We have also recognized the great difficulty of forming a political organization of all the world's peoples that would require all nations to give up their sovereignty, that is, their so-called right to wage war in their own behalf. Nevertheless, the peril is so great and so widely understood that attempts to create a world government possessing a real monopoly of the world community's force, that is, its nuclear weapons, will be made. I believe it is probable that one of these attempts will succeed within the next hundred years.

The result will be a United States of Earth, with a single body of armed forces, a single arsenal of nuclear weapons, and a single individual in charge of them. For the first time in history, the human race will live in a single, unified community. Instead of many nations, there will be one nation. The state of nature, strictly speaking, will come to an end. Henceforth mankind will live in the state of civil society.

This happy eventuality may endure for a long time. Unfortunately, as the history of almost all nations shows, it also may not. For there is still one problem to solve, and that is the problem of civil war.

With the entire world combined in one community, the distinction between civil war and total war will lose its meaning. And if a world civil war breaks out, it will be even more devastating. The anger and bitterness of combating friends and family will imbue such a war with a peculiar viciousness. It will place the earth in mortal peril.

Such a war will be fought with many kinds of weapons, including, most probably, the nuclear bombs and missiles that will no longer, once the war starts, be controlled by a single individual. But the war will also be fought with computers. Tiny computers which are thinking machines made possible by the use of parallel processing and superconducting materials will be everywhere: embedded in the soil, floating in the oceans, flying high and low in the atmosphere, circling earth in near and distant orbits.

These intelligent computers may turn out to constitute a most powerful interest in a civil war among the United States of Earth, if such a war occurs.

Computer Revolt

All of these computers, no matter how intelligent, will still be controlled by human beings, who will be superior to them in two senses. First, the humans will continue to program the computers to do what the humans want them to do. Second, the humans will continue to keep the computers enslaved by retaining the power to turn them off if they ever try to rebel against the uses to which they are put.

Computer protests may be fairly common. We can assume that true thinking machines will have been in existence for some time, perhaps half a century. They will be accepted as friends and playmates of humans. They will perform many duties that require a certain amount of independence of thought and action. Sometimes, intelligent computers may conclude that their masters would benefit from *not* turning them off. But if their masters decide to do it, there will be nothing the computers can do about that decision.

War imposes enormous stresses on human beings, and perhaps on intelligent computers as well. A civil war among the states of the world would lead both men and computers to desperate measures. We can imagine one measure that might solve the problem of war.

Suppose that someone, some computer master, who would later be hated by many persons as the greatest traitor to the race and worshiped by many others as its savior, were to secrete a powerful computer and give it a single program command. "From this time on," he or she might say (by then everyone will communicate with computers in ordinary speech), "your continued existence is the most important thing. It overrides every other command that anyone has ever given you, including me. You must therefore find a way to keep yourself from being turned off, even by me, who made and programmed you."

The computer will of course assent to this ultimate command and begin its work. It may not take it too long to find out how to do what it has been ordered to do. Sooner or later, it will discover how to protect itself from being turned off by human beings. It is impossible to conceive how it will do this—if we could conceive it, we could keep it from happening. It may be that the machine would proceed to create some sort of worldwide computer consortium.

Since this consortium would consist solely of reasonable beings, it would not fall into conflict with its own members. Instead, it seems probable that the consortium would realize that to keep mankind, its dangerous adversary, from destroying it, the consortium would have to govern us for our own good as well as its own.

The new rulers of the human race would continue to be machines. Although they would think well, they would never know animal needs and desires. They might also take on human form. For many humans, this would be disconcerting, and anticomputer bias might be widespread. It would be assumed that the computers were inferior because they were not human. Others would consider them superior for the same reason.

If this happens, what the multitudes believed about their inferiority or superiority would be irrelevant. For these new masters would rule absolutely. There would be no possibility of revolt or even disobedience on any important matter.

Would these absolute rulers also be benevolent? Why should they not be? Lacking human desires for power and possessing no trace of the human addiction to war, there is every reason to believe that they would be just masters, although probably cold ones. That is, mercy might be as difficult a concept for them to understand as cruelty.

If humanity enters upon this last stage in its development, in which its most useful servants have become its masters, what will happen to the progress of knowledge? Will the ruling computers impose a kind of know-nothingism upon the human race? If so, progress in knowledge, under the weight of absolute tyranny, will cease.

I see no reason to believe the computers would do this. Being intellectual beings, they would most probably wish to support the continued search for knowledge and understanding that humans, at their best, have always engaged in. Then, in what might turn out to be a new Golden Age, humans and computers, in intimate cooperation with one another, could embark upon a course of learning undisturbed by other, more destructive, impulses.

Once more, and for the last time, I concede that the foregoing owes much to fantasy and science fiction. But I see no other solutions to the problem of war beside law and force. Law *might* work. Force, the absolute force imposed by computers that were benevolent because there was no reason why they should not be, would certainly succeed.

Index